ISBN 978-0-331-42525-3
PIBN 11122158

This book is a reproduction of an important historical work. Forgotten Books uses
state-of-the-art technology to digitally reconstruct the work, preserving the original format
whilst repairing imperfections present in the aged copy. In rare cases, an imperfection in
the original, such as a blemish or missing page, may be replicated in our edition. We do,
however, repair the vast majority of imperfections successfully; any imperfections that
remain are intentionally left to preserve the state of such historical works.

Historic, archived document

o not assume content reflects curre
entific knowledge, policies, or practi

U. S. DEPARTMENT OF AGRICULTURE.

SECTION OF FOREIGN MARKETS—BULLETIN NO. 26.

AGRICULTURAL IMPORTS

OF THE

UNITED KINGDOM,

1896–1900.

BY

FRANK H. HITCHCOCK,

Chief, Section of Foreign Markets.

WASHINGTON:
GOVERNMENT PRINTING OFFICE.
1902.

Bulletins (to be procured, at the prices indicated, from the Superintendent of Documents, Union Building, Washington, D. C.):

No. 1.—Great Britain and Ireland. Price (including supplement), 10 cents.

No. 2.—The German Empire. Price, 5 cents.

No. 3.—France. Price, 5 cents.

No. 4.—Canada. Price, 5 cents.

No. 5.—Netherlands. Price, 5 cents.

No. 6.—Belgium. Price, 5 cents.

No. 7.—Norway. Price, 5 cents.

No. 8.—Sweden. Price, 5 cents.

No. 9.—Trade of Denmark. Price, 5 cents.

No. 10.—Our Foreign Trade in Agricultural Products during the Five Fiscal Years 1893–1897. Price, 5 cents.

No. 11.—Spain's Foreign Trade. Price, 5 cents.

No. 12.—Our Trade with Spain, 1888–1897. Price, 5 cents.

No. 13.—Trade of Puérto Rico. Price, 5 cents.

No. 14.—Trade of the Philippine Islands. Price, 10 cents.

No. 15.—Our Foreign Trade in Agricultural Products, 1894–1898. Price, 5 cents.

No. 16.—Distribution of the Agricultural Exports of the United States, 1894–1898. Price, 10 cents.

No. 17.—Sources of the Agricultural Imports of the United States, 1894–1898. Price, 10 cents.

No. 18.—Our Trade with Japan, China, and Hongkong, 1889–1899. Price, 10 cents.

No. 19.—Our Foreign Trade in Agricultural Products, 1890–1899. Price, 5 cents.

No. 20.—Agricultural Exports of the United States, by Countries, 1895–1899. Price, 10 cents.

No. 21.—Agricultural Imports of the United States, by Countries, 1895–1899. Price, 5 cents.

No. 22.—Our Trade with Scandinavia, 1890–1900. Price, 10 cents.

No. 23.—Our Foreign Trade in Agricultural Products, 1891–1900. Price, 5 cents.

No. 24.—Sources of the Agricultural Imports of the United States, 1896–1900. Price, 10 cents.

No. 25.—Distribution of the Agricultural Exports of the United States, 1896–1900. Price, 10 cents.

No. 26.—Agricultural Imports of the United Kingdom, 1896–1900.

Circulars (for free distribution; apply to the Secretary of Agriculture, Washington, D. C.):

No. 1.—Peaches and Other Fruits in England. (Exhausted.)

No. 2.—American Dried Apples in the German Empire.

No. 3.—Imports and Exports for 1893 and 1894. (Exhausted.)

No. 4.—An Example for American Farmers and Dairymen. (Exhausted.)

No. 5.—The Treaty of Shimonoseki between China and Japan of April 17, 1895, and Our Possibilities of Trade with those Countries. (Exhausted.)

No. 6.—Imports and Exports for 1893, 1894, and 1895. (Exhausted.)

No. 7.—Extension of Markets for American Feed Stuffs.

No. 8.—The Manchester District of England as a Market for American Products.

No. 9.—Imports and Exports for 1893, 1894, 1895, and 1896.

No. 10.—Course of Wheat Production and Exportation in the United States, Canada, Argentina, Uruguay, Russia, and British India from 1880 to 1896.

No. 11.—Agricultural Products Imported and Exported by the United States in the Years Ended June 30. 1892 to 1896, Inclusive. (Exhausted.)

No. 12.—Sources of the Principal Agricultural Imports of the United States during the Five Years Ended June 30, 1896. (Exhausted.)

No. 13.—Distribution of the Principal Agricultural Exports of the United States during the Five Years Ended June 30, 1896.

No. 14.—Hamburg as a Market for American Products.

No. 15.—Exports of Cotton from Egypt.

No. 16.—Our Trade with Cuba from 1887 to 1897.

No. 17.—United States Wheat for Eastern Asia.

No. 18.—Hawaiian Commerce from 1887 to 1897.

No. 19.—Austria-Hungary as a Factor in the World's Grain Trade; Recent Use of American Wheat in that Country.

No. 20.—Agricultural Imports and Exports, 1893–1897.

No. 21.—Agricultural Imports and Exports, 1894–1898.

No. 22.—Agricultural Imports and Exports, 1895–1899.

No. 23.—Agricultural Imports and Exports, 1896–1900.

. U. S. DEPARTMENT OF AGRICULTURE.

SECTION OF FOREIGN MARKETS—BULLETIN NO. 26.

AGRICULTURAL IMPORTS

OF THE

UNITED KINGDOM,

1896-1900.

BY

FRANK H. HITCHCOCK,

Chief, Section of Foreign Markets.

WASHINGTON:

GOVERNMENT PRINTING OFFICE.

·1902·

LETTER OF TRANSMITTAL.

U. S. Department of Agriculture,
Section of Foreign Markets,
Washington, D. C., November 27, 1901.

Sir: I have the honor to transmit herewith a statistical report on the agricultural imports of the United Kingdom during the five years 1896–1900, and to recommend its publication as Bulletin No. 26 of this Office.

Very respectfully,

Frank H. Hitchcock,
Chief.

Hon. James Wilson,
Secretary of Agriculture.

CONTENTS.

Value of agricultural imports—Continued.
Vegetable matter—Continued.

AGRICULTURAL IMPORTS OF THE UNiTED KiNGDOM, 1896-1900.[a]

INTRODUCTION.

The United Kingdom is the principal market for the surplus agricultural produce of exporting countries. The products of agriculture sent to that market from all sources in 1900 reached the enormous value of $1,578,000,000, forming 62 per cent of the entire import trade of Great Britain and Ireland.

The total value of the merchandise imported into the United Kingdom during each of the five years 1896–1900, and the extent to which that merchandise consisted of agricultural produce, will be seen from the following table:

Imports of the United Kingdom classified as agricultural and nonagricultural.

Calendar years.	Total imports.	Agricultural.		Nonagricultural.	
	Dollars.	*Dollars.*	*Per cent.*	*Dollars.*	*Per cent.*
1896	2,150,063,031	1,378,933,618	64.13	771,129,413	35.87
1897	2,194,932,434	1,393,546,461	63.49	801,385,973	36.51
1898	2,289,905,792	1,474,681,428	64.40	815,224,364	35.60
1899	2,360,425,665	1,469,924,839	62.27	890,500,826	37.73
1900	2,545,545,281	1,577,522,533	61.97	968,022,748	38.03
Annual average, 1896-1900	2,308,174,441	1,458,921,776	63.21	849,252,665	36.79

SOURCES OF IMPORTATION.

To this extraordinary import trade in agricultural produce the United States was the principal contributor, furnishing about 33 per cent, or nearly one-third, of the supply. About 43 per cent came from foreign countries other than the United States. The several possessions and dependencies of the United Kingdom throughout the world together contributed about 24 per cent.

[a] The statistics given in the present bulletin are based on the official import returns collected by the British customs department. Through the courtesy of Mr. A. J. Wood, the statistician of that department, it has been possible as regards certain articles to print more detailed figures than those published in the department's yearly report, entitled Annual Statement of the Trade of the United Kingdom with Foreign Countries and British Possessions. With the exception of the figures thus furnished by Mr. Wood from the records of his department, the official publication mentioned is the authority for all statistical matter here presented. To serve more satisfactorily the purposes of the bulletin, the British denominations of quantity and value have in every instance been converted into United States equivalents.

UNITED STATES.

The value of the agricultural produce received from the United States amounted to $513,000,000, leaving over $1,000,000,000 worth of such produce to be supplied from other sources.

While the United States already possesses a market of exceeding importance in the United Kingdom, selling to that country more than half of the surplus production of American farms, it will be seen from the figures just quoted that the possibilities of further trade extension there, in competition with other exporting countries, are well worth consideration.

Among the agricultural imports into the British market during 1900 there were comparatively few products in which the United States controlled the larger portion of the trade. Taking such items[a] as had a value exceeding $10,000,000, of which there were thirty-four in the year under consideration, we find that only nine of them came more extensively from the United States than from the various other sources. These nine items, with the percentage of the total supply received in each case from the United States, were as follows: Lard, 93 per cent; hams, 89 per cent; tobacco, 84 per cent; wheat flour, 83 per cent; fresh beef, 74 per cent; raw cotton, 74 per cent; cattle, 72 per cent; indian corn, 70 per cent; and bacon, 64 per cent.

It will be noticed that, with the exception of cotton, indian corn, and tobacco, the products enumerated are all articles of food. They occupy a most important place with reference to the bread and meat supply of the British people. While other countries are the chief contributors as regards the various food articles that may be properly designated as luxuries, and especially such articles as can in cases of emergency be readily dispensed with, the United States is the source from which the British people procure in large measure those staple food products that are absolutely necessary to the maintenance of life. It is this staple character of the foods in question that causes the peculiar dependence of the United Kingdom on American sources of supply.

The above-mentioned articles that are so largely furnished by the United States comprised in 1900 nearly three-fourths of all the farm produce imported from that source. The residue of the British agricultural imports for 1900 included several products that were received quite extensively from the United States, but in amounts forming less than 50 per cent of the total, as follows: Wheat, 48 per cent; oil cake, 46 per cent; oats, 28 per cent; barley, 26 per cent; cheese, 25 per cent; and tallow, 25 per cent. Although at present the principal part of the trade in each of these articles goes to competing countries, there is unquestionably abundant opportunity, in the face of this competition, to extend the sale of the American products.

Aside from the various leading items to which reference has already been made, the agricultural imports into the United Kingdom during

---

[a] See table on page 48.

the year in question embraced nineteen additional articles with values exceeding $10,000,000. In the case of these latter articles, the United States supplied only a small portion of the total importations.

Some of the products in which the American export trade is now comparatively small, as, for instance, butter, eggs, wines, oleomargarin, potatoes, and oranges, seem capable under favorable conditions of being produced in the United States in sufficient quantities to warrant much larger exportations.

Less than 2 per cent of the butter imported into the British market during 1900 was furnished by the United States. For the imports received from other sources the United Kingdom paid over $83,000,000. These figures suggest large possibilities in the way of extended trade for American butter.

The British market apparently offers the United States abundant opportunity to establish a valuable export business in eggs. The eggs imported by the United Kingdom in 1900 cost over $26,000,000. Only about 3 per cent of this sum went into the pockets of American exporters.

During 1900 the considerable sum of $25,000,000 was spent by the British people for imported wines. Less than 1 per cent of these wines came from the United States. With the rapid growth of the California wine industry the outlook for a larger export trade in that product becomes brighter.

About $12,000,000 worth of oleomargarin was imported during 1900 to supply the needs of the British people. While at present the amount of oleomargarin manufactured in the United States exceeds only slightly the domestic requirements, this article could unquestionably be produced for exportation. Of the British imports for 1900 the United States supplied less than 1 per cent.

During the year under consideration the United Kingdom spent nearly $11,000,000 for imported potatoes. Practically the entire trade went to countries other than the United States. The British market would seem to afford a promising field for the sale of American potatoes. This apparent opportunity to develop a larger export trade in potatoes suggests also the possibility of creating a foreign demand for that important American product, the yam, or sweet potato.

Oranges form another item among the British agricultural imports that could be more largely supplied from American sources. The remarkable development of orange culture in the United States, especially on the Pacific coast, and the recently improved facilities for transportation across the continent, will doubtless result in bringing the American fruit into more active competition with the product of other countries that now supply the British market. During 1900 the people of the United Kingdom spent over $10,000,000 in the importation of oranges. Less than 1 per cent of the shipments received came from the United States.

Aside from the products just mentioned, which have been selected as offering some of the most promising opportunities for development in the trade between the United States and the United Kingdom, there are numerous other agricultural products that suggest possibilities in the way of a larger sale in the British market. Many of the articles falling within this class are what are known as perishable merchandise, consisting of products that can not be transported great distances except under refrigeration. The more general introduction of refrigeration facilities on land and sea has greatly increased the opportunities for trade extension in such products, making it possible to forward them in good condition to the seaboard and transport them undamaged across the Atlantic to the British market in competition with similar products that are sent to that market by the less distant countries of Europe. It is in these perishable products, the exportation of which is made possible by modern transportation methods, that the greatest future development of American trade in the British market may be expected.

FOREIGN COUNTRIES.[a]

FRANCE.

Chief among the foreign countries that compete with the United States in supplying farm produce to the United Kingdom is the great neighboring republic of France, from which in 1900 agricultural imports were received to the value of $103,000,000, comprising 6.5 per cent of the total. Large as are the purchases made from France, however, they amount to less than a quarter of what is bought from the United States.

Sugar and wines are the leading articles of importation from France. That country also furnishes large quantities of butter and eggs, as well as fruits and vegetables in abundance. French brandies are imported quite extensively, forming another item of considerable value. Wool is also one of the leading imports from France.

GERMANY.

Next to France, the largest competitor of the United States in the British market is Germany, from which country in 1900 there was

---

[a] Unfortunately the British import returns do not always show the original sources of the articles received, it being the general practice to record imports as coming from the last country of shipment. Under this method the recorded imports from seaboard nations, such as France, Belgium, the Netherlands, and Germany, frequently include merchandise originally shipped from interior countries like Switzerland and Austria-Hungary. In the case of Switzerland, for instance, while products of that country were unquestionably imported into the United Kingdom during the years covered by the report, no such imports appear on the face of the returns. The imports from Switzerland were undoubtedly credited to the intermediate countries through which they passed. The character of the returns in this regard should be taken into consideration in making use of the statistics here presented, and especially with reference to the importations recorded from the several seaboard countries adjacent to the United Kingdom.

imported $79,000,000 worth of agricultural produce, or 5 per cent of the total. Sugar, which is the principal factor in the German trade, constituted more than half of these imports. Aside from sugar, the agricultural products purchased most extensively from Germany are eggs, wheat, oats, and oil cake. The wheat and oats, if not also the eggs and oil cake, are doubtless in large part reexports of produce received originally from other countries, and particularly from Russia.

NETHERLANDS.

The Netherlands supplied 4.4 per cent of the agricultural produce imported into the United Kingdom during 1900, the value amounting to $69,000,000. Oleomargarin, or imitation butter, formed the largest item, and sugar the second largest. Among other products that are imported in considerable quantities from the Netherlands should be mentioned butter, cheese, and milk, and also fresh pork and fresh mutton.

ARGENTINA.

Agricultural imports worth $63,000,000, or 4 per cent of the total, were received in 1900 from Argentina. Wheat is the product imported most extensively from that source. Another grain that the United Kingdom receives in large quantities from Argentina is indian corn, or maize. Recently an extensive trade has been developed in fresh mutton, and also a considerable trade in fresh beef. Argentine cattle and sheep are imported quite largely, and to some extent their products—tallow and wool. Flaxseed is another item of considerable importance among the agricultural imports received from Argentina.

RUSSIA.

During 1900 Russia kept equal pace with Argentina as a contributor to the agricultural import trade of the United Kingdom, furnishing products worth $63,000,000, or 4 per cent of the total. Grains occupy an important place among the products received from Russia. In the year mentioned oats were imported more extensively than any other variety. Wheat, barley, and indian corn followed in the order named. Flax and flaxseed are also leading imports from Russia, and within the last few years an important trade has been developed in butter and eggs.

DENMARK.

From Denmark, which is the leading source of the United Kingdom's butter imports, agricultural produce was received in 1900 to the value of $62,000,000, or 3.9 per cent of the total. After butter, the principal item received from Denmark is bacon, to the production of which Danish agriculturists have recently given much attention. In addition to butter and bacon, the Danes are now beginning to send large quantities of eggs to the British market.

EGYPT.

The large amount of cotton supplied by Egypt gives that country a place of some prominence among the sources of the United Kingdom's agricultural imports. In 1900 the agricultural products of all kinds imported from Egypt had an aggregate value of $60,000,000, forming 3.8 per cent of the total. The long-fibered Egyptian cotton, which is used so extensively by the British in the manufacture of certain lines of cotton goods, comprises by far the largest part of the trade. Of the remaining imports, cotton seed, another product of the cotton plant, is decidedly the most important.

BELGIUM.

Belgium contributed 2.2 per cent of the agricultural produce imported by the United Kingdom during 1900, the shipments for that year having a value of $34,000,000. Sugar, flax, and eggs are the articles received in largest quantities from Belgium. Other items of considerable importance in the Belgian trade are potatoes, butter, and wool. It is to be assumed that the wool furnished by Belgium was almost entirely the product of other countries, and probably in chief part of France and Argentina.

SPAIN.

From Spain agricultural imports amounting in value to $26,000,000, and forming 1.7 per cent of the total, were received during 1900. Fruits occupy the most important place among the products purchased from that country. The orange is the fruit imported most extensively, but raisins and grapes are also received in considerable quantities. Next to fruits the principal item consists of wines. Other leading imports from Spain are Spanish onions, esparto, olive oil, and almonds.

ASIATIC TURKEY.

Asiatic Turkey sent to the British market in 1900 $16,000,000 worth of agricultural produce, or 1 per cent of the total. Barley forms the largest item among the agricultural imports from that country. Other articles of considerable importance are raisins, figs, and wool.

BRITISH POSSESSIONS.

AUSTRALASIA.

Among the British possessions that contribute to the agricultural import trade of the parent country the Australasian colonies now rank foremost. In 1900 Australasia furnished about 9 per cent of all the agricultural produce imported by the United Kingdom, the combined imports from the various Australasian colonies having an aggregate value of $146,000,000. New Zealand, New South Wales, and Victoria are the leading sources, but Queensland and South Australia also make important contributions. Products of animal industry, and particularly of sheep raising, are conspicuous among the importations from Australasia. Wool forms decidedly the largest item in the trade, while fresh mutton ranks second in importance. Butter is also imported quite extensively from Australasia, and so are tallow and stearin. Beef, fresh and cured, forms another item of considerable importance.

BRITISH EAST INDIES.

Next to Australasia, the British East Indies supply the greatest amount of agricultural produce imported into the United Kingdom from its several colonial possessions. In 1900 the value of the shipments received from that source amounted to $126,000,000, forming about 8 per cent of the total. A large part of the imports received from the British East Indies comes from Bengal. After Bengal, the most important sources are Ceylon and Bombay.

The principal import into the United Kingdom from the British East Indies is tea. Jute ranks next to tea in importance, while flaxseed stands third and rice fourth. Hides and skins also form a considerable item among the articles of importation.

CANADA.

With the exception of Australasia and the British East Indies, Canada outstrips all other British possessions as a contributor to the agricultural import trade of the mother country. During 1900 the agricultural products received from Canada comprised 4.4 per cent of the total, their value being $69,000,000.

Cheese is the item of leading value among the articles supplied by Canada. Other animal products furnished quite extensively are bacon and hams, and butter and eggs. Canadian beef cattle are shipped in large numbers to the United Kingdom, forming one of the principal features of the trade. Canada also sends heavy shipments of grain to the British market, particularly wheat and indian corn, with oats in smaller quantities. Wheat flour is another important article of shipment, as are also fresh apples.

CAPE OF GOOD HOPE.

Of the remaining British dependencies that send agricultural produce to the markets of the United Kingdom, the Cape of Good Hope is the most important. During 1900 about 1 per cent of the British agricultural imports came from that source, the value amounting to $14,000,000. The principal products received from the Cape are wool, ostrich feathers, and mohair.

SUMMARY STATEMENT, BY COUNTRIES, OF AGRICULTURAL IMPORTS.

Following is a table that shows the value of the agricultural products imported into the United Kingdom from the various countries of supply during each of the five years 1896–1900:

Value of the agricultural products imported into the United Kingdom from the several countries of shipment during each calendar year from 1896 to 1900, inclusive.

Countries from which imported.	Annual average, 1896–1900.	Calendar years.					Per cent in 1900.
		1896.	1897.	1898.	1899.	1900.	
FOREIGN COUNTRIES.							
	Dollars.	*Dollars.*	*Dollars.*	*Dollars.*	*Dollars.*	*Dollars.*	
United States.	458,937,265	410,395,253	436,533,449	489,921,515	445,080,924	512,755,183	32.50
France	95,391,145	88,989,826	99,105,600	91,409,090	94,209,465	103,241,744	6.54
Germany	73,170,450	72,234,429	64,783,670	73,554,599	76,201,925	79,077,628	5.01
Netherlands	62,740,031	57,606,084	60,562,733	61,296,810	65,485,010	68,749,520	4.36
Argentina	45,029,513	43,417,568	27,720,457	37,706,250	52,981,235	63,322,053	4.01
Russia	68,809,636	82,083,769	77,792,941	64,450,131	56,438,936	63,282,404	4.01
Denmark	55,186,922	49,578,904	51,550,583	54,848,702	58,363,784	61,592,635	3.90
Egypt	48,974,309	46,097,337	44,437,795	42,126,863	52,136,196	60,073,352	3.81
Belgium	30,086,640	28,713,690	29,688,121	27,976,637	29,725,294	34,329,458	2.18
Spain	25,123,453	23,064,456	24,881,423	25,726,740	25,767,965	26,176,680	1.66
Turkey, Asiatic	14,511,025	14,129,250	16,687,194	13,125,702	12,464,522	16,148,456	1.02
Portugal	9,181,864	7,781,912	8,084,117	10,931,830	9,599,236	9,512,225	.60
Italy	9,404,556	9,240,396	9,455,980	9,208,833	9,814,141	9,303,428	.59
Greece	5,752,535	3,844,078	5,496,929	5,505,568	5,190,896	8,725,205	.55
China	9,505,225	10,093,244	8,821,094	9,348,981	11,082,584	8,180,273	.52
Philippine Islands a.	6,636,999	7,008,223	5,657,137	6,940,184	5,810,946	7,768,506	.49
Brazil	4,525,146	4,235,385	4,474,864	4,109,369	3,358,138	6,447,972	.41
Roumania	11,131,366	15,590,340	10,974,083	12,541,603	10,127,930	6,422,875	.41
Sweden	8,107,963	10,380,141	8,447,814	8,592,414	7,743,029	5,376,417	.34
Turkey, European b.	6,063,251	5,787,278	7,643,701	5,870,713	5,989,823	5,024,738	.32
Austria-Hungary	4,306,923	4,481,527	4,558,428	3,728,129	4,325,046	4,441,486	.28
Canary Islands	3,209,141	2,267,408	2,601,695	3,328,764	3,900,916	3,946,922	.25
Chile	4,749,989	6,277,223	4,171,316	4,730,122	4,651,283	3,920,002	.25
Peru	4,087,717	4,750,069	4,502,652	4,761,573	3,294,865	3,129,427	.20
Morocco	1,572,678	921,562	880,926	1,724,644	1,546,539	2,789,721	.18
Algeria	1,776,890	1,493,173	1,719,358	1,804,245	2,039,628	1,828,048	.12
Uruguay	1,334,122	1,135,526	1,418,386	1,540,083	755,665	1,820,999	.12
Norway	1,724,755	1,826,467	1,729,132	1,846,955	1,920,906	1,800,316	.11
Costa Rica	1,746,319	1,516,124	1,599,979	2,795,756	1,169,006	1,650,731	.10
Colombia	1,842,318	1,851,023	1,728,405	2,801,863	2,149,312	1,181,485	.07
Java	1,713,862	3,518,309	1,414,477	1,795,437	981,554	859,535	.05
French Indo-China..	723,162	57,931	1,730,240	242,420	787,508	797,716	.05
Tripoli	1,072,307	1,560,045	1,203,042	788,699	1,052,707	757,043	.05
Japan	1,195,448	1,419,119	1,278,127	786,513	1,766,202	727,280	.05
Ecuador	683,252	659,187	365,373	967,781	774,723	649,196	.04
Salvador	721,369	772,133	747,782	1,002,689	469,184	615,057	.04
Mexico	456,294	246,197	296,229	319,023	821,913	598,108	.04
Cyprus	476,561	401,122	475,232	651,481	333,122	521,848	.03
Guatemala	1,323,182	1,989,269	1,827,557	1,451,522	859,458	488,105	.03
Azores	398,402	350,948	358,048	456,327	413,706	412,981	.03
Tunis	512,927	293,718	295,504	891,285	689,929	394,201	.02
Pacific islands	338,127	418,095	376,015	91,773	447,777	356,976	.02
Nicaragua	321,090	162,200	637,438	289,411	179,623	336,776	.02
Persia	349,818	357,474	499,625	400,990	159,290	331,710	.02
German West Africa.	89,690	29,491	53,684	45,093	8,254	311,977	.02
Madeira Islands	284,261	252,371	343,532	284,082	283,440	257,880	.02
Liberia	c97,561	(d)	72,161	47,574	32,708	237,802	.02
French West Africa.	126,448	74,838	86,112	152,716	108,916	209,658	.01
Bulgaria	891,282	1,793,383	1,931,183	458,264	75,660	197,921	.01
Portuguese West Africa	62,263	36,367	27,141	31,120	22,771	193,914	.01
Portuguese East Africa	181,214	271,876	392,050	55,702	54,548	131,892	.01
Dutch Guiana	126,580	118,814	118,602	125,531	144,638	125,317	.01
Venezuela	163,080	228,186	227,104	147,888	107,209	105,014	.01
Madagascar	135,295	220,676	215,474	70,452	73,275	96,600	.01
French West Indies..	20,068				7,942	92,400	.01
West Africa, n. e. s..	c30,105	89,996	12,930	10,438	18,084	78,969	.01
Crete	e107,190	(f)	(f)	(f)	190,047	24,333	
Kongo Free State ...	10,311	10,663	6,716	5,329	4,784	21,065	
Spanish West Africa.	11,713	1,625	3,888	20,430	8,594	24,026	
Macao	46,074	85,460	69,026	28,343	30,776	16,765	
Dutch East Indies, n. e. s	19,271	6,395	9,641	41,998	23,967	14,356	.01
Siam	133,571	8,273	637,769		9,247	12,565	
Haiti and Santo Domingo	3,832	13,451	4,740		58	219	
Danish West Indies..	46,517	32,100	91,067	109,418			
Cuba and Porto Rico.	36,318	57,877	56,456	39,458	g27,797		
Honduras	13,766	19,466	686	48,680			

a Including the Ladrone Islands.
b Including in 1896–1898 small imports from Crete.
c Annual average, 1897–1900.
d Included in "West Africa, n. e. s."
e Annual average, 1899–1900.
f Included in European Turkey.
g Comprising imports from Cuba valued at $22,931 and from Porto Rico, $4,866.

Value of the agricultural products imported into the United Kingdom from the several countries of shipment, etc.—Continued.

Countries from which imported.	Annual average, 1896–1900.	Calendar years.					Per cent in 1900.
		1896.	1897.	1898.	1899.	1900.	
FOREIGN COUNTRIES— continued.	*Dollars.*	*Dollars.*	*Dollars.*	*Dollars.*	*Dollars.*	*Dollars.*	
German New Guinea.	9,835	49,176	......	......	......	......	......
French India........	1,061	5,304	......	......	......	......	......
Abyssinia	82	......	......	409	......	......	......
Other a	1,021,906	581,966	690,867	988,582	1,120,816	1,727,297	} 0.11
Northern whale fisheries...............	6,390	399	307	7,056	14,001	10,186	
Total foreign countries....	1,088,509,784	1,032,485,565	1,044,265,687	1,096,608,082	1,075,429,318	1,193,760,268	75.67
BRITISH POSSESSIONS.							
Australasia:							
New Zealand....	43,231,249	37,231,008	39,679,970	40,957,441	44,631,752	53,656,073	3.40
New South Wales	38,442,766	39,665,555	38,786,160	37,180,944	39,816,046	36,765,123	2.33
Victoria	24,673,301	23,219,872	23,227,379	20,269,878	26,293,319	30,356,058	1.92
Queensland	14,000,905	14,410,935	15,291,916	13,514,316	13,327,412	13,459,945	.85
South Australia .	7,009,591	8,295,964	6,249,885	5,090,866	7,580,415	7,830,827	.50
West Australia ..	1,572,192	1,714,793	1,336,969	1,289,194	1,564,614	1,955,392	.12
Tasmania	1,310,639	1,476,171	1,288,235	1,216,625	1,220,810	1,351,354	.09
Fiji Islands......	31,551	......	43,799	......	28,664	85,290	.01
Colonies not specified......	116,421	103,904	94,965	73,448	180,284	129,504	.01
Total Australasia..........	130,388,615	126,118,202	125,999,278	119,592,712	134,643,316	145,589,566	9.23
British East Indies:							
Bengal	67,144,832	62,012,933	63,976,906	69,351,916	71,282,399	69,100,005	4.38
Ceylon	22,033,972	21,469,625	21,094,331	21,306,566	21,869,909	24,429,427	1.55
Bombay..........	16,843,859	16,432,757	11,807,740	21,903,444	21,656,581	12,418,825	.79
Madras..........	6,729,680	8,997,756	5,785,325	5,491,197	6,064,901	7,309,222	.46
Straits Settlements	6,309,588	5,570,381	5,878,605	6,653,587	7,082,774	6,412,595	.41
Burma	5,929,753	5,149,233	4,911,803	7,147,809	6,610,133	5,829,787	.37
Colonies not specified......	117,813	92,368	108,042	115,987	110,725	161,943	.01
Total British East Indies..	125,109,497	119,725,053	113,562,752	131,970,506	134,627,372	125,661,804	7.97
Canada...............	62,467,278	50,371,709	58,829,928	68,334,768	65,718,193	69,081,794	4.38
Cape of Good Hope..	19,498,956	19,666,923	18,620,724	22,735,640	22,455,281	14,016,211	.89
British West Indies..	6,536,042	7,433,997	6,129,918	5,397,182	6,541,877	7,177,284	.45
Channel Islands.....	5,386,860	5,117,917	4,797,531	5,456,899	6,086,210	5,475,741	.35
Hongkong...........	3,170,210	3,075,684	2,054,078	2,916,922	3,682,122	4,172,245	.26
Niger Protectorate ..	1,548,404	962,554	1,064,587	1,117,201	979,777	3,617,902	.23
British Guiana	2,279,188	2,914,885	2,108,805	2,311,603	1,670,582	2,389,865	.15
Natal...............	3,830,761	3,649,078	3,450,776	4,789,109	3,778,899	1,035,943	.06
Lagos...............	3,608,269	4,527,223	4,093,082	3,995,723	4,456,094	969,221	.06
Mauritius	450,158	159,197	176,454	313,915	708,246	892,978	.06
Falkland Islands....	801,004	730,272	706,859	892,429	844,810	830,649	.05
Gold Coast..........	196,108	114,120	64,880	76,955	116,061	608,526	.04
Sierra Leone........	448,085	498,885	430,709	346,403	471,978	492,450	.03
Aden	594,060	738,958	638,237	619,817	527,221	446,068	.03
Malta and Gozo	186,192	158.859	185,774	238,171	150,306	197,848	.01
Gibraltar	113,588	67,713	104,751	130,860	142,414	122,203	.01
Zanzibar and Pemba.	125,060	132,345	167,778	90,229	122,096	112,854	} .01
Gambia..............	66,610	64,500	67,854	73,051	86,287	41,356	
Newfoundland and Labrador	12,069	16,693	8,044	2,068	31,924	1,616	
St. Helena..........	1,360	......	2,710	1,606	1,178	1,304	
British Honduras....	4,415	9,967	11,261	384	384	78	
Bermuda............	1,144	637	3,635	730	720	......	......
British Borneo.......	973	......	......	4,866	......	......	......
Other a	357,827	192,732	211,172	403,839	409,790	571,604	.04
Total British possessions ..	366,682,683	346,448,053	343,491,577	371,763,588	388,203,138	383,507,060	24.31
Countries not specified...............	3,729,309	......	5,789,197	6,309,758	6,292,383	255,205	.02
Total agricultural imports	1,458,921,776	1,378,933,618	1,393,546,461	1,474,681,428	1,469,924,839	1,577,522,533	100.00

a Comprising imports not credited to the countries of shipment.

GENERAL CHARACTER OF AGRICULTURAL IMPORTS.

An examination into the character of the agricultural imports of the United Kingdom for 1900 brings out the fact that about 60 per cent comprised articles of food, about 35 per cent raw materials for manu-facture, and about 5 per cent feed stuffs for the maintenance of live stock.

The amount paid by the United Kingdom for imported foods in the year under consideration reached as high as $937,000,000, or about $23 per capita. This shows how largely the British people depend on outside sources of supply for their means of sustenance.

The people of the United Kingdom also depend in great measure on foreign sources for the various raw materials that form the basis of their extensive manufacturing industries. During 1900 the imports of such materials of an agricultural nature cost $523,000,000, or $13 per capita.

The British are likewise obliged to purchase from other countries a considerable portion of the feed required for their dairy cattle and for the large number of draft animals used throughout the United Kingdom. In the importation of feed stuffs during 1900 the sum of $102,000,000 was expended.

In addition to the three great classes of imports mentioned—food products, raw materials for manufacture, and feed stuffs—about $15,000,000 worth of miscellaneous agricultural produce was imported into the British market during 1900.

Of the food products received from abroad in that year the United States supplied about 30 per cent, outlying British possessions about 20 per cent, and foreign countries other than the United States the remaining 50 per cent.

In the case of raw materials the United States was the source of 33 per cent, the British possessions of 35 per cent, and other countries of 32 per cent.

Of the feed stuffs the United States contributed 57 per cent, the British possessions less than 8 per cent, and other sources about 35 per cent.

The following table shows the value of the agricultural imports into the United Kingdom classified as food products, raw materials, and feed stuffs, and the percentage of each class received from the United States, from British possessions, and from other sources:

Value of agricultural food products, raw materials, and feed stuffs imported into the United Kingdom during 1900.

Classes imported.	Total.	From the United States.		From British posses-sions.		From other sources.	
	Dollars.	Dollars.	Per cent.	Dollars.	Per cent.	Dollars.	Per cent.
Food products	937,443,856	277,891,587	29.64	192,800,149	20.57	466,752,120	49.79
Raw materials	523,182,890	171,186,418	32.72	181,375,529	34.67	170,620,943	32.61
Feed stuffs	102,030,274	57,770,966	56.62	7,964,255	7.81	36,295,053	35.57
Miscellaneous	14,865,513	5,906,212	39.73	1,367,127	9.20	7,592,174	51.07
Total..........	1,577,522,533	512,755,183	32.50	383,507,060	24.31	681,260,290	43.19

LEADING ITEMS.

Following is a table that shows the value of the twelve principal items in the agricultural import trade of the United Kingdom during 1900, and the percentage of each item received from the United States, from British possessions, and from other sources:

Value of leading items in the agricultural import trade of the United Kingdom during 1900.

Items imported.	Total.	From the United States.		From British possessions.		From other sources.	
	Dollars.	*Dollars.*	*Per cent.*	*Dollars.*	*Per cent.*	*Dollars.*	*Per cent.*
Breadstuffs	288,412,796	157,610,276	54.65	31,815,090	11.03	98,987,430	34.32
Meat products	224,969,302	116,430,531	51.75	45,713,340	20.32	62,825,431	27.93
Cotton	200,097,380	147,245,414	73.59	3,557,952	1.78	49,294,014	24.63
Dairy products	126,815,296	10,054,398	7.93	34,915,483	27.53	81,845,415	64.54
Wool	114,645,338	111,204	.10	92,944,720	81.07	21,589,414	18.83
Sugar	93,711,460	10,424	.01	4,327,394	4.62	89,373,642	95.37
Fruits and nuts	65,470,440	5,781,764	8.75	7,428,029	11.35	52,310,647	79.90
Live animals	53,582,165	37,370,344	69.74	9,731,802	18.16	6,480,519	12.10
Tea	52,032,117	178,951	.34	47,449,314	91.19	4,403,852	8.47
Seeds	39,997,374	2,492,508	6.23	11,687,421	29.22	25,817,445	64.55
Hides and skins	32,508,596	95,909	.29	18,009,725	55.40	14,402,962	44.31
Vegetables	30,573,271	1,410,867	4.62	6,461,188	21.13	22,701,216	74.25
Other	254,706,998	34,012,593	13.36	69,466,102	27.27	151,228,303	59.37
Total	1,577,522,533	512,755,183	32.50	383,507,060	24.31	681,260,290	43.19

BREADSTUFFS.

Breadstuffs form decidedly the most important item in the British agricultural import trade. During 1900 the amount expended for imported breadstuffs was $288,000,000; of which sum $157,000,000, or 55 per cent was paid to the United States. The breadstuffs procured from foreign countries other than the United States cost $99,000,000, forming 34 per cent of the total, while from British possessions there were purchases amounting to $32,000,000, or 11 per cent. Wheat and wheat flour, corn, oats, and barley were the principal imports under the head of breadstuffs.

Wheat.—The imports of wheat into the United Kingdom during 1900 were valued at $114,000,000, amounting to 128,000,000 bushels. Nearly one-half of these imports came from the United States, from which source consignments having an aggregate value of $55,000,000, or 48 per cent of the total, were shipped to the British market. Measured in quantity, the wheat received from the United States amounted to 61,000,000 bushels. After the United States the principal source of supply in 1900 was Argentina, from which country 35,000,000 bushels, valued at about $30,000,000, or 26 per cent of the total, were imported. About 9 per cent came from Canada, the imports of Canadian wheat amounting to 12,000,000 bushels, with a value of about $11,000,000. Russia furnished 6.5 per cent of the wheat imports, sending 8,359,000 bushels, with a value of $7,428,000. Imports amounting to 7,071,000 bushels, and valued at $6,402,000, were received from Australasia, that source supplying about 5.6 per cent of the total. From Germany 3,413,000 bushels were purchased, the value being $2,917,000, or 2.6 per cent of the total. Roumania contributed shipments amounting to 1.1 per cent of the total, the quantity being 1,411,000 bushels and the value $1,278,000.

Of the several countries mentioned, the United States is the only one that shows any considerable constancy as a source of supply. In the other great wheat-exporting countries the surplus available for shipment to foreign markets from year to year is a much more variable quantity than in the United States. The imports from Argentina during 1900 were exceptionally large, while those from Russia were much smaller than in some of the preceding years. In 1896, for instance, Argentina furnished only 9,198,000 bushels, while Russia supplied 32,000,000 bushels, or nearly the reverse of the situation in 1900. The imports from Canada and from Australasia during 1900 were also much in excess of the average. The shipments received from Germany during 1900 were considerably larger than those reported for the years immediately preceding, while in the case of Roumania the 1900 figures were noticeably small when compared with the returns for 1896, in which year imports amounting to 10,000,000 bushels were recorded.

Among the various other countries contributing to the British wheat supply in 1900 Bulgaria, Cyprus, Uruguay, Denmark, and European Turkey sent the principal shipments.

Wheat flour.—The enormous quantities of wheat in the grain that are annually brought into the United Kingdom to be milled do not by any means supply the demand. The grain imports are each year supplemented by heavy importations of flour. During 1900 over 12,000,000 barrels of foreign flour were disposed of in the British market at a value of nearly $50,000,000. The principal part of these imports came from the United States, from which country about 10,000,000 barrels were procured, the value amounting to $41,000,000, or 83 per cent of the total. When contrasted with the importations from the United States the shipments received from other countries seem comparatively small. Canada, Austria-Hungary, and France were the only competitors of any considerable importance. Canada supplied 683,000 barrels, valued at $2,777,000, or 5.7 per cent of the total. From Austria-Hungary there were imports amounting to 667,000 barrels, with a value of $3,063,000, or 6.2 per cent. Owing to the exceptionally high grade of Hungarian flour, the imports from that source, although somewhat less in quantity than the imports from Canada, exceeded the latter quite noticeably in value. France, which ranked next to Canada and Austria-Hungary as a competitor of the United States in the British flour trade, supplied 432,000 barrels, the value amounting to $1,577,000, or 3.2 per cent of the total.

Of the remaining sources of supply Australasia, Argentina, and Belgium were the most important.

Corn.—During 1900 the United Kingdom expended $60,000,000 in the importation of indian corn, or maize, the quantity received amounting to 108,000,000 bushels.

Corn is imported chiefly as a feed for live stock, including poultry. The amount used for manufacturing purposes, such as distilling, the production of corn starch, etc., is comparatively small, and the amount used for human food still smaller.

The United States is naturally the principal contributor to the supply. The imports from this source during 1900 amounted to 77,000,000 bushels, having an aggregate value of $42,000,000, or 70 per cent of the total.   The leading competitors of the United States in the corn trade of 1900 were Argentina, Canada, Roumania, and Russia, named in the order of their importance.   During that year Argentine corn was imported into the British market to the extent of 13,000,000 bushels, the value amounting to $7,369,000, or about 12 per cent of the total.   The quantity imported from Canada was 9,591,000 bushels, with a value of $5,205,000, or 8.7 per cent.   From Roumania 4,553,000 bushels, valued at $2,940,000, or 4.9 per cent, were imported.   The shipments received from Russia amounted in quantity to 3,779,000 bushels, and in value to $2,344,000, forming 3.9 per cent of the total.

European Turkey, Morocco, and Uruguay stood foremost among the remaining sources from which in 1900 the United Kingdom drew its indian-corn supply.

Corn meal.—In addition to the heavy receipts of indian corn in the grain, the United Kingdom also makes annual importations, but to a very limited extent, of corn meal.   In 1900 933,000 barrels of this product were received from abroad, the value amounting to $2,221,000. Practically all of these imports were furnished by the United States.

Like the imports of corn in the grain, those of meal are used principally as feed for live stock.

Oats.—The United Kingdom is also a heavy buyer of oats, depending largely on outside sources for this important feed stuff.   During 1900 oats were imported to the extent of 70,000,000 bushels, the value amounting to $25,000,000.

Russia and the United States are the most important sources of supply.   For several years prior to 1900 the United States outstripped its chief competitor in the quantity furnished, but in 1900 Russia came to the front with exceptionally heavy shipments, supplying 37,000,000 bushels, worth $13,000,000, or 52 per cent of the total.   The imports from the United States in that year amounted to 20,000,000 bushels, with a value of $7,201,000, or 28 per cent.   After Russia and the United States, Germany and Canada are the principal contributors. In 1900 the former country furnished 5,884,000 bushels, valued at $2,289,000, or 9 per cent of the total, and the latter 5,313,000 bushels, valued at $1,991,000, or 7.8 per cent.

Among the various other sources from which the United Kingdom bought oats in 1900, the Netherlands, Sweden, and Asiatic Turkey furnished the largest shipments.

While the principal part of the oats imported into the United Kingdom is unquestionably fed to live stock, a considerable quantity of this grain is also ground up into oatmeal to be used as human food, supplementing the large imports of that breakfast cereal in its prepared form.

Oatmeal.—Unfortunately the British trade statistics do not show the exact quantity of oatmeal imported, the returns for that item being consolidated with those for groats. The combined imports of oatmeal and groats in 1900 amounted to 94,000,000 pounds and had an aggregate value of $2,549,000. Of these imports, the United States supplied 80,000,000 pounds, worth $2,255,000, or 88 per cent of the total. Presumably more than half of the imports under this head from the United States consisted of oatmeal. The presumption is strengthened by the United States export returns for the fiscal year ended June 30, 1901, which show that in the year mentioned about 54,000,000 pounds of oatmeal were shipped from this country to the United Kingdom. Aside from the United States, the only country shipping oatmeal in any considerable quantities to the British market is Canada. In 1900 the shipments of oatmeal and groats received from Canada amounted to 13,000,000 pounds, worth $270,000, or about 11 per cent of the total. An examination of the Canadian export returns shows that these shipments consisted chiefly of oatmeal.

Barley.—Barley is used quite extensively in the United Kingdom for malting, and also to some extent for bread purposes. During 1900 the imports of this grain amounted to 40,000,000 bushels, having a value of $25,000,000. The principal importations came from the United States, Russia, Asiatic Turkey, and Roumania.

The United States contributed 9,980,000 bushels, with a value of $6,569,000, or 26 per cent of the total. From Russia there were imported 11,000,000 bushels, worth $6,145,000, or 25 per cent. The imports from Asiatic Turkey were recorded at 9,355,000 bushels, having a value of $6,012,000, or 24 per cent. From Roumania 3,478,000 bushels were received, the value being $1,986,000, or about 8 per cent.

The imports from Russia and Roumania during 1900 were much smaller than in average years, while on the other hand unusually large quantities came from the United States and Asiatic Turkey.

Among numerous other sources from which the barley supply of the United Kingdom was obtained in 1900, Canada, Germany, Chile, and France were the most important.

Rye.—Another bread grain that the United Kingdom purchases in considerable quantities is rye. During 1900 the importation of this cereal amounted to 2,449,000 bushels and had a value of $1,751,000.

The quantities furnished from year to year by the several countries contributing to the supply have varied widely, and especially the imports from Russia and the United States. The two countries mentioned have alternated as the leading source of importation. In 1900 Russia furnished slightly larger shipments than the United States, the imports received from the former country amounting to 827,000 bushels and having a value of $613,000, or 35 per cent of the total, while the United States contributed 821,000 bushels, valued at $555,000, or 32 per cent. After Russia and the United States, the only important sources were Canada, Germany, and Roumania. In 1900 the imports from Canada were recorded at 510,000 bushels, with a value of $363,000, or 21 per cent. Germany supplied in that year 216,000 bushels, the value amounting to $165,000, or 9.4 per cent. The quantity of rye received from Roumania during 1900 was unusually small, amounting to only 60,000 bushels, with a value of $44,000, or 2.5 per cent. The imports from all sources other than those mentioned comprised in value less than 1 per cent of the total.

MEAT PRODUCTS.

Next to breadstuffs, the item of largest value in the agricultural import trade of the United Kingdom is that comprising the various articles of merchandise known as meat products. During 1900 the total value of this class of imports reached the enormous sum of $225,000,000.

A little over one-half of the British import trade in meat products had its source in the United States, from which country shipments were received amounting in value to $116,000,000, or 52 per cent of the total. Foreign countries other than the United States supplied 28 per cent, the value of the imports from such sources amounting to $63,000,000. From the outlying possessions of the United Kingdom there were imports valued at $46,000,000, or 20 per cent of the total.

Hog products were decidedly the leading factor in this trade, their import value in 1900 reaching as high as $102,000,000. The imports of beef products, which came next in importance, carried a value of $62,000,000. Mutton and oleomargarin were also imported quite extensively.

Bacon.—Bacon, which is so staple an article of food in the United Kingdom, was the principal item under the head of hog products. During 1900 the British people expended for imported bacon the considerable sum of $57,000,000, the quantity purchased amounting to 632,000,000 pounds. From the United States alone they imported 443,000,000 pounds, having a value of $36,000,000, or 64 per cent of the total.

Although the United States controls the principal part of the trade, it has two aggressive competitors in Denmark and Canada. During

1900 Denmark sent to the British market 123,000,000 pounds of bacon, valued at $15,000,000, or 26 per cent of the total.   Canada furnished in that year 59,000,000 pounds, worth $5,234,000, or about 9 per cent.

It will be noticed from the figures just quoted that the imports from Denmark and Canada brought proportionately a much higher price than the consignments received from the United States.   In 1900 the average import price of all bacon coming from the United States was 8.2 cents per pound, whereas the import price of the Danish bacon averaged 12.1 cents and that of the Canadian bacon 8.8 cents per pound.

While the United States furnishes a much larger portion of the British bacon supply than either Denmark or Canada, the latter countries take greater pains to produce for export the particular grade preferred in the British market, and their produce accordingly brings on the average a considerably higher price than the bacon received from the United States.

Aside from the United States, Denmark, and Canada, the only sources from which bacon was imported into the United Kingdom to any considerable extent during 1900 were the Netherlands, Sweden, and Russia, but the combined importations from these three countries amounted to only about 1 per cent of the total.

Hams.—Next to bacon, hams form the principal article of importation under the head of hog products.   In 1900 the ham imports of the United Kingdom amounted to 202,000,000 pounds and were valued at $21,000,000.   They were furnished chiefly by the United States, from which country shipments were received to the amount of 179,000,000 pounds, the value being $18,000,000, or 89 per cent of the total.   Canada was the only other country that contributed materially to the supply.   Of Canadian hams, 22,000,000 pounds were purchased, the cost being $2,175,000, or nearly 11 per cent of the total import value.

Lard.—Lard is another hog product the British supply of which is derived chiefly from the United States.   In 1900 the United Kingdom purchased from abroad 216,000,000 pounds of this article, paying therefor the sum of $16,000,000.   Of these imports, 201,000,000 pounds were furnished by the United States, the value amounting to $15,000,000, or 93 per cent of the total.   The only other source from which lard was imported in any considerable quantities was Canada, that country supplying 13,000,000 pounds, valued at $987,000, or about 6 per cent.   The small additional imports received came principally from Denmark, Germany, and the Netherlands.

Pork.—Although pork is not imported into the United Kingdom as extensively as some of the other hog products, it nevertheless forms an item of considerable importance in the trade.   During 1900 there were imports of fresh pork amounting to 78,000,000 pounds, and valued at $7,277,000.   Salted or pickled pork was purchased from abroad to the extent of 28,000,000 pounds, the value being $1,467,000.

The fresh pork came chiefly from the Netherlands and the United States. The former country contributed 44,000,000 pounds, worth $4,009,000, or 55 per cent of the total, and the United States 27,000,000 pounds, worth $2,446,000, or 34 per cent. Among the additional sources of importation Belgium and Denmark ranked foremost.

The imports of pork in a salted or pickled condition were received chiefly from the United States and Denmark. The United States sent to the British market in 1900 14,000,000 pounds, valued at $865,000, or 59 per cent of the total, while Denmark supplied about 9,248,000 pounds, valued at $409,000, or 28 per cent. Of the remaining sources of supply, Canada and Germany were the most important.

Fresh beef.—Among the beef products imported fresh beef forms the leading item. During 1900 there were sent to the British market from abroad 462,000,000 pounds of this article, the value amounting to $40,000,000. The United States was the principal source of supply, furnishing 321,000,000 pounds, with a value of $29,000,000, or 74 per cent of the total. After the United States, the Australasian colonies were the principal contributors, supplying 81,000,000 pounds, worth $5,685,000, or 14 per cent. Queensland and New Zealand controlled the largest part of the Australasian trade in fresh beef. Argentina was another country from which this product was purchased in considerable quantities. The imports from Argentina in 1900 amounted to 46,000,000 pounds, and had a value of $3,247,000, forming about 8 per cent of the total. Among other countries engaged in this trade Denmark and Canada were the most prominent.

Preserved beef.—Beef in its various preserved forms is not imported by the United Kingdom nearly so extensively as fresh beef. During 1900 there were imports of salted or pickled beef to the extent of 22,000,000 pounds, valued at $1,248,000, and of other cured beef, consisting chiefly of the canned article, to the extent of 58,000,000 pounds, valued at $7,092,000.

The salted or pickled beef was received chiefly from the United States, that country supplying 21,000,000 pounds, worth $1,191,000, or 95 per cent of the total. The remaining imports came largely from Canada.

The United States was also the principal source of supply as regards the cured beef imported by the United Kingdom, furnishing 32,000,000 pounds in 1900, valued at $3,447,000, or 49 per cent of the total. Australasia contributed 30 per cent, supplying 17,000,000 pounds, worth $2,129,000. The Australasian shipments came chiefly from Queensland and New South Wales. Belgium, Argentina, and Canada ranked foremost among the remaining countries from which imports were received.

Tallow.—Tallow is another meat product that the United Kingdom imports in large quantities. The British import returns for 1900 show that in that year 244,000,000 pounds of tallow and stearin were received from abroad.   Unfortunately the amount of stearin included in these figures can not be separately stated, but it was presumably a comparatively small portion of the whole.   The combined imports had a value of $14,000,000.   They came chiefly from the Australasian colonies and from the United States.   Australasia furnished 136,000,000 pounds, worth $7,737,000, or 56 per cent of the total.   New South Wales and New Zealand contributed the principal part of these shipments.   From the United States 64,000,000 pounds were imported, the value being $3,417,000, or 25 per cent.   Argentina also contributed quite largely, supplying 20,000,000 pounds, valued at $1,164,000, or about 8 per cent.   Of the remaining sources of importation France, Belgium, the Netherlands, and Canada were the most important.

Mutton.—During 1900 the British people imported 380,000,000 pounds of fresh mutton, at a cost of $28,000,000.   More than half of these imports came from the Australasian colonies, the shipments received from that source amounting to 217,000,000 pounds, and having a value of $16,000,000, or 58 per cent of the total.   Aside from Australasia the only important sources of supply were Argentina and the Netherlands, the former country contributing 125,000,000 pounds and the latter country 37,000,000 pounds.   The imports from Argentina were valued at $8,220,000, or 29 per cent of the total, and the imports from the Netherlands at $3,589,000, or 13 per cent.

Oleomargarin, or imitation butter.—Another article of importation classified under the head of meat products is oleomargarin, or imitation butter.   During 1900 the British people spent about $12,000,000 for imports of this product, the quantity received amounting to 103,000,000 pounds.   The oleomargarin imported into the United Kingdom comes chiefly from the Netherlands.   In 1900 that country supplied 97,000,000 pounds, valued at $11,000,000, or 93 per cent of the total.   Among the remaining countries of supply, France and Germany were the largest contributors.   The United States furnished only about 75,000 pounds, worth a little over $5,000.

COTTON.

After the two large groups of merchandise known as breadstuffs and meat products, the most important factor in the agricultural import trade of the United Kingdom is cotton, enormous quantities of which are annually purchased to supply the British mills with raw material.   For this staple article, which is the basis of one of their greatest manufacturing industries, the British people are largely dependent upon the United States.   During 1900 there were shipped to the British market from all sources 1,779,000,000 pounds of cotton, having an aggregate value of about $200,000,000.   Of these imports 1,760,000,000 pounds, worth over $199,000,000, consisted of raw cotton, and 19,000,000 pounds, worth $656,000, of waste cotton.

Of the raw cotton imported the United States furnished 1,365,000,000 pounds, valued at $147,000,000, or 74 per cent of the total. Next to the United States the most important source of supply was Egypt. The peculiar, long-fibered cotton of that country was imported to the extent of 312,000,000 pounds, the value amounting to $44,000,000, or 22 per cent. The British East Indies also supplied cotton in considerable quantities. From that source 37,000,000 pounds were procured, the value being $3,387,000, or 1.7 per cent. Madras furnished the principal part of these shipments. About 30,000,000 pounds, valued at $3,259,000, or 1.6 per cent, came from Brazil. Peru, Chile, and China stood foremost among the countries from which additional imports were received.

DAIRY PRODUCTS.

Next to the enormous imports of breadstuffs and meat products required to feed the British people the most important group of food stuffs received from abroad is that comprising the several products of the dairy—butter, cheese, and milk. In the importation of these three products the people of the United Kingdom expended during 1900 nearly $127,000,000.

The part played by the United States as a contributor to the British supply of these articles was strikingly insignificant, particularly when contrasted with the situation just described as regards breadstuffs and meat products. Of the sum paid by the British for imported dairy products in 1900 the United States received only about $10,000,000, or less than 8 per cent. The outlying possessions of the United Kingdom were paid $35,000,000, or about 28 per cent. The bulk of the trade, however, was controlled by foreign countries other than the United States, the amount paid to such countries reaching as high as $82,000,000, and forming nearly 65 per cent of the total.

Butter.—Among the dairy products imported, butter was of course the principal item. The butter imported by the British people in 1900 cost them $85,000,000, the quantity received amounting to 378,000,000 pounds. Denmark was the leading source of supply. The imports from that country during 1900 amounted to 166,000,000 pounds, and had a value of $39,000,000, forming 46 per cent of the total.

After Denmark, the principal sources from which the United Kingdom purchases butter are Australasia, France, the Netherlands, Sweden, and Russia. During 1900 the Australasian colonies sent to the British market 58,000,000 pounds, the import value amounting to $12,000,000, or 14 per cent. Victoria contributed the largest portion of these shipments, but considerable quantities were also received from New Zealand and New South Wales. The amount of butter imported from France in 1900 was 36,000,000 pounds, having a value of $8,689,000, or 10 per cent. The Netherlands contributed 32,000,000 pounds, worth $6,883,000, or 8.1 per cent. From Sweden there were imports valued at $4,934,000, or 5.8 per cent, the quantity being 22,000,000 pounds. From Russia, including Finland, butter was purchased to the extent of 23,000,000 pounds, the value being $4,773,000, or 5.6 per cent.

Among the various other countries that contributed during 1900 to the British butter supply should be mentioned Canada, Belgium, and the United States. The quantity supplied by the United States was surprisingly small, amounting to only 6,277,000 pounds, with a value of $1,206,000, or 1.4 per cent.

Butter is one of the agricultural products of the United States for which there should be an exceptional opportunity in the way of increased export trade, provided proper care is taken to supply an article that can successfully compete with the high-grade product now furnished by competing countries.

Cheese.—Another dairy product for which the United Kingdom depends quite largely on outside sources of supply is cheese. During 1900 303,000,000 pounds of this product were imported into the British market, at a cost of $33,000,000. More than half of this sum went to Canada, that country supplying shipments to the value of $18,000,000, or 56 per cent of the total. The quantity received from Canada was 169,000,000 pounds. The United States ranked second as a source of supply, contributing 76,000,000 pounds, worth $8,471,000, or 25 per cent. Cheese was also purchased quite extensively from the Netherlands, that country sending shipments to the amount of 37,000,000 pounds, the value being $3,891,000, or about 12 per cent. From Australasia 9,072,000 pounds, having a value of $1,063,000, or about 3 per cent, were imported, these shipments coming chiefly from New Zealand. Among the remaining sources from which the United Kingdom procured its cheese supply in 1900 Belgium and France were the most important.

Milk.—The British people consume large quantities of condensed milk. The imports of this product in 1900 amounted to 111,000,000 pounds, with a value of $8,486,000. In addition to the condensed milk imported, 1,751,000 pounds of fresh milk were purchased from foreign countries at a cost of $131,000. France, Denmark, and the Netherlands were the principal contributors to the fresh-milk supply.

Of the condensed milk procured from abroad consignments amounting to 43,000,000 pounds, with a value of $3,748,000, or 44 per cent of the total, were recorded as coming from France, but unquestionably a large part of these consignments originated in Switzerland. From the Netherlands there were imports valued at $2,930,000, or 35 per cent, the quantity amounting to 44,000,000 pounds. Norway supplied 12,000,000 pounds, valued at $908,000, or 11 per cent. From the United States shipments amounting to 4,178,000 pounds were received, the value being $377,000, or 4.5 per cent. Of the remaining countries from which condensed milk was imported, Belgium, Germany, and Italy sent the largest shipments.

WOOL.

After cotton and wheat the largest single item in point of value among the agricultural products imported into the United Kingdom during 1900 was wool. The amount expended in the importation of this raw material was $115,000,000. Of the sum mentioned, $93,000,000, or 81 per cent, went to the various British possessions, the amount of wool imported into the United Kingdom from foreign sources being a comparatively small portion of the total. In 1900 the receipts from countries not under the British flag had a value of about $22,000,000, forming about 19 per cent.

Under the general head of wool the British import returns include mohair, other goats' hair, hair of the alpaca, vicuña, and llama, etc. The principal part of the item, however, consists of sheep's wool, of which 553,000,000 pounds were imported in 1900, with an aggregate value of $106,000,000. About three-fourths of the wool sent to the British market in that year came from the Australasian colonies. The imports from this source amounted to 386,000,000 pounds, and were valued at $79,000,000, or 75 per cent of the total. New South Wales, New Zealand, and Victoria were the largest contributors, but considerable shipments were also received from the other colonies. Of the remaining British possessions, the Cape of Good Hope and the British East Indies were the principal sources of supply. From the Cape of Good Hope 29,000,000 pounds were imported, having a value of $4,849,000, or 4.6 per cent of the total. The British East Indies furnished 31,000,000 pounds, valued at $4,034,000, or 3.8 per cent, Bombay alone supplying $3,700,000 worth.

Among the foreign countries that contributed to the British import trade in wool, France, Argentina, Asiatic Turkey, and Chile were the leading factors. From France 20,000,000 pounds were imported, the value being $4,221,000, or about 4 per cent of the total. The imports from Argentina amounted to 11,000,000 pounds, and had a value of $1,710,000, or 1.6 per cent. Asiatic Turkey supplied 13,000,000 pounds, worth $1,673,000, or 1.6 per cent. From Chile there were imports amounting to 12,000,000 pounds, with a value of $1,635,000, or 1.5 per cent.

Belgium, Russia, Uruguay, and Germany were foremost among the various other countries from which the United Kingdom imported wool during 1900. The United States, although a heavy importer of wool, annually contributes small shipments to the British import trade. During 1900 these shipments amounted to 701,000 pounds, and were valued at $92,000.

The quantity of mohair imported by the United Kingdom in 1900 was 18,000,000 pounds, the value being $5,973,000. These imports came chiefly from the Cape of Good Hope and from European Turkey. Other goats' hair, and hair of the alpaca, vicuña, and llama were imported in much smaller amounts.

SUGAR.

Sugar is another important food product for which the United Kingdom depends almost entirely on foreign sources of supply. In 1900 imported sugar cost the British people $94,000,000, and of this sum about $89,000,000, or 95 per cent of the total, was paid to foreign countries. The sugar received from British possessions amounted in value to only $4,327,000, or less than 5 per cent.

Of the sugar imported into the British market during 1900 2,156,000,000 pounds had been refined, while 1,482,000,000 pounds were received in the raw state. The refined sugar was valued at $60,000,000 and the unrefined at $34,000,000. More than half of the refined sugar came from Germany, that country contributing 1,329,000,000 pounds, with a value of $37,000,000, or 61 per cent. From France 485,000,000 pounds were received, the value amounting to $13,000,000, or 22 per cent. The Netherlands furnished 253,000,000 pounds, and Belgium 68,000,000 pounds. The imports from the former country were valued at $7,274,000, or 12 per cent, and the imports from the latter country at $1,900,000, or 3.2 per cent. Among other sources of supply the most important were Austria-Hungary and Russia. Small shipments, amounting to 210,000 pounds, and valued at $9,600, were recorded from the United States.

Of the unrefined sugar imported 1,147,000,000 pounds, worth $25,000,000, consisted of beet sugar, and 335,000,000 pounds, worth $8,743,000, of cane sugar.

France, Germany, and Belgium were the principal sources of the raw beet sugar. From France 480,000,000 pounds were received, the value amounting to $11,000,000, or 44 per cent of the total. Germany supplied 358,000,000 pounds, worth $7,625,000, or 31 per cent. The imports from Belgium, amounting to 232,000,000 pounds, were valued at $4,848,000, or 19 per cent. The Netherlands and Austria-Hungary were foremost among the remaining sources of importation.

Of the unrefined cane sugar imported nearly one-half came from the British tropical possessions, among which the British West Indies, British Guiana, the British East Indies, and Mauritius were the principal contributors. From the British West Indies 55,000,000 pounds were imported, the value being $1,784,000, or 20 per cent of the total. The imports from British Guiana amounted to 38,000,000 pounds, and had a value of $1,232,000, or 14 per cent. The British East Indies furnished 42,000,000 pounds, valued at $909,000, or 10 per cent. Mauritius contributed 19,000,000 pounds, worth $400,000, or 4.6 per cent.

Among the foreign sources from which the United Kingdom received its largest imports of raw cane sugar in 1900 were France, Peru, Argentina, and the Philippine Islands. From France 50,000,000 pounds were purchased, the amount paid being $1,402,000, or 16 per cent of the total. The consignments received from France consisted of sugar originally imported into that country from tropical sources, and probably in chief part from the French West Indies. From Peru the United Kingdom bought 27,000,000 pounds, valued at $629,000, or 7.2 per cent. Argentina furnished 24,000,000 pounds, and the Philippine Islands about the same amount. The imports from Argentina were valued at $523,000, or about 6 per cent, and the imports from the Philippines at $479,000 or 5.5 per cent. Among other sources from which the United Kingdom received unrefined cane sugar in considerable quantities should be mentioned Java, Brazil, Chile, and Egypt. From the United States 33,000 pounds were imported, the value being $866.

To supplement the enormous sugar supply required by the people of the United Kingdom that country annually procures from abroad large quantities of molasses.[a] The imports of this product in 1900 amounted to 151,000,000 pounds and were valued at $1,694,000. They were furnished chiefly by the United States, from which source 124,000,000 pounds were received, the value being $1,483,000, or 88 per cent of the total.

FRUITS AND NUTS.

Fruits and nuts form an important class among the agricultural products the British people are obliged to procure from beyond seas. The importations under this head during 1900 were exceptionally large, having a total value of $65,000,000. They were supplied chiefly by foreign countries other than the United States, the imports from such sources amounting in value to $52,000,000, and forming 80 per cent of the total. The British possessions furnished shipments to the value of $7,428,000, or about 11 per cent. The imports from the United States were valued at $5,732,000, or about 9 per cent.

Of the $65,000,000 expended for fruits and nuts, about $56,000,000 represents the sum paid for fruits and about $9,000,000 the sum paid for nuts. Fresh fruits were imported to the value of about $32,000,000, and fruits that had been dried or otherwise preserved to the value of about $24,000,000. Oranges, apples, grapes, bananas, and lemons were the varieties of fresh fruit imported most extensively.

---

[a] Including sirup.

Oranges.—Of oranges 570,000,000 pounds were received, the value being about $10,000,000. Spain was the principal source of supply, the imports from that country amounting to 494,000,000 pounds and having a value of $8,768,000, or 85 per cent of the total. The remaining shipments came chiefly from Asiatic Turkey, Italy, Portugal, and Egypt. The United States supplied only 426,000 pounds, valued at $14,000.

Apples.—In 1900 there were imported into the British market 238,000,000 pounds of fresh apples, worth nearly $6,000,000. Of these imports the United States furnished 101,000,000 pounds and Canada 90,000,000 pounds. The shipments received from the United States were valued at $2,486,000, or 42 per cent of the total, and those from Canada at $2,082,000, or 35 per cent. After the United States and Canada the principal sources of supply were Australasia, Belgium, France, the Netherlands, and Portugal.

Grapes.—The amount of grapes imported by the United Kingdom during 1900 was 66,000,000 pounds, having a value of $2,896,000. A large part of these shipments came from Spain, that country supplying 53,000,000 pounds, worth about $2,000,000, or 69 per cent of the total. The remaining imports were received chiefly from the Channel Islands, Portugal, and Belgium.

Bananas.—The Canary Islands supply most of the bananas purchased by the United Kingdom. Of the total importation for 1900, amounting to 1,287,000 bunches, worth $2,671,000, these islands furnished 1,244,000 bunches, the value being $2,572,000, or 96 per cent of the total. Next to the Canaries, the Madeira Islands sent the largest shipments.

Lemons.—The British imports of lemons, including limes and citrons, amounted in 1900 to 106,000,000 pounds, having a value of $2,048,000. Italy, which was the principal source of supply, furnished 92,000,000 pounds, the value amounting to $1,716,000, or 84 per cent of the total. The remaining imports came largely from Spain, although shipments of some importance were also received from Germany, Portugal, and France.

Other fresh fruits purchased by the United Kingdom in considerable quantities were plums, pears, and cherries. Of fresh plums there were imports to the amount of 47,000,000 pounds, having a value of $1,911,000. Pears were imported to the extent of 53,000,000 pounds, worth $1,785,000. The imports of cherries were recorded at 27,000,000 pounds, with a value of $1,501,000. Each of these varieties came in largest quantities from France.

Among the dried fruits imported in 1900, currants and raisins were leading items.

Currants.—The imports of dried currants amounted to 92,000,000 pounds, and had a value of $8,857,000. The principal part of these imports came from Greece, that country sending to the British market 87,000,000 pounds in 1900, the value being $8,488,000, or 96 per cent of the total.   The Netherlands, France, Belgium, and Germany stood foremost among the remaining sources of supply.

Raisins.—Raisins were imported during 1900 to the extent of 74,000,000 pounds, the value amounting to $6,414,000.   Spain and Asiatic Turkey were the largest contributors.   From Spain 45,000,000 pounds were received and from Asiatic Turkey 24,000,000 pounds. The imports from the former country had a value of $3,765,000, or 59 per cent of the total, and those from the latter country a value of $2,298,000, or 36 per cent.   Of the remaining sources of importation Greece and France sent the largest consignments.   From the United States 288,000 pounds were recorded, the value being $28,000.

Figs. —Another dried fruit that is imported to a considerable extent is the fig.   In 1900 the imports of this fruit, including fig cake, amounted to 18,000,000 pounds, and had a value of $1,319,000.   They came chiefly from Asiatic Turkey.

Nuts.—As regards the nuts imported, a distinction is made between those used for food and those for other purposes.   The importations of food nuts during 1900 amounted in value to $5,704,000.   The principal item was almonds, of which shipments worth $2,773,000 were received, the quantity being about 16,000,000 pounds.   Spain and Morocco were the leading sources of supply.   From Spain 5,928,000 pounds were purchased, and from Morocco 4,515,000 pounds.   The imports from the former country cost $1,052,000, or 38 per cent of the total, and the imports from the latter $821,000, or 30 per cent.   The remaining importations came chiefly from Italy, Portugal, France, and the Canary Islands.

Among the nuts imported for purposes other than food, the leading item was that comprising the various oil nuts, of which shipments amounting to 127,000,000 pounds were received in 1900, the value being $3,478,000.   The oil nuts came from numerous sources, but principally from the Niger Protectorate, the British East Indies, Australasia, Sierra Leone, and the Pacific islands.   The United States supplied 224,000 pounds, worth $7,000.

LIVE ANIMALS.

Another important item in the agricultural import trade of the United Kingdom is that comprising the various kinds of live animals. The imports under this head during 1900 amounted in value to nearly $54,000,000.   Cattle formed the principal part of the item, but horses and sheep were also imported quite extensively.

A large part of the British import trade in live stock is controlled by the United States.   During 1900 that country sent shipments valued at $37,000,000, or about 70 per cent of the total.   Other foreign countries supplied 12 per cent, the imports from such sources having a value of $6,481,000. From the British possessions shipments were received to the value of $9,731,000, or 18 per cent.

Cattle.—During 1900 there were imported into the British market 496,000 head of cattle, having an aggregate value of $44,000,000. Of these cattle 350,000 head came from the United States, the imports from that source amounting in value to $32,000,000, or 72 per cent of the total. The remaining importations had their origin chiefly in Canada and Argentina. From the former country 105,000 head were received, and from the latter 39,000 head. The imports from Canada were valued at $8,790,000, or 20 per cent, and those from Argentina at $3,248,000, or 7.4 per cent. The only other sources from which imports came in 1900 were the Channel Islands and Uruguay.

Horses.—The United States also supplies most of the horses imported into the United Kingdom. The total number of horses sent to the British market from abroad during 1900 was 52,000, worth $6,572,000. Of these horses 30,000 were received from the United States, their value being $4,638,000, or 71 per cent of the total. After the United States Russia was the principal source of supply in 1900, the horses imported from that country numbering 12,000, and having a value of $569,000, or 8.7 per cent of the total. Among the remaining countries that shipped horses to the British market in 1900, France, Canada, the Netherlands, and Denmark stood foremost.

Sheep.—Sheep were imported into the United Kingdom during 1900 to the value of $2,969,000, the number received being 383,000 head. Of these imports 179,000 head came from Argentina and 143,000 head from the United States. The sheep purchased from Argentina cost $1,406,000, or 47 per cent of the total, and those from the United States $1,094,000, or 37 per cent. Other sheep imported in that year were received principally from Canada and Denmark. A small number also came from Uruguay.

TEA.

Tea, which forms the favorite table drink of the British people, was imported in 1900 to the extent of nearly 300,000,000 pounds, costing about $52,000,000. The United Kingdom derives the principal part of its tea supply from the British dependencies in the East Indies, and especially from Bengal and Ceylon, which together furnished in 1900 nearly nine-tenths of all the tea sent to the British market. The imports from Bengal amounted to 151,000,000 pounds, worth $27,000,000, and those from Ceylon to 114,000,000 pounds, worth $20,000,000. The quantity received from all British possessions was 271,000,000 pounds, with an aggregate value of $47,000,000, or 91 per cent of the total. The receipts from countries other than British territory amounted to only 28,000,000 pounds, valued at $4,583,000, or 9 per cent. China was the principal foreign contributor to the supply, furnishing 19,000,000 pounds, worth $2,991,000, or 5.8 per cent.

Considering the prominence of China as a tea-exporting country, it is surprising that larger shipments from that source are not sent to the United Kingdom. During 1900 China supplied little more than one-twentieth of the British tea requirements. In the tea import trade of the United States, on the other hand, China is decidedly the most important factor, contributing fully half of the entire supply. Japan, which ranks next to China among the sources from which the United States purchases tea, sells a comparatively insignificant amount to the United Kingdom. The consignments to the British market from Japan in 1900 fell short of 100,000 pounds, and were valued at less than $18,000.

It is doubtless a fact, however, that quantities of tea from Japan as well as from China are included in the British import trade with the United States. During 1900 American houses in the tea business sent to the United Kingdom consignments amounting to 1,031,000 pounds and valued at $179,000. As the United States procures most of its tea from China and Japan, these shipments probably consisted largely of the Chinese and Japanese article.

SEEDS.

During 1900 the British people expended about $40,000,000 in the importation of seeds. They came chiefly from foreign countries other than the United States, the shipments from such sources having a value of $26,000,000, and forming 65 per cent of the total. The United States furnished only about 6 per cent, the value being $2,493,000. From British possessions there were imports worth about $12,000,000, or 29 per cent.

The seed imports of the United Kingdom consist largely of oilseeds. During 1900 such seeds were purchased from abroad to the value of $36,000,000, most of which sum was paid for flaxseed and cotton seed.

Flaxseed.—Of flaxseed 14,000,000 bushels, worth $20,000,000, were imported. Nearly half of these imports originated in the British East Indies, from which source 6,291,000 bushels were received, the value being $9,536,000, or 47 per cent of the total. Bengal furnished most of the East Indian consignments. After the British East Indies the leading sources of supply were Russia and Argentina. From the former country there were imports amounting to 3,155,000 bushels, and having a value of $4,855,000, or 24 per cent. Argentina contributed 2,564,000 bushels, worth $3,320,000, or 16 per cent. Among the other countries from which flaxseed was imported in 1900, Germany, the United States, European Turkey, and the Netherlands stood foremost. The United States supplied 536,000 bushels, valued at $787,000, or about 4 per cent.

Cotton seed.—Of cotton seed the United Kingdom imported during the year mentioned 911,000,000 pounds, valued at $13,000,000. Decidedly the largest part of these imports came from Egypt, that country sending to the British market 782,000,000 pounds, valued at $11,000,000, or 88 per cent of the total. Next to Egypt the most important sources of importation were Brazil, the United States, and Asiatic Turkey. From Brazil shipments amounting to 53,000,000 pounds were received, the value being $562,000, or 4.4 per cent. The United States furnished 40,000,000 pounds, worth $524,000, or 4.1 per cent. The importations from Asiatic Turkey amounted to 22,000,000 pounds, with a value of $231,000, or 1.8 per cent. Cotton seed also came in considerable quantities from the South American countries of Peru, Chile, and Colombia.

Rape seed.—Among the various other oilseeds imported into the United Kingdom during 1900, rape seed stood foremost as regards value. The imports for that year had a valuation of $1,200,000 and amounted in quantity to 1,108,000 bushels. They came chiefly from the British East Indies and from Russia.

Grass seed.—In addition to the oilseeds there were several other kinds of seeds imported, grass seed forming the principal item. During 1900 the grass-seed imports amounted to 29,000,000 pounds, and had a value of $2,477,000. The United States was the leading source of supply. From that country 12,000,000 pounds were received, the value amounting to $1,125,000, or 45 per cent of the total. Large imports came also from Germany, Australasia, and France. Germany furnished 4,157,000 pounds, worth $425,000, or 17 per cent. From Australasia there were imports to the value of $363,000, or about 15 per cent, the quantity received being 4,458,000 pounds. The Australasian shipments came chiefly from New Zealand. France contributed 5,072,000 pounds, with a value of $274,000, or 11 per cent. Additional sources of supply included the Netherlands, Chile, Belgium, and Canada.

HIDES AND SKINS.

Among the various classes of raw materials that figure extensively in the agricultural import trade of the United Kingdom, hides and skins occupy a place of considerable importance. During 1900 hides and skins were imported to the value of nearly $33,000,000. The major portion of the supply came from British possessions, the shipments received from such sources having a value of $18,000,000, or 55 per cent of the total. The United States furnished only about $96,000 worth, or less than 1 per cent. From other foreign countries there were imports to the value of $14,000,000, or about 44 per cent.

According to the official import returns of hides and skins for 1900, consignments came in under the designation of hides to the value of $17,000,000 and under the designation of skins to the value of $16,000,000.

Hides.—The quantity of hides imported was 155,000,000 pounds, the value being, as stated above, $17,000,000. From the British East Indies, which formed the leading source of supply, there was an importation of 65,000,000 pounds, with a value of $7,145,000, or 43 per cent of the total. Bombay and Bengal contributed the principal part of these shipments.

After the British East Indies the countries that sent the largest consignments were Italy, Belgium, and Germany. The imports from Italy amounted to 11,000,000 pounds and had a value of $1,453,000, or 8.7 per cent. Belgium supplied 13,000,000 pounds, worth $1,396,000, or 8.4 per cent. From Germany 12,000,000 pounds were procured, the value amounting to $1,175,000, or 7.1 per cent. The Netherlands, France, Australasia, Russia, and Denmark stood foremost among the various other sources of supply. From the United States 476,000 pounds were imported, the value being $53,000, or much less than 1 per cent of the total.

The consignments received under the designation of skins consisted chiefly of sheepskins and goatskins, the only other item of importance being rabbit skins.

Sheepskins.—About 15,000,000 sheepskins, having an aggregate value of $7,784,000, were imported into the United Kingdom during 1900. From Australasia, which was decidedly the most important source of importation, 6,769,000 were received, their value amounting to $3,306,000, or 42 per cent of the total. While each of the Australasian colonies contributed to these imports, New Zealand sent by far the largest shipments.

Next to Australasia, the principal sources of supply were the Cape of Good Hope and Argentina, the former country contributing 2,681,000 and the latter 1,419,000. The imports from the Cape were valued at $1,454,000, or 19 per cent of the total, and the imports from Argentina at $1,164,000, or 15 per cent. Among the numerous other countries engaged in this trade France, Germany, and Spain held leading positions. Imports of 73,000 sheepskins, worth $22,000, were recorded as coming from the United States.

Goatskins.—The number of goatskins imported into the United Kingdom during 1900 was about 15,000,000, their aggregate value amounting to $6,876,000. The British East Indies ranked foremost as a source of supply. The goatskins received from that source numbered 7,617,000, and had a value of $3,114,000, or 45 per cent of the total. Bengal furnished the principal part of these shipments.

Aside from the British East Indies there were many additional sources of importation, chief among them being Russia, France, and the Cape of Good Hope.   Russia sent 1,984,000 skins, having a value of $993,000, or 14 per cent of the total. · From France 1,471,000 were imported, the value being $771,000, or 11 per cent.   The Cape of Good Hope supplied 1,022,000, worth $536,000, or 7.8 per cent.   Among other countries from which imports came in 1900 should be mentioned Morocco, China, and the Netherlands.   Small shipments were recorded from the United States, the skins received from that country numbering 35,000, with a value of $16,000.

Rabbit skins.—The United Kingdom affords a large market for rabbit skins.   The number received from abroad during 1900 was 33,000,000, having a total import value of $1,046,000.   The trade is controlled largely by Australasia, from which source 24,000,000 skins were imported in 1900, the value being $673,000, or 64 per cent of the total.   Victoria, New Zealand, and South Australia were the principal factors in the trade.

Outside of Australasia the country from which rabbit skins were imported most extensively was Belgium.   The number of skins received from Belgium in 1900 was 6,312,000, valued at $243,000, or 23 per cent.   The only other countries that sent shipments of any considerable size were France, Germany, and the Netherlands.

VEGETABLES.

Vegetables form another item of considerable importance among the various classes of imported agricultural produce that make up the food supply of the British people.   During 1900 the sum expended in the importation of vegetables amounted to $31,000,000.   The part played by the United States as a contributor to the supply was comparatively small, the imports received from that source having a value of only $1,411,000, or less than 5 per cent of the total.   From the various other foreign countries there were importations valued at $23,000,000, or 74 per cent.   The outlying possessions of the United Kingdom contributed 21 per cent, sending shipments worth $6,461,000.

Measured in value more than two-thirds of the vegetables procured from abroad during 1900 were imported fresh.   The aggregate value of the fresh vegetables received in that year amounted to about $23,000,000.   Potatoes, onions, and tomatoes were the principal varieties.   Dried vegetables, consisting largely of peas and beans, with smaller quantities of vetches and lentils, were imported to the value of $6,763,000.   Preserved vegetables were purchased much less extensively.

Potatoes.—Of potatoes about 17,000,000 bushels, worth $11,000,000, were imported.   France, the Channel Islands, Belgium, and Germany were the leading sources of importation.   From France shipments were received to the value of $3,001,000, or 28 per cent of the total, the quantity being 4,093,000 bushels. The imports from the Channel Islands were recorded at 1,968,000 bushels, with a value of $2,622,000,[a] or 24 per cent. Belgium contributed 5,610,000 bushels, worth $2,424,000, or 22 per cent. From Germany 2,480,000 bushels were received, the value amounting to $1,196,000, or 11 per cent. Of the remaining sources of supply the most important were the Netherlands, Portugal, and the Canary Islands.

Onions.—The quantity of onions imported during 1900 was 7,310,000 bushels, and the value $4,149,000. Spain, Egypt, and the Netherlands were the principal contributors. From Spain 2,394,000 bushels were received, having a value of $1,502,000, or 36 per cent of the total. Egypt supplied 1,587,000 bushels, valued at $1,023,000, or 25 per cent. The imports from the Netherlands amounted to 1,887,000 bushels, and were valued at $825,000, or 20 per cent. Among other sources of supply should be mentioned France, Belgium, Portugal, and Germany.

Tomatoes.—The tomato imports were recorded at 93,000,000 pounds, with a value of $3,856,000. They came chiefly from the Channel Islands, the Canaries, France, and Spain. From the Channel Islands there were shipments valued at $1,397,000,[a] or about 36 per cent of the total, the quantity received from that source amounting to 17,000,000 pounds. The Canary Islands supplied 21,000,000 pounds, worth $1,002,000, or 26 per cent. The imports from France amounted to 16,000,000 pounds and were valued at $529,000, or 14 per cent. Spain furnished 23,000,000 pounds, with a value of $429,000, or 11 per cent. Among other countries contributing to the supply Italy, the United States, and Portugal stood foremost. From the United States 5,700,000 pounds, worth $195,000, or about 5 per cent, were received.

Peas.—Of dried peas 4,198,000 bushels were consigned to the British market in 1900, the import value amounting to $3,797,000. Canada and the United States furnished the largest shipments. The imports from Canada amounted to 1,586,000 bushels, worth $1,346,000, or 35 per cent of the total. The United States sent 1,085,000 bushels, having a value of $972,000, or 26 per cent. Of the remaining sources of supply the Netherlands, Russia, the British East Indies, and Germany were the most important.

Beans.—Dried beans were imported by the United Kingdom during 1900 to the amount of 3,206,000 bushels, having a value of $2,613,000. They came in largest quantities from Egypt, Morocco, and Asiatic Turkey. Egypt contributed 1,043,000 bushels, Morocco 731,000

---

[a] The exceptionally high price of the potatoes imported from the Channel Islands is explained by the fact that these imports consist chiefly of early potatoes that are sent into the British market before the general crop becomes available. For a similar reason the tomatoes imported from the Channel Islands bring an unusually high price.

bushels, and Asiatic Turkey 675,000 bushels. The imports from Egypt were valued at $783,000, or 30 per cent of the total; those from Morocco at $630,000, or 24 per cent; and those from Asiatic Turkey at $555,000, or 21 per cent. Germany and Russia stood foremost among the additional sources of supply.

Vetches and lentils.—The imports of vetches and lentils in 1900 amounted to 408,000 bushels and had a value of $354,000. They were received chiefly from Germany, Egypt, and Russia.

EGGS.

It necessitates the importation of a vast number of eggs to meet the requirements of the British people for this article of food. During 1900 as many as 169,000,000 dozens were imported, their aggregate value amounting to $26,000,000. The principal contributors to the supply were Russia, Germany, Denmark, France, and Belgium. Russia, which has recently come into prominence as an exporter of eggs, shipped to the British market about 40,000,000 dozens, with an import value of $5,400,000, or 21 per cent of the total. Germany sent shipments amounting to 35,000,000 dozens, and having a value of $4,950,000, or 19 per cent. Denmark supplied 24,000,000 dozens, worth $4,494,000, or 17 per cent; France, 23,000,000 dozens, worth $4,222,000, or 16 per cent; and Belgium 24,000,000 dozens, worth $3,569,000, or 14 per cent. Additional sources of importation included Canada, the United States, Egypt, and Morocco. The United States furnished 4,259,000 dozens, valued at $760,000, or about 3 per cent.

WINES.

The people of the United Kingdom annually consume about 20,000,-000 gallons of imported wines. To meet the British wants in this direction it cost during 1900 the considerable sum of $25,000,000. The wines imported in that year came chiefly from three countries—France, Portugal, and Spain. From France 6,461,000 gallons were procured, the import value amounting to $13,000,000, or 53 per cent of the total. Portugal supplied 4,635,000 gallons, worth $5,404,000, or 21 per cent. From Spain there was an importation of 5,490,000 gallons, valued at $3,417,000, or 14 per cent. The remaining imports were received principally from the Netherlands, Australasia, Germany, and Italy. It is probable that the wines recorded as coming from the Netherlands were largely of German origin. The United States shipped to the British market 199,000 gallons, worth $115,000.

JUTE.

Among the raw materials the United Kingdom has to import in considerable quantities to supply the needs of domestic manufacture should be mentioned jute. Of this product 281,000 tons were purchased during 1900, the import value amounting to about $20,000,000.

he principal part of the jute imports originated in the British East
ndies, from which source 278,000 tons were procured, coming chiefly
rom Bengal.   The jute received from the British East Indies cost
19,965,000, or over 99 per cent of the entire sum spent in importation.
s regards the comparatively small shipments that came from other
urces, China was the largest contributor.

HEMP.

Hemp is another raw material that is imported quite extensively by the
nited Kingdom.   The consignments received under the designation
f hemp in 1900 amounted to about 100,000 tons, worth $16,000,000,
nd doubtless consisted in chief part of Manila fiber, a product of the
hilippine Islands.   Other fibers included in the import returns of
emp were New Zealand flax, sisal grass, and sunn.

The statistics of hemp importation for 1900 show receipts from the
'hilippines to the extent of 38,000 tons, valued at $6,969,000, or 44
er cent of the total.   Manila fiber undoubtedly formed the principal
art of the consignments to which these figures relate.   This is prob-
bly true also as regards imports received from Hongkong, amounting
o 11,000 tons, with a value of $2,125,000, or 13 per cent.   The ship-
ents recorded as coming from Hongkong unquestionably included
eexports of Manila fiber originally sent to that port by the Philip-
ines.

Under the designation of hemp Australasia contributed about 13,000
ons, worth $1,735,000, or 11 per cent.   These consignments presum-
bly consisted in the main of New Zealand flax.

From Italy there were hemp imports amounting to 11,000 tons and
aving a value of $1,628,000, or 10 per cent.

The additional sources from which shipments were received under
he designation of hemp included Germany, Russia, the British East
ndies, and Mauritius.

TOBACCO.

It annually costs the British people between $10,000,000 and
20,000,000 for their tobacco supply.   The sum paid during 1900 for
mports of this product in its unmanufactured forms was about
14,000,000, the consignments received aggregating 98,000,000 pounds.

The trade in tobacco is controlled very largely by the United States.
n 1900 the shipments from that country to the Bristish market
mounted to 89,000,000 pounds and had a value of $12,000,000, form-
ng 84 per cent of the total.

The residue of the tobacco imported by the United Kingdom is pur-
hased principally from the Netherlands and consists in the main of
umatra tobacco brought from the Dutch East Indies.   The consign-
nents received from the Netherlands in 1900 aggregated 5,729,000
ounds and were valued at $1,311,000, or about 9 per cent.

Among the other countries from which the United Kingdom procured its tobacco supply in 1900 should be mentioned Germany and France.

OIL CAKE.

Within the last few years the use of oil cake in the United Kingdom as a feed for live stock has become so extensive that enormous importations are now required to meet the demand. During 1900 more than $12,000,000 worth of this product was disposed of in the British market. Measured in value, over half of the shipments received consisted of flaxseed oil cake. Cotton-seed oil cake was also imported quite extensively.

Flaxseed oil cake.—Of flaxseed oil cake there were imports amounting to 420,000,000 pounds and valued at $6,793,000. Germany, Russia, and the United States were the leading sources of supply. From Germany 141,000,000 pounds were received, the value being $2,315,000, or 34 per cent of the total. Russia supplied 119,000,000 pounds, worth $1,984,000, or 29 per cent. The imports from the United States were recorded at 118,000,000 pounds, with a value of $1,818,000, or 27 per cent.

Among the various other countries from which the United Kingdom purchased this kind of oil cake in 1900 the most important were the British East Indies, Canada, Spain, and Argentina.

Cotton-seed oil cake.—In quantity the imports of cotton-seed oil cake brought into the British market during 1900 almost exactly equaled the imports of flaxseed-oil cake, recorded at 420,000,000 pounds. The value of the cotton-seed oil cake, however, was considerably less, amounting to only $5,117,000. The cotton-seed variety came in chief part from the United States, that country furnishing 283,000,000 pounds, valued at $3,728,000, or 73 per cent of the total. Aside from the United States, the principal source of supply was Egypt, from which country 97,000,000 pounds were received, having a value of $966,000, or 19 per cent. Among the additional sources from which this product came Mexico and France were the most important.

COFFEE.

While the people of the United Kingdom do not drink nearly so much coffee as tea, there is nevertheless a considerable consumption of the former product. The imports of raw coffee into the United Kingdom during the year 1900 were recorded at 85,000,000 pounds, with a value of $12,000,000. Of this coffee 12,000,000 pounds, worth $2,162,000, or 17 per cent of the total, came from the British East Indies, which form one of the leading sources of supply. Bombay and Madras furnish most of the East Indian coffee.

A considerable portion of the coffee imported by the United Kingdom, however, instead of being received directly from the country of production, finds its way to the British market through intermediate channels. The United States, which is one of the most important of these intermediate points of shipment, forwarded in 1900 12,000,000 pounds, worth $1,896,000; or 15 per cent. Through the ports of Germany indirect shipments were received to the extent of 14,000,000 pounds, the value being $1,878,000, or 15 per cent.

After the British East Indies the largest direct importations in 1900 came from Costa Rica, the consignments from that source amounting to 11,000,000 pounds, having a value of $1,651,000, or 13 per cent.

Other sources of supply included, in the order of their importance, Colombia, France, Salvador, Guatemala, Brazil, Nicaragua, and Chile.

RICE.

Rice finds considerable favor in the United Kingdom as an article of food. During 1900 this product in its various forms, including rice meal and flour, was imported to the extent of 705,000,000 pounds. The total import value was about $12,000,000. The bulk of the rice imported in that year came from the British East Indies, from which source 525,000,000 pounds were received, the value amounting to $8,119,000, or 69 per cent of the total. A large part of the East Indian shipments came from Burma and Bengal. Rice was also purchased quite extensively from the Netherlands, that country being a large importer from the East Indies. The quantity of rice procured from the Netherlands was 65,000,000 pounds, and its value $1,697,000, or 14 per cent. French Indo-China was one of the important sources of supply. Among other countries from which considerable shipments were received should be mentioned Germany and Asiatic Turkey. Imports amounting to 1,471,000 pounds, and valued at $36,000, were recorded as coming from the United States.

FLAX.

In addition to the large quantities of jute and hemp that are imported into the United Kingdom to supply the peculiar needs of the manufacturing industries in which these fibers are utilized, there is a considerable importation of flax. During 1900 flax, not including flax tow, was procured from abroad to the amount of 58,000 tons, the value amounting to $11,000,000. Russia and Belgium contributed the principal part of these imports. From the former country 43,000 tons were received and from the latter 11,000 tons. The importations from Russia were valued at $6,616,000, or 60 per cent of the total, and those from Belgium at $3,481,000, or 32 per cent. Aside from Russia and Belgium the leading sources of supply were the Netherlands and Germany.

Of flax tow, about 13,000 tons were imported during 1900, costing $1,207,000. The imports of this product, like the imports of flax fiber proper, came chiefly from Russia and Belgium.

TABLE OF LEADING AGRICULTURAL IMPORTS.

The following table enumerates the leading articles in the agricultural import trade of the United Kingdom for 1900, arranged in the order of their value, and shows in each instance the percentage received from the United States, from British possessions, and from other sources:

Leading articles in the agricultural import trade of the United Kingdom for 1900.

Articles imported.	Total.	From the United States.		From British possessions.		From other sources.	
	Dollars.	*Dollars.*	*Per cent.*	*Dollars.*	*Per cent.*	*Dollars.*	*Per cent.*
Cotton, raw............	199,441,794	146,951,331	73.68	3,434,795	1.72	49,055,668	24.60
Wheat	113,612,963	54,637,500	48.09	17,152,154	15.10	41,823,309	36.81
Wool, sheep's	106,266,310	92,123	.09	89,745,044	84.45	16,429,143	15.46
Butter	84,922,542	1,205,549	1.42	15,352,046	18.08	68,364,947	80.50
Sugar, refined.........	60,047,748	9,558	.02	1,508	....	60,036,682	99.98
Corn (maize)	59,993,526	41,833,271	69.73	5,205,043	8.68	12,955,212	21.59
Bacon.................	57,298,020	36,459,540	63.63	5,233,838	9.13	15,604,642	27.24
Tea	52,032,117	178,951	.34	47,449,314	91.19	4,403,852	8.47
Wheat flour...........	49,164,050	40,714,385	82.81	3,179,168	6.47	5,270,497	10.72
Cattle................	43,857,842	31,635,870	72.13	8,954,764	20.42	3,267,208	7.45
Fresh beef............	39,724,500	29,489,900	74.24	6,153,850	15.49	4,080,750	10.27
Sugar, unrefined	33,663,712	866	....	4,325,886	12.85	29,336,960	87.15
Cheese...............	33,276,558	8,471,355	25.46	19,553,816	58.76	5,251,387	15.78
Fresh mutton..........	28,427,981	29,145	.10	16,450,780	57.87	11,948,056	42.03
Eggs	26,308,396	759,992	2.89	1,444,241	5.49	24,104,163	91.62
Oats.................	25,482,984	7,201,140	28.26	2,030,878	7.97	16,250,966	63.77
Wines	25,271,292	114,684	.45	748,171	2.96	24,408,437	96.59
Barley	25,076,963	6,568,880	26.20	943,503	3.76	17,564,580	70.04
Hams	20,545,433	18,311,248	89.13	2,178,153	10.60	56,032	.27
Flaxseed, or linseed	20,255,084	787,380	3.89	9,676,885	47.78	9,790,819	48.33
Jute.................	20,120,004	3,747	.02	19,965,201	99.23	151,056	.75
Hides	16,634,398	52,836	.32	8,393,214	50.46	8,188,348	49.22
Lard	15,896,821	14,765,146	92.88	990,620	6.23	141,055	.89
Hemp (except tow).....	15,822,232	118,168	.75	4,867,186	30.76	10,836,878	68.49
Tobacco..............	14,281,031	12,056,126	84.42	39,311	.28	2,185,594	15.30
Tallow and stearin......	13,797,584	3,417,383	24.77	7,934,848	57.51	2,445,353	17.72
Cotton seed	12,771,886	524,000	4.10	10,142	.08	12,237,744	95.82
Oil cake.............	12,397,608	5,702,565	46.00	469,977	3.79	6,225,066	50.21
Coffee, raw...........	12,367,514	1,895,852	15.33	2,764,931	22.36	7,706,731	62.31
Oleomargarin..........	11,995,071	5,193	.04	949	.01	11,988,929	99.95
Rice.................	11,718,868	35,920	.31	8,161,987	69.65	3,520,961	30.04
Flax (except tow)	11,016,739	....	....	44,816	.41	10,971,923	99.59
Potatoes	10,874,530	453	....	2,743,762	25.23	8,130,315	74.77
Oranges..............	10,320,825	14,123	.14	67,523	.65	10,239,179	99.21
Other articles..........	282,837,607	48,711,003	17.22	67,838,756	23.99	166,287,848	58.79
Total	1,577,522,533	512,755,183	32.50	383,507,060	24.31	681,260,290	43.19

AGRICULTURAL IMPORTS IN DETAIL.

Following is a detailed statement showing the value of all of the various agricultural products imported into the United Kingdom during each year from 1896 to 1900, inclusive, together with the annual average for the period mentioned:

Value of the agricultural imports of the United Kingdom during the five calendar years 1896–1900.

Articles imported.	Annual average, 1896–1900.	Calendar years.				
		1896.	1897.	1898.	1899.	1900.
• ANIMAL MATTER.						
Albumen.....................	a$59,317	(b)	$75,041	$49,283	$57,050	$55,892
Animals, live:						
Cattle—						
Oxen and bulls......	45,091,710	$44,973,541	50,490,872	45,364,895	41,222,988	43,406,255
Cows	404,861	302,847	412,455	374,482	488,670	445,849
Calves	5,352	6,662	5,110	4,716	4,535	5,738
Total cattle....	45,501,923	45,283,050	50,908,437	45,744,093	41,716,193	43,857,842
Horses—						
Stallions.............	249,423	162,312	225,115	182,338	213,620	463,729
Mares	2,297,305	1,719,787	2,540,454	2,291,640	2,259,170	2,675,475
Geldings............	3,217,159	3,119,378	3,338,784	3,104,608	3,090,057	3,432,970
Total horses ...	5,763,887	5,001,477	6,104,353	5,578,586	5,562,847	6,572,174
Sheep	4,468,040	5,516,830	4,472,781	4,792,836	4,588,579	2,969,173
Swine	1,003	49	....	4,964	....	....
Other c	260,180	224,847	422,709	244,167	226,200	182,976
Total live animals........	55,995,033	56,026,253	61,908,280	56,364,646	52,093,819	53,582,165
Bones:						
For fertilizers	1,295,033	1,225,706	1,058,911	1,195,402	1,526,422	1,468,724
Other, including animal charcoal..............	154,322	155,733	112,771	133,542	115,725	253,837
Total	1,449,355	1,381,439	1,171,682	1,328,944	1,642,147	1,722,561
Bristles.....................	2,591,950	2,706,105	2,501,980	2,238,434	2,958,929	2,554,304
Dairy products:						
Butter..................	79,700,632	74,673,347	77,459,677	77,678,017	83,769,576	84,922,542
Cheese	27,346,802	23,847,514	28,641,888	24,187,683	26,780,369	33,276,558
Milk—						
Condensed	7,011,044	5,695,518	6,805,134	6,988,056	7,080,918	8,485,594
Other	67,678	26,712	47,925	54,957	78,195	130,602
Total milk	7,078,722	5,722,230	6,853,059	7,043,013	7,159,113	8,616,196
Total dairy products.....	114,126,156	104,243,091	112,954,624	108,908,713	117,709,058	126,815,296
Eggs.......................	22,822,913	20,364,628	21,202,401	21,690,560	24,548,582	26,308,396
Egg yolks and liquid eggs...	d45,685	(b)	34,275	57,094	(b)	(b)
Feathers and downs:						
For beds e	481,718	425,454	442,389	468,347	517,041	555,360
For ornament..........	6,639,212	5,544,160	5,876,357	7,007,765	7,834,442	6,933,337
Total	7,120,930	5,969,614	6,318,746	7,476,112	8,351,483	7,488,697
Fibers, animal:						
Silk—						
Raw	5,724,830	5,180,764	5,417,573	6,514,365	7,051,685	4,459,763
Waste	2,628,367	2,650,646	2,239,052	2,654,608	2,938,106	2,659,425
Total silk......	8,353,197	7,831,410	7,656,625	9,168,973	9,989,791	7,119,188

a Annual average, 1897–1900.   c Exclusive of poultry.   e Including feather beds.
b Not stated.   d Annual average, 1897–1898.

Value of the agricultural imports of the United Kingdom, etc.—Continued.

Articles imported.	Annual average, 1896–1900.	Calendar years.				
		1896.	1897.	1898.	1899.	1900.
ANIMAL MATTER—cont'd.						
Fibers, animal—Continued.						
Wool and hair of the goat, alpaca, etc.—						
Goats' hair—						
Mohair	$6,601,800	$4,507,678	$6,731,119	$7,204,357	$8,592,351	$5,973,497
Other	208,516	150,920	220,433	224,287	145,440	301,499
Total goats' hair	6,810,316	4,658,598	6,951,552	7,428,644	8,737,791	6,274,996
Hair of the alpaca, vicuña, and llama	1,268,311	1,439,306	1,205,043	1,090,096	1,265,587	1,341,524
Sheep's wool	115,368,345	121,459,791	118,922,033	114,785,654	115,407,933	106,266,310
Other, including flocks	602,147	429,352	507,007	505,532	806,335	762,508
Total wool	124,049,119	127,987,047	127,585,635	123,809,926	126,217,646	114,645,338
Total animal fibers	132,402,316	135,818,457	135,242,260	132,978,899	136,207,437	121,764,526
Glue, size, and gelatin	a2,276,520	(b)	2,144,535	2,255,545	2,448,779	2,257,219
Glue stock	a474,525	(b)	272,865	393,471	635,044	596,720
Greaves	c83,417	(b)	92,337	74,496	(b)	(b)
Hair:						
Cattle d	409,087	401,783	485,944	331,156	457,290	369,260
Horse	1,095,240	956,564	1,226,416	1,039,494	1,252,141	1,001,584
Other	1,337,644	1,127,953	1,378,806	1,239,055	1,394,160	1,548,248
Total	2,841,971	2,486,300	3,091,166	2,609,705	3,103,591	2,919,092
Hides and skins:						
Hides—						
Dry	6,688,619	4,406,251	6,877,172	7,080,441	5,587,662	9,491,568
Wet	7,022,543	6,421,424	6,506,467	7,061,433	7,980,563	7,142,830
Total hides	13,711,162	10,827,675	13,383,639	14,141,874	13,568,225	16,634,398
Skins—						
Goatskins	5,991,314	4,086,896	5,310,841	5,820,134	7,862,463	6,876,238
Rabbit skins	1,004,612	992,829	990,450	811,168	1,182,219	1,046,395
Sheepskins	6,857,271	5,964,455	6,368,122	6,835,642	7,333,801	7,784,337
Other e	f 93,304	75,732	97,374	101,505	98,605	167,228
Total skins	13,961,287	11,119,912	12,766,787	13,568,449	16,477,088	15,874,198
Total hides and skins	27,672,449	21,947,587	26,150,426	27,710,323	30,045,313	32,508,596
Honey	132,185	142,569	107,360	134,656	131,999	144,340
Horns, horn tips, horn strips, and hoofs	928,308	891,893	870,349	898,945	943,322	1,037,032
Meat products:						
Beef products—						
Beef, fresh	31,375,602	24,472,791	28,146,215	28,788,778	35,745,727	39,724,500
Beef, salted or pickled	1,245,791	1,477,956	1,050,682	1,328,574	1,123,884	1,247,858
Beef, other cured	5,443,250	5,129,067	4,867,376	4,951,566	5,176,185	7,092,058
Tallow and stearin g	11,027,746	10,602,410	9,100,009	10,056,296	11,582,431	13,797,584
Total beef products	49,092,389	41,682,224	43,164,282	45,125,214	53,628,227	61,862,000
Hog products—						
Bacon	47,903,496	38,223,997	43,155,373	50,230,427	50,609,663	57,298,020
Hams	18,521,123	15,261,777	17,918,288	18,954,234	19,925,884	20,545,433
Pork, fresh	5,368,901	3,344,458	3,723,495	5,671,322	6,827,899	7,277,330
Pork, salted or pickled	1,433,297	1,420,853	1,234,597	1,556,200	1,488,317	1,466,515
Lard	13,125,139	11,040,594	9,699,630	14,053,484	14,935,167	15,896,821
Total hog products	86,351,956	69,291,679	75,731,383	90,465,667	93,786,930	102,484,119
Mutton—						
Fresh	25,042,499	22,962,804	23,494,820	23,856,454	26,470,436	28,427,981
Cured, other than salted	842,436	982,264	785,833	950,179	759,193	734,710
Total mutton	25,884,935	23,945,068	24,280,653	24,806,633	27,229,629	29,162,691

a Annual average, 1897–1900.
b Not stated.
c Annual average, 1897–1898.
d Including elk hair.
e In 1900 including "Skins in any way dressed (not leather)."
f Annual average, 1896–1899.
g Including mutton tallow and mutton stearin.

Value of the agricultural imports of the United Kingdom, etc.—Continued.

Articles imported.	Annual average, 1896–1900.	Calendar years.				
		1896.	1897.	1898.	1899.	1900.
ANIMAL MATTER—cont'd.						
Ieat products—Continued.						
Oleo, oleomargarin, etc.—						
Oleo oil..............	$1,221,812	$1,032,603	$1,079,687	$1,253,586	$1,282,006	$1,461,181
Oleomargarin (imitation butter)	12,051,868	12,158,585	12,095,053	11,603,605	12,407,025	11,995,071
Imitation cheese	63,905	3,494	93,164	74,589	49,327	98,951
Total oleo, oleomargarin, etc.........*l.*	13,337,585	13,194,682	13,267,904	12,931,780	13,738,358	13,555,203
Poultry and game *a*	3,766,046	3,433,209	3,556,073	3,102,355	3,821,633	4,916,961
Rabbits.................	2,809,721	1,954,455	2,644,914	2,786,572	3,108,015	3,554,647
Sausage casings, including bladders..........	*b* 744,177	(*c*)	622,206	780,377	694,834	879,289
Other—						
Fresh or salted	3,853,872	2,696,352	3,539,274	3,955,189	4,298,818	4,779,725
Cured, other than salted.............	3,018,980	2,529,174	2,631,107	2,869,829	3,290,124	3,774,667
Total meat products	188,710,825	158,726,843	169,437,796	186,823,616	203,596,568	224,969,302
Oils, animal, n. e. s., except whale and fish.............	398,221	404,917	348,315	305,149	362,705	570,018
Silkworm gut................	*d* 16,858	(*c*)	12,439	4,015	(*c*)	34,119
Wax. *e*	908,233	947,167	804,359	891,820	913,549	984,269
Total animal matter.......	560,410,889	512,056,863	544,741,236	553,194,426	585,749,375	606,312,544
VEGETABLE MATTER.						
Beer and ale. (*See* Malt liquors.)						
Breadstuffs:						
Cereals—						
Unground—						
Barley...........	26,556,672	27,785,433	22,780,447	33,050,698	24,089,817	25,076,963
Buckwheat......	216,400	176,946	228,331	281,551	226,151	169,023
Corn (maize)	53,725,616	45,854,786	44,716,847	54,905,362	63,157,559	59,993,526
Oats	21,494,474	20,567,372	19,654,883	21,329,174	20,437,957	25,482,984
Rye.............	1,444,890	1,145,117	1,218,971	1,416,370	1,693,026	1,750,967
Wheat..........	113,697,885	105,500,800	113,698,487	127,245,621	108,431,552	113,612,963
Total unground	217,135,937	201,030,454	202,297,966	238,228,776	218,036,062	226,086,426
Ground—						
Corn(maize)meal	1,633,101	600,103	1,270,740	1,846,764	2,226,589	2,221,309
Oatmeal and groats	2,346,424	1,610,646	2,115,331	2,997,399	2,459,841	2,548,902
Wheat flour	49,810,087	44,907,444	46,716,726	56,185,898	52,076,319	49,164,050
Other *f*	572,316	578,325	881,795	271,006	717,356	413,098
Total ground..	54,361,928	47,696,518	50,984,592	61,301,067	57,480,105	54,347,359
Total cereals ..	271,497,865	248,726,972	253,282,558	299,529,843	275,516,167	280,433,785
Sago, sago meal, and sago flour..............	858,803	1,006,100	757,354	796,437	844,547	889,577
Other, and preparations of *g*	6,908,970	6,055,639	6,051,108	7,021,999	8,326,669	7,089,434
Total breadstuffs	279,265,638	255,788,711	260,091,020	307,348,279	284,687,383	288,412,796
Carob beans (locust beans)..	*h* 872,817	(*i*)	(*i*)	(*i*)	940,607	805,026
Cider and perry	70,594	53,707	84,044	70,632	67,090	77,499
Chicory root. (*See* under "Coffee substitutes.")						

a Including live poultry and game.
b Annual average, 1897–1900.
c Not stated.
d Annual average for the three years 1897, 1898, and 1900.
e Including ozokerite and earth wax.
f Including ground beans and peas.
g Prior to 1900 including rice meal and rice flour.
h Annual average, 1899–1900.
i Included in " Beans, dried."

Value of the agricultural imports of the United Kingdom, etc.—Continued.

Articles imported.	Annual average, 1896–1900.	Calendar years.				
		1896.	1897.	1898.	1899.	1900.
VEGETABLE MATTER—cont'd.						
Cocoa and chocolate:						
Cocoa—						
Crude	$6,148,185	$5,129,106	$4,514,263	$6,559,468	$6,416,067	$8,122,018
Husks and shells	6,139	3,703	8,258	11,728	3,806	3,202
Butter...............	209,074	54,987	317,919	143,849	138,505	390,108
Cocoa, ground or prepared, and chocolate ..	2,719,653	1,765,800	2,905,505	2,975,344	2,448,365	3,503,252
Cocoa and chocolate, containing distilled spirits	39,759	24,284	33,501	45,375	49,833	45,803
Total	9,122,810	6,977,880	7,779,446	9,735,764	9,056,576	12,064,383
Coffee:						
Raw	16,127,587	17,318,637	17,446,617	17,470,677	16,034,490	12,367,514
Kiln-dried, roasted, or ground	6,393	3,445	3,071	4,297	4,755	16,395
Total	16,133,980	17,322,082	17,449,688	17,474,974	16,039,245	12,383,909
Coffee substitutes:						
Chicory root—						
Raw or kiln-dried...	205,734	225,022	202,432	198,539	202,427	200,252
Roasted or ground ..	9,245	16,590	10,974	6,813	5,465	6,385
Chicory root and coffee (mixed), roasted and ground	964	1,932	1,017	1,037	477	355
Other...............	696	2,949	268	141	107	15
Total coffee substitutes...	216,639	246,493	214,691	206,530	208,476	207,007
Dextrin	a 52,842	(b)	68,238	41,920	48,368	(b)
Fibers, vegetable:						
Cotton—						
Raw	166,675,443	176,517,878	156,677,805	166,072,009	134,667,730	199,441,794
Waste c.............	573,037	610,639	707,258	415,667	476,036	655,586
Total cotton...	167,248,480	177,128,517	157,385,063	166,487,676	135,143,766	200,097,380
Esparto and other vegetable fibers for paper making...............	3,890,776	3,877,058	4,015,811	3,741,263	3,924,122	3,895,624
Flax, and tow of—						
Flax.................	12,816,003	13,526,198	13,890,504	12,933,035	12,713,541	11,016,739
Tow of..............	1,484,518	1,644,220	1,697,790	1,338,687	1,534,909	1,206,984
Total flax, and tow of	14,300,521	15,170,418	15,588,294	14,271,722	14,248,450	12,223,723
Hemp, and tow of—						
Hemp d..............	11,244,242	9,029,348	8,200,622	10,798,958	12,370,049	15,822,232
Tow of ....,.....	468,251	467,656	380,974	435,260	597,455	459,913
Total hemp, and tow of...	11,712,493	9,497,004	8,581,596	11,234,218	12,967,504	16,282,145
Jute	19,177,996	20,283,533	19,186,712	18,500,413	17,799,316	20,120,004
Kapok..................	e 47,667	(b)	36,445	25,116	(b)	81,441
Piassava and other vegetable fibers for brush making...............	f 984,989	(b)	847,885	1,150,557	983,091	958,423
All other	405,110	447,772	416,616	369,669	313,325	478,168
Total vegetable fibers	217,551,968	226,404,302	206,058,422	215,780,634	185,379,574	254,136,908
Flowers:						
Fresh...................	g 976,147	(b)	1,035,684	1,065,773	1,027,347	976,147
Everlasting...........	g 58,729					58,729
Total	f 1,040,920	(b)	1,035,684	1,065,773	1,027,347	1,034,876
Fruit juices, nonalcoholic...	f 398,235	(b)	477,267	366,657	344,830	404,187

a Annual average, 1897–1899.
b Not stated.
c Probably including cop and mill waste as well as the waste of raw cotton.
d Including Manila hemp, New Zealand flax, sisal grass, sunn, etc.
e Annual average for the three years 1897, 1898, and 1900.
f Annual average, 1897–1900.
g Statistics for 1900 only.

Value of the agricultural imports of the United Kingdom, etc.—Continued.

Articles imported.	Annual average, 1896–1900.	Calendar years.				
		1896.	1897.	1898.	1899.	1900.
VEGETABLE MATTER—cont'd.						
Fruits and nuts:						
Fruits—						
Fresh—						
Apples............	$6,120,747	$7,701,212	$5,778,010	$5,392,355	$5,772,365	$5,959,793
Apricots and peaches	a 125,780	(b)	(b)	(b)	(b)	125,780
Bananas.........	a 2,671,494	(c)	(c)	(c)	(c)	2,671,494
Cherries.........	950,695	514,929	866,875	1,123,324	747,699	1,500,649
Currants........	a 424,213	(c)	(c)	(c)	(c)	424,213
Gooseberries.....	a 71,177	(c)	(c)	(c)	(c)	71,177
Grapes..........	2,599,514	2,155,022	2,409,000	2,674,205	2,863,775	2,895,568
Lemons, limes, and citrons....	2,109,881	2,161,845	1,995,995	2,137,780	2,205,683	2,048,101
Oranges	10,202,440	9,370,032	11,031,966	9,669,541	10,619,837	10,320,825
Pears	1,401,128	1,005,779	1,839,050	1,079,288	1,296,197	1,785,324
Plums d	a 1,911,055	1,176,632	2,422,461	2,115,302	1,431,004	1,911,055
Strawberries.....	a 418,271	(c)	(c)	(c)	(c)	418,271
Other............	a 1,410,068	2,874,963	3,382,991	4,237,315	4,500,651	1,410,068
Total fresh	29,219,080	26,960,414	29,726,348	28,429,110	29,437,211	31,542,318
Dried or preserved—						
Currants........	5,600,445	3,639,018	5,193,646	5,271,295	5,041,232	8,857,035
Figs and fig cake.	1,011,135	1,013,415	1,034,744	647,498	1,041,207	1,318,812
Plums and prunes—						
Prunes	172,304	150,599	150,681	177,194	181,365	201,682
French plums and prunelloes.	366,396	374,575	193,993	474,883	247,033	541,495
Other plums, including dried apricots........	334,307	193,984	448,229	287,362	446,720	295,241
Raisins	4,993,581	4,222,735	4,907,729	4,293,966	5,129,953	6,413,521
Other—						
Dried........	1,606,825	1,206,021	1,959,496	1,187,713	1,594,747	2,086,147
Preserved without sugar......	3,280,761	2,581,469	2,582,038	3,054,780	3,631,358	4,554,158
Total dried or preserved...	17,365,754	13,381,816	16,470,556	15,394,691	17,313,615	24,268,091
Total fruits	46,584,834	40,342,230	46,196,904	43,823,801	46,750,826	55,810,409
Nuts—						
For food—						
Almonds	2,436,401	2,090,006	2,123,877	2,693,272	2,501,493	2,773,355
Other............	2,783,838	2,834,318	2,439,849	2,801,026	2,913,345	2,930,655
Total for food..	5,220,239	4,924,324	4,563,726	5,494,298	5,414,838	5,704,010
Oil nuts	3,168,726	3,234,957	2,874,997	2,941,133	3,314,451	3,478,092
All other	559,904	608,098	576,310	577,873	559,307	477,929
Total nuts.....	8,948,869	8,767,379	8,015,033	9,013,304	9,288,596	9,660,031
Total fruits and nuts	55,533,703	49,109,609	54,211,937	52,837,105	56,039,422	65,470,440
Fruits and vegetables, preserved in sugar............	1,481,621	1,221,214	1,334,691	1,735,744	2,003,412	1,113,042
Ginger. (See under "Spices.")						
Glucose and grape sugar	3,305,234	3,030,671	2,828,410	3,560,949	3,477,786	3,628,355
Grass and moss	e 39,032	(f)	(f)	(f)	53,040	25,024
Hay	1,935,869	1,729,282	1,996,311	1,927,290	2,091,617	1,934,847
Hops	3,651,179	2,878,934	2,551,491	5,013,176	3,941,096	3,871,199
Husks and bran for packing.	g 23,586	(f)	21,748	25,423	(f)	(f)
Indigo......................	5,278,476	7,463,858	7,156,548	4,335,093	4,798,807	2,638,076
Kapok. (See under "Fibers, vegetable.")						
Lard substitutes.............	348,792	231,334	161,373	433,240	438,034	479,978
Locust beans. (See Carob beans.)						

a Statistics for 1900 only.
b Included in "Plums, fresh."
c Included in "Other fresh fruits."
d Prior to 1900 including fresh apricots and peaches.
e Annual average, 1899–1900.
f Not stated.
g Annual average, 1897–1898.

Value of the agricultural imports of the United Kingdom, etc.—Continued.

Articles imported.	Annual average, 1896–1900.	Calendar years.				
		1896.	1897.	1898.	1899.	1900.
VEGETABLE MATTER—cont'd.						
Madder, madder root, garancin, and munjeet.......	a $24,621	$37,394	$23,899	$21,354	$15,836	(b)
Malt......................	12,466	29,535	10,419	6,983	5,446	$9,947
Malt liquors:-						
Mum, spruce, or black beer, Berlin white beer, etc..............	44,932	49,171	48,169	39,613	44,641	43,064
Other..................	572,242	503,624	520,404	532,235	598,229	706,718
Total	617,174	552,795	568,573	571,848	642,870	749,782
Nursery stock (plants, shrubs, trees, and flower roots).....................	2,091,114	1,941,957	2,056,038	2,124,787	2,163,480	2,169,306
Oil cake:						
Cotton-seed..............	3,635,088	1,963,122	2,562,894	3,726,761	4,805,401	5,117,261
Flaxseed, or linseed	6,710,584	5,658,961	6,230,989	7,132,975	7,736,771	6,793,225
Other....................	268,079	111,827	134,826	256,538	350,081	487,122
Total	10,613,751	7,733,910	8,928,709	11,116,274	12,892,253	12,397,608
Oils, vegetable:						
Essential or perfumed...	1,375,556	1,588,362	1,526,465	1,387,512	1,177,771	1,197,670
Fixed or expressed—						
Castor	719,904	934,704	680,799	837,481	762,829	383,709
Cocoanut............	2,016,926	1,214,839	1,292,873	1,674,602	2,655,367	3,246,948
Olive	2,677,450	2,982,561	2,508,832	2,959,426	2,692,566	2,243,865
Palm	5,163,643	5,862,570	4,873,157	4,746,915	5,047,850	5,287,720
Seed (cotton-seed, linseed, etc.)	3,894,522	3,382,193	3,400,194	3,357,564	4,278,486	5,054,172
Other...............	1,071,795	1,439,199	1,282,912	1,097,829	1,005,361	533,675
Total fixed or expressed ...	15,544,240	15,816,066	14,038,767	14,673,817	16,442,459	16,750,089
Total vegetable oils	16,919,796	17,404,428	15,565,232	16,061,329	17,620,230	17,947,759
Opium......................	1,370,026	1,214,581	1,021,079	1,080,538	1,456,981	2,076,949
Rice, rice meal, and rice flour c	10,435,872	8,216,117	10,295,368	9,760,350	12,188,655	11,718,868
Safflower..................	a 3,611	9,261	4,297	584	302	(b)
Seeds:						
Garden seeds	375,185	412,183	433,644	395,384	318,663	316,050
Grass seed, including clover seed	2,999,382	3,837,420	2,818,959	3,188,584	2,675,324	2,476,625
Oilseeds—						
Cotton seed	10,107,693	8,416,656	9,369,721	10,069,329	9,910,871	12,771,886
Flaxseed, or linseed.	17,011,260	19,576,353	14,543,550	14,213,265	16,468,051	20,255,084
Rape seed	1,338,452	951,532	1,256,691	1,789,587	1,494,273	1,200,176
Other...............	1,608,371	810,486	1,965,336	1,652,707	1,729,321	1,884,007
Total oilseeds .	30,065,776	29,755,027	27,135,298	27,724,888	29,602,516	36,111,153
All other	1,056,752	938,232	997,063	1,173,080	1,081,838	1,093,546
Total seeds	34,497,095	34,942,862	31,384,964	32,481,936	33,678,341	39,997,374
Spices:						
Cinnamon..............	275,302	211,479	263,628	316,731	386,561	198,110
Ginger..................	748,870	853,754	834,804	721,459	701,165	633,171
Pepper	2,509,369	1,469,401	2,159,534	2,947,960	2,992,109	2,977,841
Other..................	1,078,941	1,117,806	1,054,634	994,075	1,164,889	1,063,301
Total	4,612,482	3,652,440	4,312,600	4,980,225	5,244,724	4,872,423
Spirits, distilled:						
Brandy—						
Bottled.............	d 2,641,274	} 6,140,550	6,693,209	5,593,234	5,549,158	{ 2,641,274
Unbottled	d 3,226,786					3,226,786
Total brandy..	5,968,842	6,140,550	6,693,209	5,593,234	5,549,158	5,868,060

a Annual average, 1896–1899.
b Not stated.
c Prior to 1900 rice meal and rice flour were included in "Other breadstuffs, and preparations of."
d Statistics for 1900 only.

Value of the agricultural imports of the United Kingdom, etc.—Continued.

Articles imported.	Annual average, 1896–1900.	Calendar years.				
		1896.	1897.	1898.	1899.	1900.
EGETABLE MATTER—cont'd.						
pirits, distilled—Continued.						
Gin—						
Bottled	*a* $217,450	$298,083	$305,300	$306,385	$330,270	$217,450
Unbottled	*a* 105,369					105,369
Total gin	312,571	298,083	305,300	306,385	330,270	322,819
Rum—						
Bottled	*a* 1,927	1,676,246	1,590,431	1,683,400	1,792,965	1,927
Unbottled	*a* 2,346,296					2,346,296
Total rum	1,818,253	1,676,246	1,590,431	1,683,400	1,792,965	2,348,223
Imitation rum—						
Bottled	*a* 243	7,013	8,361	6,273	16,648	243
Unbottled	*a* 16,644					16,644
Total imitation rum	11,036	7,013	8,361	6,273	16,648	16,887
Other, not sweetened or mixed—						
Bottled	*a* 60,973	310,862	316,629	299,611	395,135	60,973
Unbottled	*a* 327,452					327,452
Total not sweetened or mixed	342,133	310,862	316,629	299,611	395,135	388,425
Sweetened or mixed (tested)—						
Bottled	*a* 915,836	760,503	905,344	929,949	1,032,978	915,836
Unbottled	*a* 73,377					73,377
Total sweetened or mixed (tested)	923,598	760,503	905,344	929,949	1,032,978	989,213
Liqueurs, cordials, etc. (not tested)—						
Bottled	*a* 112,986	115,487	112,022	104,897	105,535	112,986
Unbottled	*a* 759					759
Total liqueurs, cordials, etc. (not tested)	110,337	115,487	112,022	104,897	105,535	113,745
Perfumed—						
Bottled	*a* 565,721	619,768	639,341	648,544	655,289	565,721
Unbottled	*a* 64,131					64,131
Total perfumed	638,559	619,768	639,341	648,544	655,289	629,852
Total distilled spirits	10,125,329	9,928,512	10,570,637	9,572,293	9,877,978	10,677,224
Straw	795,531	832,994	1,027,435	790,159	706,188	620,878
Sugar and molasses:						
Molasses	1,459,759	823,816	1,198,337	1,688,272	1,894,193	1,694,175
Sugar—						
Unrefined—						
Beet	21,675,727	20,285,927	18,870,019	21,564,415	22,737,801	24,920,475
Cane and other	12,776,807	20,273,240	11,414,069	12,759,588	10,693,900	8,743,237
Total unrefined	34,452,534	40,559,167	30,284,088	34,324,003	33,431,701	33,663,712
Refined—						
In lumps and loaves	8,836,254	9,492,176	8,198,130	8,204,758	8,624,080	9,662,129
Other, including sugar candy	43,197,330	39,344,451	39,143,051	41,282,106	45,831,422	50,385,619
Total refined	52,033,584	48,836,627	47,341,181	49,486,864	54,455,502	60,047,748
Total sugar	86,486,118	89,395,794	77,625,269	83,810,867	87,887,203	93,711,460
Total sugar and molasses	87,945,877	90,219,610	78,823,606	85,499,139	89,781,396	95,405,635

a Statistics for 1900 only.

Value of the agricultural imports of the United Kingdom, etc.—Continued.

Articles imported.	Annual average, 1896–1900.	1896.	1897.	1898.	1899.	1900.
VEGETABLE MATTER—cont'd.						
Tea:						
For the manufacture of caffein	a $14,054	} $51,403,735	$50,636,341	{ $11,241	$6,653	$24,269
Other	a 51,329,506			50,298,407	51,682,264	52,007,848
Total	51,214,152	51,403,735	50,636,341	50,309,648	51,688,917	52,032,117
Teazels	b 34,132	(c)	48,232	20,031	(c)	(c)
Tobacco:						
Leaf	a 14,490,980	} 11,732,883	11,416,527	{ 11,859,782	17,336,410	14,276,749
Stems	a 4,592			7,280	2,214	4,282
Total	13,327,225	11,732,883	11,416,527	11,867,062	17,338,624	14,281,031
Vegetables:						
Fresh—						
Onions	3,828,637	3,318,705	3,701,265	3,858,692	4,115,852	4,148,672
Potatoes	7,625,329	4,418,660	5,841,396	9,314,053	7,678,004	10,874,530
Tomatoes	d 3,855,918	(e)	(e)	(e)	(e)	3,855,918
Other	d 3,729,656	6,252,250	7,089,035	8,179,545	8,489,892	3,729,656
Total fresh	18,973,225	13,989,615	16,631,696	21,352,290	20,283,748	22,608,776
Dried—						
Beans f	3,290,377	g 4,075,290	g 3,709,611	g 3,261,329	2,792,841	2,612,814
Peas	3,885,946	4,149,343	3,752,339	3,356,761	4,374,745	3,796,542
Vetches and lentils	334,412	336,718	255,472	347,356	378,468	354,048
Total dried	7,510,735	8,561,351	7,717,422	6,965,446	7,546,054	6,763,404
Preserved in salt or vinegar, including pickles	777,834	678,035	676,823	737,669	933,025	861,117
Sauces and condiments h	326,008	271,594	322,230	363,104	333,136	339,974
Total vegetables	27,587,802	23,500,595	25,348,171	29,418,509	29,095,963	30,573,271
Vinegar	55,209	48,587	52,500	49,852	62,031	63,073
Wines:						
Sparkling—						
Champagne	10,959,340	10,948,131	12,611,136	12,403,487	9,465,367	9,368,577
Saumur	370,328	330,688	346,758	398,221	398,946	377,027
Burgundy	53,987	48,782	49,672	56,904	62,510	52,067
Hock	230,884	222,248	234,122	250,279	274,787	172,985
Moselle	188,627	174,357	195,662	210,695	199,405	163,018
Other	17,010	24,459	24,187	9,573	11,047	15,782
Total sparkling	11,820,176	11,748,665	13,461,537	13,329,159	10,412,062	10,149,456
Still—						
Bottled	2,179,231	2,612,342	2,739,976	2,399,506	1,853,017	1,291,316
Unbottled	14,984,724	14,576,642	15,109,227	16,271,936	15,135,292	13,830,520
Total still	17,163,955	17,188,984	17,849,203	18,671,442	16,988,309	15,121,836
Total wines	28,984,131	28,937,649	31,310,740	32,000,601	27,400,371	25,271,292
Yeast	1,816,413	2,078,833	1,878,849	1,794,317	1,672,168	1,657,900
Total vegetable matter	898,510,887	866,876,755	848,805,225	921,487,002	884,175,464	971,209,989
Total agricultural imports	1,458,921,776	1,378,933,618	1,393,546,461	1,474,681,428	1,469,924,839	1,577,522,533

a Annual average, 1898–1900.
b Annual average, 1897–1898.
c Not stated.
d Statistics for 1900 only.
e Included in "Other fresh vegetables."
f Exclusive of kidney, haricot, and French beans.
g Including carob beans.
h Including table salt.

The annual quantity of the various agricultural imports enumerated in the preceding table will be seen from the following statistics:

Quantity of the agricultural imports of the United Kingdom during the five calendar years 1896–1900.

Articles imported.	Annual average, 1896-1900.	Calendar years.				
		1896.	1897.	1898.	1899.	1900.
ANIMAL MATTER.						
Animals, live:						
Cattle—	*Number.*	*Number.*	*Number.*	*Number.*	*Number.*	*Number.*
Oxen and bulls......	544,719	558,361	613,080	564,390	497,432	490,333
Cows	4,896	3,987	5,038	4,500	5,879	5,073
Calves...............	203	205	203	176	193	239
Total cattle....	549,818	562,553	618,321	569,066	503,504	495,645
Horses—						
Stallions.............	702	498	492	689	933	900
Mares	17,892	14,309	19,927	17,058	17,014	21,150
Geldings.............	27,166	25,870	29,100	25,174	25,952	29,736
Total horses ...	45,760	40,677	49,519	42,921	43,899	51,786
Sheep...................	607,086	769,592	611,504	663,747	607,755	382,833
Swine	91	4	....	450	....	....
Bones:	*Tons. (a)*	*Tons. (a)*	*Tons. (a)*	*Tons. (a)*	*Tons. (a)*	*Tons. (a)*
For fertilizers	64,474	66,681	59,228	59,406	68,915	68,137
Other, including animal charcoal...............	6,952	7,098	5,296	6,519	3,991	11,858
Total	71,426	73,779	64,524	65,925	72,906	79,995
	Pounds.	*Pounds.*	*Pounds.*	*Pounds.*	*Pounds.*	*Pounds.*
Bristles	4,031,225	4,056,279	4,007,693	3,778,749	4,578,248	3,735,156
Dairy products:						
Butter...................	363,620,096	340,224,416	360,393,824	359,425,136	379,663,312	378,393,792
Cheese	275,007,085	251,386,800	291,555,936	262,018,624	267,015,728	303,058,336
Milk—						
Condensed	89,520,570	68,469,520	84,699,216	91,534,688	92,355,088	110,544,336
	Pounds.	*Gallons. (b)*	*Pounds.*	*Pounds.*	*Pounds.*	*Pounds.*
Other...............	c 1,237,432	27,338	1,120,672	1,197,392	880,208	1,751,456
Total milk	c 96,020,764	(d)	85,819,888	92,732,080	93,235,296	112,295,792
Total dairy products.....	c 246,401,936	(d)	737,769,648	714,175,840	739,914,336	793,747,920
	Dozens.	*Dozens.*	*Dozens.*	*Dozens.*	*Dozens.*	*Dozens.*
Eggs.......................	149,516,400	132,450,110	140,317,540	144,246,010	161,747,560	168,820,780
Feathers and downs:	*Pounds.*	*Pounds.*	*Pounds.*	*Pounds.*	*Pounds.*	*Pounds.*
For beds e	4,050,973	2,983,344	4,024,944	4,390,288	4,281,536	4,574,752
For ornament..........	1,276,160	1,166,512	1,218,964	1,398,674	1,420,173	1,176,477
Total	5,327,133	4,149,856	5,243,908	5,788,962	5,701,709	5,751,229
Fibers, animal:						
Silk—						
Raw	1,864,854	1,697,668	1,805,608	2,138,912	2,268,762	1,413,320
Waste	7,313,466	7,047,376	6,134,688	7,931,952	8,652,672	6,800,640
Total silk......	9,178,320	8,745,044	7,940,296	10,070,864	10,921,434	8,213,960
Wool and hair of the goat, alpaca, etc.—						
Goats' hair—						
Mohair	20,752,339	14,986,979	22,880,450	21,198,515	26,650,852	18,044,898
Other.............	3,070,812	2,156,233	3,259,050	3,664,005	2,422,995	3,851,770
Total goats' hair	23,823,151	17,143,212	26,139,506	24,862,520	29,073,847	21,896,668
Hair of the alpaca, vicuña, and llama.	5,239,702	4,962,080	5,121,543	4,853,594	5,465,498	5,795,796
Sheep's wool :.......	672,082,119	713,575,173	735,627,420	694,701,454	663,351,817	553,154,732
Other, including flocks.............	2,205,700	1,660,617	2,618,808	1,537,995	2,318,934	2,892,146
Total wool.....	703,350,672	737,341,082	769,507,277	725,955,563	700,210,096	583,739,342

a Tons of 2,240 pounds.   e Annual average, 1897–1900.   e Including feather beds.
b United States standard gallons.   d Not stated.

Quantity of the agricultural imports of the United Kingdom, etc.—Continued.

Articles imported.	Annual average, 1896–1900.	Calendar years.				
		1896.	1897.	1898.	1899.	1900.
ANIMAL MATTER—cont'd.	*Pounds.*	*Pounds.*	*Pounds.*	*Pounds.*	*Pounds.*	*Pounds.*
Glue, size, and gelatin	a23,874,256	(b)	(b)	(b)	(b)	23,874,256
Glue stock..................	a16,889,824	(b)	(b)	(b)	(b)	16,889,824
Hair:						
Cattle c..................	7,482,182	7,195,664	8,315,664	6,542,256	8,404,480	6,952,848
Horse..................	3,588,906	2,902,928	4,353,216	3,434,816	3,904,656	3,348,912
Hides and skins:						
Hides—						
Dry..................	59,669,882	41,335,056	62,393,744	60,839,744	50,033,200	83,747,664
Wet	74,755,699	67,730,208	71,530,816	77,745,248	85,517,376	71,254,848
Total hides....	134,425,581	109,065,264	133,924,560	138,584,992	135,550,576	155,002,512
Skins—	*Number.*	*Number.*	*Number.*	*Number.*	*Number.*	*Number.*
Goatskins	14,223,188	9,982,054	13,523,056	14,569,660	18,165,381	14,875,790
Rabbit skins.........	29,549,307	30,157,616	30,213,971	23,626,911	30,332,788	33,415,248
Sheepskins..........	14,703,515	13,364,634	14,539,056	15,077,072	15,478,816	15,057,995
Other d..............	e201,369	164,033	241,561	226,862	173,021	315,630
Total skins....	58,700,231	53,668,337	58,517,644	53,500,505	64,150,006	63,664,663
	Pounds.	*Pounds.*	*Pounds.*	*Pounds.*	*Pounds.*	*Pounds.*
Honey......................	2,048,502	2,237,200	1,691,984	2,336,768	1,862,784	2,113,776
Horns, horn tips, horn strips, and hoofs..................	*Tons.* (f) 6,299	*Tons.* (f) 6,385	*Tons.* (f) 6,267	*Tons.* (f) 6,132	*Tons.* (f) 6,472	*Tons.* (f) 6,241
Meat products:						
Beef products—	*Pounds.*	*Pounds.*	*Pounds.*	*Pounds.*	*Pounds.*	*Pounds.*
Beef, fresh...........	374,123,254	297,886,400	337,163,344	347,291,952	425,924,016	462,350,560
Beef, salted or pickled............	22,456,762	27,724,032	19,592,832	23,401,840	19,956,496	21,608,608
Beef, other cured....	43,464,288	45,019,632	41,740,944	31,510,528	41,031,088	58,019,248
Tallow and stearin g.	229,863,043	229,571,888	218,503,600	226,457,392	230,847,344	243,934,992
Total beef products.....	669,907,347	600,201,952	617,000,720	628,661,712	717,758,944	785,913,408
Hog products—						
Bacon..............	598,339,482	509,546,912	560,550,480	639,668,064	650,113,296	631,818,656
Hams..............	200,230,957	163,454,144	193,298,000	220,897,488	221,606,112	201,899,040
Pork, fresh	57,545,533	33,534,032	38,933,104	62,451,424	74,924,864	77,884,240
Pork, salted or pickled............	29,164,486	28,597,968	26,567,072	30,911,216	31,888,640	27,857,536
Lard..................	217,327,600	194,819,856	194,932,416	235,969,552	245,061,488	215,854,688
Total hog products	1,102,608,058	929,952,912	1,014,281,072	1,189,897,744	1,223,594,400	1,155,314,160
Mutton—						
Fresh..............	363,805,277	324,257,696	357,646,912	371,168,112	385,954,464	379,999,200
Cured, other than salted	11,012,825	13,725,712	11,090,464	13,251,168	9,777,040	7,219,744
Total mutton..	374,818,102	337,983,408	368,737,376	384,419,280	395,731,504	387,218,944
Oleo, oleomargarin, etc.—						
Oleo oil..............	17,721,066	13,483,344	16,729,776	19,445,552	18,612,608	20,334,048
Oleomargarin (imitation butter)	103,861,609	103,704,608	104,892,316	100,868,880	106,755,600	103,086,144
Imitation cheese	903,482	47,152	1,331,120	1,138,480	641,872	1,358,784
Total oleo, oleomargarin, etc	122,486,157	117,235,104	122,953,712	121,452,912	126,010,080	124,778,976
Rabbits..................	36,113,325	19,137,776	30,963,296	35,212,576	42,258,832	52,994,144
Other—						
Fresh or salted	46,023,846	31,291,680	40,860,064	46,477,424	52,053,008	59,427,056
Cured, other than salted	21,788,950	19,850,656	22,173,200	19,631,248	22,263,024	25,026,624
Oils, animal, n. e. s., except whale and fish	7,494,032	7,204,176	6,187,328	6,352,976	6,089,776	11,635,904
Wax h.....................	5,302,013	4,834,816	4,684,960	5,457,984	5,751,312	5,780,992

a Statistics for 1900 only.
b Not stated.
c Including elk hair.
d In 1900 including "Skins in any way dressed (not leather)."
e Annual average, 1896–1899.
f Tons of 2,240 pounds.
g Including mutton tallow and mutton stearin.
h Including ozokerite and earth wax.

Quantity of the agricultural imports of the United Kingdom, etc.—Continued. ·

Articles imported.	Annual average, 1896–1900.	Calendar years.				
		1896.	1897.	1898.	1899.	1900.
VEGETABLE MATTER.						
and ale. (*See* Malt						
¡uors.)						
¡dstuffs:						
Cereals—						
Unground—	*Bushels.(a)*	*Bushels.(a)*	*Bushels. (a)*	*Bushels. (a)*	*Bushels.(a)*	*Bushels.(a)*
Barley...........	46,730,784	52,447,085	44,237,013	57,066,343	40,108,502	39,794,977
Buckwheat......	350,644	318,631	397,283	442,820	337,167	257,320
Corn (maize)....	111,847,877	103,544,200	107,570,760	114,338,584	125,482,700	108,303,140
Oats	59,512,411	61,553,555	56,408,835	54,522,650	54,693,555	70,383,460
Rye	2,190,864	1,965,400	2,037,880	2,115,540	2,386,660	2,448,840
Wheat...........	124,431,873	130,715,163	117,115,003	121,758,803	124,387,346	128,183,048
Ground—						
Corn (m a i z e)	*Barrels.(b)*	*Barrels.(b)*	*Barrels.(b)*	*Barrels.(b)*	*Barrels.(b)*	*Barrels.(b)*
meal	719,940	210,343	588,172	830,743	1,037,009	933,431
Oatmeal and	*Pounds.*	*Pounds.*	*Pounds.*	·*Pounds.*	*Pounds.*	*Pounds.*
groats	87,449,040	62,132,000	82,039,440	110,821,760	88,458,720	93,793,280
	Barrels.(b)	*Barrels.(b)*	*Barrels.(b)*	*Barrels.(b)*	*Barrels.(b)*	*Barrels.(b)*
·Wheat flour	12,058,493	12,182,971	10,674,668	12,009,777	13,111,833	12,313,218
	Pounds.	*Pounds.*	*Pounds.*	*Pounds.*	*Pounds.*	*Pounds.*
Other *c*	57,758,221	60,104,464	97,440,448	24,103,968	70,209,104	36,933,120
Sago, sago meal, and						
sago flour.........	53,399,942	·70,177,856	49,914,928	51,214,352	45,613,232	50,079,344
b beans (locust beans)..	*d* 78,366,680	(*e*)	(*e*)	(*e*)	78,195,600	78,537,760
	Gallons. (f)	*Gallons. (f)*	*Gallons. (f)*	*Gallons. (f)*	*Gallons. (f)*	*Gallons. (f)*
er and perry	488,271	385,316	601,061	470,204	460,733	524,041
cory root. (*See* under						
Coffee substitutes.")						
oa and chocolate:						
Cocoa—	*Pounds.*	*Pounds.*	*Pounds.*	*Pounds.*	*Pounds.*	*Pounds.*
Crude	42,353,977	38,281,803	34,533,531	42,833,993	43,473,241	52,647,318
Husks and shells....	477,008	267,008	434,896	1,089,424	344,848	248,864
Butter...............	866,979	242,940	1,601,132	737,550	·493,452	1,259,821
Cocoa, ground or pre-						
pared, and chocolate..	6,744,576	3,794,422	8,992,943	8,027,995	5,152,640	7,754,879
Cocoa and chocolate,						
containing distilled						
spirits	88,375	51,603	75,233	99,196	109,754	106,087
Total	50,530,915	42,637,776	45,637,735	52,788,158	49,573,935	62,016,969
ĩee:						
Raw	92,419,600	79,908,416	84,725,984	103,273,856	109,176,816	85,012,928
Kiln-dried, roasted, or						
ground	26,937	13,572	12,054	18,359	-22,155	68,547
Total	92,446,537	79,921,988	84,738,038	103,292,215	109,198,971	85,081,475
ĩee substitutes:						
Chicory root—·						
Raw or kiln-dried...	10,878,224	11,553,920	11,002,432	10,565,520	·10,323,930	10,945,312
Roasted òr ground ..	167,157	355,009	188,658	· 108,769	79,024	104,322
Chicory root and coffee						
(mixed), roasted and						
ground	10,015	21,541	13,629	9,489	3,450	1,966
Other....................	8,579	37,856	2,352	1,456	1,120	112
Total coffee						
substitutes...	11,063,975	11,968,326	11,207,071	10,685,234	10,407,530	11,051,712
)ers, vegetable:						
Cotton—						
Raw	1,798,810,518	1,754,890,256	1,724,160,368	2,128,548,352	1,626,246,944	1,760,206,672
Waste *g*	17,328,710	19,503,049	20,966,005	13,644,422	14,028,104	18,501,970
Total cotton ...	1,816,139,228	1,774,393,305	1,745,126,373	2,142,192,774	1,640,275,048	1,778,708,642
Esparto and other veg-						
etable fibers for paper	*Tons. (h)*	*Tons. (h)*	*Tons. (h)*	*Tons. (h)*	*Tons. (h)*	*Tons. (h)*
making................	· 199,416	187,278	204,579	197,341	207,604	200,280

·For barley and buckwheat, bushels of 48 pounds; for corn and rye, bushels of 56 pounds; for oats,
₃hels of 32 pounds; and for wheat, bushels of 60 pounds.
Barrels of 196 pounds.
Including ground beans and peas.
ⁱAnnual average, 1899–1900.
⁝Included in "Beans, dried."
ⁱUnited States standard gallons.
·Probably including cop and mill waste as well as the waste of raw cotton.
·Tons of 2,240 pounds.

*Quantity of the agricultural imports of the United Kingdom, etc.—*Continued.

Articles imported.	Annual average, 1896–1900.	Calendar years.				
		1896.	1897.	1898.	1899.	1900.
VEGETABLE MATTER—cont'd.						
Fibers, vegetable—Cont'd.						
Flax, and tow of—	*Tons.* (a)	*Tons.* (a)	*Tons.* (a)	*Tons.* (a)	*Tons.* (a)	*Tons.* (a)
Flax..............	75,555	76,099	80,188	82,069	80,979	58,442
Tow of	16,823	19,100	18,614	15,184	18,073	13,144
Total flax, and tow of	92,378	95,199	98,802	97,253	99,052	71,586
Hemp, and tow of—						
Hemp b..............	89,253	86,518	84,413	89,600	85,543	100,188
Tow of..............	5,223	5,200	4,606	4,842	6,430	5,039
Total hemp, and tow of...	94,476	91,718	89,019	94,442	91,973	105,227
Jute	321,493	340,649	336,919	362,137	286,839	280,919
Piassava and other vegetable fibers for brush making.................	c 8,209	(d)	(d)	(d)	(d)	8,209
All other	5,726	6,444	5,898	5,620	4,183	6,484
	Gallons. (e)	*Gallons.* (e)	*Gallons.* (e)	*Gallons.* (e)	*Gallons.* (e)	*Gallons.* (e)
Fruit juices, nonalcoholic...	c 1,224,138	(d)	(d)	(d)	(d)	1,224,138
Fruits and nuts:						
Fruits—						
Fresh—	*Pounds.*	*Bushels.* (f)	*Bushels.* (f)	*Bushels.* (f)	*Bushels.* (f)	*Pounds.*
Apples...........	c238,396,592	6,371,530	4,332,270	3,567,666	3,982,799	238,396,592
Apricots and peaches	c 1,533,168	(g)	(g)	(g)	(g)	1,533,168
	Bunches.	*Bunches.*	*Bunches.*	*Bunches.*	*Bunches.*	*Bunches.*
Bananas..........	c 1,287,442	(h)	(h)	(h)	(h)	1,287,442
	Pounds.	*Bushels.* (f)	*Bushels.* (f)	*Bushels.* (f)	*Bushels.* (f)	*Pounds.*
Cherries........	c 27,162,800	226,277	322,131	414,467	290,095	27,162,800
Currants........	c 7,219,744	(h)	(h)	(h)	(h)	7,219,744
Gooseberries.....	c 2,917,040	(h)	(h)	(h)	(h)	2,917,040
Grapes ...:......	c 66,399,984	911,066	1,025,015	1,171,535	1,194,113	66,399,984
Lemons, limes, and citrons....	c106,163,792	1,712,719	1,597,709	1,683,041	1,741,691	106,163,792
Oranges	c570,123,232	7,458,231	9,074,315	7,503,453	8,823,155	570,123,232
Pears...........	c 53,412,912	499,063	1,085,011	507,157	589,845	53,412,912
Plums i..........	c 47,378,128	577,893	1,076,699	951,299	575,859	47,378,128
Strawberries	c 5,849,200	(h)	(h)	(h)	(h)	5,849,200
Other...........	c 55,408,864	1,472,059	1,779,457	2,245,712	2,318,590	55,408,864
Dried or preserved—	*Pounds.*	*Pounds.*	*Pounds.*	*Pounds.*	*Pounds.*	*Pounds.*
Currants........	120,437,789	110,505,584	129,151,904	139,039,824	131,144,608	92,347,024
Figs and fig cake.	15,532,070	16,053,968	16,338,672	11,201,008	16,078,608	17,988,096
Plums and prunes—						
Prunes	2,705,002	2,694,944	2,358,944	2,709,280	2,560,656	3,201,184
French plums and prunelloes.	4,196,483	3,671,696	1,381,632	6,049,456	1,914,976	7,964,656
Other plums, including dried apricots........	5,031,331	2,934,064	6,571,488	4,494,896	6,944,000	4,212,208
Raisins ..:.......	72,719,383	69,383,216	75,219,424	66,546,032	78,710,688	73,737,552
Other—						
Dried........	49,714,582	34,659,072	58,950,528	32,194,512	51,808,400	70,960,400
Preserved without sugar	81,933,344	62,986,516	65,816,306	75,850,332	93,549,823	111,463,744
Total dried or preserved....	352,269,984	302,889,060	355,788,898	338,085,340	382,711,759	381,874,864
Nuts—						
For food—						
Almonds	17,191,328	16,566,816	18,229,792	19,070,688	16,369,136	15,720,208
Other...........	c 85,489,040	(d)	(d)	(d)	(d)	85,489,040
Total for food...	c101,209,248	(d)	(d)	(d)	(d)	101,209,248
Oil nuts	126,419,760	140,060,480	121,434,880	115,610,880	128,056,320	126,936,320

a Tons of 2,240 pounds.
b Including Manila hemp, New Zealand flax, sisal grass, sunn, etc.
c Statistics for 1900 only.
d Not stated.
e United States standard gallons.
f Winchester bushels.
g Included in "Plums, fresh."
h Included in "Other fresh fruits."
i Prior to 1900 including fresh apricots and peaches.

Quantity of the agricultural imports of the United Kingdom, etc.—Continued.

Articles imported.	Annual average, 1896–1900.	Calendar years.				
		1896.	1897.	1898.	1899.	1900.
GETABLE MATTER—cont'd.						
uits and vegetables, pre-served in sugar...........	*Pounds.* 22,715,795	*Pounds.* 16,679,376	*Pounds.* 19,655,664	*Pounds.* 30,876,384	*Pounds.* 32,927,328	*Pounds.* 13,440,224
nger. (*See* under "Spices.")						
ucose and grape sugar	194,978,538	172,382,224	180,332,880	211,349,152	204,468,208	206,360,224
iy	*Tons. (a)* 117,376	*Tons. (a)* 107,987	*Tons. (a)* 121,541	*Tons. (a)* 116,107	*Tons. (a)* 131,546	*Tons. (a)* 109,698
)ps	*Pounds.* 22,266,899	*Pounds.* 23,188,592	*Pounds.* 18,385,248	*Pounds.* 27,343,232	*Pounds.* 20,186,096	*Pounds.* 22,231,328
digo......................	7,149,162	10,073,392	9,242,912	6,029,856	6,605,424	3,794,224
.rd substitutes...........	6,825,683	4,442,256	3,470,656	9,458,848	8,767,472	7,989,184
cust beans. (*See* Carob beans.)						
adder, madder root, garancin, and munjeet.........	*b* 404,208	584,304	424,816	331,632	276,080	(*c*)
alt......................	*Bushels. (d)* 12,682	*Bushels. (d)* 32,026	*Bushels. (d)* 11,165	*Bushels. (d)* 6,833	*Bushels. (d)* 5,727	*Bushels. (d)* 7,658
alt liquors:						
Mum, spruce, or black beer, Berlin white beer, etc....................	*Gallons. (e)* 63,615	*Gallons. (e)* 67,755	*Gallons.. (e)* 65,594	*Gallons. (e)* 59,069	*Gallons. (e)* 64,471	*Gallons. (e)* 61,187
Other...................	2,028,929	1,884,518	1,929,760	1,966,403	2,125,462	2,238,502
Total	2,092,544	1,952,273	1,995,354	2,025,472	2,189,933	2,299,689
il cake:.	*Pounds.*	*Pounds.*	*Pounds.*	*Pounds.*	*Pounds.*	*Pounds.*
Cotton-seed	332,426,304	200,988,480	250,481,280	355,425,280	434,795,200	420,441,280
Flaxseed, or linseed.....	483,869,568	494,148,480	488,315,520	493,588,480	523,474,560	419,820,800
Other...................	26,189,632	12,866,560	15,854,720	26,272,960	31,662,400	44,291,520
Total	842,485,504	708,003,520	754,651,520	875,286,720	989,932,160	884,553,600
ils, vegetable:						
Essential or perfumed...	1,839,746	2,038,324	1,888,436	1,893,405	1,620,234	1,758,331
Fixed or expressed—						
Castor	12,802,451	18,680,928	12,046,384	14,089,600	13,221,824	5,973,520
Cocoanut	39,873,568	24,550,176	27,185,872	34,395,312	51,329,264	61,907,216
Olive	*Gallons. (e)* 4,858,974	*Gallons. (e)* 5,702,580	*Gallons. (e)* 4,670,229	*Gallons. (e)* 5,457,877	*Gallons. (e)* 4,821,165	*Gallons. (e)* 3,643,921
Palm	*Pounds.* 110,074,115	*Pounds.* 128,378,992	*Pounds.* 108,982,720	*Pounds.* 102,020,800	*Pounds.* 105,892,864	*Pounds.* 105,095,200
Seed (cotton-seed, linseed, etc.)	85,236,032	75,299,840	74,307,520	80,467,520	103,971,840	92,133,440
pium.....................	557,672	489,235	443,219	426,042	596,536	833,330
ice, rice meal, and rice flour *f*	589,062,813	507,530,016	580,032,208	509,199,376	643,923,392	704,629,072
afflower...................	*b* 25,732	60,032	35,056	5,600	2,240	(*c*)
eeds:						
Garden seeds	2,295,412	2,675,056	2,545,511	2,146,771	2,039,204	2,070,518
Grass seed, including clover seed	36,054,166	45,429,104	33,593,952	38,390,576	33,518,016	29,339,184
Oilseeds—						
Cotton seed	885,345,216	825,258,560	924,842,240	964,167,680	801,946,880	910,510,720
Flaxseed, or linseed .	*Bushels. (d)* 15,911,366	*Bushels. (d)* 21,280,786	*Bushels. (d)* 15,749,916	*Bushels. (d)* 13,933,626	*Bushels. (d)* 14,844,416	*Bushels. (d)* 13,748,088
Rape seed	1,593,963	1,483,132	1,528,534	2,136,864	1,713,511	1,107,773
Other.................	1,431,636	834,913	1,730,741	1,416,992	1,602,497	1,573,038
All other	*Pounds.* 66,053,434	*Pounds.* 53,551,120	*Pounds.* 61,422,480	*Pounds.* 78,515,808	*Pounds.* 72,121,168	*Pounds,* 64,656,592
pices:						
Cinnamon..............	1,820,721	1,318,980	1,554,260	1,811,672	2,770,341	1,648,352
Ginger..................	9,343,802	10,776,304	11,273,024	9,934,288	8,492,512	6,242,880
Pepper	26,612,301	26,113,001	31,053,164	29,715,185	23,903,914	22,276,242
Other..................	9,863,303	10,720,928	9,650,652	8,131,915	11,314,715	9,495,305
Total	47,640,127	48,929,213	53,531,100	49,596,060	46,481,482	39,662,779

a Tons of 2,240 pounds.
b Annual average, 1896–1899.
c Not stated.

d Winchester bushels.
e United States Standard gallons.
f Prior to 1900, exclusive of rice meal and flour.

Quantity of the agricultural imports of the United Kingdom, etc.—Continued.

Articles imported.	Annual average, 1896–1900.	Calendar years.				
		1896.	1897.	1898.	1899.	1900.
VEGETABLE MATTER—cont'd.						
Spirits, distilled:						
Brandy—	*Pf. gals.* (a)	*Pf. gals.* (a)	*Pf. gals.* (a)	*Pf. gals.* (a)	*Pf. gals.* (a)	*Pf. gals.* (a)
Bottled	b 641,682	3,300,374	3,708,048	3,018,501	2,958,886	641,682
Unbottled	b 2,474,615					2,474,615
Total brandy..	3,220,421	3,300,374	3,708,048	3,018,501	2,958,886	3,116,297
Gin—						
Bottled	b 276,646	431,013	430,113	422,909	494,007	276,646
Unbottled	b 219,128					219,128
Total gin	454,763	431,013	430,113	422,909	494,007	495,774
Rum—						
Bottled	b 1,117	6,418,700	5,903,883	6,564,551	6,694,887	1,117
Unbottled	b 7,436,598					7,436,598
Total rum	6,603,947	6,418,700	5,903,883	6,564,551	9,694,887	7,437,715
Imitation rum—						
Bottled	b 99	31,597	34,390	20,795	59,632	99
Unbottled	b 51,075					51,075
Total imitation rum	39,518	31,597	34,390	20,795	59,632	51,174
Other, not sweetened or mixed—						
Bottled	b 29,783	1,595,799	1,641,962	1,219,256	1,510,419	29,783
Unbottled	b 1,686,538					1,686,538
Total not sweetened or mixed	1,536,751	1,595,799	1,641,962	1,219,256	1,510,419	1,716,321
Sweetened or mixed (tested)—						
Bottled	b 102,476	100,729	115,843	130,302	135,947	102,476
Unbottled	b 19,878					19,878
Total sweetened or mixed (tested)	121,035	100,729	115,843	130,302	135,947	122,354
Liqueurs, cordials, etc. (not tested)—	*Gallons.* (c)	*Gallons.* (c)	*Gallons.* (c)	*Gallons.* (c)	*Gallons.* (c)	*Gallons.* (c)
Bottled	b 17,493	16,603	16,647	15,473	17,492	17,493
Unbottled	b 764					764
Total liqueurs, cordials, etc. (not tested)..	16,894	16,603	16,647	15,473	17,492	18,257
Perfumed—						
Bottled	b 59,103	65,198	65,182	67,210	67,919	59,103
Unbottled	b 5,221					5,221
Total perfumed	65,967	65,198	65,182	67,210	67,919	64,324
Straw	*Tons.* (d) 71,629	*Tons.* (d) 73,793	*Tons.* (d) 91,724	*Tons.* (d) 71,966	*Tons.* (d) 64,827	*Tons.* (d) 55,835
Sugar and molasses: Molasses	*Pounds.* 140,063,571	*Pounds.* 86,977,632	*Pounds.* 130,544,288	*Pounds.* 151,557,056	*Pounds.* 180,270,608	*Pounds.* 150,968,272
Sugar— Unrefined—						
Beet	1,029,576,733	903,158,816	973,794,080	1,071,370,832	1,052,729,664	1,146,830,272
Cane and other..	546,190,467	860,132,896	544,200,944	574,234,640	416,901,744	335,482,112
Total unrefined	1,575,767,200	1,763,291,712	1,517,995,024	1,645,605,472	1,469,631,408	1,482,312,384

a United States standard proof gallons.
b Statistics for 1900 only.
c United States standard gallons.
d Tons of 2,240 pounds.

Quantity of the agricultural imports of the United Kingdom, etc.—Continued.

Articles imported.	Annual average, 1896–1900.	Calendar years.				
		1896.	1897.	1898.	1899.	1900.
GETABLE MATTER—cont'd.						
gar and molasses—Cont'd.						
Sugar—Continued.						
Refined—						
In lumps and loaves	*Pounds.* 295,965,421	*Pounds.* 296,313,248	*Pounds.* 281,439,312	*Pounds.* 285,175,856	*Pounds.* 294,464,464	*Pounds.* 322,434,224
Other, including sugar candy ...	1,589,784,179	1,358,702,800	1,491,605,696	1,565,092,592	1,700,157,088	1,833,362,720
Total refined ..	1,885,749,600	1,655,016,048	1,773,045,008	1,850,268,448	1,994,621,552	2,155,796,944
Total sugar....	3,461,516,800	3,418,307,760	3,291,040,032	3,495,873,920	3,464,252,960	3,638,109,328
Total sugar and molasses.	3,601,580,371	3,505,285,392	3,421,584,320	3,647,430,976	3,644,523,568	3,789,077,600
a:						
For the manufacture of caffein................	a 425,449	}265,394,122	266,800,411	{ 367,348	194,009	714,991
Other....................	a286,472,045			{271,593,683	288,922,251	298,900,200
Total	278,577,403	265,394,122	266,800,411	271,961,031	289,116,260	299,615,191
bacco:						
Leaf....................	a 18,897,539	} 83,558,757	80,728,432	{ 79,451,961	119,014,671	98,225,986
Stems...................	a 120,907			{ 179,994	60,214	122,514
Total	92,268,506	83,558,757	80,728,432	79,631,955	119,074,885	98,348,500
getables:						
Fresh—	*Bushels.* (b)	*Bushels.* (b)	*Bushels.* (b)	*Bushels.* (b)	*Bushels.* (b)	*Bushels.* (b)
Onions..............	6,664,263	6,278,642	6,301,355	6,191,594	7,239,375	7,310,349
Potatoes............	10,075,346	4,189,970	7,319,583	12,603,226	9,630,154	16,683,796
	Pounds.	*Pounds.*	*Pounds.*	*Pounds.*	*Pounds.*	*Pounds.*
Tomatoes............	c93,299,360	(d)	(d)	(d)	(d)	93,299,360
Dried—	*Bushels.* (e)	*Bushels.* (e)	*Bushels.* (e)	*Bushels.* (e)	*Bushels.* (e)	*Bushels.* (e)
Beans f	4,417,043	g 5,792,248	g 5,301,427	g 4,280,913	3,504,144	3,206,485
Peas	4,860,843	5,634,826	5,264,252	4,067,825	5,138,840	4,198,473
Vetches and lentils..	373,251	406,440	267,816	356,661	427,453	407,883
Preserved in salt or vinegar, including pickles.	*Gallons.* (h) 2,999,646	*Gallons.* (h) 2,694,430	*Gallons.* (h) 2,557,099	*Gallons.* (h) 2,678,161	*Gallons.* (h) 3,468,982	*Gallons.* (h) 3,599,560
Sauces and condiments i.	*Pounds.* 5,222,675	*Pounds.* 4,523,611	*Pounds.* 4,770,757	*Pounds.* 5,191,851	*Pounds.* 5,794,301	*Pounds.* 5,832,855
inegar	*Gallons.* (h) 231,187	*Gallons.* (h) 223,540	*Gallons.* (h) 239,456	*Gallons.* (h) 208,419	*Gallons.* (h) 252,439	*Gallons.* (h) 232,083
ines:						
Sparkling—						
Champagne	1,916,527	1,935,664	2,165,622	2,156,479	1,663,934	1,660,936
Saumur	177,661	165,467	169,578	183,333	186,099	183,828
Burgundy	17,752	16,454	16,261	17,481	20,874	17,690
Hock	62,003	57,033	59,175	62,595	69,362	61,853
Moselle.............	54,559	48,292	52,932	55,603	55,333	60,633
Other...............	5,145	6,988	6,976	2,830	3,792	5,138
Total sparkling	2,233,647	2,229,898	2,470,544	2,478,321	1,999,394	1,990,078
Still—						
Bottled	1,025,000	1,184,837	1,239,714	1,093,688	987,009	669,751
Unbottled	17,527,205	16,624,946	17,366,150	18,201,016	17,934,106	17,509,807
Total still......	18,552,205	17,809,783	18,605,864	19,294,704	18,871,115	18,179,558
Total wines....	20,785,852	20,039,681	21,076,408	21,773,025	20,870,509	20,169,636
	Pounds.	*Pounds.*	*Pounds.*	*Pounds.*	*Pounds.*	*Pounds.*
east.......................	17,165,658	19,318,544	17,874,752	17,051,440	16,044,784	15,538,768

a Annual average, 1898–1900.
b For onions, Winchester bushels, and for potatoes, bushels of 60 pounds.
c Statistics for 1900 only.
d Not stated.
e For beans and peas, bushels of 60 pounds, and for vetches and lentils, Winchester bushels.
f Exclusive of kidney, haricot, and French beans.
g Including carob beans.
h United States standard gallons.
i Including table salt.

SOURCES OF AGRICULTURAL IMPORTS IN DETAIL.

The two series of tables presented on the following pages embrace all the agricultural imports of the United Kingdom, exhibiting for each article the value, and when possible the quantity, of the annual importations received from the various sources of supply during the five calendar years 1896–1900. To facilitate comparison, cross references are given from each table of values to the corresponding table of quantities and vice versa. Where values only are given, it is because the official returns do not specify the quantity. An index to the articles covered by the tables is printed on pages 223–227. In the arrangement of the tables those relating to animal matter come first, followed by those relating to vegetable matter. The tables are as follows:

Value of the agricultural imports of the United Kingdom (animal matter), by articles and countries, during the five calendar years 1896–1900.(ª)

CATTLE.(b)

Countries from which imported.	Annual average, 1896–1900.	Calendar years.					Per ct. in 1900.
		1896.	1897.	1898.	1899.	1900.	
FOREIGN COUNTRIES.							
	Dollars.	Dollars.	Dollars.	Dollars.	Dollars.	Dollars.	
United States.........	31,386,863	32,778,403	35,188,951	30,362,016	26,969,077	31,635,870	72.13
Argentina.............	5,341,965	4,494,884	5,613,542	6,575,926	6,777,083	3,248,389	7.41
Uruguay	17,110	23,350	1,839			18,819	.04
Other c	511	2,555					
Total foreign countries.....	36,746,449	37,299,192	40,804,332	36,937,942	33,787,701	34,903,078	79.58
BRITISH POSSESSIONS.							
Canada..............	8,594,436	7,824,840	9,953,010	8,636,870	7,767,406	8,790,057	20.04
Channel Islands......	160,483	156,244	151,095	169,281	161,086	164,707	.38
Other d.............	555	2,774					
Total British possessions ...	8,755,474	7,983,858	10,104,105	8,806,151	7,928,492	8,954,764	20.42
Total	45,501,923	45,283,050	50,908,437	45,744,093	41,716,193	43,857,842	100.00

ª As the subdivision of certain articles in the British import returns seemed to be carried out too minutely for the general purposes of the present report, it was thought best in showing the imports of these articles by countries to consolidate the separate items into which each article is divided, and thus bring the articles into closer conformity with the corresponding items published in the United States trade returns. The articles treated in this manner are as follows: Cattle; horses; hides; malt liquors; brandy; gin; rum; imitation rum; distilled spirits, n. e. s., not sweetened or mixed; distilled spirits, sweetened or mixed (tested); liqueurs, cordials, etc. (not tested); distilled spirits, perfumed; refined sugar; tea; tobacco; and champagne and other sparkling wines.

For the following items no statistics are available as to the countries of origin, the British returns showing only the totals of importation: Albumen; egg yolks and liquid eggs; greaves; silkworm gut; dextrin; kapok; flowers, everlasting; grass and moss; husks and bran for packing; and teazels.

For the following items no statistics are available as to the countries of origin prior to 1900: Glue, size, and gelatin; glue stock; sausage casings; piassava and other vegetable fibers for brush making; and fruit juices.

b For quantities, see page 146.
c Including in 1896 cows from Norway valued at $316.
d Including in 1896 oxen and bulls from Queensland valued at $1,557.

Value of the agricultural imports of the United Kingdom (animal matter), etc.—Cont'd.

HORSES. (a)

	Annual average, 1896-1900.	Calendar years.					Per ct. in 1900.
		1896.	1897.	1898.	1899.	1900.	
'OREIGN COUNTRIES.							
	Dollars.	*Dollars.*	*Dollars.*	*Dollars.*	*Dollars.*	*Dollars.*	
nited States.........	3,746,828	2,592,010	3,861,884	3,791,291	3,851,397	4,637,561	70.56
ussia................	324,450	166,410	265,657	265,438	355,580	569,166	8.66
rance	185,354	58,062	61,537	127,731	215,542	463,899	7.06
etherlands..........	185,148	170,736	174,386	196,616	197,298	186,703	2.84
enmark.............	102,752	105,535	107,175	89,573	124,758	86,721	1.32
rgentina............	38,228	58,140	30,333	25,452	22,167	55,050	.84
ermany.............	91,146	161,368	98,021	68,632	74,589	53,118	.81
elgium..............	33,324	34,421	32,328	45,580	31,116	23,174	.35
ther................	10,008	12,643	11,067	10,181	7,971	8,176	.13
Total foreign countries.....	4,717,238	3,359,325	4,642,388	4,620,494	4,880,418	6,083,568	92.57
BRITISH POSSESSIONS.							
anada...............	965,360	1,550,657	1,364,844	864,290	632,587	414,421	6.31
ustralasia:							
Victoria..........	11,601	12,653	243	20,926	....	24,186	
New South Wales.	33,686	50,636	60,685	34,552	14,599	7,957	
New Zealand.....	7,737	15,086	3,893	9,003	5,840	4,866	.56
South Australia ..	1,304	681	....	....	5,840	....	
Queensland	49	243	....	....	....	....	
ritish East Indies b..	9,453	3,582	5,577	6,536	2,326	29,243	.44
hannel Islands......	3,978	4,793	3,047	4,657	4,034	3,358	.05
ape of Good Hope...	9,091	730	18,980	10,682	12,020	3,042	.05
[alta and Gozo	1,056	779	4,015	195	....	292	.02
ther................	8,334	2,312	681	7,251	5,183	1,241	
Total British possessions ...	1,046,649	1,642,152	1,461,965	958,092	682,429	488,606	7.43
Total	5,763,887	5,001,477	6,104,353	5,578,586	5,562,847	6,572,174	100.00

SHEEP. (c)

FOREIGN COUNTRIES.							
	Dollars.	*Dollars.*	*Dollars.*	*Dollars.*	*Dollars.*	*Dollars.*	
Argentina	2,486,921	2,441,581	2,572,466	3,101,849	2,912,289	1,406,419	47.37
United States.........	1,272,316	1,974,840	1,325,737	1,069,199	897,607	1,094,198	36.85
Denmark.............	203,619	375,134	93,383	202,636	159,947	186,995	6.30
Uruguay.............	15,697	21,189	15,909	....	33,593	7,796	.26
Chile	26,193	5,655	....	28,372	96,936	....	......
Norway	16,108	80,541	....	....	....	....	......
Total foreign countries.....	4,020,854	4,898,940	4,007,495	4,402,056	4,100,372	2,695,408	90.78
BRITISH POSSESSIONS.							
Canada...............	429,633	612,965	465,247	307,981	488,207	273,765	9.22
Falkland Islands.....	16,560	....	....	82,799	....	....	......
Australasia	919	4,594	....	....	....	....	......
Other................	74	331	39	....	....	....	......
Total British possessions ...	447,186	617,890	465,286	390,780	488,207	273,765	9.22
Total	4,468,040	5,516,830	4,472,781	4,792,836	4,588,579	2,969,173	100.00

a For quantities, see page 146.
b Including stallions and mares from Bombay valued at $2,608 in 1896 and $759 in 1897; from Madras, $243 in 1896 and $292 in 1897; and from Bengal, $243 in 1896 and $900 in 1897.
c For quantities, see page 147.

Value of the agricultural imports of the United Kingdom (animal matter), etc.—Cont'd.

SWINE. (a)

Countries from which imported.	Annual average, 1896–1900.	Calendar years.					Per ct. in 1900.
		1896.	1897.	1898.	1899.	1900.	
FOREIGN COUNTRIES.	Dollars.	Dollars.	Dollars.	Dollars.	Dollars.	Dollars.	
United States.........	993	....	....	4,964	....	....	......
Other.................	10	49	....	....	....	....	......
Total	1,003	49	....	4,964	....	....	......

LIVE ANIMALS (b) NOT ELSEWHERE SPECIFIED.

	Annual average.	1896.	1897.	1898.	1899.	1900.	Per ct.
FOREIGN COUNTRIES.	Dollars.	Dollars.	Dollars.	Dollars.	Dollars.	Dollars.	
Belgium..............	41,147	46,256	37,847	38,703	31,910	51,020	27.88
France	76,266	70,238	178,328	52,626	31,851	48,285	26.39
Netherlands..........	33,174	30,318	28,888	35,647	38,411	32,606	17.82
Germany.............	29,154	27,043	26,206	43,799	20,707	28,012	15.31
United States........	30,216	8,653	114,304	22,191	3,217	2,715	1.49
Egypt	2,029	4,385	2,618	803	1,280	1,061	.58
Argentina............	1,327	24	487	360	5,669	97	.05
China	1,941	341	....	2,745	6,531	88	.05
Madagascar	993	4,964	....	....	....	....	......
Other c	7,532	6,638	6,015	14,303	5,777	4,925	2.69
Total foreign countries.....	223,779	198,860	394,693	211,177	145,353	168,809	92.26
BRITISH POSSESSIONS.							
British East Indies:							
Bengal	7,748	10,079	11,933	7,645	4,467	4,614	
Straits Settlements	3,875	414	1,105	7,577	8,249	2,029	
Bombay	1,757	5,076	827	963	341	1,577	5.04
Burma	3,136	3,811	4,063	3,212	3,815	779	
Ceylon	24	....	....	....	....	122	
Madras...........	165	243	....	487	....	97	
Channel Islands......	2,127	2,321	3,071	2,190	930	2,122	1.16
Cape of Good Hope...	12,591	545	1,659	3,426	56,232	1,095	.60
Australasia	1,692	2,316	487	4,049	915	691	.37
Aden	1,038	97	229	....	4,866	....	......
Other................	2,248	1,085	4,642	3,441	1,032	1,041	.57
Total British possessions ...	36,401	25,987	28,016	32,990	80,847	14,167	7.74
Total	260,180	224,847	422,709	244,167	226,200	182,976	100.00

a For quantities, see page 147.
b Exclusive of poultry.
c Including imports from Spain valued at $1,061 in 1896, $1,908 in 1897, $910 in 1898, and $745 in 1899.

Value of the agricultural imports of the United Kingdom (animal matter), etc.—Cont'd.

BONES FOR FERTILIZERS. (a)

Countries from which imported.	Annual average, 1896–1900.	1896.	1897.	1898.	1899.	1900.	Per ct. in 1900.
FOREIGN COUNTRIES.	*Dollars.*	*Dollars.*	*Dollars.*	*Dollars.*	*Dollars.*	*Dollars.*	
rgentina	171,985	236,614	150,029	231,082	160,001	82,249	5.60
ruguay	42,522	63,182	48,378	10,468	14,677	75,908	5.17
etherlands	39,611	36,353	42,699	50,787	38,864	29,350	2.00
razil	41,587	44,679	38,479	29,686	84,113	10,979	.75
ermany	19,295	7,898	26,167	22,892	29,442	10,078	.69
pain	10,007	8,560	13,938	15,266	4,424	7,845	.53
urkey, Asiatic	10,581	9,767	4,253	9,494	22,118	7,271	.49
gypt	23,360	23,510	15,787	37,175	33,983	6,346	.43
rance	9,416	1,966	23,388	7,796	7,777	6,151	.42
enmark	7,708	5,509	8,765	10.356	8,210	5,699	.39
hile	5,762	6,565	6,794	2,433	7,889	5,129	.35
elgium	10,052	2,341	19,077	13,441	11,470	3,932	.27
orway	3,348	....	1,036	7,670	6,477	1,557	.10
nited States	2,483	5,275	2,039	1,139	3,577	384	.03
urkey, European	4,142	161	....	438	19,831	282	.02
ussia	24,809	2,711	5,514	42,076	73,742	....	....
orocco	12,797	21,091	73	26,323	16,497	....	....
ther b	3,046	3,144	3,007	4,166	2,083	2,882	.19
Total foreign countries	442,511	479,326	409,423	522,638	545,175	255,992	17.43
BRITISH POSSESSIONS.							
ritish East Indies:							
Bombay	642,494	529,222	429,157	502,291	743,523	1,008,275	
Bengal	197,025	186,767	209,999	160,225	230,852	197,283	82.27
Burma	3,462	6,078	2,453	3,299	2,677	2,803	
Madras	88	....	....	....	438	....	
ape of Good Hope	1,177	1,368	501	1,577	871	1,567	.11
hannel Islands	1,550	1,961	1,489	1,382	1,372	1,548	.10
ustralasia c	5,395	19,427	3,480	2,360	453	1,256	.09
ibraltar	968	1,557	1,655	1,630	....	....	
Other	363	....	754	....	1,061	....	
Total British possessions	852,522	746,380	649,488	672,764	981,247	1,212,732	82.57
Total	1,295,033	1,225,706	1,058,911	1,195,402	1,526,422	1,468,724	100.00

BONES (EXCEPT FOR FERTILIZERS), INCLUDING ANIMAL CHARCOAL. (d)

	Annual average, 1896–1900.	1896.	1897.	1898.	1899.	1900.	Per ct. in 1900.
FOREIGN COUNTRIES.	*Dollars.*	*Dollars.*	*Dollars.*	*Dollars.*	*Dollars.*	*Dollars.*	
Argentina	21,162	9,684	11,962	12,692	3,368	68,107	26.83
Brazil	41,838	36,888	50,130	54,169	23,194	44,811	17.65
Uruguay	12,043	12,838	....	9,125	905	37,350	14.71
Germany	5,331	6,278	195	1,401	2,029	16,751	6.60
United States	8,243	11,212	3,820	6,531	5,353	14,298	5.63
Netherlands	6,393	5,124	2,268	3,976	7,976	12,619	4.97
France	9,603	9,826	954	11,071	19,690	6,472	2.55
Belgium	7,032	12,230	8,988	4,589	6,672	2,681	1.06
Other e	4,496	2,920	861	2,638	10,740	5,319	2.10
Total foreign countries	116,141	107,000	79,178	106,192	79,927	208,408	82.10
BRITISH POSSESSIONS.							
Australasia:							
New South Wales	18,410	24,736	14,969	13,981	21,228	17,135	
Victoria	5,260	5,168	6,448	4,823	5,723	4,141	
Queensland	5,250	8,229	5,786	5,840	2,657	3,737	
New Zealand	519	467	336	584	842	365	10.11
South Australia	757	1,426	122	1,587	375	273	
West Australia	24	122	....	....	....	....	
Tasmania	18	88	....	....	....	....	
British East Indies	5,876	7,913	5,173	....	3,046	13,247	5.22
Other	2,067	584	759	535	1,927	6,531	2.57
Total British possessions	38,181	48,733	33,593	27,350	35,798	45,429	17.90
Total	154,322	155,733	112,771	133,542	115,725	253,837	100.00

a For quantities, see page 147.
b Including in 1896 imports from Cyprus valued at $1,489.
c Including in 1896 imports from Queensland valued at $9,660 and from Victoria $5,144.
d For quantities, see page 148.
e Including imports from Colombia valued at $584 in 1896 and $34 in 1898.

Value of the agricultural imports of the United Kingdom (animal matter), etc.—Cont'd.

BRISTLES. (a)

Countries from which imported.	Annual average, 1896-1900.	Calendar years.					Per ct. in 1900.
		1896.	1897.	1898.	1899.	1900.	
FOREIGN COUNTRIES.	Dollars.	Dollars.	Dollars.	Dollars.	Dollars.	Dollars.	
Russia................	759,379	674,643	696,056	687,306	1,041,407	697,481	27.31
China	726,040	819,115	748,672	704,022	818,151	540,240	21.15
Netherlands..........	331,632	332,338	278,155	225,348	395,427	426,894	16.71
Germany.............	337,891	466,298	307,329	254,537	335,492	325,798	12.75
France	113,659	89,836	82,492	87,801	116,956	191,210	7.49
Belgium.............	22,592	19,174	15,913	18,546	17,184	42,144	1.65
United States........	7,655	9,470	5,952	5,256	11,120	6,477	.25
Japan	6,570	2,867	5,621	6,852	13,383	4,127	.16
Italy	8,611	....	....	13,062	26,999	2,993	.12
Other b	2,171	1,664	3,640	4,195	1,046	311	.01
Total foreign countries.....	2,316,200	2,415,405	2,143,830	2,006,925	2,777,165	2,237,675	87.60
BRITISH POSSESSIONS.							
British East Indies:							
Bengal	152,268	157,626	232,560	88,200	88,235	194,718	} 7.76
Ceylon	389	....	....	....	....	1,947	
Bombay	5,895	2,414	14,332	4,336	6,823	1,572	
Hongkong...........	116,273	130,660	106,878	138,973	86,706	118,149	4.63
Other..............	925	....	4,380	....	....	243	.01
Total British possessions ...	275,750	290,700	358,150	231,509	181,764	316,629	12.40
Total	2,591,950	2,706,105	2,501,980	2,238,434	2,958,929	2,554,304	100.00

BUTTER. (a)

	Annual average, 1896-1900.	1896.	1897.	1898.	1899.	1900.	Per ct. in 1900.
FOREIGN COUNTRIES.	Dollars.	Dollars.	Dollars.	Dollars.	Dollars.	Dollars.	
Denmark.............	35,018,816	30,602,562	32,839,935	35,816,618	36,758,796	39,076,170	46.01
France	10,459,538	12,349,693	11,341,748	10,627,682	9,289,409	8,689,155	10.23
Netherlands..........	6,493,463	5,629,207	6,586,073	6,469,710	6,898,950	6,883,377	8.11
Sweden..............	6,756,620	8,101,190	7,376,178	7,307,867	6,064,326	4,933,536	5.81
Russia..............	4,158,164	3,674,597	4,721,790	4,285,566	3,335,952	4,772,917	5.62
Belgium.............	1,136,449	927,282	739,319	847,958	1,381,166	1,786,521	2.10
United States........	2,421,734	3,005,185	3,083,166	1,388,456	3,426,313	1,205,549	1.42
Germany.............	1,353,648	2,609,641	1,280,362	1,041,655	907,958	928,626	1.09
Norway	624,477	400,333	672,545	660,842	749,134	639,531	.75
Argentina	416,984	359,766	256,163	347,541	488,266	633,185	.75
Italy................	19,383	35,068	33,598	7,747	....	20,503	} .03
Other...............	4,348	1,479	599	14,259	3,975	1,426	
Total foreign countries.....	68,863,624	67,696,003	68,931,476	68,815,901	69,304,245	69,570,496	81.92
BRITISH POSSESSIONS.							
Australasia:							
Victoria	4,418,297	3,745,721	3,973,006	2,947,206	5,116,434	6,309,116	} 14.38
New Zealand.....	2,248,980	1,352,390	1,785,791	1,646,824	2,644,296	3,815,599	
New South Wales.	902,459	183,423	546,109	815,713	1,047,631	1,919,421	
South Australia ..	74,314	27,019	3,971	39,867	169,719	130.996	
Queensland	56,689	....	34,679	167,748	43,886	37,131	
Canada.............	3,115,784	1,653,364	2,164,921	3,221,307	5,421,067	3,118,259	3.67
British East Indies ...	11,380	6,492	10,492	13,232	9,733	16,950	.02
Channel Islands......	6,173	8,682	9,027	6,258	3,158	3,742	} .01
Other c	2,932	253	205	3,961	9,407	832	
Total British possessions ...	10,837,008	6,977,344	8,528,201	8,862,116	14,465,331	15,352,046	18.08
Total	79,700,632	74,673,347	77,459,677	77,678,017	83,769,576	84,922,542	100.00

a For quantities, see page 149.
b Including imports from Denmark valued at $506 in 1896. $1.986 in 1897. and $3.859 in 1898.
c Including imports from Newfoundland and Labrador valued at $462 in 1898 and $1,051 in 1899.

Value of the agricultural imports of the United Kingdom (animal matter), etc.—Cont'd.

CHEESE. (a)

ountries from which imported.	Annual average, 1896–1900.	Calendar years.					Per ct. in 1900.
		1896.	1897.	1898.	1899.	1900.	
FOREIGN COUNTRIES.	Dollars.	Dollars.	Dollars.	Dollars.	Dollars.	Dollars.	
nited States.........	6,594,166	6,005,441	6,876,749	4,898,551	6,718,734	8,471,355	25.46
etherlands..........	3,715,519	3,574,984	3,641,364	3,527,901	3,941,938	3,891,409	11.69
elgium..............	527,755	381,480	459,909	513,528	558,854	725,002	2.18
rance.	540,127	679,032	535,738	457,947	502,023	525,898	1.58
:aly................	32,160	19,048	25,471	6,653	13,451	96,177	.29
ermany.............	6,761	5,611	8,156	6,195	5,874	7,971	.02
ther b	4,460	5,850	3,197	4,657	3,665	4,930	.02
Total foreign countries.....	11,420,948	10,671,446	11,550,584	9,415,432	11,744,539	13,722,742	41.24
BRITISH POSSESSIONS.							
anada..............	15,276,879	12,600,833	16,300,347	14,325,638	14,668,658	18,488,919	55.56
Australasia:							
New Zealand.....	630,982	561,365	782,373	441,752	350,811	1,018,612	} 3.19
Victoria	8,751	511	2,973	1,849	959	37,462	
New South Wales.	1,778	102	1,937	34	165	6,652	
Newfoundland and Labrador..........	6,759	12,434	3,455	1,606	14,682	1,616	} .01
Other................	705	823	219	1,372	555	555	
Total British possessions ...	15,925,854	13,176,068	17,091,304	14,772,251	15,035,830	19,553,816	58.76
Total	27,346,802	23,847,514	28,641,888	24,187,683	26,780,369	33,276,558	100.00

CONDENSED MILK. (a)

	Annual average, 1896–1900.	1896.	1897.	1898.	1899.	1900.	Per ct. in 1900.
FOREIGN COUNTRIES.	Dollars.	Dollars.	Dollars.	Dollars.	Dollars.	Dollars.	
France	3,200,183	2,983,904	3,107,080	3,032,652	3,129,598	3,747,682	44.17
Netherlands..........	2,353,616	1,735,603	2,228,750	2,434,394	2,439,362	2,929,969	34.53
Norway	798,475	500,420	775,701	933,005	872,442	907,806	10.70
United States........	296,469	151,962	388,488	279,678	284,739	377,480	4.45
Belgium..............	251,883	245,734	235,383	231,889	226,112	320,298	3.77
Germany.............	64,746	55,585	42,304	45,954	75,737	104,148	1.23
Italy	35,395	12,069	9,460	19,812	47,862	87,772	1.03
Denmark.............	3,808	827	13,529	3,343	715	628	} .01
Other................	933	448	526	3,027	472	190	
Total foreign countries.....	7,005,508	5,689,552	6,801,221	6,983,754	7,077,039	8,475,973	99.89
BRITISH POSSESSIONS.							
Total British possessions...............	5,536	5,966	3,913	4,302	3,879	9,621	.11
Total	7,011,044	5,695,518	6,805,134	6,988,056	7,080,918	8,485,594	100.00

MILK, OTHER THAN CONDENSED. (c)

	Annual average, 1896–1900.	1896.	1897.	1898.	1899.	1900.	Per ct. in 1900.
FOREIGN COUNTRIES.	Dollars.	Dollars.	Dollars.	Dollars.	Dollars.	Dollars.	
France	22,651	29	10,653	12,074	9,455	81,042	62.05
Denmark............	14,938	1,494	1,289	11,110	37,808	22,989	17.60
Netherlands.........	7,230	312	847	3,110	9,704	22,177	16.98
United States........	2,375	....	11,860	....	....	14	.01
Sweden	15,550	24,556	20,376	23,851	8,969	....	......
Other................	4,101	29	2,876	3,732	9,490	4,380	3.36
Total foreign countries.....	66,845	26,420	47,901	53,877	75,426	130,602	100.00
BRITISH POSSESSIONS.							
Total British possessions d..............	833	292	24	1,080	2,769	....	......
Total	67,678	26,712	47,925	54,957	78,195	130,602	100.00

a For quantities, see page 150.
b Including imports from Russia valued at $2,973 in 1896, $1,567 in 1897, $1,007 in 1898, and $1,367 in 1899.
c For quantities, see page 151.
d Comprising in 1896 imports from Victoria valued at $292.

Value of the agricultural imports of the United Kingdom (animal matter), etc.—Cont'd.

EGGS. (*a*)

Countries from which imported.	Annual average, 1896–1900.	Calendar years.					Per ct. in 1900.
		1896.	1897.	1898.	1899.	1900.	
FOREIGN COUNTRIES.							
	Dollars.	*Dollars.*	*Dollars.*	*Dollars.*	*Dollars.*	*Dollars.*	
Russia................	4,575,544	3,066,148	3,953,043	4,701,667	5,757,220	5,399,640	20.52
Germany.............	4,251,128	3,806,192	3,956,572	3,838,909	4,704,158	4,949,810	18.81
Denmark.............	3,442,375	2,545,107	2,901,806	3,335,728	3,934,775	4,494,461	17.08
France	4,719,349	6,196,028	4,977,792	3,977,566	4,223,514	4,221,844	16.05
Belgium.............	3,587,584	3,378,918	3,737,847	3,556,915	3,694,890	3,569,349	13.57
United States.........	327,040	78,336	206,082	326,153	264,635	759,992	2.89
Egypt	230,414	15,631	65,143	175,462	305,933	589,902	2.24
Morocco.............	164,206	73,192	55,094	117,696	157,723	417,327	1.59
Netherlands..........	115,245	49,677	82,657	99,515	173,929	170,449	.65
Spain................	114,451	117,979	71,411	165,948	60,233	156,682	.60
Portugal.............	99,458	91,539	85,641	141,907	62,510	115,691	.44
Sweden	16,842	29,228	17,320	10,468	15,534	11,660	.04
Austria-Hungary.....	6,582	....	28,493	....	584	3,835	.02
Italy................	8,377	1,158	38,397	1,762	34	535	} .01
Other................	7,136	3,742	12,122	3,148	13,689	2,978	
Total foreign countries.....	21,665,731	19,452,875	20,189,420	20,452,844	23,369,361	24,864,155	94.51
BRITISH POSSESSIONS.							
Canada..............	1,116,645	870,768	944,091	1,224,947	1,137,267	1,406,151	5.34
Channel Islands......	26,558	34,732	52,665	9,971	17,704	17,719	.07
Gibraltar............	7,977	2,448	9,387	2,798	9,957	15,295	.06
Malta and Gozo	2,442	2,657	6,429	....	117	3,008	.01
Australasia...........	2,137	574	....	....	10,113	....	....
Other................	1,423	574	409	....	4,063	2,068	.01
Total British possessions ...	1,157,182	911,753	1,012,981	1,237,716	1,179,221	1,444,241	5.49
Total	22,822,913	20,364,628	21,202,401	21,690,560	24,548,582	26,308,396	100.00

FEATHERS AND DOWNS FOR BEDS. (*b*) (*c*)

	Annual average, 1896–1900.	1896.	1897.	1898.	1899.	1900.	Per ct. in 1900.
FOREIGN COUNTRIES.							
	Dollars.	*Dollars.*	*Dollars.*	*Dollars.*	*Dollars.*	*Dollars.*	
France	130,104	93,933	126,140	130,797	160,351	139,299	25.08
Germany.............	110,985	159,991	109,219	78,156	105,905	101,656	25.30
China...............	69,739	52,626	29,734	102,440	76,881	87,013	15.67
United States.........	31,756	27,476	28,352	3,869	22,580	76,501	13.78
Japan	19,630	10,473	15,792	10,312	28,381	33,194	5.98
Netherlands..........	21,159	19,982	22,517	23,349	17,802	22,143	3.99
Belgium.............	15,685	16,605	12,731	22,425	14,624	12,040	2.17
Russia...............	6,722	11,388	2,788	12,449	3,134	3,849	.69
Other *d*	6,034	4,832	6,419	5,309	5,446	8,166	1.47
Total foreign countries.....	411,814	397,306	353,692	389,106	435,104	483,861	87.13
BRITISH POSSESSIONS.							
Hongkong............	64,416	22,970	79,236	75,640	78,136	66,097	11.90
Other................	5,488	5,178	9,461	3,601	3,801	5,402	.97
Total British possessions ...	69,904	28,148	88,697	79,241	81,937	71,499	12.87
Total	481,718	425,454	442,389	468,347	517,041	555,360	100.00

a For quantities, see page 151.
b For quantities, see page 152.
c Including feather beds.
d Including imports from Portugal valued at $1.095 in 1896, $1.752 in 1897, $642 in 1898, and $3,699 in 1899, and from European Turkey $2,219 in 1896, and $3,071 in 1897.

Value of the agricultural imports of the United Kingdom (animal matter), etc.—Cont'd.

FEATHERS AND DOWNS FOR ORNAMENT.(a)

Countries from which imported.	Annual average, 1896–1900.	Calendar years.					Per ct. in 1900.
		1896.	1897.	1898.	1899.	1900.	
FOREIGN COUNTRIES.	*Dollars.*	*Dollars.*	*Dollars.*	*Dollars.*	*Dollars.*	*Dollars.*	
France	1,943,455	2,011,719	2,082,127	2,066,846	1,979,828	1,576,756	22.74
Netherlands	592,044	444,161	461,271	491,512	910,118	653,157	9.42
Germany	116,244	15,972	19,033	209,581	176,654	159,981	2.31
Venezuela	135,041	203,707	179,481	114,538	91,106	86,371	1.24
Egypt	31,792	17,325	18,249	32,873	34,917	55,595	.80
United States	40,206	47,696	17,515	32,581	49,882	53,356	.77
Tripoli	14,488	15,889	6,059	5,353	16,814	28,323	.41
Dutch East Indies, n. e. s.	18,927	4,672	9,641	41,998	23,967	14,356	.21
China	22,645	2,331	17,957	23,315	57,649	11,972	.17
Colombia	18,056	44,874	11,130	18,746	7,392	8,137	.12
Brazil	15,120	13,271	14,575	22,702	18,128	6,925	.10
Belgium	15,958	17,573	19,850	22,133	14,118	6,117	.09
Argentina	11,003	10,633	22,313	5,450	13,383	3,226	.05
Turkey, Asiatic	2,876	5,231	1,027	3,465	1,810	2,847	.04
Japan	5,785	1,226	11,115	8,721	5,085	2,779	.04
Portuguese East Africa	7,202	36,012					
Morocco	2,769	49	3,407	4,404	5,986		
Uruguay	2,267	409	2,725	5,913	2,287		
Other	9,806	7,713	6,828	10,843	16,298	7,349	.10
Total foreign countries	3,005,684	2,900,463	2,904,303	3,120,974	3,425,422	2,677,257	38.61
BRITISH POSSESSIONS.							
Cape of Good Hope	3,450,536	2,393,155	2,771,657	3,701,260	4,263,346	4,123,264	59.47
British East Indies:							
Bengal	60,170	98,045	74,199	53,118	33,384	42,105	
Bombay	39,919	75,523	52,777	36,839	16,347	18,108	
Straits Settlements	13,824	22,916	10,949	21,559	3,504	10,191	} 1.05
Madras	899	58	248	628	959	2,604	
Ceylon	647	677	457	1,460	584	58	
Malta and Gozo	22,436	7,052	15,101	26,571	42,679	20,775	.30
Hongkong	13,426	1,844	7,874	15,602	25,856	15,952	.23
Australasia	11,356	11,003	12,327	7,966	11,815	14,171	.20
British West Indies	6,872	4,687	15,203	5,597	2,248	6,623	.10
Aden	7,330	4,059	10,366	14,804	5,645	1,776	.03
Natal	5,537	24,576	774	292	1,995	49	} .01
Other	576	102	122	1,095	1,158	404	
Total British possessions	3,633,528	2,643,697	2,972,054	3,886,791	4,409,020	4,256,080	61.39
Total	6,639,212	5,544,160	5,876,357	7,007,765	7,834,442	6,933,337	100.00

SILK, RAW.(b)

FOREIGN COUNTRIES.	*Dollars.*	*Dollars.*	*Dollars.*	*Dollars.*	*Dollars.*	*Dollars.*	
China	1,839,775	1,321,503	1,451,044	1,883,506	2,940,480	1,602,339	35.93
France	2,721,012	2,659,109	2,965,645	3,534,700	3,055,758	1,389,848	31.16
Japan	152,639	241,680	35,180	128,821	182,241	175,272	3.93
Italy	113,608	108,749	152,740	102,503	106,270	102,780	2.31
Turkey, Asiatic	4,266	12,677	803	973		6,876	.15
Greece	5,083		9,806	9,285		6,326	.14
Turkey, European	19,205	29,900	26,153	11,801	22,176	5,996	.14
United States	1,999		5,290			4,706	.11
Belgium	4,220	901	1,703	16,225	1,713	560	.01
Other	4,572	389		7,290	5,840	9,339	.21
Total foreign countries	4,866,379	4,369,908	4,648,364	5,695,104	6,314,478	3,304,042	74.09
BRITISH POSSESSIONS.							
British East Indies:							
Bengal	660,755	465,685	609,407	721,011	636,908	870,763	} 20.53
Ceylon	10,696	1,460	3,893	98	2,920	45,108	
Bombay	1,565	7,592	234				
Hongkong	181,493	336,119	155,675	78,443	97,379	239,850	5.38
Other	3,942			19,709			
Total British possessions	858,451	810,856	769,209	819,261	737,207	1,155,721	25.91
Total	5,724,830	5,180,764	5,417,573	6,514,365	7,051,685	4,459,763	100.00

a For quantities, see page 152.   b For quantities, see page 153.

Value of the agricultural imports of the United Kingdom (animal matter), etc.—Cont'd.

SILK WASTE.(a)

Countries from which imported.	Annual average, 1896–1900.	Calendar years.					Per ct. in 1900.
		1896.	1897.	1898.	1899.	1900.	
FOREIGN COUNTRIES.	Dollars.	Dollars.	Dollars.	Dollars.	Dollars.	Dollars.	
China	908,220	791,478	655,980	1,078,207	1,047,864	967,572	36.38
France	348,335	393,773	295,654	326,197	378,881	347,171	13.06
Belgium	187,688	207,790	216,759	205,838	171,262	136,792	5.14
Germany	43,938	1,265	20,644	24,493	40,426	132,860	5.00
Japan	224,059	316,853	158,891	304,166	221,684	118,699	4.46
Netherlands	11,590	1,869	2,543	2,686	20,235	29,618	1.11
Turkey, European	22,935	15,870	36,265	28,026	11,018	23,496	.88
Russia	5,355	9,820	1,071	818	11,913	3,154	.12
United States	9,284	4,735	7,815	4,370	27,092	2,409	.09
Spain	5,883	11,475	6,346	2,711	6,638	2,243	.09
Macao	595			1,942	1,032		
Other b	11,513	12,278	9,144	10,575	13,178	12,390	.47
Total foreign countries	1,779,395	1,767,206	1,412,112	1,990,029	1,951,223	1,776,404	66.80
BRITISH POSSESSIONS.							
Hongkong	680,902	668,482	543,199	545,715	860,592	786,524	29.57
British East Indies:							
Bengal	54,363	30,099	55,600	64,515	67,941	53,663	
Bombay	28,310	48,894	5,514	9,670	41,833	35,637	
Burma	2,321	2,243		1,139	2,939	5,285	
Madras	5,531	5,013	16,239	2,618	1,874	1,912	3.63
Ceylon	75,194	127,760	206,388	40,922	900		
Straits Settlements	2,044				10,220		
Other	307	949			584		
Total British possessions	848,972	883,440	826,940	664,579	986,883	883,021	33.20
Total	2,628,367	2,650,646	2,239,052	2,654,608	2,938,106	2,659,425	100.00

MOHAIR.(c)

	Annual average, 1896–1900.	1896.	1897.	1898.	1899.	1900.	Per ct. in 1900.
FOREIGN COUNTRIES.	Dollars.	Dollars.	Dollars.	Dollars.	Dollars.	Dollars.	
Turkey, European	3,200,314	1,687,731	3,453,565	3,714,458	4,375,105	2,770,713	46.38
Turkey, Asiatic	127,500	155,003	158,366	174,464	17,262	132,403	2.21
Germany	2,926	6,049	49	59	3,202	5,270	.09
France	5,803	5,723	5,519	11,568	4,614	1,591	.03
Russia	29,709	423		146,019	2,102		
China	6,039	6,618			23,578		
Italy	3,994	4,351	15,621				
Other d	8,850	10,220	9,869	5,402	10,502	8,258	.14
Total foreign countries	3,385,135	1,876,118	3,642,989	4,051,970	4,436,365	2,918,235	48.85
BRITISH POSSESSIONS.							
Cape of Good Hope	2,977,509	2,389,126	2,779,068	2,962,180	3,871,077	2,886,092	48.32
British East Indies:							
Madras	29,230			4,380	39,628	102,143	1.71
Bombay	19	97					
Natal	209,268	241,013	308,332	185,535	244,994	66,467	1.11
Other	639	1,324	730	292	287	560	.01
Total British possessions	3,216,665	2,631,560	3,088,130	3,152,387	4,155,986	3,055,262	51.15
Total	6,601,800	4,507,678	6,731,119	7,204,357	8,592,351	5,973,497	100.00

a For quantities, see page 153.
b Including in 1896 imports from Italy valued at $7,908.
c For quantities, see page 154.
d Including in 1900 imports from the United States valued at $4,842.

Value of the agricultural imports of the United Kingdom (animal matter), etc.—Cont'd.

GOATS' HAIR, OTHER THAN MOHAIR. (a)

ountries from which imported.	Annual average, 1896-1900.	Calendar years.					Per ct. in 1900.
		1896.	1897.	1898.	1899.	1900.	
FOREIGN COUNTRIES.							
	Dollars.	*Dollars.*	*Dollars.*	*Dollars.*	*Dollars.*	*Dollars.*	
hina	72,001	93,529	74,248	63,941	48,140	80,146	26.58
rance	12,420	910	15,388	9,670	7,611	28,523	9.46
ermany	6,985	1,275	6,662	19	5,129	21,841	7.24
elgium.............	15,147	11,499	30,591	14,838	11,908	6,896	2.29
nited States........	3,361	8,176	297	2,297	....	6,034	2.00
urkey, European....	99	....	341	....	98	58	.02
urkey, Asiatic.......	354	....	1,513	10	209	39	.01
ussia...............	6,071	....	28,995	1,362	....	....	
:aly	1,364	1,324	....	5,173	321	....	
ther...............	8,351	404	7,509	6,463	13,013	14,366	4.77
Total foreign countries	126,153	117,117	165,544	103,773	86,429	157,903	52.37
BRITISH POSSESSIONS.							
ritish East Indies:							
Madras..........	25,280	170	24	38,046	9,762	78,395	
Bombay..........	51,060	29,876	49,273	67,080	44,601	64,471	47.52
Ceylon	78	....	....	....		389	
Bengal	599	122	97	2,774	....	....	
atal...............	3,426	....	5,305	11,826	....	....	
ther...............	1,920	3,635	190	788	4,648	341	.11
Total British possessions ...	82,363	33,803	54,889	120,514	59,011	143,596	47.63
Total	208,516	150,920	220,433	224,287	145,440	301,499	100.00

HAIR OF THE ALPACA, VICUÑA, AND LLAMA. (a)

FOREIGN COUNTRIES.							
	Dollars.	*Dollars.*	*Dollars.*	*Dollars.*	*Dollars.*	*Dollars.*	
Peru...................	1,011,467	1,063,403	1,084,227	898,847	1,009,142	1,001,716	74.67
Chile	199,505	231,125	96,381	174,187	247,077	248,756	18.54
Germany	35,608	42,387	18,785	16,819	9,368	90,682	6.76
United States........	21,200	102,391	3,606	....	....	....	
Other.................	531	....	2,044	243	....	370	.03
Total	1,268,311	1,439,306	1,205,043	1,090,096	1,265,587	1,341,524	100.00

SHEEP'S WOOL. (b)

FOREIGN COUNTRIES.							
	Dollars.	*Dollars.*	*Dollars.*	*Dollars.*	*Dollars.*	*Dollars.*	
France	4,604,105	3,987,771	4,482,830	4,288,885	6,039,769	4,221,270	3.97
Argentina	1,709,313	1,053,977	1,727,695	2,327,355	1,727,802	1,709,783	1.61
Turkey, Asiatic.......	1,806,828	1,872,960	3,024,126	1,430,055	1,034,443	1,672,553	1.57
Chile	1,362,732	859,434	979,456	1,573,310	1,766,778	1,634,682	1.54
Belgium..............	2,035,917	2,779,798	1,996,988	1,898,441	2,001,640	1,502,717	1.42
Russia...............	1,678,201	1,689,741	2,032,474	1,965,696	1,263,742	1,439,350	1.36
Uruguay	445,984	282,997	453,655	370,793	113,545	1,008,932	.95
Germany.............	709,345	563,833	970,166	570,894	451,421	990,411	.93
Egypt ....:....	410,105	516,048	448,375	371,533	341,064	373,504	.35
Turkey, European.....	299,178	249,092	406,041	270,865	198,977	370,915	.35
Peru.................	330,316	409,896	379,417	239,227	315,928	307,110	.29
Portugal.............	368,621	464,532	587,367	297,880	258,231	235,144	.22
Italy	203,767	70,992	97,320	238,921	419,337	192,266	.18
Denmark.............	248,499	196,573	322,664	198,519	361,688	163,052	.15
Netherlands..........	234,542	316,746	333,574	187,083	175,155	160,152	.15
China	179,436	278,719	185,647	252,494	70,871	109,448	.10
Portuguese East Africa...............	36,693	6,326	47,108	22,668	5,071	102,294	.10
United States........	481,828	673,757	114,518	155,791	1,372,952	92,123	.09
Morocco	149,745	89,617	290,292	197,697	86,921	84,200	.08
Persia	123,971	54,271	250,085	181,102	56,544	77,854	.07
Spain................	111,905	97,714	260,528	82,176	66,087	53,020	
Austria-Hungary.....	14,452	20,123	36,319	10,955	3,971	890	.05
Brazil	4,106	9,417	....	....	10,940	175	

a For quantities, see page 154.   b For quantities, see page 155.

Value of the agricultural imports of the United Kingdom (animal matter), etc.—Cont'd.

SHEEP'S WOOL—Continued.

Countries from which imported.	Annual average, 1896-1900.	Calendar years.					Per ct. in 1900.
		1896.	1897.	1898.	1899.	1900.	
FOREIGN COUNTRIES— continued.	Dollars.	Dollars.	Dollars.	Dollars.	Dollars.	Dollars.	
Tripoli	6,470		32,352				
Roumania	6,145	22,454	8,273				
Canary Islands	2,787	13,879		58			
Pacific islands	2,495		12,473				
Other a	9,769	3,090	10,502	8,254	7,528	19,471	0.02
Total foreign countries	17,577,255	16,583,757	19,490,245	17,140,602	18,150,405	16,521,266	15.55
BRITISH POSSESSIONS.							
Australasia:							
New South Wales	26,925,237	27,949,429	27,196,012	26,308,956	27,704,736	25,467,052	⎫
New Zealand	22,431,729	22,298,897	22,253,887	23,043,880	21,138,090	23,423,890	⎪
Victoria	15,177,275	15,949,779	15,353,467	14,254,942	11,435,046	15,893,142	⎬74.79
Queensland	8,084,255	8,284,710	9,553,879	7,718,152	7,155,629	7,708,906	⎪
South Australia	5,036,015	7,076,806	5,160,802	3,839,299	4,607,690	4,495,478	⎪
West Australia	1,459,327	1,653,174	1,290,026	1,209,145	1,381,741	1,762,549	⎪
Tasmania	842,673	1,048,546	881,489	807,060	752,672	723,595	⎭
Cape of Good Hope	9,744,920	11,355,053	9,331,397	11,382,466	11,807,020	4,848,664	4 56
British East Indies:							
Bombay	4,529,908	5,313,615	4,655,138	4,642,641	4,337,984	3,700,161	⎫
Bengal	310,580	312,935	385,738	326,591	230,721	296,662	⎪
Madras	20,756	20,264	13,149	27,578	9,115	83,671	⎬3.80
Straits Settlements	66,422	18,999	82,229	106,182	121,390	3,309	⎪
Ceylon	511		1,397	1,022	136		⎭
Falkland Islands	718,622	657,605	651,512	786,782	772,275	724,933	.68
Natal	2,401,270	2,923,798	2,588,647	3,105,484	2,758,288	630,134	.59
Hongkong	2,880					14,400	.01
Canada	10,885	2,861		4,083	32,708	12,273	⎫
British West Indies	17,876	5,577	4,005	69,761	5,017	5,022	⎪
St. Helena	239		180	720		297	⎬.02
Gibraltar	2,909	1,110	9,986	3,363		88	⎪
Malta and Gozo	3,495	185	16,449	341	501		⎭
Other	3,856	2,691	2,399	6,604	6,769	818	
Total British possessions	97,791,090	104,876,034	99,431,788	97,645,052	97,257,528	89,745,044	84.45
Total	115,368,345	121,459,791	118,922,033	114,785,654	115,407,933	106,266,310	100.00

WOOL, ETC., NOT ELSEWHERE SPECIFIED, INCLUDING FLOCKS. (b)

FOREIGN COUNTRIES.	Dollars.	Dollars.	Dollars.	Dollars.	Dollars.	Dollars.	
France	270,976	147,124	232,278	226,112	447,095	302,273	39.64
Belgium	171,187	142,204	131,590	163,660	187,759	230,721	30.26
Germany	80,788	69,494	75,942	42,786	83,655	132,062	17.32
Netherlands	58,293	37,355	43,925	52,023	74,769	83,392	10.94
United States	12,211	18,624	8,740	18,551	6,935	8,205	1.07
Other	4,421	3,309	8,152	1,110	4,497	5,037	.66
Total foreign countries	597,876	418,110	500,627	504,242	804,710	761,690	99.89
BRITISH POSSESSIONS.							
Total British possessions	4,271	11,242	6,380	1,290	1,625	818	.11
Total	602,147	429,352	507,007	505,532	806,335	762,508	100.00

a Including imports from Greece valued at $1,601 in 1896, $428 in 1897, $662 in 1898, and $560 in 1899.
b For quantities, see page 156.

Value of the agricultural imports of the United Kingdom (animal matter), etc.—Cont'd.

GLUE, SIZE, AND GELATIN. (a) (b)

Countries from which imported.	Calendar year 1900.	Per cent.	Countries from which imported.	Calendar year 1900.	Per cent.
FOREIGN COUNTRIES.	*Dollars.*		FOREIGN COUNTRIES—cont'd.	*Dollars.*	
France	910,722	40.35	Other	24,644	1.09
Germany	401,525	17.79			
Belgium	350,276	15.52	Total foreign countries.	2,253,652	99.84
Netherlands	250,892	11.11			
United States	194,529	8.62	BRITISH POSSESSIONS.		
Austria-Hungary	92,395	4.09			
Russia	28,669	1.27	Total British possessions	3,567	.16
			Total	2,257,219	100.00

GLUE STOCK. (a) (b)

FOREIGN COUNTRIES.	*Dollars.*		BRITISH POSSESSIONS—cont'd.		
France	78,935	13.23	Australasia:	*Dollars.*	
Germany	60,928	10.21	New South Wales	52,889	
Belgium	54,422	9.12	Victoria	11,611	
Argentina	30,722	5.15	Queensland	10,166	12.98
United States	6,745	1.13	New Zealand	1,509	
Other	33,691	5.64	South Australia	1,124	
			West Australia	170	
Total foreign countries.	265,443	44.48	Other	1,499	.25
BRITISH POSSESSIONS.			Total British possessions	331,277	55.52
British East Indies:					
Madras	140,856		Total	596,720	100.00
Bengal	90,274				
Bombay	20,653	42.29			
Straits Settlements	326				
Burma	200				

CATTLE HAIR. (c) (d)

Countries from which imported.	Annual average, 1896–1900.	Calendar years.					Per ct. in 1900.
		1896.	1897.	1898.	1899.	1900.	
FOREIGN COUNTRIES.	*Dollars.*	*Dollars.*	*Dollars.*	*Dollars.*	*Dollars.*	*Dollars.*	
France	149,178	146,486	202,607	122,753	161,840	112,202	30.38
Germany	71,483	53,342	88,546	65,518	79,489	70,520	19.10
United States	24,584	29,982	11,217	16,113	28,255	37,355	10.11
Netherlands	48,304	74,214	49,828	33,715	47,979	35,783	9.69
Russia	27,600	7,971	69,971	3,124	35,195	21,739	5.89
Belgium	18,852	25,486	6,633	24,094	23,311	14,736	3.99
Italy	9,329	3,621	8,803	6,609	15,918	11,694	3.17
Argentina	5,184	6,774	3,976	5,100	4,691	5,378	1.46
Uruguay	6,486	19,875	209	5,217	3,806	3,324	.90
Spain	2,034	4,565	2,020	....	900	2,686	.73
Other	11,559	3,733	13,140	10,823	17,378	12,721	3.44
Total foreign countries	374,593	376,049	456,950	293,066	418,762	328,138	88.86
BRITISH POSSESSIONS.							
Australasia:							
New South Wales	18,505	14,999	17,952	21,437	21,058	17,077	
New Zealand	1,529	1,148	1,080	706	2,015	2,696	
South Australia	1,183	234	555	1,314	1,825	1,986	
Victoria	2,613	2,141	925	3,504	5,421	1,075	6.38
Queensland	1,587	2,881	2,321	1,621	696	418	
West Australia	100	....		204	....	297	
Tasmania	99	263	....	170	63	....	
British East Indies	7,745	3,377	5,509	8,735	6,550	14,551	3.94
Other e	1,133	691	652	399	900	3,022	.82
Total British possessions	34,494	25,734	28,994	38,090	38,528	41,122	11.14
Total	409,087	401,783	485,944	331,156	457,290	369,260	100.00

a For quantities, see page 156.
b Prior to 1900 not stated by countries.
c For quantities, see page 157.
d Including elk hair.
e Including imports from Canada valued at $496 in 1896, $58 in 1897, and $1,655 in 1900.

*Value of the agricultural imports of the United Kingdom (animal matter), etc.—*Cont'd.

HORSEHAIR. (*a*)

Countries from which imported.	Annual average, 1896–1900.	Calendar years.					Per ct. in 1900.
		1896.	1897.	1898.	1899.	1900.	
FOREIGN COUNTRIES.							
	Dollars.	*Dollars.*	*Dollars.*	*Dollars.*	*Dollars.*	*Dollars.*	
Russia	369,417	253,749	426,432	380,346	531,227	255,331	25.49
China	206,114	250,902	234,935	168,629	236,945	139,162	13.90
France	102,960	108,752	79,796	98,581	99,325	128,344	12.81
Belgium	68,586	57,960	44,193	55,196	87,145	98,435	9.83
Germany	108,311	91,042	152,813	123,234	77,786	96,678	9.65
Argentina	54,252	48,519	82,312	42,446	32,761	65,221	6.51
United States	22,603	24,513	6,691	14,609	16,186	51,015	5.09
Uruguay	17,746	3,027	14,687	17,865	23,354	29,797	2.98
Italy	8,784	87	12,264	9,821	13,208	8,541	.85
Brazil	9,935	18,634	8,988	4,832	11,407	5,815	.58
Netherlands	8,599	7,120	15,665	13,110	3,222	3,879	.39
Other *b*	6,672	2,419	3,796	4,059	16,551	6,536	.65
Total foreign countries	983,979	866,724	1,082,572	932,728	1,149,117	888,754	88.73
BRITISH POSSESSIONS.							
Australasia:							
New South Wales.	50,598	37,321	66,077	51,502	49,468	48,621	
Victoria	26,588	21,924	38,820	27,311	25,827	19,057	
New Zealand	9,436	8,098	11,087	9,168	10,171	8,706	
South Australia	6,564	8,876	8,190	5,553	5,232	4,969	} 8.20
Queensland	1,403	3,465	1,689	998	521	341	
Tasmania	104				209	312	
West Australia	112	243		122	97	97	
Canada	8,749	8,073	11,988	4,136	3,119	16,478	1.65
Hongkong	855	813		1,411		2,054	.20
Other	6,852	1,027	6,093	6,565	8,380	12,195	1.22
Total British possessions	111,261	89,840	143,844	106,766	103,024	112,830	11.27
Total	1,095,240	956,564	1,226,416	1,039,494	1,252,141	1,001,584	100.00

HAIR NOT ELSEWHERE SPECIFIED.

	Annual average, 1896–1900.	1896.	1897.	1898.	1899.	1900.	Per ct. in 1900.
FOREIGN COUNTRIES.							
	Dollars.	*Dollars.*	*Dollars.*	*Dollars.*	*Dollars.*	*Dollars.*	
Russia	445,932	387,587	490,212	421,152	419,269	511,440	33.03
China	426,233	332,338	477,774	306,555	523,431	491,069	31.72
United States	292,991	229,655	220,365	309,466	311,894	393,573	25.42
France	64,325	61,727	63,454	81,592	55,259	59,595	3.85
Italy	24,200	14,415	29,004	29,325	16,921	31,335	2.03
Germany	29,780	41,351	35,589	28,445	25,345	18,172	1.17
Netherlands	10,651	11,675	12,191	8,224	9,159	12,006	.78
Belgium	15,946	23,495	31,379	9,645	5,606	9,606	.62
Denmark	3,351	9,577	1,562	832	905	3,879	.25
Uruguay	1,402			6,677		331	.02
Turkey, Asiatic	2,450	754		11,422	73		
Other *c*	10,178	8,142	8,492	20,245	3,489	10,521	.68
Total foreign countries	1,327,439	1,120,716	1,370,022	1,233,580	1,371,351	1,541,527	99.57
BRITISH POSSESSIONS.							
Hongkong	1,309	73	2,239			4,234	.27
Canada	3,017	2,769	5,339	2,210	3,431	1,338	.09
Australasia *d*	2,046	3,446	1,187	3,202	1,542	852	.05
British East Indies	3,590	229		29	17,427	263	} .02
Other	243	720	19	34	409	34	
Total British possessions	10,205	7,237	8,784	5,475	22,809	6,721	.43
Total	1,337,644	1,127,953	1,378,806	1,239,055	1,394,160	1,548,248	100.00

a For quantities, see page 157.
b Including imports from Denmark valued at $404 in 1896 and $200 in 1897.
c Including imports from Argentina valued at $545 in 1896 and $759 in 1897.
d Including imports from New Zealand valued at $1,548 in 1896, $136 in 1897, $993 in 1898, $492 in 1899, and $156 in 1900.

due of the agricultural imports of the United Kingdom (animal matter), etc.—Cont'd.

HIDES. (a)

	Annual average, 1896-1900.	Calendar years.					Per ct. in 1900.
		1896.	1897.	1898.	1899.	1900.	
REIGN COUNTRIES.	*Dollars.*	*Dollars.*	*Dollars.*	*Dollars.*	*Dollars.*	*Dollars.*	
ly	1,179,653	1,018,490	890,287	1,139,579	1,397,396	1,452,514	8.73
lgium	1,308,084	1,523,190	1,183,616	1,056,444	1,381,079	1,396,092	8.39
rmany	1,075,974	762,036	1,075,341	1,075,657	1,292,270	1,174,569	7.06
therlands	974,914	857,395	928,421	1,020,169	1,114,273	954,311	5.74
ance	921,582	719,439	784,772	907,120	1,271,208	925,370	5.56
ıssia	290,730	119,122	169,724	305,008	418,889	440,905	2.65
nmark	340,278	85,013	248,011	480,693	496,592	391,082	2.35
azil	258,432	151,470	153,786	307,188	381,908	297,810	1.79
rtugal	247,324	183,360	252,571	304,560	265,263	230,867	1.39
ina	184,502	134,826	93,656	162,702	318,829	212,496	1.28
gentina	257,391	323,613	426,943	254,250	167,953	114,197	.69
'eden	118,120	54,889	74,603	181,735	175,223	104,148	.63
rway	73,965	51,945	34,100	61,877	132,675	89,227	.54
lombia	67,456	53,371	20,746	76,419	100,240	86,502	.52
ypt	33,813	24,761	11,485	5,616	68,423	58,778	.35
ıited States	170,309	560,932	88,215	51,468	98,094	52,836	.32
uguay	187,457	161,986	339,229	327,063	61,391	47,614	.29
ench West Africa	15,259	....	311	23,958	22,006	30,021	.18
ench Indo-China	61,254	57,381	70,788	93,773	61,260	22,517	.14
ıstria-Hungary	11,119	4,901	13,393	8,502	6,677	22,123	.13
ile	40,133	54,150	43,589	37,015	46,981	18,931	.11
ain	13,111	8,049	12,483	8,984	17,670	18,371	.11
pan	19,844	12,502	20,587	20,984	27,763	17,432	.10
uador	7,240	6,716	1,071	3,382	9,217	15,816	.09
ru	6,879	7,640	4,584	7,314	4,224	10,633	.06
ıdagascar	29,500	59,323	48,918	8,477	22,668	8,112	.05
tch Guiana	7,896	6,764	12,147	6,823	10,122	3,625	.02
rtuguese East Africa	61,137	95,271	198,125	10,950	292	1,046	.01
orocco	6,179	8,696	5,017	15,928	764	491	} .20
her b	18,543	4,876	11,003	21,778	22,498	32,562	
orthern whale fisheries	6,390	399	307	7,056	14,001	10,186	.06
Total foreign countries	7,994,468	7,113,056	7,217,779	7,992,472	9,407,849	8,241,184	49.54
RITISH POSSESSIONS.							
ritish East Indies:							
Bombay	840,854	94,829	239,305	163,782	415,142	3,291,214	
Bengal	1,806,315	1,082,456	2,404,285	1,253,391	1,389,799	2,901,641	
Straits Settlements	594,136	506,481	745,178	459,986	617,953	641,088	} 42.96
Burma	189,534	193,151	271,672	126,568	175,194	181,083	
Madras	91,950	70,832	117,691	77,231	75,329	118,865	
Ceylon	6,479	5,124	8,351	4,579	2,789	11,553	
ustralasia:							
New South Wales	579,928	533,505	493,215	489,477	665,158	718,286	
Queensland	82,856	95,169	78,545	103,866	71,148	65,552	
New Zealand	7,191	866	9,787	1,275	857	23,169	} 4.96
Victoria	31,919	26,620	68,394	41,103	9,061	14,415	
South Australia	4,421	6,944	4,613	3,499	8,995	3,056	
West Australia	225	282	15	....	....	827	
ape of Good Hope	914,551	745,241	1,302,718	2,216,199	208,359	100,235	.60
atal	387,084	212,072	253,014	1,060,294	314,682	95,359	.57
ritish West Indies	71,960	62,184	73,757	62,593	71,192	90,074	.54
ibraltar	32,366	9,417	20,337	37,010	46,198	48,869	.29
[alta and Gozo	9,259	399	706	2,453	27,389	15,349	.90
hannel Islands	9,401	11,680	10,059	7,816	9,188	8,263	.05
alkland Islands	3,640	3,869	1,752	1,679	3,226	7,675	.05
den	8,953	6,589	9,723	7,879	13,373	7,203	.04
ierra Leone	15,340	31,068	30,386	6,156	4,307	4,784	.03
anzibar and Pemba	4,116	7,650	1,733	4,336	2,385	4,477	.03
[auritius	4,202	3,640	4,628	803	8,945	2,993	.02
ambia	1,673	1,319	1,309	1,562	2,214	1,961	.01
t. Helena	802	....	1,557	691	857	905	.01
ongkong	2,584	560	5,441	3,319	3,601	....	
ther c	14,955	2,672	7,694	11,855	18,035	34,518	.21
Total British possessions	5,716,694	3,714,619	6,165,860	6,149,402	4,160,376	8,393,214	50.46
Total	13,711,162	10,827,675	13,383,639	14,141,874	13,568,225	16,634,398	100.00

a For quantities, see page 158.
b Including dry hides from Asiatic Turkey valued at $5,324 in 1897, $7,499 in 1898, $5,426 in 1899, nd $15,213 in 1900.
c Including wet hides from Canada valued at $764 in 1896, $1,523 in 1897, $6,541 in 1898, $2,798 in 399, and $15,461 in 1900, and from Newfoundland and Labrador, $15 in 1896 and $574 in 1899.

Value of the agricultural imports of the United Kingdom (animal matter), etc.—Cont'd.

GOATSKINS. (a)

Countries from which imported.	Annual average, 1896-1900.	Calendar years.					Per ct. in 1900.
		1896.	1897.	1898.	1899.	1900.	
FOREIGN COUNTRIES.	Dollars.	Dollars.	Dollars.	Dollars.	Dollars.	Dollars.	
Russia	853,634	640,110	807,878	813,080	1,014,423	992,664	14.44
France	692,990	405,399	616,138	429,634	1,242,369	771,408	11.22
Morocco	312,922	72,248	183,326	473,798	447,630	387,607	5.64
China	277,144	313,923	319,476	256,951	162,726	332,645	4.84
Netherlands	216,122	177,953	282,082	245,797	242,795	131,984	1.92
Turkey, Asiatic	88,884	54,923	98,177	150,122	31,953	109,243	1.59
Germany	115,194	147,951	116,762	67,309	153,222	90,726	1.32
Egypt	29,926	13,378	10,482	20,838	33,136	71,796	1.04
Belgium	61,616	77,786	79,261	31,559	59,965	59,508	.86
Italy	24,684	29,379	36,027	10,580	4,380	43,054	.62
Brazil	9,637	146	....	195	6,813	41,030	.60
Turkey, European	31,784	41,652	1,090	26,776	60,247	29,155	.42
United States	32,634	72,667	10,205	34,070	29,905	16,322	.24
Norway	10,062	12,225	6,375	11,660	10,288	9,762	.14
Cyprus	9,244	4,667	16,098	11,509	6,609	7,339	.11
Algeria	36,985	4,774	114,489	30,961	28,985	5,718	.08
Spain	11,969	24,897	24,284	4,560	2,238	3,864	.06
Portuguese West Africa	4,382	....	8,823	6,458	2,779	3,849	.05
Tripoli	7,051	24,333	....	....	9,426	1,494	.02
Austria-Hungary	6,332	22,250	8,030	214	....	1,168	.02
Greece	3,010	14,668	....	....	....	384	} .01
Chile	7,315	20,201	8,390	7,864	....	122	
Japan	4,821	7,689	....	....	16,415	....	
Madagascar	1,342	900	5,811	....	....	....	
Other b	17,221	13,290	1,333	9,840	20,142	41,502	.60
Total foreign countries	2,866,905	2,197,409	2,754,537	2,643,775	3,586,459	3,152,344	45.84
BRITISH POSSESSIONS.							
British East Indies:							
Bengal	2,081,449	952,865	1,737,165	2,272,339	3,182,214	2,262,660	} 45.29
Madras	229,909	8,142	26,922	19,646	300,506	794,330	
Bombay	25,545	20,332	42,850	10,351	2,404	51,789	
Burma	2,285	....	....	49	6,857	4,521	
Straits Settlements	16,538	38,547	9,976	8,108	25,452	608	
Cape of Good Hope	597,665	659,941	583,493	627,170	581,805	535,913	7.79
Aden	154,917	191,176	140,506	220,175	158,288	64,442	.94
Natal	8,503	14,488	8,404	14,341	3,012	2,268	.03
Zanzibar and Pemba	1,916	2,852	4,959	1,771	....	....	
Other	5,682	1,144	2,029	2,409	15,466	7,363	.11
Total British possessions	3,124,409	1,889,487	2,556,304	3,176,359	4,276,004	3,723,894	54.16
Total	5,991,314	4,086,896	5,310,841	5,820,134	7,862,463	6,876,238	100.00

RABBIT SKINS. (a)

FOREIGN COUNTRIES.	Dollars.	Dollars.	Dollars.	Dollars.	Dollars.	Dollars.	
Belgium	174,508	48,631	166,936	206,807	207,391	242,775	23.20
France	96,206	66,924	116,324	120,217	92,790	84,771	8.10
Germany	18,528	37,131	18,663	6,292	9,485	21,072	2.02
Netherlands	12,591	23,408	12,317	2,278	9,222	15,729	1.50
United States	7,189	22,834	3,630	9,052	170	258	.03
Japan	92	462	....	....	....	....	.....
Chile	8	39	....	....	....	....	.....
Other	1,549	200	....	....	....	7,543	.72
Total foreign countries	310,671	199,629	317,870	344,646	319,058	372,151	35.57

a For quantities, see page 159.
b Including imports from Argentina valued at $190 in 1896 and $1,703 in 1898, and from Peru, $195 in 1896, $467 in 1897, and $691 in 1898.

alue of the agricultural imports of the United Kingdom (animal matter), etc.—Cont'd.

RABBIT SKINS—Continued.

	Annual average, 1896-1900.	Calendar years.					Per ct. in 1900.
		1896.	1897.	1898.	1899.	1900.	
BRITISH POSSESSIONS.							
Australasia:	Dollars.	Dollars.	Dollars.	Dollars.	Dollars.	Dollars.	
Victoria	305,141	311,066	246,873	213,021	398,406	356,340	
New Zealand	235,608	301,572	270,986	157,679	276,091	171,715	
South Australia	56,495	55,108	23,048	25,520	91,641	87,159	
New South Wales	69,607	95,111	103,209	44,665	64,481	40,567	}64.31
Tasmania	24,903	29,209	26,260	23,053	29,277	16,716	
Queensland	50					248	
West Australia	37					185	
Other	2,100	1,134	2,204	2,584	3,265	1,314	.12
Total British possessions	693,941	793,200	672,580	466,522	863,161	674,244	64.43
Total	1,004,612	992,829	990,450	811,168	1,182,219	1,046,395	100.00

SHEEPSKINS. (a)

	Annual average, 1896-1900.	1896.	1897.	1898.	1899.	1900.	Per ct. in 1900.
FOREIGN COUNTRIES.	Dollars.	Dollars.	Dollars.	Dollars.	Dollars.	Dollars.	
Argentina	977,054	494,563	946,164	965,509	1,315,094	1,163,940	14.95
France	172,128	26,746	44,344	94,118	352,315	343,117	4.41
Germany	141,995	66,350	166,025	100,912	133,824	242,867	3.12
Spain	137,817	100,790	103,180	126,252	170,235	188,630	2.42
Chile	67,059	37,224	30,513	78,109	71,460	122,991	1.58
Russia	110,651	84,366	124,957	134,179	124,115	85,636	1.10
Turkey, Asiatic	84,458	74,623	98,075	106,202	72,423	70,968	.91
Uruguay	40,613	48,178	27,710	63,411	11,091	52,675	.68
Denmark	38,295	34,839	35,618	37,813	38,460	44,743	.57
Netherlands	54,454	37,633	73,898	66,413	49,882	44,446	.57
Belgium	20,258	11,154	25,165	10,093	12,775	42,105	.54
Brazil	43,224		34	123,307	50,952	41,828	.54
China	18,689	32,177	12,395	9,324	8,769	30,781	.40
Egypt	25,676	25,520	45,409	18,006	8,711	30,732	.40
United States	14,841	33,885	10,945	4,341	2,910	22,123	.28
Turkey, European	6,062	11,193	5,699	185	3,480	9,752	.13
Portuguese East Africa	47,074	101,617	121,594	6,054		6,103	.08
Morocco	10,577	5,285	6,691	24,308	11,923	4,677	.06
Persia	16,541	8,030	33,044	23,311	18,030	292	
Madagascar	1,977	5,168	4,647			68	}.71
Other	28,300	15,359	19,685	20,945	30,323	55,186	
Total foreign countries	2,057,743	1,254,700	1,935,792	2,007,792	2,486,772	2,603,660	33.45
BRITISH POSSESSIONS.							
Australasia:							
New Zealand	1,238,561	838,245	1,059,213	1,348,288	1,401,328	1,545,732	
South Australia	574,026	584,043	526,857	633,146	467,023	659,060	
Victoria	388,618	358,199	357,678	363,771	309,446	553,998	
New South Wales	285,230	290,428	291,343	221,255	323,019	300,103	}42.47
West Australia	111,342	60,948	45,964	79,222	182,776	187,798	
Queensland	74,371	237,086	53,658	31,686	8,098	41,326	
Tasmania	16,831	10,677	15,855	21,666	18,050	17,909	
Cape of Good Hope	1,694,167	2,004,253	1,731,681	1,696,681	1,584,275	1,453,945	18.68
Aden	168,882	171,218	178,941	154,526	152,613	187,112	2.40
British East Indies b	69,627	35,516	46,524	70,442	86,779	108,873	1.40
Falkland Islands	42,120	32,606	50,125	15,996	43,619	68,253	.88
Natal	131,583	83,889	68,413	187,565	264,723	53,327	}.68
St. Helena	318		973	195	321	102	
Hongkong	175				876		
Other	3,677	2,647	5,105	3,411	4,083	3,139	.04
Total British possessions	A,799,528	4,709,755	4,432,330	4,827,850	4,847,029	5,180,677	66.55
Total	6,857,271	5,964,455	6,368,122	6,835,642	7,333,801	7,784,337	100.00

a For quantities, see page 160.
b Including imports from Bengal valued at $7,976 in 1896, $11,728 in 1897, $25,364 in 1898, $57,678 in 1899, and $63,698 in 1900.

Value of the agricultural imports of the United Kingdom (animal matter), etc.—Cont'd.

SKINS NOT ELSEWHERE SPECIFIED.(a)

Countries from which imported.	Annual average, 1896-1900.	Calendar years.					Per ct. in 1900.
		1896.	1897.	1898.	1899.	1900.	
FOREIGN COUNTRIES.							
	Dollars. (b)	Dollars.	Dollars.	Dollars.	Dollars.	Dollars.(c)	
China	1,718	243	4,852	1,192	584	64,632	38.65
France	3,588	671	3,212	5,426	5,042	16,371	9.79
Germany	8,305	4,935	7,144	10,551	10,589	15,729	9.40
Netherlands	263	10	112	389	540	7,519	4.50
United States	13,730	6,141	6,214	15,855	26,712	4,370	2.61
Russia	5,982	4,599	13,208	25	6,098	1,635	.98
Chile	2,722	146	204	10,526	10	146	.09
Other d.	5,280	7,451	5,981	3,893	3,796	19,130	11.44
Total foreign countries	41,588	24,196	40,927	47,857	53,371	129,532	77.46
BRITISH POSSESSIONS.							
British East Indies:							
Madras	3,304	1,840	1,192	4,789	5,397	7,217	⎫
Straits Settlements	6,612	6,263	2,862	6,584	10,740	6,794	
Burma	12	....	....	....	49	2,589	⎬10.12
Bengal	561	735	44	1,338	127	190	
Bombay	219	....	248	....	628	122	
Ceylon	12	....	49	....	....	19	⎭
Australasia:							
New South Wales.	26,309	15,811	41,029	24,654	23,744	15,261	⎫
Victoria	6,415	8,555	2,905	13,062	1,139	214	
Queensland	468	....	657	1,216	....	195	
South Australia ..	3,570	12,736	1,543	....	....	....	⎬9.37
West Australia ...	256	....	925	97	....	....	
New Zealand	15	....	....	....	58	....	
Tasmania	10	....	19	....	19	....	⎭
Hongkong	....	....	....	....	....	2,774	1.66
Canada	1,430	1,927	1,212	146	2,433	....	......
Other	2,523	3,669	3,762	1,762	900	2,321	1.39
Total British possessions ...	51,716	51,536	56,447	53,648	45,234	37,696	22.54
Total	93,304	75,732	97,374	101,505	98,605	167,228	100.00

HONEY. (a)

FOREIGN COUNTRIES.	Dollars.	Dollars.	Dollars.	Dollars.	Dollars.	Dollars.	
United States	38,979	53,595	31,092	36,577	31,476	42,154	29.20
Chile	30,417	35,209	18,975	33,676	32,177	32,051	22.20
France	13,730	15,704	13,407	11,826	13,320	14,395	9.97
Peru	7,876	8,594	8,001	9,597	2,302	10,886	7.54
Italy	4,593	4,808	4,365	5,509	4,609	3,674	2.55
Germany	1,989	2,969	813	272	2,662	3,227	2.24
Cuba and Porto Rico .	1,029	2,467	2,677	....	....	....	......
Haiti and Santo Domingo	815	409	3,664	....	....	....	......
Other	1,675	2,156	1,781	1,659	861	1,917	1.33
Total foreign countries	101,103	125,911	84,775	99,116	87,407	108,304	75.03
BRITISH POSSESSIONS.							
British West Indies...	17,533	9,154	14,799	13,709	24,192	25,812	17.88
Australasia:							
New South Wales.	3,943	1,085	2,647	6,925	6,784	2,273	⎫
Queensland	1,296	350	1,012	2,740	861	1,518	
New Zealand	2,444	3,966	2,672	2,019	2,156	1,406	⎬3.77
Victoria	198	710	29	15	15	219	
South Australia ..	251	54	1,061	10	112	20	⎭
Canada	5,311	1,324	365	9,874	10,448	4,545	3.15
Other	106	15	....	248	24	243	.17
Total British possessions ...	31,082	16,658	22,585	35,540	44,592	36,036	24.97
Total	132,185	142,569	107,360	134,656	131,999	144,340	100.00

a For quantities, see page 161.
b Annual average, 1896–1899.
c Including "Skins in any way dressed (not leather)."
d Including imports from Argentina valued at $487 in 1897, $44 in 1898, and $7,480 in 1900 (the figures for the last two years including dressed skins); from Brazil $2,604 in 1896 and $68 in 1897; and from Asiatic Turkey $49 in 1896.

ilue of the agricultural imports of the United Kingdom (animal matter), etc.—Cont'd.

HORNS, HORN TIPS, HORN STRIPS, AND HOOFS. (a)

	Annual average, 1896–1900.	Calendar years.					Per ct. in 1900.
		1896.	1897.	1898.	1899.	1900.	
REIGN COUNTRIES.							
	Dollars.	*Dollars.*	*Dollars.*	*Dollars.*	*Dollars.*	*Dollars.*	
ance	144,561	83,529	96,410	132,174	225,893	184,800	17.82
rmany	52,695	25,189	37,019	52,174	72,044	77,046	7.43
gentina	32,900	22,980	49,351	34,951	16,011	41,209	3.97
therlands	34,515	81,621	18,454	13,831	18,916	39,754	3.83
iited States	44,271	52,670	52,597	43,872	37,170	35,044	3.38
lgium	19,173	29,841	28,625	12,293	8,765	16,342	1.58
azil	7,985	5,178	7,412	7,713	9,913	9,709	.94
ru	4,929	6,078	3,324	4,356	3,587	7,300	.70
rtugal	2,340	1,859	730	910	939	7,261	.70
rway	3,707	2,214	3,733	6,273	2,341	3,976	.38
ypt	4,155	4,579	2,321	5,309	5,012	3,553	.34
eden	3,108	1,450	3,343	1,864	5,616	3,265	.32
ile	4,512	4,755	7,563	3,110	4,618	2,516	.24
ina	3,682	10,336	3,630	97	3,129	1,217	.12
uguay	7,547	11,694	12,195	10,808	3,087	....	
rtuguese East Af- ica	4,514	7,412	14,838	321	....	....	
her	9,731	7,665	8,035	5,932	13,694	13,329	1.29
Total foreign countries	384,325	359,050	349,580	335,988	430,685	446,321	43.04
RITISH POSSESSIONS.							
itish East Indies:							
Bombay	104,440	90,950	94,610	70,929	92,945	172,766	⎫
Bengal	122,428	143,820	110,255	106,508	133,936	117,623	⎪
Madras	62,661	31,666	66,900	67,430	73,348	73,961	⎬ 40.92
Ceylon	24,195	22,410	20,104	21,646	21,598	35,219	⎪
Burma	23,951	26,459	17,544	28,674	25,612	21,466	⎪
Straits Settlements	5,827	12,911	6,297	2,974	3,616	3,338	⎭
stralasia:							
New South Wales.	76,755	79,066	86,526	66,569	62,467	89,149	⎫
Victoria	23,000	24,050	22,542	18,819	23,583	26,007	⎪
Queensland	11,962	16,984	19,378	9,285	5,465	8,696	⎬ 13.11
South Australia	6,087	3,937	5,280	7,105	6,628	7,485	⎪
New Zealand	2,204	2,292	2,224	2,380	1,299	2,823	⎪
West Australia	451	....	39	404	....	1,810	⎪
Tasmania	532	964	....	769	925	....	⎭
ape of Good Hope	53,667	60,700	57,269	103,520	29,958	16,887	1.63
atal	18,443	13,836	7,718	48,412	15,753	6,497	.62
ongkong	836	1,168	263	754	900	1,095	.10
ther	6,544	1,630	3,820	6,779	14,604	5,889	.58
Total British possessions	543,983	532,843	520,769	562,957	512,637	590,711	56.96
Total	928,308	891,893	870,349	898,945	943,322	1,037,032	100.00

FRESH BEEF. (a)

	Annual average, 1896–1900.	1896.	1897.	1898.	1899.	1900.	Per ct. in 1900.
'OREIGN COUNTRIES.							
	Dollars.	*Dollars.*	*Dollars.*	*Dollars.*	*Dollars.*	*Dollars.*	
nited States	24,599,290	20,518,366	22,430,331	22,762,718	27,795,137	29,489,900	74.24
rgentina	1,182,799	337,726	623,778	729,201	975,884	3,247,406	8.17
enmark	386,419	17,607	369,333	374,925	444,594	725,634	1.83
etherlands	67,773	248	58,457	16,634	172,824	90,702	.23
elgium	10,151	....	25,788	24,965	....	....	
weden	5,501	....	....	27,369	136	....	
rance	4,476	....	21,729	....	652	....	
ther	9,508	3,056	24	13,091	14,361	17,008	.04
Total foreign countries	26,265,917	20,877,003	23,529,440	23,948,903	29,403,588	33,570,650	84.51

a For quantities, see page 162.

Value of the agricultural imports of the United Kingdom (animal matter), etc.—Cont'd.

FRESH BEEF—Continued.

Countries from which imported.	Annual average, 1896–1900.	Calendar years.					Per ct. in 1900.
		1896.	1897.	1898.	1899.	1900.	
BRITISH POSSESSIONS.							
	Dollars.	*Dollars.*	*Dollars.*	*Dollars.*	*Dollars.*	*Dollars.*	
Australasia:							
Queensland	3,377,737	3,016,354	3,529,989	3,593,487	3,768,360	2,980,498	
New Zealand.....	1,009,503	203,439	572,685	710,557	1,044,512	2,516,321	
New South Wales.	347,223	287,080	428,957	334,314	559,029	126,733	}14.31
Victoria..........	29,324	778	29,199	1,061	53,760	61,824	
South Australia ..	9,745	....	....	....	48,723	....	
Canada..............	336,099	88,137	55,945	200,349	867,619	468,445	}1.18
Other..............	54	....	....	107	136	29	
Total British possessions ...	5,109,685	3,595,788	4,616,775	4,839,875	6,342,139	6,153,850	15.49
Total	31,375,602	24,472,791	28,146,215	28,788,778	35,745,727	39,724,500	100.00

BEEF, SALTED OR PICKLED. (*a*)

FOREIGN COUNTRIES.							
	Dollars.	*Dollars.*	*Dollars.*	*Dollars.*	*Dollars.*	*Dollars.*	
United States.........	1,211,815	1,433,432	1,032,593	1,297,701	1,103,927	1,191,422	95.48
Other *b*	12,759	5,519	9,018	19,505	12,774	16,979	1.36
Total foreign countries.....	1,224,574	1,438,951	1,041,611	1,317,206	1,116,701	1,208,401	96.84
BRITISH POSSESSIONS.							
Canada..............	20,222	38,786	5,689	11,096	6,541	38,995	3.12
Other *c*	995	219	3,382	272	642	462	.04
Total British possessions ...	21,217	39,005	9,071	11,368	7,183	39,457	3.16
Total	1,245,791	1,477,956	1,050,682	1,328,574	1,123,884	1,247,858	100.00

BEEF, CURED, NOT ELSEWHERE SPECIFIED. (*a*)

FOREIGN COUNTRIES.							
	Dollars.	*Dollars.*	*Dollars.*	*Dollars.*	*Dollars.*	*Dollars.*	
United States.........	2,168,265	2,137,785	1,589,462	1,597,234	2,069,956	3,446,888	48.60
Belgium.............	784,837	798,885	787,921	757,451	639,857	940,072	13.26
Argentina...........	222,546	230,969	172,352	287,386	140,374	281,649	3.97
Uruguay.............	32,482	6,911	5,348	80,127	4,098	65,926	.93
Germany............	30,516	8,740	30,528	21,383	32,338	59,590	.84
France	9,150	8,594	5,416	14,434	3,635	13,670	.19
Netherlands.........	4,567	7,188	1,372	3,947	6,706	3,621	.05
Norway	1,427	4,492	1,085	380	647	530	} .01
Brazil	2,722	4,307	7,295	1,630	112	268	
Japan	1,411	7,056	....	....	....	....	
Other..............	2,161	1,348	1,908	4,638	2,205	706	.01
Total foreign countries.....	3,260,084	3,216,275	2,602,687	2,768,610	2,899,928	4,812,920	67.86
BRITISH POSSESSIONS.							
Australasia:							
Queensland	933,246	909,155	1,022,583	769,282	909,271	1,055,938	
New South Wales.	1,045,765	721,162	1,065,360	1,250,773	1,190,638	1,000,893	
New Zealand.....	32,803	14,191	18,624	32,820	37,701	60,680	}30.01
South Australia ..	5,476	14	29	9,679	6,998	10,658	
Victoria...........	6,586	2,428	10,916	3,767	15,471	346	
Canada.............	155,991	265,842	145,372	116,572	107,068	145,104	2.05
Other..............	3,299	....	1,805	63	9,110	5,519	.08
Total British possessions ...	2,183,166	1,912,792	2,264,689	2,182,956	2,276,257	2,279,138	32.14
Total	5,443,250	5,129,067	4,867,376	4,951,566	5,176,185	7,092,058	100.00

a For quantities, see page 163.
b Including imports from Argentina valued at $1,961 in 1896, $988 in 1897, $4,088 in 1898, and $3,883 in 1899, and from Germany $1,859 in 1896, $1,348 in 1897, $1,290 in 1898, and $1,032 in 1899.
c Including imports from South Australia valued at $219 in 1896; from New South Wales, $3,139 in 1897, from New Zealand, $204 in 1897, from Queensland, $39 in 1897; and from total Australasia, $272 in 1898 and $331 in 1899.

Value of the agricultural imports of the United Kingdom (animal matter), etc.—Cont'd.

TALLOW AND STEARIN. (a)

Countries from which imported.	Annual average, 1896–1900.	Calendar years.					Per ct. in 1900.
		1896.	1897.	1898.	1899.	1900.	
FOREIGN COUNTRIES.	*Dollars.*	*Dollars.*	*Dollars.*	*Dollars.*	*Dollars.*	*Dollars.*	
United States.........	2,402,791	1,885,725	1,170,963	2,619,360	2,920,523	3,417,383	24.77
Argentina............	796,554	684,176	518,414	868,485	747,197	1,164,495	8.44
France	411,670	304,750	304,638	477,073	530,035	441,854	3.20
Belgium.............	244,644	187,122	175,179	239,904	273,327	347,687	2.52
Netherlands.........	134,114	127,351	109,263	104,819	168,751	160,385	1.16
Uruguay	167,957	261,886	171,466	217,260	54,334	134,841	.98
Germany............	78,017	38,416	62,053	70,452	90,254	128,909	.93
China	44,861	79,927	57,546	32,085	12,502	42,246	.31
Chile...............	7,028	20,610	5,450	3,460	....	5,621	.04
Russia..............	6,256	28,737	876	73	487	1,109	.01
Turkey, European....	3,422	15,573	185	1,314	....	39	} .13
Other b	19,847	15,962	17,383	21,437	26,284	18,167	
Total foreign countries.....	4,317,161	3,650,235	2,593,416	4,655,722	4,823,694	5,862,736	42.49
BRITISH POSSESSIONS.							
Australasia:							
New South Wales.	3,024,101	3,515,885	3,217,740	2,465,789	3,169,449	2,751,694	}
New Zealand.....	1,602,997	976,765	1,390,276	1,564,482	1,722,673	2,360,788	
Victoria..........	973,083	1,015,152	1,090,033	658,428	787,405	1,314,398	} 56.08
Queensland	912,461	1,192,370	666,307	600,463	815,163	1,288,002	
South Australia ..	60,754	146,477	79,528	....	55,313	22,454	
Tasmania	139	696	....	....	....	....	
Canada.............	83,489	23,194	5,129	92,576	157,903	138,642	1.00
Falkland Islands.....	20,056	36,192	3,470	5,139	25,690	29,788	.22
British East Indies c..	28,541	43,317	45,224	8,263	23,170	22,731	.16
Channel Islands......	2,119	1,027	5,168	3,815	414	170	} .05
Other d	2,845	1,100	3,718	1,669	1,557	6,181	
Total British possessions ...	6,710,585	6,952,175	6,506,593	5,400,574	6,758,737	7,934,848	57.51
Total	11,027,746	10,602,410	9,100,009	10,056,296	11,582,431	13,797,584	100.00

BACON. (a)

Countries from which imported.	Annual average, 1896–1900.	1896.	1897.	1898.	1899.	1900.	Per ct. in 1900.
FOREIGN COUNTRIES.	*Dollars.*	*Dollars.*	*Dollars.*	*Dollars.*	*Dollars.*	*Dollars.*	
United States.........	29,104,292	19,790,635	26,053,411	31,331,690	31,886,184	36,459,540	63.63
Denmark............	13,861,617	13,586,266	13,355,769	13,144,962	14,335,526	14,885,563	25.98
Netherlands.........	271,689	268,178	224,316	218,632	248,873	398,445	.70
Sweden..............	561,259	1,010,071	674,497	574,987	409,234	137,508	.24
Russia..............	127,176	172,376	291,761	96,118	5,032	70,593	.12
Other e	31,657	8,954	3,626	18,454	14,716	112,533	.20
Total foreign countries.....	43,957,690	34,836,480	40,603,380	45,384,843	46,899,565	52,064,182	90.87
BRITISH POSSESSIONS.							
Canada..............	3,943,587	3,385,347	2,546,129	4,845,209	3,707,597	5,233,653	9.13
Newfoundland and Labrador...........	1,749	1,820	4,589	....	2,336	....	......
Other.................	470	350	1,275	375	165	185	......
Total British possessions ...	3,945,806	3,387,517	2,551,993	4,845,584	3,710,098	5,233,838	9.13
Total	47,903,496	38,223,997	43,155,373	50,230,427	50,609,663	57,298,020	100.00

a For quantities, see page 164.
b Including in 1896 imports from Asiatic Turkey valued at $7,786.
c Including imports from the Straits Settlements valued at $42,475 in 1896, $39,589 in 1897, $4,867 in 1898, $15,388 in 1899, and $17,870 in 1900.
d Comprising in 1896 imports from Newfoundland and Labrador valued at $1,100.
e Including imports from Germany valued at $4,852 in 1896 and $482 in 1897.

Value of the agricultural imports of the United Kingdom (animal matter), etc.—Cont'd.

HAMS. (a)

Countries from which imported.	Annual average, 1896–1900.	Calendar years.					Per ct. in 1900.
		1896.	1897.	1898.	1899.	1900.	
FOREIGN COUNTRIES.							
	Dollars.	*Dollars.*	*Dollars.*	*Dollars.*	*Dollars.*	*Dollars.*	
United States	16,901,518	13,424,114	16,602,352	17,769,606	18,400,271	18,311,248	89.13
Germany	18,704	18,415	20,590	17,145	18,220	19,150	.09
Denmark	17,045	27,496	14,127	12,108	20,264	11,232	.06
Spain	6,494	4,871	6,292	5,528	8,852	6,925	.03
Other b	12,233	8,263	8,118	14,580	11,480	18,725	.09
Total foreign countries	16,955,994	13,483,159	16,651,479	17,818,967	18,459,087	18,367,280	89.40
BRITISH POSSESSIONS.							
Canada	1,564,210	1,778,326	1,266,614	1,135,218	1,465,848	2,175,043	10.59
Other	919	292	195	49	949	3,110	.01
Total British possessions	1,565,129	1,778,618	1,266,809	1,135,267	1,466,797	2,178,153	10.60
Total	18,521,123	15,261,777	17,918,288	18,954,234	19,925,884	20,545,433	100.00

FRESH PORK.(a)

	Annual average, 1896–1900.	1896.	1897.	1898.	1899.	1900.	Per ct. in 1900.
FOREIGN COUNTRIES.							
	Dollars.	*Dollars.*	*Dollars.*	*Dollars.*	*Dollars.*	*Dollars.*	
Netherlands	2,989,205	2,708,339	2,378,526	2,308,969	3,541,045	4,009,149	55.
United States	1,701,768	72,005	590,856	2,707,083	2,692,907	2,445,991	33.
Belgium	484,871	478,571	450,492	429,507	447,699	618,084	8.
Denmark	60,819	25,753	20,138	13,753	98,980	145,469	2.09
France	87,749	48,568	273,161	112,173	165	4,677	.00
Argentina	6,193	4,964	7,241	8,181	6,005	4,575	} .06
Other	195	287	565	102	....	19	
Total foreign countries	5,330,800	3,338,487	3,720,979	5,579,768	6,786,801	7,227,964	99.32
BRITISH POSSESSIONS.							
Canada	33,748	....	876	91,077	40,392	36,397	.50
Australasia	4,017	5,893	1,139	263	389	12,400	.17
Other	336	78	501	214	317	569	.01
Total British possessions	38,101	5,971	2,516	91,554	41,098	49,366	.68
Total	5,368,901	3,344,458	3,723,495	5,671,322	6,827,899	7,277,330	100.00

PORK, SALTED OR PICKLED.(a)

	Annual average, 1896–1900.	1896.	1897.	1898.	1899.	1900.	Per ct. in 1900.
FOREIGN COUNTRIES.							
	Dollars.	*Dollars.*	*Dollars.*	*Dollars.*	*Dollars.*	*Dollars.*	
United States	920,386	856,888	815,139	1,092,695	972,570	864,636	58.96
Denmark	363,615	423,035	293,182	333,253	359,659	408,947	27.89
Germany	36,127	22,328	29,214	30,338	45,648	53,108	3.62
Netherlands	4,575	6,472	3,708	2,555	2,993	7,144	.49
France	3,656	5,086	6,409	2,890	1,066	2,827	.19
Sweden	2,793	11,159	1,217	1,591	....	....	
Other	1,263	2,005	2,954	229	379	750	.05
Total foreign countries	1,332,415	1,326,973	1,151,823	1,463,551	1,382,315	1,337,412	91.20
BRITISH POSSESSIONS.							
Canada	100,739	93,880	82,755	92,649	105,807	128,602	8.77
Other c	143	....	19	....	195	501	.03
Total British possessions	100,882	93,880	82,774	92,649	106,002	129,103	8.80
Total	1,433,297	1,420,853	1,234,597	1,556,200	1,488,317	1,466,515	100.00

a For quantities, see page 165.

b Including imports from Belgium valued at $3,932 in 1896, $3,261 in 1897, $2,964 in 1898, and $3,635 in 1899.

c Comprising in 1897 imports from Australasia valued at $19.

Value of the agricultural imports of the United Kingdom (animal matter), etc.—Cont'd.

LARD.(a)

Countries from which imported.	Annual average, 1896–1900.	Calendar years.					Per ct. in 1900.
		1896.	1897.	1898.	1899.	1900.	
FOREIGN COUNTRIES.							
	Dollars.	Dollars.	Dollars.	Dollars.	Dollars.	Dollars.	
United States.........	12,418,597	10,183,828	9,378,534	13,608,233	14,157,242	14,765,146	92.88
Denmark..............	48,686	122,548	13,402	26,425	33,983	47,069	.30
Germany..............	28,206	7,835	10,653	7,144	70,496	44,903	.28
Netherlands..........	38,281	22,800	39,214	18,167	79,679	31,545	.20
Belgium..............	26,015	9,640	29,360	56,413	21,899	12,765	.08
France	4,954	12,366	165	3,051	4,545	4,642	} .03
Otherb..............	1,916	7,280	268	1,664	239	131	
Total foreign countries.....	12,566,655	10,366,297	9,471,596	13,721,097	14,368,083	14,906,201	93.77
BRITISH POSSESSIONS.							
Canada..............	554,636	673,548	226,136	332,387	553,803	987,306	6.21
Newfoundland and Labrador..........	2,656	....	....	....	13,281	....	......
Otherc..............	1,192	749	1,898	....		3,314	.02
Total British possessions ...	558,484	674,297	228,034	332,387	567,084	990,620	6.23
Total	13,125,139	11,040,594	9,699,630	14,053,484	14,935,167	15,896,821	100.00

FRESH MUTTON.(a)

FOREIGN COUNTRIES.	Dollars.	Dollars.	Dollars.	Dollars.	Dollars.	Dollars.	
Argentina............	6,602,965	5,216,358	5,718,765	6,608,347	7,251,455	8,219,898	28.92
Netherlands..........	2,977,788	2,510,452	2,882,253	2,845,827	3,061,223	3,589,185	12.63
Denmark.............	77,117	69,129	50,032	52,402	150,287	63,736	.22
France	16,644	....	5,115	3,956	36,002	38,144	.13
United States.........	15,222	2,764	13,524	6,249	24,480	29,145	.10
Belgium.............	6,769	1,110	1,041	8,356	....	23,340	.08
Germany.............	21,372	44,042	28,051	13,699	7,314	13,753	.05
Other...............	2,594	6,880	506	4,891	692	....	....
Total foreign countries.....	9,720,471	7,850,735	8,699,287	9,543,727	10,531,403	11,977,201	42.13
BRITISH POSSESSIONS.							
Australasia:							
New Zealand.....	10,963,966	9,392,131	10,109,901	10,260,903	12,124,418	12,932,480	}
New South Wales.	3,302,480	4,555,214	3,825,750	3,122,980	2,843,934	2,164,575	
Victoria	682,339	748,828	672,015	485,988	512,691	992,172	} 57.87
South Australia ..	116,867	64,184	16,259	72,180	211,172	220,540	
Queensland	255,517	351,502	171,544	368,905	245,457	140,175	
Otherd..............	859	210	64	1,821	1,361	838	}
Total British possessions ...	15,322,028	15,112,069	14,795,533	14,312,727	15,939,033	16,450,780	57.87
Total	25,042,499	22,962,804	23,494,820	23,856,454	26,470,436	28,427,981	100.00

a For quantities, see page 166.
b Including imports from Russia valued at $2,365 in 1896 and $10 in 1898.
c Comprising imports from Australasia valued at $749 in 1896 and $1,898 in 1897.
d Including in 1898 imports from the Falkland Islands valued at $34.

Value of the agricultural imports of the United Kingdom (animal matter), etc.—Cont'd.

MUTTON, CURED, OTHER THAN SALTED.(*a*)

Countries from which imported.	Annual average, 1896–1900.	Calendar years.					Per ct. in 1900.
		1896.	1897.	1898.	1899.	1900.	
FOREIGN COUNTRIES.							
	Dollars.	*Dollars.*	*Dollars.*	*Dollars.*	*Dollars.*	*Dollars.*	
United States	24,253	31,160	35,136	9,217	17,933	27,817	3.79
Argentina	16,177	18,702	24,313	16,410	5,655	15,806	} 2.15
Germany	394	78	93	58	1,732	10	
France	487	2,433					
Belgium	355		1,776				
Uruguay	248	735	506				
Other	83	93	185	34	54	49	.01
Total foreign countries	41,997	53,201	62,009	25,719	25,374	43,682	5.95
BRITISH POSSESSIONS.							
Australasia:							
New South Wales	461,120	538,877	378,059	553,866	431,284	403,515	
New Zealand	208,804	139,581	201,064	298,667	206,607	198,101	
Queensland	70,593	188,715	69,805	26,600	47,424	25,418	}88.32
Victoria	36,138	47,589	51,298	31,774	28,099	21,904	
South Australia	4,437	9,149	13,037				
Canada	17,826	10,152	8,079	13,553	15,271	42,076	} 5.73
Other	1,526		2,482		5,134	14	
Total British possessions	800,439	929,063	723,824	924,460	733,819	691,028	94.05
Total	842,436	982,264	785,833	950,179	759,193	734,710	100.00

OLEO OIL.(*a*)

	Annual average, 1896–1900.	1896.	1897.	1898.	1899.	1900.	Per ct. in 1900.
FOREIGN COUNTRIES.							
	Dollars.	*Dollars.*	*Dollars.*	*Dollars.*	*Dollars.*	*Dollars.*	
United States	734,836	608,122	644,373	814,131	595,120	1,014,436	69.43
France	170,914	148,195	130,091	154,891	224,837	196,558	13.45
Netherlands	243,268	195,288	219,212	262,460	406,041	133,337	9.12
Germany	15,395	14,745	35,170	16,863	10,195		
Other *b*	9,409	511			2,847	43,687	2.99
Total foreign countries	1,173,822	964,861	1,028,846	1,248,345	1,239,040	1,388,018	94.99
BRITISH POSSESSIONS.							
Canada	34,255	59,809	31,769		23,286	56,412	3.86
Australasia	13,735	7,933	19,072	5,241	19,680	16,751	1.15
Total British possessions	47,990	67,742	50,841	5,241	42,966	73,163	5.01
Total	1,221,812	1,032,603	1,079,687	1,253,586	1,282,006	1,461,181	100.00

OLEOMARGARIN (IMITATION BUTTER).(*a*)

	Annual average, 1896–1900.	1896.	1897.	1898.	1899.	1900.	Per ct. in 1900.
FOREIGN COUNTRIES.							
	Dollars.	*Dollars.*	*Dollars.*	*Dollars.*	*Dollars.*	*Dollars.*	
Netherlands	11,173,638	11,214,046	11,153,025	10,754,036	11,577,618	11,169,464	93.12
France	496,605	508,822	516,360	512,486	501,585	443,771	3.70
Germany	199,509	257,438	184,173	181,657	157,567	216,710	1.81
Norway	123,064	136,758	144,949	110,951	110,246	112,416	.94
Belgium	48,780	35,267	76,691	39,438	50,115	42,387	.35
United States	4,757	1,801	14,405		2,385	5,193	.04
Other	3,816	4,025	5,450	1,445	3,981	4,181	.03
Total foreign countries	12,050,169	12,158,157	12,095,053	11,600,013	12,403,497	11,994,122	99.99
BRITISH POSSESSIONS.							
Total British possessions	1,699	428		3,592	3,528	949	.01
Total	12,051,868	12,158,585	12,095,053	11,603,605	12,407,025	11,995,071	100.00

a For quantities, see page 167.
b Comprising in 1896 imports from Egypt valued at $511.

Value of the agricultural imports of the United Kingdom (animal matter), etc.—Cont'd.

IMITATION CHEESE. (a)

untries from which imported.	Annual average, 1896-1900.	Calendar years.					Per ct. in 1900.
		1896.	1897.	1898.	1899.	1900.	
OREIGN COUNTRIES.							
	Dollars.	Dollars.	Dollars.	Dollars.	Dollars.	Dollars.	
ited States.........	55,672	....	83,353	66,360	36,056	92,590	93.57
her b	6,621	1,771	9,811	8,229	13,271	25	.03
Total foreign countries	62,293	1,771	93,164	74,589	49,327	92,615	93.60
RITISH POSSESSIONS.							
tal British possessions c	1,612	1,723	....			6,336	6.40
Total	63,905	3,494	93,164	74,589	49,327	98,951	100.00

POULTRY AND GAME. (d)

	Annual average, 1896-1900.	1896.	1897.	1898.	1899.	1900.	Per ct. in 1900.
OREIGN COUNTRIES.							
	Dollars.	Dollars.	Dollars.	Dollars.	Dollars.	Dollars.	
rance	1,368,910	1,474,073	1,246,374	1,059,452	1,443,185	1,621,469	32.98
elgium	798,138	697,798	798,977	622,537	806,880	1,039,499	21.14
ussia...............	811,755	698,751	909,184	800,530	680,502	969,806	19.72
nited States........	281,411	92,561	126,904	189,151	241,700	756,741	15.39
etherlands.........	204,806	208,140	186,372	203,308	249,661	176,547	3.59
ermany	104,868	102,046	155,071	84,341	93,339	89,544	1.82
gypt	38,569	10,560	2,706	389	96,006	83,183	1.69
orway	21,687	31,900	14,809	13,237	25,929	22,561	.46
enmark	27,966	59,726	30,104	23,028	14,853	12,118	.25
ther...............	1,108	1,679	1,810	701	526	822	.02
Total foreign countries	3,654,218	3,377,234	3,472,311	2,996,674	3,652,581	4,772,290	97.06
BRITISH POSSESSIONS.							
Canada...............	72,024	30,503	40,869	61,800	134,895	92,055	1.87
Australasia e	37,914	25,243	42,105	42,772	31,603	47,847	.97
Other f...............	1,890	229	788	1,109	2,554	4,769	.10
Total British possessions ...	111,828	55,975	83,762	105,681	169,052	144,671	2.94
Total	3,766,046	3,433,209	3,556,073	3,102,355	3,821,633	4,916,961	100.00

RABBITS (DEAD). (a)

	Annual average, 1896-1900.	1896.	1897.	1898.	1899.	1900.	Per ct. in 1900.
FOREIGN COUNTRIES.							
	Dollars.	Dollars.	Dollars.	Dollars.	Dollars.	Dollars.	
Belgium..............	1,056,021	1,222,022	1,105,630	1,113,825	1,054,366	784,261	22.06
France	183,073	206,802	150,151	163,091	199,707	195,614	5.50
Netherlands.........	166,951	137,669	168,902	170,225	187,599	170,357	} 4.80
Other g	338	58	102	....	1,411	121	
Total foreign countries	1,406,383	1,566,551	1,424,785	1,447,141	1,443,083	1,150,353	32.36
BRITISH POSSESSIONS.							
Australasia:							
New Zealand	644,413	85,894	489,166	746,107	822,643	1,078,256	} 67.64
Victoria	554,037	270,183	556,587	350,797	544,756	1,047,860	
South Australia...	61,426	....	13,334	74,842	47,074	171,880	
New South Wales.	141,035	31,827	153,791	164,755	250,459	104,342	
Queensland	2,427	....	7,251	2,930	....	1,956	
Total British possessions ...	1,403,338	387,904	1,220,129	1,339,431	1,664,932	2,404,294	67.64
Total	2,809,721	1,954,455	2,644,914	2,786,572	3,108,015	3,554,647	100.00

a For quantities, see page 168.
b Comprising in 1896 imports from the Netherlands valued at $1,771.
c Comprising in 1896 imports from Canada valued at $1,723.
d Including live poultry and game.
e Including imports from New South Wales valued at $3,032 in 1896, $24,308 in 1897, $27,608 in 1898, $13,047 in 1899, and $24,936 in 1900.
f Comprising in 1896 imports from the Channel Islands valued at $229.
g Comprising in 1896 imports from the United States valued at $58.

Value of the agricultural imports of the United Kingdom (animal matter), etc.—Cont'd.

SAUSAGE CASINGS, INCLUDING BLADDERS. (a)

Countries from which imported.	Calendar year 1900.	Per cent.	Countries from which imported.	Calendar year 1900.	Per cent.
FOREIGN COUNTRIES.	*Dollars.*		BRITISH POSSESSIONS.		
United States.................	500,617	56.93	Australasia:	*Dollars.*	
Netherlands..................	26,775	3.05	New Zealand............	243,364	
Germany....................	24,800	2.82	New South Wales........	993	
Turkey, Asiatic	21,924	2.49	Queensland	769	27.95
Other........................	46,431	5.28	South Australia	535	
			Victoria	97	
Total foreign countries.	620,547	70.57	Canada....................	12,872	1.47
			Other......................	112	.01
			Total British possessions	258,742	29.43
			Total	879,289	100.00

MEAT, FRESH OR SALTED, NOT ELSEWHERE SPECIFIED.(b)

Countries from which imported.	Annual average, 1896–1900.	Calendar years.					Per ct. in 1900.
		1896.	1897.	1898.	1899.	1900.	
FOREIGN COUNTRIES.	*Dollars.*	*Dollars.*	*Dollars.*	*Dollars.*	*Dollars.*	*Dollars.*	
Netherlands..........	2,361,100	1,680,266	2,296,784	2,518,448	2,561,098	2,748,906	57.51
United States.........	805,993	482,066	616,654	762,610	1,042,808	1,125,826	23.55
Argentina............	135,754	88,366	99,520	103,963	126,763	260,158	5.44
Denmark.............	129,736	83,339	104,206	98,269	145,435	217,430	4.55
France	206,687	238,011	221,148	213,089	190,922	170,264	3.56
Belgium.............	43,584	27,422	40,499	50,480	48,378	51,142	1.07
Germany.............	13,241	9,470	10,317	11,086	14,059	21,272	.45
Other................	2,675	1,090	3,927	2,939	3,660	1,757	.04
Total foreign countries.....	3,698,770	2,610,030	3,393,055	3,760,884	4,133,123	4,596,755	96.17
BRITISH POSSESSIONS.							
Australasia:							
New Zealand.....	86,813	41,672	100,902	95,880	94,522	101,091	
New South Wales.	14,083	14,176	13,475	18,025	8,079	16,658	
Victoria	4,880	1,951	3,407	1,723	4,195	13,125	2.95
Queensland	18,511	7,480	15,583	26,508	33,881	9,105	
South Australia ..	745	....	....	297	2,292	1,134	
Canada...............	29,770	19,719	12,833	51,780	22,702	41,818	.88
Other c...............	300	1,324	19	92	24	39	
Total British possessions ...	155,102	86,322	146,219	194,305	165,695	182,970	3.83
Total	3,853,872	2,696,352	3,539,274	3,955,189	4,298,818	4,779,725	100.00

MEAT, CURED, NOT ELSEWHERE SPECIFIED.(d)

FOREIGN COUNTRIES.	*Dollars.*	*Dollars.*	*Dollars.*	*Dollars.*	*Dollars.*	*Dollars.*	
United States........	1,801,646	1,264,701	1,361,077	1,891,127	2,005,310	2,486,012	65.86
Uruguay	141,585	82,789	142,642	139,119	176,128	167,247	4.43
Belgium.............	115,914	87,568	71,552	114,007	144,525	161,918	4.29
Argentina............	161,369	230,906	149,995	124,938	144,618	156,390	4.14
France	88,493	69,932	68,700	82,604	102,527	118,704	3.14
Germany.............	42,991	27,977	28,664	52,694	38,100	67,518	1.79
Netherlands..........	40,689	31,165	39,584	28,401	40,830	63,464	1.68
Russia...............	22,421	18,785	21,150	22,912	25,676	23,583	.63
Norway	4,861	4,200	4,823	5,898	2,594	6,789	.18
Other e	5,203	3,450	1,616	2,730	7,212	11,008	.29
Total foreign countries.....	2,425,172	1,821,473	1,889,803	2,464,430	2,687,520	3,262,633	86.43

a Prior to 1900 not stated by countries.
b For quantities, see page 168.
c Comprising in 1896 imports from Newfoundland and Labrador valued at $1,324.
d For quantities, see page 169.
e Including imports from Italy valued at $964 in 1896 and $39 in 1897.

Value of the agricultural imports of the United Kingdom (animal matter), etc.—Cont'd.

MEAT, CURED, NOT ELSEWHERE SPECIFIED—Continued.

Countries from which imported.	Annual average, 1896–1900.	Calendar years.					Per ct. in 1900.
		1896.	1897.	1898.	1899.	1900.	
BRITISH POSSESSIONS.							
Australasia:	*Dollars.*	*Dollars.*	*Dollars.*	*Dollars.*	*Dollars.*	*Dollars.*	
Victoria	236,009	283,109	337,813	131,391	172,722	255,009	
Queensland	58,784	67,396	37,438	37,949	96,269	54,870	
New South Wales.	74,100	54,291	86,935	86,229	88,784	54,262	
South Australia ..	37,016	2,092	23,140	36,912	74,647	48,290	}11.74
New Zealand	73,645	139,732	118,733	26,148	53,556	30,056	
West Australia ...	122	....	....	....	....	608	
Canada	113,481	160,886	135,493	86,220	116,426	68,379	1.81
Other	651	195	1,752	550	200	560	.02
Total British possessions ...	593,808	707,701	741,304	405,399	602,604	512,034	13.57
Total	3,018,980	2,529,174	2,631,107	2,869,829	3,290,124	3,774,667	100.00

ANIMAL OILS NOT ELSEWHERE SPECIFIED, EXCEPT WHALE AND FISH. (a)

FOREIGN COUNTRIES.	*Dollars.*	*Dollars.*	*Dollars.*	*Dollars.*	*Dollars.*	*Dollars.*	
United States	307,699	372,350	309,188	286,135	340,489	230,331	40.41
Belgium	20,978	1,679	5,981	2,959	....	94,269	16.54
France	14,134	97	268	428	234	69,644	12.22
Netherlands	12,489	1,640	3,056	3,450	7,884	46,417	8.14
Germany	4,395	2,852	3,927	4,599	1,523	9,076	1.59
Argentina	5,036	3,475	3,655	6,901	5,815	5,334	.93
Other	1,070	175	1,674	44	....	3,455	.61
Total foreign countries	365,801	382,268	327,749	304,516	355,945	458,526	80.44
BRITISH POSSESSIONS.							
Australasia:							
Victoria	13,569	190	506	....	453	66,695	
Queensland	4,209	1,134	2,205	....	15	17,690	
South Australia ..	1,630	....	1,217	....	....	6,935	}16.69
New Zealand	836	555	....	98	....	3,528	
New South Wales.	966	628	2,900	....	998	302	
Canada	11,103	20,142	13,227	535	5,270	16,342	2.87
Other	107	....	511	....	24	....	
Total British possessions ...	32,420	22,649	20,566	633	6,760	111,492	19.56
Total	398,221	404,917	348,315	305,149	362,705	570,018	100.00

WAX (INCLUDING OZOKERITE AND EARTH WAX). (b)

FOREIGN COUNTRIES.	*Dollars.*	*Dollars.*	*Dollars.*	*Dollars.*	*Dollars.*	*Dollars.*	
Germany	201,245	140,369	170,065	207,425	224,273	264,090	26.83
Brazil	138,760	256,391	71,727	123,984	73,382	168,318	17.10
France	46,860	27,627	26,026	36,698	79,343	64,608	6.56
Morocco	36,624	26,926	24,323	57,561	24,040	50,271	5.11
United States	80,337	124,295	76,273	62,885	88,103	50,130	5.09
Chile	39,632	50,081	37,964	37,399	34,946	37,769	3.84
Japan	30,054	7,757	29,281	35,895	41,351	35,988	3.66
Italy	34,496	33,146	31,165	40,523	32,547	35,097	3.56
Portuguese East Africa	18,743	1,178	10,322	15,709	47,959	18,546	1.88
Spain	14,816	17,125	18,167	11,062	13,096	14,629	1.49
Madagascar	45,649	69,119	86,157	43,823	15,320	13,826	1.40
Netherlands	10,440	5,295	12,093	17,476	9,821	7,514	.76
China	3,210	73	6,555	3,436	....	5,986	.61
Peru	6,378	4,205	5,178	10,151	7,271	5,085	.52
French West Africa ..	5,754	3,042	4,273	10,570	6,472	4,414	.45
Belgium	4,007	7,397	6,443	1,226	2,268	3,002	
Portugal	4,966	3,986	856	18,804	1,168	14	} .31
Abyssinia	82	....	....	409	....	....	
Other c	11,447	10,473	12,794	8,998	15,232	9,738	.99
Total foreign countries	733,560	788,485	629,662	744,034	716,592	789,025	80.16

a For quantities, see page 169.
b For quantities, see page 170.
c Including in 1896 imports from Portuguese West Africa valued at $1,703 and from the Canary Islands $49.

Value of the agricultural imports of the United Kingdom (animal matter), etc.—Cont'd.

WAX (INCLUDING OZOKERITE AND EARTH WAX)—Continued.

Countries from which imported.	Annual average, 1896–1900.	Calendar years.					Per ct. in 1900.
		1896.	1897.	1898.	1899.	1900.	
BRITISH POSSESSIONS.							
	Dollars.	*Dollars.*	*Dollars.*	*Dollars.*	*Dollars.*	*Dollars.*	
British East Indies:							
Bengal	40,345	41,579	47,215	29,763	38,319	44,850	
Bombay	12,608	10,059	6,307	5,120	16,556	24,999	
Madras	3,379	8,550	535	2,798	1,572	3,441	
Straits Settlements	946	39	1,017	....	3,625	49	} 7.45
Ceylon	728	....	49	3,163	428	....	
Burma	253	535	....	730	....	....	
Zanzibar and Pemba.	32,949	14,089	31,603	36,956	37,998	44,100	4.48
British West Indies...	28,073	24,294	38,051	27,058	30,664	20,298	2.06
Australasia:							
New South Wales.	10,720	7,421	10,677	7,402	14,867	13,232	
Queensland	390	365	691	472	....	423	
South Australia ..	2,126	3,869	3,285	1,718	1,411	345	} 1.45
Victoria	4,618	7,675	8,750	3,260	3,139	263	
New Zealand	241	647	185	....	375	....	
Tasmania	103	282	24	122	88	....	
Gambia	16,812	25,398	13,101	11,514	26,269	7,777	.79
Gibraltar	6,014	4,093	4,083	10,020	8,584	3,290	} .34
Sierra Leone	1,361	3,431	1,655	88	1,616	14	
Mauritius	1,676	618	2,603	414	4,745	....	
Other *a*	11,331	5,738	4,866	7,188	6,701	32,163	3.27
Total British possessions ...	174,673	158,682	174,697	147,786	196,957	195,244	19.84
Total	908,233	947,167	804,359	891,820	913,549	984,269	100.00

Value of the agricultural imports of the United Kingdom (vegetable matter), by articles and countries, during the five calendar years 1896–1900.

BARLEY.(*b*)

Countries from which imported.	Annual average, 1896–1900.	Calendar years.					Per ct. in 1900.
		1896.	1897.	1898.	1899.	1900.	
FOREIGN COUNTRIES.							
	Dollars.	*Dollars.*	*Dollars.*	*Dollars.*	*Dollars.*	*Dollars.*	
United States	4,441,627	4,413,818	4,572,018	3,868,220	2,785,200	6,568,880	26.20
Russia	8,926,515	9,870,912	7,266,775	11,719,024	9,631,217	6,144,647	24.50
Turkey, Asiatic	5,006,777	4,559,263	4,602,638	5,493,203	4,366,783	6,011,996	23.97
Roumania	3,262,797	3,423,875	3,411,460	5,757,872	1,734,975	1,985,800	7.92
Germany	515,166	704,406	271,089	483,842	342,358	774,134	3.09
Chile	945,359	1,678,237	820,555	642,806	865,750	719,444	2.87
France	525,284	338,684	134,515	853,341	587,713	712,168	2.84
Netherlands	248,598	274,329	303,918	263,098	234,799	166,843	.67
Mexico	96,777	....	....	32,070	286,919	164,897	.66
Turkey, European....	275,431	251,535	54,597	573,220	334,883	162,921	.65
Denmark	269,106	587,041	154,322	178,109	267,794	158,263	.63
Cyprus	104,894	29,978	80,949	227,562	56,943	129,040	.51
Austria-Hungary	290,423	212,729	432,924	393,520	309,758	103,184	.41
Tripoli	403,871	967,942	430,870	277,060	265,721	77,762	.31
Bulgaria	88,934	27,642	38,231	279,999	34,708	64,092	.26
Egypt	212,554	203,950	64,058	311,164	437,270	46,329	.18
Algeria	130,927	....	....	223,698	390,337	40,601	.16
Tunis	187,435	....	....	493,254	406,246	37,676	.15
Argentina	17,341	16,580	8,030	7,679	19,398	35,034	.14
Morocco	6,629	....	....	....	21,023	12,122	.05
Persia	8,770	30,790	5,120	....	....	7,942	.03
Belgium	13,606	1,358	40,927	18,026	54	7,665	.03
Sweden	3,958	1,202	....	....	17,057	1,533	} .01
Spain	187,228	....	....	742,020	193,633	487	
Italy	6,380	24,479	....	7,421	....	....	
Other	2,019	....	6,419	545	3,129	....	....
Total foreign countries	26,178,409	27,618,750	22,699,415	32,846,753	23,593,668	24,133,460	96.24

a Including imports from Natal valued at $1,976 in 1896, $1,056 in 1897, $1,056 in 1898, and $2,497 in 1899, and from the Cape of Good Hope $540 in 1896 and $2,789 in 1897.
b For quantities, see page 171.

ue of the agricultural imports of the United Kingdom (vegetable matter), etc.—Cont'd.

BARLEY—Continued.

ries from which imported.	Annual average, 1896–1900.	Calendar years.					Per ct. in 1900.
		1896.	1897.	1898.	1899.	1900.	
ITISH POSSESSIONS.	*Dollars.*	*Dollars.*	*Dollars.*	*Dollars.*	*Dollars.*	*Dollars.*	
ada................	355,658	161,159	81,032	200,213	489,297	846,591	3.37
tralasia:							
New Zealand.....	19,733	....	....	....	3,037	95,627	
South Australia ..	115	487	....	....	....	88	
West Australia ...	16	....	....	....	....	78	} .39
New South Wales.	1,202	5,037	....	....	973	....	
er.................	1,539	....	....	8,732	2,842	1,119	
Total British possessions ...	378,263	166,683	81,032	203,945	496,149	943,503	3.76
Total	26,556,672	27,785,433	22,780,447	33,050,698	24,089,817	25,076,963	100.00

BUCKWHEAT. (a)

₹EIGN COUNTRIES.							
	Dollars.	*Dollars.*	*Dollars.*	*Dollars.*	*Dollars.*	*Dollars.*	
nce	79,895	128,033	89,081	21,198	89,373	71,791	42.48
ısia................	36,515	28,445	10,278	14,080	77,825	51,998	30.76
ted States........	40,315	34	26,581	130,388	38,222	6,351	3.76
herlands..........	2,503	2,618	9,894	....	....	....	
er.................	2,666	6,219	1,669	380	4,638	423	.25
Total foreign countries.....	161,894	165,349	137,503	165,996	210,058	130,563	77.25
ITISH POSSESSIONS.							
nada...............	53,966	11,378	88,414	115,555	16,025	38,460	22.75
annel Islands......	540	219	2,414	....	68	....	
Total British possessions ...	54,506	11,597	90,828	115,555	16,093	38,460	22.75
Total	216,400	176,946	228,331	281,551	226,151	169,023	100.00

CORN (MAIZE). (b)

OREIGN COUNTRIES.							
	Dollars.	*Dollars.*	*Dollars.*	*Dollars.*	*Dollars.*	*Dollars.*	
ıited States........	34,738,887	24,587,037	32,231,949	35,598,131	39,443,795	41,833,271	69.73
gentina	7,012,481	13,573,321	2,859,283	3,507,953	7,752,442	7,369,404	12.28
›umania...........	4,863,938	3,503,938	4,653,045	5,507,997	7,715,091	2,939,619	4.90
ıssia..............	2,095,817	1,321,216	1,246,379	2,766,829	2,800,573	2,344,086	3.91
ırkey, European	24,016	5,499	1,728	7,495	11,067	94,293	.16
›rocco.............	27,906	....	1,460	17,125	87,175	83,772	.14
‘uguay	55,148	114,236	58,622	15,198	25,398	62,286	.10
ırkey, Asiatic	14,656	1,183	25,281	....	....	46,816	.08
‘rmany	12,932	25,038	10,448	14,269	7,198	7,709	} .01
;ypt	16,819	53,556	....	2,920	27,179	438	
ılgaria............	8,190	....	....	....	40,952	....	
her................	7,583	9,782	11,300	2,823	7,222	6,789	.01
Total foreign countries.....	48,878,323	43,194,806	41,099,495	47,440,740	57,868,092	54,788,483	91.32
RITISH POSSESSIONS.							
nada...............	4,836,066	2,624,041	3,604,174	7,463,989	5,283,175	5,204,951	
·itish East Indies:							
Bengal	1,149	....	....	....	5,655	92	} 8.68
Bombay	6,809	33,408	....	....	637	....	
ıtal	2,636	....	13,178	....	....	....	
her................	633	2,531	....	633	....	....	
Total British possessions ...	4,847,293	2,659,980	3,617,352	7,464,622	5,289,467	5,205,043	8.68
Total	53,725,616	45,854,786	44,716,847	54,905,362	63,157,559	59,993,526	100.00

a For quantities, see page 171.　　　　b For quantities, see page 172.

Value of the agricultural imports of the United Kingdom (vegetable matter), etc.—Cont'd.

OATS. (a)

Countries from which imported.	Annual average, 1896-1900.	Calendar years. 1896.	1897.	1898.	1899.	1900.	Per ct. in 1900.
FOREIGN COUNTRIES.							
	Dollars.	Dollars.	Dollars.	Dollars.	Dollars.	Dollars.	
Russia	8,651,985	11,906,515	7,041,412	4,872,208	6,140,822	13,298,967	52.19
United States	8,347,636	5,118,108	9,311,941	11,146,076	8,960,915	7,201,140	28.26
Germany	973,749	529,490	329,228	518,545	1,202,245	2,289,236	8.98
Netherlands	238,568	302,429	307,908	257,861	117,823	206,821	.81
Sweden	589,970	1,084,368	250,167	421,619	1,027,532	166,162	.65
Turkey, Asiatic	189,845	402,970	81,324	159,597	172,138	133,196	.52
Argentina	24,222	17,120	....	3,942	38,698	61,352	.24
Chile	14,553	17,860	2,900	....	14,108	37,895	.15
Roumania	104,675	31,146	21,997	251,107	189,453	29,671	.12
Turkey, European	114,116	66,457	67,678	196,266	219,051	21,130	.08
Denmark	26,440	9,261	23,671	23,437	71,426	4,404	.02
France	7,254	3,290	161	20,250	12,570	....	
Cyprus	2,907	7,777	6,477	282	....	....	
Other b	3,098	1,620	195	3,431	8,112	2,132	.01
Total foreign countries	19,289,018	19,498,411	17,445,059	17,874,621	18,174,893	23,452,106	92.03
BRITISH POSSESSIONS.							
Canada	2,058,139	915,476	2,160,205	3,417,412	1,807,073	1,990,530	7.81
Australasia:							
New Zealand	133,215	153,485	48,212	22,984	410,090	31,306	
Victoria	3,617	....	1,407	7,636	6,317	2,725	
West Australia	10	....	....	....	....	49	} .13
New South Wales	7,909	....	....	....	39,545	....	
South Australia	8	....	....	....	39	....	
Other	2,558	....	....	6,521	....	6,268	.03
Total British possessions	2,205,456	1,068,961	2,209,824	3,454,553	2,263,064	2,030,878	7.97
Total	21,494,474	20,567,372	19,654,883	21,329,174	20,437,957	25,482,984	100.00

RYE. (c)

	Annual average, 1896-1900.	1896.	1897.	1898.	1899.	1900.	Per ct. in 1900.
FOREIGN COUNTRIES.							
	Dollars.	Dollars.	Dollars.	Dollars.	Dollars.	Dollars.	
Russia	317,522	383,514	112,655	78,609	399,657	613,179	35.02
United States	576,644	348,091	605,636	722,047	652,607	554,839	31.69
Germany	78,128	49,030	46,061	13,884	116,587	165,077	9.43
Roumania	154,376	217,319	220,418	88,760	201,512	43,871	2.50
Other d	16,122	6,166	54	34,031	29,199	11,159	.64
Total foreign countries	1,142,792	1,004,120	984,824	937,331	1,399,562	1,388,125	79.28
BRITISH POSSESSIONS.							
Canada	302,098	140,997	234,147	479,039	293,464	362,842	20.72
Total	1,444,890	1,145,117	1,218,971	1,416,370	1,693,026	1,750,967	100.00

WHEAT. (c)

	Annual average, 1896-1900.	1896.	1897.	1898.	1899.	1900.	Per ct. in 1900.
FOREIGN COUNTRIES.							
	Dollars.	Dollars.	Dollars.	Dollars.	Dollars.	Dollars.	
United States	59,510,924	47,229,139	63,774,363	74,431,979	57,481,638	54,637,500	48.09
Argentina	12,870,998	7,009,318	1,551,786	8,535,374	17,626,769	29,631,743	26.08
Russia	15,119,018	25,243,703	26,469,147	12,362,798	4,091,700	7,427,739	6.54
Germany	1,834,539	1,711,845	2,332,723	1,470,437	740,214	2,917,476	2.57
Roumania	2,405,348	8,254,411	2,068,360	372,501	53,775	1,277,690	1.12
Bulgaria	792,441	1,765,741	1,892,952	169,685	....	133,829	.12
Cyprus	43,594	14,697	4,643	101,136	....	97,495	.09
Uruguay	127,178	6,789	110,314	259,341	162,989	96,459	.08
Denmark	19,142	....	....	3,504	11,543	80,662	.07
Turkey, European	856,427	1,973,653	2,120,806	109,151	1,363	77,163	.07
Persia	10,918	21,364	....	....	....	33,224	.03
Turkey, Asiatic	470,140	953,377	1,055,768	270,976	38,105	32,474	.03

a For quantities, see page 172.
b Including imports from Norway valued at $769 in 1896 and $195 in 1897.
c For quantities, see page 173.
d Including imports from France valued at $3,747 in 1896 and $54 in 1897

alue of the agricultural imports of the United Kingdom (vegetable matter), etc.—Cont'd.

WHEAT—Continued.

ıtries from which imported.	Annual average, 1896-1900.	Calendar years.					Per ct. in 1900.
		1896.	1897.	1898.	1899.	1900.	
ƆREIGN COUNTRIES— continued.	Dollars.	Dollars.	Dollars.	Dollars.	Dollars.	Dollars.	
etherlands.........	12,014	6,370	9,762	29,150	8,249	6,541	⎫
hile	1,347,367	2,895,548	1,820,519	1,607,171	409,370	4,224	⎪
elgium.............	18,283	832	1,114	58,773	27,218	3,480	⎬ 0.01
rance	23,517	3,669	5,047	106,625	19	2,224	⎪
gypt	53,145	41,862	42,489	145,547	34,941	886	⎭
reece...............	13,166	....	65,829	....	....	....	.....
pain	12,061	-321	59,581	....	404	....	.....
razil	5,645	....	....	28,226	....	....	.....
ripoli	2,409	....	12,045	....	....	....	.....
ther................	1,824	....	1,092	8,030	....	....	.....
Total foreign countries.....	95,550,098	97,132,639	103,398,340	100,070,404	80,688,297	96,460,809	84.90
BRITISH POSSESSIONS.							
΄anada..............	8,686,126	5,316,029	9,124,970	9,480,657	8,769,204	10,739,771	9.45
ustralasia:							
Victoria.........	1,293,802	10,122	....	331,375	3,437,126	2,690,386	⎫
New Zealand.....	596,751	....	....	10,872	1,126,342	1,846,540	⎪
South Australia ..	587,364	...:......	....	....	1,397,459	1,539,362	⎪
New South Wales.	73,840	....	....	45,915	83,860	239,427	⎬ 5.64
Tasmania	18,062	....	....	....	5,149	85,159	⎪
West Australia ...	179	....	....	....	....	895	⎪
Queensland	4,442	....	....	....	22,211	....	⎭
ritish East Indies:							
Bengal	1,815,940	101,783	44	5,356,484	3,611,016	10,371	⎫ .01
Bombay ...·......	5,071,071	2,940,227	1,174,958	11,949,089	9,290,888	243	⎬
ther................	210	....	175	875	....	....	.....
Total British possessions ...	18,147,787	8,368,161	10,300,147	27,175,217	27,743,255	17,152,154	15.10
Total	113,697,885	105,500,800	113,698,487	127,245,621	108,431,552	113,612,963	100.00

CORN (MAIZE) MEAL. (a)

	Annual average, 1896-1900.	1896.	1897.	1898.	1899.	1900.	Per ct. in 1900.
FOREIGN COUNTRIES.	Dollars.	Dollars.	Dollars.	Dollars.	Dollars.	Dollars.	
United States.........	1,623,975	598,526	1,269,611	1,835,888	2,204,967	2,210,934	99.53
Other.................	4,105	1,085	871	2,711	7,908	7,947	.36
Total foreign countries.....	1,628,080	599,611	1,270,482	1,838,549	2,212,875	2,218,881	99.89
BRITISH POSSESSIONS.							
Total British possessions b..............	5,021	492	258	8,215	13,714	2,428	.11
Total	1,633,101	600,103	1,270,740	1,846,764	2,226,589	2,221,309	100.00

OATMEAL AND GROATS. (a)

	Annual average, 1896-1900.	1896.	1897.	1898.	1899.	1900.	Per ct. in 1900.
FOREIGN COUNTRIES.	Dollars.	Dollars.	Dollars.	Dollars.	Dollars.	Dollars.	
United States.........	2,072,149	1,335,207	1,886,246	2,663,119	2,220,993	2,255,180	88.48
Other.................	19,225	7,879	14,760	11,071	39,093	23,320	.91
Total foreign countries.....	2,091,374	1,343,086	1,901,006	2,674,190	2,260,086	2,278,500	89.39
BRITISH POSSESSIONS.							
Canada..............	254,882	267,560	214,325	323,170	198,952	270,402	10.61
Other................	168	....	....	39	803	....	.....
Total British possessions ...	255,050	267,560	214,325	323,209	199,755	270,402	10.61
Total	2,346,424	1,610,646	2,115,331	2,997,399	2,459,841	2,548,902	100.00

a For quantities, see page 174.   b Comprising in 1896 imports from Canada valued at $492.

Value of the agricultural imports of the United Kingdom (vegetable matter), etc.—Cont'd.

WHEAT FLOUR. (a)

Countries from which imported.	Annual average, 1896–1900.	Calendar years.					Per ct. in 1900.
		1896.	1897.	1898.	1899.	1900.	
FOREIGN COUNTRIES.	*Dollars.*	*Dollars.*	*Dollars.*	*Dollars.*	*Dollars.*	*Dollars.*	
United States	39,200,890	33,026,989	34,499,076	46,087,862	41,676,141	40,714,385	82.81
Austria-Hungary	3,157,798	3,739,370	3,598,845	2,643,804	2,744,370	3,062,600	6.23
France	2,327,273	3,544,028	4,060,082	1,116,234	1,338,682	1,577,340	3.21
Argentina	97,105	57,050	8,215	32,873	145,961	241,427	.49
Belgium	199,877	148,886	142,170	268,198	255,700	184,481	.38
Germany	185,540	320,999	150,535	252,464	125,853	77,849	.16
Netherlands..........	60,308	28,104	46,636	95,505	60,018	71,275	.15
Russia	127,692	24,512	156,652	423,614	4,862	28,819	.06
Chile	9,925	195	....	28,557	13,714	7,159	.01
Italy................	5,695	3,003	7,752	2,311	8,477	6,930	.01
Denmark	40,902	25,749	102,440	54,768	15,062	6,492	.01
Roumania	2,418	....	10,980	29	....	1,129	} .01
Other	7,092	12,677	7,003	5,397	5,339	5,046	
Total foreign countries	45,422,515	40,931,562	42,790,336	51,011,616	46,394,179	45,984,882	93.53
BRITISH POSSESSIONS.							
Canada	4,285,176	3,973,434	3,909,693	5,148,402	5,617,138	2,777,214	5.65
Australasia:							
New South Wales.	41,399	....	....	8,370	12,609	186,017	
Victoria	44,648	....	....	15,515	34,207	173,515	
South Australia..	8,288	....	....	....	2,574	38,864	} .82
New Zealand.....	1,054	....	....	....	2,302	2,969	
Tasmania	214	....	....	....	1,071	....	
Natal	4,802	....	12,157	....	11,855	....	.....
Other	1,991	2,448	4,540	1,995	384	589	.....
Total British possessions ...	4,387,572	3,975,882	3,926,390	5,174,282	5,682,140	3,179,168	6.47
Total	49,810,087	44,907,444	46,716,726	56,185,898	52,076,319	49,164,050	100.00

Total &
comm
Total P
Total ....

FOREIGN COU
United States.
Netherlands...

GROUND CEREALS (b) NOT ELSEWHERE SPECIFIED. (c)

FOREIGN COUNTRIES.							
	Dollars.	*Dollars.*	*Dollars.*	*Dollars.*	*Dollars.*	*Dollars.*	
Chile	100,366	82,361	77,538	57,011	145,508	139,411	33.75
United States........	250,289	214,437	614,931	54,714	304,254	63,109	15.28
Germany	64,931	79,158	42,397	75,509	75,260	52,334	12.67
Argentina	44,156	94,838	35,185	4,044	44,129	42,587	10.31
Russia	25,698	25,515	29,812	24,371	7,786	41,005	9.92
France	26,365	33,793	16,123	25,462	31,253	25,194	6.10
Denmark	7,407	8,619	3,898	8,317	7,241	8,959	2.17
Belgium.............	4,128	822	1,878	4,083	12,930	925	.22
Uruguay	1,787	97	....	....	8,838	....	.....
Turkey, Asiatic......	1,454	7,271	....	....	....	....	.....
Other d	7,770	3,149	7,295	6,044	3,772	18,590	4.50
Total foreign countries	534,351	550,060	829,057	259,555	640,971	392,114	94.92
BRITISH POSSESSIONS.							
Canada..............	28,764	27,715	52,738	5,835	46,534	10,998	2.66
British East Indies:							
Bombay	8,481	....	....	5,110	27,462	9,830	} 2.38
Bengal...........	579	....	....	506	2,389	....	
Other e	141	550	....	....	....	156	.04
Total British possessions ...	37,965	28,265	52,738	11,451	76,385	20,984	5.08
Total	572,316	578,325	881,795	271,006	717,356	413,098	100.00

French Indus'
Other..

comm

British East In

Total

Total..

a For quant
b Including
$1,363 in 189
d Prior to 18

a For quantities, see page 174.
b Including ground beans and peas.
c For quantities, see page 175.
d Including imports from the Netherlands valued at $1,071 in 1896, $837 in 1897, $2,209 in 1898, and $448 in 1899; from Austria-Hungary, $97 in 1897 and $1,363 in 1898; from Cyprus, $1,290 in 1896; and from European Turkey, $730 in 1897 and $273 in 1898.
e Comprising in 1896 imports from Australasia valued at $550.

Value of the agricultural imports of the United Kingdom (vegetable matter), etc.—Cont'd.

SAGO, SAGO MEAL, AND SAGO FLOUR.(a)

Countries from which imported.	Annual average, 1896–1900.	Calendar years.					Per ct. in 1900.
		1896.	1897.	1898.	1899.	1900.	
FOREIGN COUNTRIES.	*Dollars.*	*Dollars.*	*Dollars.*	*Dollars.*	*Dollars.*	*Dollars.*	
Java	1,299				2,117	4,380	0.49
Netherlands	2,019	49		6,652	1,995	1,397	.16
Philippine Islands b..	2,502	12,507					
Spain	613				3,066		
Other c	1,039	1,489	1,217	117	1,883	491	.05
Total foreign countries	7,472	14,045	1,217	6,769	9,061	6,268	.70
BRITISH POSSESSIONS.							
British East Indies:							
Straits Settlements	851,136	992,055	756,137	789,668	834,512	883,309	}99.30
Bombay	195				974		
Total British possessions	851,331	992,055	756,137	789,668	835,486	883,309	99.30
Total	858,803	1,006,100	757,354	796,437	844,547	889,577	100.00

BREADSTUFFS NOT ELSEWHERE SPECIFIED, AND PREPARATIONS OF.(d)

	Annual average, 1896–1900.	1896.	1897.	1898.	1899.	1900.	Per ct. in 1900.
FOREIGN COUNTRIES.	*Dollars.*	*Dollars.*	*Dollars.*	*Dollars.*	*Dollars.*	*Dollars.*	
United States	1,239,163	761,257	1,137,763	1,100,666	1,631,441	1,564,687	22.07
Germany	1,360,035	1,519,881	1,013,385	1,258,929	1,623,216	1,384,763	19.53
Netherlands	941,494	830,458	1,054,288	976,877	862,899	982,945	13.87
Belgium	464,073	373,105	388,863	497,697	494,913	565,789	7.98
Italy	303,346	289,980	232,784	321,004	351,215	321,749	4.54
France	238,777	194,042	202,549	232,716	289,552	275,025	3.88
Java	69,232	20,916	7,762	55,084	122,855	139,542	1.97
Austria-Hungary	56,911	67,348	46,081	43,531	61,104	66,491	.94
Brazil	17,477	47,473	17,252	10,823	2,214	9,621	.14
China	5,857	10,624	1,129	6,322	1,771	9,441	.13
Japan	4,914	5,285	1,046	477	9,679	8,083	.11
French Indo-China...	14,016				70,078		
Other	16,238	7,893	11,003	12,682	14,235	35,379	.50
Total foreign countries	4,731,533	4,128,262	4,113,905	4,516,808	5,535,172	5,363,515	75.66
BRITISH POSSESSIONS.							
British East Indies:							
Straits Settlements	1,092,291	1,080,358	899,840	1,061,520	1,269,324	1,150,411	
Bombay	1,974	4,146	1,903	3,076	68	677	
Bengal	1,555	1,436	24	1,290	4,842	185	}16.24
Madras	125		219	233	78	97	
Burma	773,275	672,424	899,198	1,222,202	1,072,552		
Ceylon	170	584	243		24		
British West Indies...	170,161	138,525	119,808	112,572	156,074	323,827	4.57
Canada	124,277	18,210	5,611	98,600	265,983	232,979	3.29
Natal	4,412	8,497	4,721	3,192	3,217	2,433	.03
Other	9,197	3,197	5,636	2,506	19,335	15,310	.21
Total British possessions	2,177,437	1,927,377	1,937,203	2,505,191	2,791,497	1,725,919	24.34
Total	6,908,970	6,055,639	6,051,108	7,021,999	8,326,669	7,089,434	100.00

a For quantities, see page 175.
b Including the Ladrone Islands.
c Including imports from Germany valued at $1,217 in 1897, $949 in 1899, and $58 in 1900; from Italy $1,363 in 1896; from the United States $876 in 1899; and from Belgium $24 in 1898.
d Prior to 1900 including rice meal and rice flour.

Value of the agricultural imports of the United Kingdom (vegetable matter), etc.—Cont'd.

CAROB BEANS (LOCUST BEANS).(a)

Countries from which imported.	Annual average, 1896–1900.	Calendar years.					Per ct. in 1900.
		1896.	1897.	1898.	1899.	1900.	
FOREIGN COUNTRIES.	Dollars.(b)	Dollars.	Dollars.	Dollars.	Dollars.	Dollars.	
Cyprus	263,991				263,122	264,859	32.90
Portugal	289,909				337,414	242,405	30.11
Algeria	71,063				64,865	77,261	9.60
Turkey, Asiatic	44,370				12,273	76,467	9.50
Italy	79,702	(c)	(c)	(c)	102,192	57,211	7.11
Morocco	23,374				....	46,748	5.81
Spain	47,755				88,483	7,027	.87
France	6,621				9,782	3,460	.43
Russia	22,201				44,402	....	......
Other	23,831				18,074	29,588	3.67
Total	872,817	(c)	(c)	(c)	940,607	805,026	100.00

CIDER AND PERRY.(a)

FOREIGN COUNTRIES.	Dollars.	Dollars.	Dollars.	Dollars.	Dollars.	Dollars.	
United States	63,381	50,329	80,662	49,117	64,106	72,691	93.80
France	2,703	2,901	2,857	1,830	2,628	3,300	4.26
Netherlands	1,183	117	243	5,144	97	311	.40
Other	498	141	151	1,139	166	895	1.15
Total foreign countries	67,765	53,488	83,913	57,230	66,997	77,197	99.61
BRITISH POSSESSIONS.							
Canada	2,674	....	19	13,354	....	....	......
Other d	155	219	112	48	93	302	.39
Total British possessions	2,829	219	131	13,402	93	302	.39
Total	70,594	53,707	84,044	70,632	67,090	77,499	100.00

COCOA, CRUDE.(a)

FOREIGN COUNTRIES.	Dollars.	Dollars.	Dollars.	Dollars.	Dollars.	Dollars.	
Portugal	948,605	547,389	165,524	1,050,449	1,246,530	1,733,136	21.34
France	571,469	380,726	514,248	743,085	384,570	834,717	10.28
Ecuador	602,543	564,582	300,599	833,247	754,098	560.188	6.90
Brazil	365,202	252,153	437,080	244,162	345,249	547,364	6.74
Germany	371,650	270,801	280,354	406,489	411,365	489,244	6.02
Colombia	98,066	31,929	41,287	124,081	168,687	124,344	1.53
United States	50,212	46,334	50,816	56,777	25,505	71,630	.88
Netherlands	108,104	135,104	77,810	141,289	120,801	65,484	.81
Dutch Guiana	13,099	8,652	19,836	10,516	10,040	16,449	.20
Venezuela	12,331	17,286	9,173	18,785	6,687	9,723	.12
Spanish West Africa	2,919	195	613	9,227	3,071	1,489	} .02
Belgium	16,784	73	14,381	3,952	65,367	146	
Guatemala	4,016	....	896	2,638	16,546	....	......
Other	5,934	5,815	5.723	4,448	6,998	6,686	.08
Total foreign countries	3,170,934	2,261,039	1,918,370	3,649,145	3,565,514	4,460,600	54.92
BRITISH POSSESSIONS.							
British West Indies	2,353,585	2,355,624	2,039,044	2,172,883	2,152,774	3,047,596	37.52
British East Indies:							
Ceylon	569,793	475,978	514,350	674,112	637,969	546,556	}
Straits Settlements	1,070	311	3,645	715	97	584	
Bombay	1,187	725	165	3,864	925	258	} 6.74
Burma	545	....	....	2,725	....	....	
Bengal	392	....	1,947	15	....	....	
Madras	65	15	39	272	....	....	

a For quantities, see page 176.
b Annual average, 1899–1900.
c Included in "Beans, dried."
d Comprising in 1896 imports from the Channel Islands valued at $219.

Value of the agricultural imports of the United Kingdom (vegetable matter), etc.—Cont'd.

COCOA, CRUDE—Continued.

	Annual average, 1896-1900.	Calendar years.					Per ct. in 1900.
		1896.	1897.	1898.	1899.	1900.	
BRITISH POSSESSIONS—continued.	*Dollars.*	*Dollars.*	*Dollars.*	*Dollars.*	*Dollars.*	*Dollars.*	
Niger Protectorate ...	13,869	8,312	7,957	14,502	17,091	21,481	0.27
Gold Coast............	8,915	2,453	735	8,137	14,619	18,629	.23
British Guiana	16,841	19,724	23,330	13,500	15,145	12,507	.15
Lagos.................	7,605	4,755	4,448	5,149	11,417	12,254	.15
Sierra Leone..........	131	39	....	107	326	185	} .02
Other.................	3,253	131	233	14,342	190	1,367	
Total British possessions ...	2,977,251	2,868,067	2,595,893	2,910,323	2,850,553	3,661,418	45.08
Total	6,148,185	5,129,106	4,514,263	6,559,468	6,416,067	8,122,018	100.00

COCOA HUSKS AND SHELLS.(a)

	Annual average, 1896-1900.	1896.	1897.	1898.	1899.	1900.	Per ct. in 1900.
FOREIGN COUNTRIES.	*Dollars.*	*Dollars.*	*Dollars.*	*Dollars.*	*Dollars.*	*Dollars.*	
Total foreign countries b.............	6,117	3,645	8,248	11,718	3,772	3,202	100.00
BRITISH POSSESSIONS.							
Total British possessions	22	58	10	10	34	....	......
Total	6,139	3,703	8,258	11,728	3,806	3,202	100.00

COCOA BUTTER.(a)

	Annual average, 1896-1900.	1896.	1897.	1898.	1899.	1900.	Per ct. in 1900.
FOREIGN COUNTRIES.	*Dollars.*	*Dollars.*	*Dollars.*	*Dollars.*	*Dollars.*	*Dollars.*	
Netherlands..........	193,650	52,651	305,612	141,781	126,471	341,735	87.60
Germany	13,518	2,336	11,154	1,255	4,900	47,945	12.29
Belgium	515	....	1,046	49	1,051	428	.11
Other.................	1,391	....	107	764	6,083	....	......
Total	209,074	54,987	317,919	143,849	138,505	390,108	100.00

COCOA, GROUND OR PREPARED, AND CHOCOLATE.(a)

	Annual average, 1896-1900.	1896.	1897.	1898.	1899.	1900.	Per ct. in 1900.
FOREIGN COUNTRIES.	*Dollars.*	*Dollars.*	*Dollars.*	*Dollars.*	*Dollars.*	*Dollars.*	
Netherlands..........	1,921,772	1,404,515	2,410,042	2,388,220	1,519,185	1,886,898	53.86
France	401,422	107,730	133,795	244,936	491,755	1,028,895	29.37
Belgium	375,510	233,553	336,080	325,520	415,117	567,278	16.19
Germany	13,915	9,300	17,364	10,210	17,714	14,989	.43
United States........	4,579	6,083	5,275	3,952	3,222	4,365	.13
Other.................	1,241	959	2,715	1,333	783	413	.01
Total foreign countries	2,718,439	1,762,140	2,905,271	2,974,171	2,447,776	3,502,838	99.99
BRITISH POSSESSIONS.							
British Guiana	339	1,694	....	....	....	....	.....
Other.................	875	1,966	234	1,173	589	414	.01
Total British possessions ...	1,214	3,660	234	1,173	589	414	.01
Total	2,719,653	1,765,800	2,905,505	2,975,344	2,448,365	3,503,252	100.00

a For quantities, see page 177.
b Including imports from Spain valued at $2,969 in 1896 and $5,898 in 1897, and from the United States, $214 in 1900.

Value of the agricultural imports of the United Kingdom (vegetable matter), etc.—Cont'd.

COCOA AND CHOCOLATE, CONTAINING DISTILLED SPIRITS.(a)

Countries from which imported.	Annual average, 1896–1900.	Calendar years.					Per ct. in 1900.
		1896.	1897.	1898.	1899.	1900.	
FOREIGN COUNTRIES.							
	Dollars.	*Dollars.*	*Dollars.*	*Dollars.*	*Dollars.*	*Dollars.*	
Belgium..............	35,106	18,907	28,357	42,226	46,022	40,017	87.37
Germany.............	2,833	1,572	2,954	2,555	3,596	3,489	7.62
Netherlands.........	1,106	2,360	1,149	10	15	1,995	4.35
Other b	714	1,445	1,041	584	200	302	.66
Total	39,759	24,284	33,501	45,375	49,833	45,803	100.00

COFFEE, RAW.(a)

	Annual average, 1896–1900.	1896.	1897.	1898.	1899.	1900.	Per ct. in 1900.
FOREIGN COUNTRIES.							
	Dollars.	*Dollars.*	*Dollars.*	*Dollars.*	*Dollars.*	*Dollars.*	
United States........	2,124,072	2,831,729	2,758,089	1,631,139	1,503,549	1,895,852	15.33
Germany.............	1,378,539	570,276	966,068	1,981,361	1,497,281	1,877,710	15.18
Costa Rica...........	1,746,819	1,516,124	1,599,979	2,795,756	1,169,006	1,650,731	13.35
Colombia............	1,535,689	1,600,285	1,578,780	1,960,523	1,679,609	859,249	6.95
France	1,523,027	1,108,282	1,780,107	1,898,894	2,095,637	732,214	5.92
Salvador	503,558	461,811	486,762	769,452	297,445	502,320	4.06
Guatemala	1,309,966	1,989,269	1,824,641	1,404,905	842,912	488,105	3.95
Brazil	760,575	908,780	925,964	828,157	698,070	441,903	3.57
Nicaragua...........	315,215	158,064	617,724	288,486	175,233	336,567	2.72
Chile	176,581	20,542	10,565	4,954	510,622	336,222	2.72
Netherlands.........	835,265	1,103,897	196,363	155,509	84,994	135,561	1.10
Mexico..............	126,171	70,652	119,054	125,483	209,089	106,576	.86
Peru................	74,360	63,084	111,686	65,620	56,398	75,012	.61
Ecuador	45,280	54,680	63,177	25,160	10,191	73,192	.59
Belgium.............	102,780	86,536	322,016	54,553	8,969	41,828	.34
Liberia	c 24,779	(d)	43,974	21,889	14,556	18,697	.15
Egypt	14,451	1,299	2,521	49,098	6,779	12,556	.10
Venezuela...........	13,440	3,918	35,671	13,952	5,971	7,689	.06
Portuguese East Africa...............	5,771	23,661	63	....	1,226	3,903	.03
Portugal............	37,040	107,238	52,183	12,857	11,918	1,003	.0
Haiti and Santo Domingo..............	3,017	13,042	1,076	....	58	910	
Austria-Hungary.....	10,287	1,071	7,533	63	42,524	243	
Portuguese West Africa...............	11,258	21,330	13,899	15,407	5,416	238	} .0
West Africa, n.e.s....	c 29	50,670	....	....	....	117	
German West Africa..	21	....	....	....	10	97	
French West Africa ..	68	....	214	....	102	24	
Honduras	13,766	19,466	686	48,680	....	....	......
Java................	4,510	3,660	18,478	414	....	....	......
Kongo Free State.....	391	1,368	589	....	....	....	......
Spanish West Africa..	9	29	15	....	....	....	......
Other...............	9,779	9,606	13,802	17,544	3,879	4,064	.0
Total foreign countries	12,211,186	12,800,369	13,551,679	14,169,856	10,931,444	9,602,583	
BRITISH POSSESSIONS.							
British East Indies:							
Bombay	1,608,463	1,425,778	991,335	1,105,041	3,259,976	1,260,185	
Madras...........	1,167,407	1,728,654	1,545,571	1,120,920	762,722	679,169	
Ceylon	279,189	335,628	305,519	177,691	361,201	215,907	} 17.4
Straits Settlements	35,640	75,596	59,055	30,250	8,069	5,227	
Bengal	3,074	3,562	3,499	2,239	4,891	1,178	
British West Indies...	408,398	445,733	547,370	449,562	365,333	233,991	1.8
Aden	241,697	364,525	266,840	222,433	169,150	185,535	1.5
Natal...............	136,438	109,905	155,942	93,714	148,939	173,690	1.4
Niger Protectorate ...	4,689	7,178	5,105	6,273	2,784	2,107	.0
Gold Coast	2,513	4,832	3,319	1,407	2,433	574	} .0
Other...............	28,893	16,877	11,383	91,291	17,548	7,368	
Total British possessions ...	3,916,401	4,518,268	3,894,938	3,300,821	5,103,046	2,764,931	
Total	16,127,587	17,318,637	17,446,617	17,470,677	16,034,490	12,367,514	100.0

a For quantities, see page 178.
b Including in 1900 imports from the United States valued at $49.
c Annual average, 1897–1900.
d Included in "West Africa, n.e.s."

alue of the agricultural imports of the United Kingdom (vegetable matter), etc.—Cont'd.

COFFEE, KILN-DRIED, ROASTED, OR GROUND.(a)

hich	Annual average, 1896–1900.	Calendar years.					Per ct. in 1900.
		1896.	1897.	1898.	1899.	1900.	
OREIGN COUNTRIES.	*Dollars.*	*Dollars.*	*Dollars.*	*Dollars.*	*Dollars.*	*Dollars.*	
ited States........	1,916	219	34	34	122	9,169	55.93
lgium..............	685	277	312	229	389	2,219	13.53
rmany.............	1,761	1,251	1,616	2,336	2,112	1,489	9.08
etherlands.........	622	404	185	321	1,085	1,114	6.79
ance.	668	930	540	545	472	852	5.20
her................	276	355	209	302	385	131	.80
Total foreign countries.....	5,928	3,436	2,896	3,767	4,565	14,974	91.33
RITISH POSSESSIONS.							
tal British possesions	465	9	175	530	190	1,421	8.67
Total ..., ...	6,393	3,445	3,071	4,297	4,755	16,395	100.00

CHICORY ROOT, RAW OR KILN-DRIED.(a)

OREIGN COUNTRIES.	*Dollars.*	*Dollars.*	*Dollars.*	*Dollars.*	*Dollars.*	*Dollars.*	
elgium..............	205,342	223,669	202,393	197,969	202,427	200,252	100.00
ermany.............	57	5	39	244	....	....	......
ther................	335	1,348	....	326	....	....	......
Total	205,734	225,022	202,432	198,539	202,427	200,252	100.00

ROOT, ROASTED OR GROUND.(a)

OREIGN COUNTRIES.	*Dollars.*	*Dollars.*	*Dollars.*	*Dollars.*	*Dollars.*	*Dollars.*	
elgium.............	3,714	5,032	5,485	2,998	1,723	3,329	52.14
etherlands.........	1,993	2,317	2,166	1,951	2,059	1,474	23.09
ermany.............	1,369	1,382	1,328	1,528	1,280	1,329	20.81
rance	455	1,114	321	268	321	253	3.96
ther................	40	97	....	44	58	....	......
Total foreign countries.....	7,571	9,942	9,300	6,789	5,441	6,385	100.00
RITISH POSSESSIONS.							
hannel Islands......	1,665	6,648	1,674	5	....	....	......
ritish West Indies...	9	....	....	19	24	....	......
Total British possessions ...	1,674	6,648	1,674	24	24	....	......
Total	9,245	16,590	10,974	6.813	5,465	6,385	100.00

CHICORY ROOT AND COFFEE (MIXED), ROASTED AND GROUND. (a)

FOREIGN COUNTRIES.	*Dollars.*	*Dollars.*	*Dollars.*	*Dollars.*	*Dollars.*	*Dollars.*	
ermany.............	227	267	112	360	121	277	78.03
enmark.............	489	1,251	628	458	107	....	......
ther................	36	49	9	....	122	....	......
Total foreign countries.....	752	1,567	749	818	350	277	78.03
RITISH POSSESSIONS.							
hannel Islands......	115	316	258	....	....	....	......
ther................	97	49	10	219	127	78	21.97
Total British possessions ...	212	365	268	219	127	78	21.97
Total	964	1,932	1,017	1,037	477	355	100.00

a For quantities, see page 179.

Value of the agricultural imports of the United Kingdom (vegetable matter), etc.—Cont'd.

COFFEE SUBSTITUTES, OTHER THAN CHICORY ROOT. (a)

Countries from which imported.	Annual average, 1896–1900.	Calendar years.					Per ct. in 1900.
		1896.	1897.	1898.	1899.	1900.	
FOREIGN COUNTRIES.	*Dollars.*	*Dollars.*	*Dollars.*	*Dollars.*	*Dollars.*	*Dollars.*	
Total foreign countries	696	2,949	268	141	107	15	100.00

COTTON, RAW. (a)

FOREIGN COUNTRIES.	*Dollars.*	*Dollars.*	*Dollars.*	*Dollars.*	*Dollars.*	*Dollars.*	
United States	125,941,529	136,092,767	119,509,137	133,892,170	93,262,239	146,951,331	73.68
Egypt	35,047,761	33,254,327	31,556,576	28,621,814	37,684,283	44,121,806	22.12
Brazil	1,333,029	981,033	1,476,618	476,391	472,518	3,258,584	1.65
Peru	867,414	788,597	765,077	933,448	899,086	950,861	.48
Chile	82,231	25,734	46,655	65,956	72,530	200,281	.10
China	42,121	48,271	5,460	44	6,638	150,190	.08
Turkey, Asiatic	37,839	78,565	18,240		2,336	90,055	.04
Colombia	33,245	20,177	14,050	36,596	37,487	57,916	.03
Germany	38,829	9,908	48,392	47,682	37,321	50,840	.03
Netherlands	17,662	63	1,825	52,986	8,292	25,145	.01
France	20,642	20,157	13,981	9,757	37,628	21,685	.01
Belgium	7,419	23,778	389	1,110	3,064	8,156	}.01
Italy	6,731	17,884	7,300	2,531		5,942	
Pacific islands	11,429	14,064	33,993	1,606	4,258	3,226	
Java	2,042			10,210			
Russia	1,897	78	5,937	764	204		
Other b	30,782	17,870	5,903	5,431	13,724	110,981	.06
Total foreign countries	163,522,102	171,393,273	153,509,533	164,158,496	132,542,208	196,006,999	98.28
BRITISH POSSESSIONS.							
British East Indies:							
Madras	1,371,755	1,423,257	739,903	939,488	1,313,770	2,442,360	
Bombay	1,324,316	3,113,222	1,807,004	705,886	388,201	607,266	
Ceylon	38,594	97		10,414		182,460	
Bengal	349,592	522,959	544,980	176,489	357,089	146,443	}1.70
Straits Settlements	10,438	23,155	6,940	7,796	5,928	8,370	
Burma	14				68		
British West Indies	27,041	33,287	19,159	24,162	22,089	36,508	}.02
Canada	18,329		14,697	43,998	32,941	10	
Aden	6,326		31,632				
Other c	6,936	8,628	3,957	5,280	5,436	11,378	
Total British possessions	3,153,341	5,124,605	3,168,272	1,913,513	2,125,522	3,434,795	1.72
Total	166,675,443	176,517,878	156,677,805	166,072,009	134,667,730	199,441,794	100.00

WASTE COTTON. (a) (d)

FOREIGN COUNTRIES.	*Dollars.*	*Dollars.*	*Dollars.*	*Dollars.*	*Dollars.*	*Dollars.*	
United States	191,703	151,694	310,687	89,894	112,158	294,083	44.86
France	71,489	71,139	109,331	57,887	41,935	77,154	11.77
Belgium	38,847	36,265	45,988	31,316	36,285	44,382	6.77
Netherlands	18,846	13,412	26,158	7,329	9,757	37,574	5.73
Portugal	13,268	10,799	11,626	12,721	8,852	22,342	3.41
Italy	33,320	74,019	34,766	34,192	3,368	20,254	3.09
Germany	5,722	8,711	7,645	3,129	1,105	8,020	1.22
Sweden	3,823	7,066	4,570	2,642	3,260	1,577	.24
Other e	17,664	14,054	13,174	17,841	16,205	27,043	4.12
Total foreign countries	394,682	387,159	563,945	256,951	232,925	532,429	81.21

a For quantities, see page 180.
b Including imports from Cyprus valued at $1,606 in 1896, $4,010 in 1897, $462 in 1898, and $1,119 in 1899
c Including imports from Australasia valued at $6,438 in 1896, $3,567 in 1897, $1,275 in 1898, and $2,30 in 1899.
d This item probably includes cop and mill waste as well as the waste of raw cotton.
e Including in 1896 imports from Spain valued at $5,504.

Value of the agricultural imports of the United Kingdom (vegetable matter), etc.—Cont'd.

WASTE COTTON—Continued.

	Annual average, 1896–1900.	Calendar years.					Per ct. in 1900.
		1896.	1897.	1898.	1899.	1900.	
BRITISH POSSESSIONS.							
British East Indies:	*Dollars.*	*Dollars.*	*Dollars.*	*Dollars.*	*Dollars.*	*Dollars.*	
Bombay	172,021	206,500	137,761	158,692	240,731	116,422	
Bengal	5,933	16,376	5,372		2,380	5,538	} 18.61
Madras	13					63	
Other	388	604	180	24		1,134	.18
Total British possessions	178,355	223,480	143,313	158,716	243,111	123,157	18.79
Total	573,087	610,639	707,258	415,667	476,036	655,586	100.00

ESPARTO AND OTHER VEGETABLE FIBERS FOR PAPER MAKING. (a)

	Annual average, 1896–1900.	1896.	1897.	1898.	1899.	1900.	Per ct. in 1900.
FOREIGN COUNTRIES.	*Dollars.*	*Dollars.*	*Dollars.*	*Dollars.*	*Dollars.*	*Dollars.*	
Algeria	1,494,285	1,377,088	1,495,631	1,481,956	1,483,110	1,633,640	41.94
Spain	1,435,149	1,652,722	1,497,417	1,355,856	1,412,219	1,257,528	32.28
Tripoli	632,572	551,881	721,716	501,697	742,448	645,118	16.56
Tunis	325,492	293,718	295,504	398,031	283,683	356,525	9.15
Other	2,952	1,260	5,105	2,920	2,662	2,813	.07
Total foreign countries	3,890,450	3,876,669	4,015,373	3,740,460	3,924,122	3,895,624	100.00
BRITISH POSSESSIONS.							
Total British possessions b	326	389	438	803			
Total	3,890,776	3,877,058	4,015,811	3,741,263	3,924,122	3,895,624	100.00

FLAX (EXCEPT TOW). (a)

	Annual average, 1896–1900.	1896.	1897.	1898.	1899.	1900.	Per ct. in 1900.
FOREIGN COUNTRIES.	*Dollars.*	*Dollars.*	*Dollars.*	*Dollars.*	*Dollars.*	*Dollars.*	
Russia	7,888,275	7,747,862	8,515,246	8,390,561	8,171,525	6,616,182	60.06
Belgium	4,102,000	4,836,177	4,606,244	3,845,236	3,741,117	3,481,226	31.60
Netherlands	605,017	654,816	604,940	567,882	590,219	607,227	5.51
Germany	125,933	170,055	71,231	79,275	87,855	221,246	2.01
France	52,020	51,016	72,083	37,097	64,627	35,277	.32
Turkey, European	6,707	16,020	10,507	2,638		4,370	.04
Turkey, Asiatic	4,613	14,050	5,718	1,912		1,387	.01
United States	5,310	17,179	4,535	3,840	998		
Other c	1,935	487		3,718	462	5,008	.04
Total foreign countries	12,791,810	13,507,662	13,890,504	12,932,159	12,656,803	10,971,923	99.59
BRITISH POSSESSIONS.							
Australasia:							
New Zealand	23,487	18,536		715	56,738	41,448	
New South Wales	662					3,309	} .41
Victoria	12					59	
Other	32			161			
Total British possessions	24,193	18,536		876	56,738	44,816	.41
Total	12,816,003	13,526,198	13,890,504	12,933,035	12,713,541	11,016,739	100.00

a For quantities, see page 181.
b Comprising in 1896 imports from Malta and Gozo valued at $389.
c Comprising in 1896 imports from Brazil valued at $487.

Value of the agricultural imports of the United Kingdom (vegetable matter), etc.—Cont'd.

FLAX, TOW OF. (a)

Countries from which imported.	Annual average, 1896–1900.	Calendar years.					Per ct. in 1900.
		1896.	1897.	1898.	1899.	1900.	
FOREIGN COUNTRIES.							
	Dollars.	*Dollars.*	*Dollars.*	*Dollars.*	*Dollars.*	*Dollars.*	
Russia	1,111,923	1,116,580	1,210,367	1,030,837	1,281,899	919,929	76.22
Belgium	269,613	410,976	378,054	209,488	156,507	193,039	15.99
Germany	45,664	46,183	45,258	44,091	49,147	43,643	3.62
France	27,314	30,386	26,235	23,622	30,021	26,308	2.18
Netherlands	27,414	28,372	37,039	30,649	17,335	23,676	1.96
Other b	621	1,878	837	....	....	389	.03
Total foreign countries	1,482,549	1,634,375	1,697,790	1,338,687	1,534,909	1,206,984	100.00
BRITISH POSSESSIONS.							
Australasia: New Zealand	1,969	9,845	....	....	....	....	
Total	1,484,518	1,644,220	1,697,790	1,338,687	1,534,909	1,206,984	100.00

HEMP (c) (EXCEPT TOW). (a)

	Annual average, 1896–1900.	1896.	1897.	1898.	1899.	1900.	Per ct. in 1900.
FOREIGN COUNTRIES.							
	Dollars.	*Dollars.*	*Dollars.*	*Dollars.*	*Dollars.*	*Dollars.*	
Philippine Islands d	4,781,415	3,560,492	3,694,214	4,925,088	4,758,400	6,968,882	44.05
Italy	1,684,997	1,616,598	1,987,790	1,665,355	1,527,546	1,627,693	10.29
Germany	997,957	911,997	823,830	903,918	1,368,338	981,700	6.20
Russia	846,132	1,103,902	705,750	725,318	720,291	975,398	6.16
United States	128,537	46,967	32,221	224,662	220,666	118,168	.75
France	67,049	1,440	6,078	43,706	183,462	100,561	.64
Mexico	61,575	17,636	17,081	15,597	184,431	73,129	.46
Austria-Hungary	26,262	54,310	13,616	11,446	18,454	33,486	.21
Spain	47,403	63,921	19,588	12,600	108,236	32,669	.21
China	10,013	2,462	14,556	89	11,641	21,369	.14
Egypt	3,325	2,253	842	....	7,154	6,375	.04
Denmark	14,703	33,005	11,753	12,030	11,470	5,256	.03
Belgium	7,172	9,081	3,246	11,105	8,896	3,533	.02
Netherlands	9,812	3,115	949	21,807	21,485	1,703	.01
Japan	14,940	49,410	20,186	....	5,105	....	
Madagascar	902	....	....	4,511	....	....	
Other e	5,998	2,253	9,168	8,385	5,061	5,124	.03
Total foreign countries	8,708,192	7,478,542	7,360,868	8,585,567	9,160,636	10,955,046	69.24
BRITISH POSSESSIONS.							
Hongkong	1,251,191	961,562	229,704	1,318,773	1,621,216	2,124,699	13.43
Australasia:							
New Zealand	557,962	83,339	101,043	235,582	775,754	1,594,095	} 10.96
New South Wales	28,154	....	....	....	....	140,769	
British East Indies:							
Bengal	234,778	149,723	288,622	201,561	219,226	314,756	
Straits Settlements	77,122	10,570	63	98,907	111,784	164,288	
Bombay	161,883	199,857	152,283	171,364	129,644	156,268	} 4.28
Madras	43,346	75,903	10,901	57,717	40,348	31,861	
Ceylon	14,122	341	2,643	4,243	52,850	10,531	
Mauritius	151,567	67,683	53,746	119,745	251,223	265,438	1.68
British Borneo	973	....	....	4,866	....	....	
Other	14,952	1,528	749	633	7,368	64,481	.41
Total British possessions	2,536,050	1,550,506	839,754	2,213,391	3,209,413	4,867,186	30.76
Total	11,244,242	9,029,348	8,200,622	10,798,958	12,370,049	15,822,232	100.00

a For quantities, see page 182.
b Comprising in 1900 imports from the United States valued at $389.
c Including Manila hemp, New Zealand flax, sisal grass, sunn, etc.
d Including the Ladrone Islands.
e Including imports from European Turkey valued at $453 in 1896, $1,275 in 1897, and $58 in 1899, and from Asiatic Turkey $983 in 1898.

alue of the agricultural imports of the United Kingdom (vegetable matter), etc.—Cont'd.

HEMP, TOW OF. (a)

‹ from which ported.	Annual average, 1896–1900.	Calendar years.					Per ct. in 1900.
		1896.	1897.	1898.	1899.	1900.	
OREIGN COUNTRIES.							
	Dollars.	Dollars.	Dollars.	Dollars.	Dollars.	Dollars.	
ermany	163,310	194,144	158,448	126,831	133,600	203,527	44.25
ussia	239,959	225,426	157,772	255,613	391,466	169,520	36.86
taly	48,764	37,861	52,062	33,700	50,923	69,274	15.06
ther b	9,536	9,261	6,765	14,035	13,738	3,883	.85
Total foreign countries	461,569	466,692	375,047	430,179	589,727	446,204	97.02
RITISH POSSESSIONS.							
ritish East Indies c..	3,775	964	5,927	5,081	5,815	1,085	.24
ther	2,907				1,913	12,624	2.74
Total British possessions	6,682	964	5,927	5,081	7,728	13,709	2.98
Total	468,251	467,656	380,974	435,260	597,455	459,913	100.00

JUTE. (a)

?OREIGN COUNTRIES.	Dollars.	Dollars.	Dollars.	Dollars.	Dollars.	Dollars.	
hina	26,884	462	4,010	26,269	24,741	78,935	0.39
ermany	79,869	56,651	81,061	34,216	180,479	46,937	.23
etherlands	7,980	657	9,879	1,616	19,330	8,419	.04
rance	2,834	102	316	375	8,370	5,008	.03
nited States	2,868	7,786		170	2,638	3,747	.02
elgium	3,056	774	623	1,260	9,903	2,720	.01
ther	2,802	1,256	195	745	2,779	9,037	.05
Total foreign countries	126,293	67,688	96,084	64,651	248,240	154,803	.77
BRITISH POSSESSIONS.							
British East Indies:							
Bengal	19,023,433	20,193,819	19,077,420	18,423,187	17,499,121	19,923,616	} 99.23
Madras	17,298	2,098	12,965	3,655	32,547	35,224	
Ceylon	2,561			6,487		6,317	
Bombay	5,600	19,928	243		7,786	44	
Straits Settlements	2,149				487	10,259	
Hongkong	662				1,946	1,363	
Total British possessions	19,051,703	20,215,845	19,090,628	18,435,762	17,551,076	19,965,201	99.23
Total	19,177,996	20,283,533	19,186,712	18,500,413	17,799,316	20,120,004	100.00

PIASSAVA AND OTHER VEGETABLE FIBERS FOR BRUSH MAKING. (a) (d)

Countries from which imported.	Calendar year 1900.	Per cent.	Countries from which imported.	Calendar year 1900.	Per cent.
FOREIGN COUNTRIES.			BRITISH POSSESSIONS.		
	Dollars.				
Brazil	213,396	22.27	British East Indies:	Dollars.	
Liberia	117,492	12.26	Ceylon	227,222	} 37.95
Germany	57,167	5.96	Bombay	⸾9,461	
United States	37,010	3.86	Madras	44,037	
France	32,396	3.38	Straits Settlements	2,910	
Belgium	26,814	2.80	Burma	127	
West Africa, n. e. s.	25,948	2.71	Niger Protectorate	19,086	1.99
Italy	20,551	2.14	Other	9,246	.97
French West Africa	6,906	.72	Total British possessions	392,089	40.91
Other	28,654	2.99			
Total foreign countries	566,334	59.09	Total	958,423	100.00

a For quantities, see page 183.
b Including imports from France valued at $2,565 in 1896, $229 in 1897, $545 in 1898, and $2,983 in 1899.
c Including imports from Bengal valued at $964 in 1896, $5,343 in 1897, $3,241 in 1898, $5,815 in 1899, and $949 in 1900, and from Ceylon $487 in 1898.
d Prior to 1900 not stated by countries.

Value of the agricultural imports of the United Kingdom (vegetable matter), etc.—Cont'd.

VEGETABLE FIBERS NOT ELSEWHERE SPECIFIED. (a)

Countries from which imported.	Annual average, 1896–1900.	Calendar years.					Per ct. in 1900.
		1896.	1897.	1898.	1899.	1900.	
FOREIGN COUNTRIES.							
	Dollars.	*Dollars.*	*Dollars.*	*Dollars.*	*Dollars.*	*Dollars.*	
Madagascar	54,933	81,202	69,941	13,641	35,287	74,594	15.60
France	24,060	36,056	8,220	9,986	21,909	44,129	9.23
China	17,040	13,286	23,564	13,451	7,767	27,131	5.67
Germany	9,050	4,808	8,638	9,003	1,844	20,955	4.38
Mexico	47,984	101,676	70,691	29,233	19,972	18,347	3.84
Belgium	8,799	3,411	9,475	12,322	4,944	13,845	2.90
United States	51,643	98,990	62,671	26,444	60,530	9,582	2.00
Algeria	5,411	12,035	6,151	2,565	2,093	4,210	.88
Japan	3,630		3,280	13,811	584	477	.10
Russia	1,999	9,830	165				
Other	4,311	1,917	7,212	6,940	2,570	2,915	.61
Total foreign countries	228,860	363,211	270,008	137,396	157,500	216,185	45.21
BRITISH POSSESSIONS.							
British East Indies:							
Ceylon	86,321	41,604	67,742	136,501	78,876	106,883	⎫
Bombay	25,750	9,899	19,164	36,051	25,680	37,954	
Madras	21,354	11,777	38,475	26,123	12,629	17,763	⎬34.40
Bengal	8,115	9,947	6,005	18,410	4,745	1,469	
Burma	608	1,285		949	482	326	
StraitsSettlements	233	180		895		92	⎭
Mauritius	25,423	5,835	7,606	10,682	20,303	82,687	17.29
Hongkong	228	350		15		774	.16
Otherᵇ	8,218	3,684	7,616	2,647	13,110	14,035	2.94
Total British possessions	176,250	84,561	146,608	232,273	155,825	261,983	54.79
Total	405,110	447,772	416,616	369,669	313,325	478,168	100.00

FLOWERS, FRESH. (c)

Countries from which imported.	Calendar year 1900.	Per cent.	Countries from which imported.	Calendar year 1900.	Per cent.
FOREIGN COUNTRIES.			BRITISH POSSESSIONS.		
	Dollars.			*Dollars.*	
France	609,427	62.43	Channel Islands	334,538	34.27
Netherlands	26,746	2.74	Total	976,147	100.00
Other	5,436	.56			
Total foreign countries	641,609	65.73			

FRUIT JUICES, NONALCOHOLIC. (a) (c)

FOREIGN COUNTRIES.			BRITISH POSSESSIONS.		
	Dollars.			*Dollars.*	
Italy	146,496	36.25	British West Indies	168,021	41.57
United States	17,612	4.36	Canada	57,210	14.15
Other	13,675	3.38	Other	1,173	.29
Total foreign countries	177,783	43.99	Total British possessions	226,404	56.01
			Total	404,187	100.00

a For quantities, see page 184.
b Including imports from Natal valued at $73 in 1896 and $24 in 1897.
c Prior to 1900 not stated by countries.

lue of the agricultural imports of the United Kingdom (vegetable matter), etc.—Cont'd.

APPLES, FRESH. (a)

:s from which ported.	Annual average, 1896-1900.	Calendar years.					Per ct. in 1900.
		1896.	1897.	1898.	1899.	1900.	
ЭREIGN COUNTRIES.	*Dollars.*	*Dollars.*	*Dollars.*	*Dollars.*	*Dollars.*	*Dollars.*	
ıited States.........	2,407,524	3,271,471	2,446,497	1,956,912	1,877,033	2,485,706	41.71
lgium..............	348,393	336,353	437,231	220,204	353,303	394,873	6.62
ance..............	244,557	255,073	268,402	241,777	308,006	149,528	2.51
:therlands..........	194,007	67,965	495,463	134,792	145,484	126,330	2.12
rtugal..........~....	170,437	181,691	184,012	166,872	233,441	86,171	1.45
rmany.............	36,473	19,471	39,190	50,106	26,922	46,679	.78
)ain...............	19,681	6,750	50,704	22,493	15,149	3,309	} .06
adeira Islands......	1,752	199	3,587	1,231	3,572	170	
aly................	1,652	1,051	6,453	239	516	....	......
ther*b*..............	5,209	4,122	2,642	1,368	13,120	4,794	.08
Total foreign countries....	3,429,685	4,144,116	3,934,181	2,795,994	2,976,546	3,297,560	55.33
RITISH POSSESSIONS.							
anada..............	2,211,710	3,145,034	1,357,457	2,182,698	2,291,650	2,081,709	34.93
ustralasia:							
Tasmania........	399,958	379,193	364,583	346,928	413,112	495,974	
South Australia ..	20,621	2,453	37,740	7,674	24,016	31,223	
Victoria..........	22,928	14,337	56,150	5,027	14,361	24,765	} 9.26
New South Wales.	2,536	462	487	3,947	7,665	117	
New Zealand.....	864	156	....	10	4,156	....	
hannel Islands......	28,823	15,261	27,398	41,682	35,744	24,031	.40
ther................	3,622	170	14	8,395	5,115	4,414	.08
Total British possessions ...	2,691,062	3,557,066	1,843,829	2,596,361	2,795,819	2,662,233	44.67
Total..........	6,120,747	7,701,212	5,778,010	·5,392,355	5,772,365	5,959,793	100.00

APRICOTS AND PEACHES, FRESH. (a) (c)

Countries from which imported.	Calendar year 1900.	Per ,cent.	Countries from which imported.	Calendar year 1900.	Per cent.
FOREIGN COUNTRIES.	*Dollars.*		BRITISH.POSSESSIONS.	*Dollars.*	
₣rance......................	108,888	86.57	Total British possessions	2,477	1.97
∪nited States................	13,641	10.84			
Эther......................	774	·62	Total	125,780	100.00
Total foreign countries	123,303	98.03			

BANANAS. (a) (d)

FOREIGN COUNTRIES.	*Dollars.*		BRITISH POSSESSIONS.	*Dollars.*	
ℭanary Islands...............	2,572,140	96.28	British West Indies..........	4,253	} 0.16
Madeira Islands.............	93,841	3.51	Other......................	15	
∪nited States................	68	} .05			
Эther......................	1,177		Total British possessions	4,268	.16
Total foreign countries	2,667,226	99.84	Total	2,671,494	100.00

a For quantities, see page 185.
b Including imports from Denmark valued at $1,226 in 1896 and $1,324 in 1897.
c Prior to 1900 included in "Plums, fresh."
d Prior to 1900 included in "Fresh fruits not elsewhere specified."

Value of the agricultural imports of the United Kingdom (vegetable matter), etc.—Cont'd.

CHERRIES. (a)

Countries from which imported.	Annual average, 1896–1900.	Calendar years.					Per ct. in 1900.
		1896.	1897.	1898.	1899.	1900.	
FOREIGN COUNTRIES.	*Dollars.*	*Dollars.*	*Dollars.*	*Dollars.*	*Dollars.*	*Dollars.*	
France	705,798	285,299	665,689	857,667	573,541	1,146,791	76.4?
Germany	95,089	72,822	99,793	83,976	67,440	151,412	10.0
Netherlands	92,444	115,409	70,462	99,958	54,505	121,886	8.12
Belgium	57,176	41,399	30,352	81,723	52,130	80,278	5.35
Other	166	....	579	....	83	170	.01
Total foreign countries	950,673	514,929	866,875	1,123,324	747,699	1,500,537	99.99
BRITISH POSSESSIONS.							
Total British possessions	22	....	....	....	....	112	.01
Total	950,695	514,929	866,875	1,123,324	747,699	1,500,649	100.00

CURRANTS (FRESH).(a) (b)

Countries from which imported.	Calendar year 1900.	Per cent.	Countries from which imported.	Calendar year 1900.	Per cent.
FOREIGN COUNTRIES.	*Dollars.*		FOREIGN COUNTRIES—cont'd.	*Dollars.*	
France	301,417	71.05	Other	472	0.11
Netherlands	91,957	21.68			
Belgium	18,439	4.35	Total	424,213	100.00
Germany	11,928	2.81			

GOOSEBERRIES.(a) (b)

FOREIGN COUNTRIES.	*Dollars.*		FOREIGN COUNTRIES—cont'd.	*Dollars.*	
Netherlands	56,427	79.28	Other	1,591	2.23
France	13,159	18.49			
			Total	71,177	100.00

GRAPES. (a)

Countries from which imported.	Annual average, 1896–1900.	Calendar years.					Per ct. in 1900.
		1896.	1897.	1898.	1899.	1900.	
FOREIGN COUNTRIES.	*Dollars.*	*Dollars.*	*Dollars.*	*Dollars.*	*Dollars.*	*Dollars.*	
Spain	1,741,174	1,362,090	1,579,924	1,825,599	1,938,755	1,999,499	69.05
Portugal	232,002	154,156	188,144	296,253	298,506	222,949	7.70
Belgium	114,092	75,557	124,908	120,811	132,189	116,996	4.04
France	34,780	21,213	30,742	79,922	26,484	15,539	.54
Italy	2,906	1,241	9,854	....	939	2,496	.08
Netherlands	1,550	6,112	696	477	268	199	.01
Other c	5,311	2,657	6,701	6,210	6,385	4,604	.16
Total foreign countries	2,131,815	1,623,026	1,940,969	2,329,272	2,403,526	2,362,282	81.58
BRITISH POSSESSIONS.							
Channel Islands	444,374	499,220	433,444	335,672	445,937	507,596	17.53
Cape of Good Hope	14,165	16,843	14,264	5,879	11,130	22,712	.79
Canada	3,538	....	14,196	1,139	837	1,518	.05
Other d	5,622	15,933	6,127	2,243	2,345	1,460	.05
Total British possessions	467,699	531,996	468,031	344,933	460,249	533,286	18.42
Total	2,599,514	2,155,022	2,409,000	2,674,205	2,863,775	2,895,568	100.00

a For quantities, see page 186.
b Prior to 1900 included in " Fresh fruits not elsewhere specified."
c Including in 1900 imports from the United States valued at $209.
d Including in 1896 imports from the British West Indies valued at $13,032.

lue of the agricultural imports of the United Kingdom (vegetable matter), etc.—Cont'd.

LEMONS, LIMES, AND CITRONS. (a)

ntries from which imported.	Annual average, 1896–1900.	Calendar years.					Per ct. in 1900.
		1896.	1897.	1898.	1899.	1900.	
OREIGN COUNTRIES.	Dollars.	Dollars.	Dc.lars.	Dollars.	Dollars.	Dollars.	
ily..................	1,807,826	1,882,961	1,695,912	1,840,189	1,903,911	1,716,157	83.79
ain..................	251,866	238,658	243,943	245,301	259,667	271,760	13.27
rmany..............	14,487	8,798	9,719	19,549	13,592	20,775	1.01
ortugal..............	14,549	14,789	13,889	15,514	16,313	12,239	.60
ance	3,390	905	....	4,862	19	11,164	.54
urkey, Asiatic	6,413	2,404	10,492	1,557	8,434	9,178	.45
iited States.........	4,845	229	18,653	4,866	321	156	.01
her.................	2,507	1,864	462	3,061	2,657	4,492	.22
Total foreign countries.....	2,105,883	2,150,608	1,993,070	2,134,899	2,204,914	2,045,921	99.89
RITISH POSSESSIONS.							
otal British possessions...............	3,998	11,237	2,925	2,881	769	2,180	.11
Total	2,109,881	2,161,845	1,995,995	2,137,780	2,205,683	2,048,101	100.00

	Annual average, 1896–1900.	1896.	1897.	1898.	1899.	1900.	Per ct. in 1900.
OREIGN COUNTRIES.	Dollars.	Dollars.	Dollars.	Dollars.	Dollars.	Dollars.	
pain.................	8,753,108	7,966,212	9,668,718	8,023,749	9,338,984	8,767,876	84.95
urkey, Asiatic.......	458,416	351,541	479,039	479,735	418,947	562,820	5.45
aly..................	367,935	345,006	319,680	390,692	393,106	391,189	3.79
ortugal..............	188,667	218,301	119,190	203,941	134,520	267,385	2.59
gypt	133,636	179,253	149,148	112,017	117,862	109,900	1.07
rance	85,054	111,073	67,674	106,241	63,123	77,158	.75
anary Islands.......	27,905	23,578	37,949	28,639	21,617	27,744	.27
ermany..............	21,575	749	17,417	15,222	49,074	25,413	.25
Jnited States.........	34,411	56,174	40,893	50,787	10,079	14,123	.14
zores	54,890	49,011	75,893	120,874	23,276	5,397	.05
razil	8,626	4,643	14,741	16,692	6,200	852	.01
ther.................	2,520	1,747	760	1,533	5,115	3,445	.03
Total foreign countries	10,136,743	9,307,288	10,991,102	9,550,122	10,581,903	10,253,302	99.35
BRITISH POSSESSIONS.							
ritish West Indies...	30,673	38,621	15,427	24,289	23,846	51,181	.49
Malta and Gozo.......	10,707	16,347	8,983	10,633	9,222	8,351	.08
Australasia:							
South Australia ..	3,641	462	7,957	555	3,431	5,801	
New South Wales.	13,470	5,752	7,582	51,960	784	1,275	
West Australia ...	11	24	....	....	....	29	
Tasmania	3,310	24	....	16,351	175	....	.07
Victoria	2,852	63	199	13,952	44	....	
New Zealand	8	....	39	....	....	....	
Queensland	2	....	10	....	....	....	
ther.................	1,023	1,451	667	1,679	432	886	.01
Total British possessions ...	65,697	62,744	40,864	119,419	37,934	67,523	.65
Total	10,202,440	9,370,032	11,031,966	9,669,541	10,619,837	10,320,825	100.00

a For quantities, see page 187.

Value of the agricultural imports of the United Kingdom (vegetable matter), etc.—Cont'd.

PEARS, FRESH. (a)

Countries from which imported.	Annual average, 1896–1900.	Calendar years.					Per ct. in 1900.
		1896.	1897.	1898.	1899.	1900.	
FOREIGN COUNTRIES.							
	Dollars.	*Dollars.*	*Dollars.*	*Dollars.*	*Dollars.*	*Dollars.*	
France	771,165	609,773	647,425	713,395	729,357	1,155,877	64.74
Belgium.............	291,963	182,479	680,142	111,039	164,429	321,724	18.02
United States.........	182,964	112,499	251,958	134,919	218,880	196,563	11.01
Netherlands.........	84,103	68,939	206,013	34,163	68,613	42,786	2.40
Germany.............	22,443	3,158	33,710	14,818	43,920	16,609	.93
Other.................	6,044	4,599	3,061	3,825	15,539	3,197	.18
Total foreign countries.....	1,358,682	981,447	1,822,309	1,012,159	1,240,738	1,736,756	97 28
BRITISH POSSESSIONS.							
Channel Islands......	25,640	22,211	9,631	27,150	30,717	38,489	2.16
Canada...............	14,439	19	5,358	39,322	18,566	8,930	.50
Other.................	2,367	2,102	1,752	657	6,176	1,149	.06
Total British possessions ...	42,446	24,332	16,741	67,129	55,459	48,568	2.72
Total	1,401,128	1,005,779	1,839,050	1,079,288	1,296,197	1,785,324	100.00

PLUMS, FRESH. (a)

FOREIGN COUNTRIES.							
	Dollars. (b)	*Dollars.* (c)	*Dollars.* (c)	*Dollars.* (c)	*Dollars.* (c)	*Dollars.*	
France	1,475,061	731,089	1,585,880	1,487,835	1,030,219	1,475,061	77.18
Germany.............	159,903	200,159	460,488	404,455	300,813	159,903	8.37
Belgium.............	142,900	117,434	142,078	91,149	6,818	142,900	7.48
Netherlands.........	96,522	100,406	208,461	103,316	43,618	96,522	5.05
United States.........	28,489	15,388	16,838	10,565	28,318	28,489	1.49
Other.................	180	219	2,974	1,543	380	180	.01
Total foreign countries.....	1,903,055	1,164,695	2,416,719	2,098,863	1,410,166	1,903,055	99.58
BRITISH POSSESSIONS.							
Cape of Good Hope...	7,217	11,937	4,949	10,098	7,723	7,217	.38
Other.................	783	....	793	6,341	13,115	783	.04
Total British possessions ...	8,000	11,937	5,742	16,439	20,838	8,000	.42
Total	1,911,055	1,176,632	2,422,461	2,115,302	1,431,004	1,911,055	100.00

STRAWBERRIES.(a) (d)

Countries from which imported.	Calendar year 1900.	Per cent.	Countries from which imported.	Calendar year 1900.	Per cent.
FOREIGN COUNTRIES.			BRITISH POSSESSIONS.		
	Dollars.			*Dollars.*	
France	377,879	90.34	Total British possessions	136	0.03
Netherlands................	40,251	9.63	Total	418,271	100.00
Other.....................	5				
Total foreign countries	418,135	99.97			

a For quantities, see page 188.
b Statistics for 1900 only.
c Including fresh apricots and peaches.
d Prior to 1900 included in "Fresh fruits not elsewhere specified."

'alue of the agricultural imports of the United Kingdom (vegetable matter), etc.—Cont'd.

FRESH FRUITS NOT ELSEWHERE SPECIFIED. (a)

	Annual average, 1896–1900.	Calendar years.					Per ct. in 1900.
		1896.	1897.	1898.	1899.	1900.	
FOREIGN COUNTRIES.							
	Dollars. (b)	Dollars. (c)	Dollars. (c)	Dollars. (c)	Dollars. (c)	Dollars.	
pain..................	582,077	461,490	545,476	697,769	633,881	582,077	41.28
zores................	405,837	299,051	254,017	334,314	388,123	405,837	28.78
ermany	181,934	251,072	195,176	233,120	195,857	181,934	12.90
etherlands..........	83,266	231,066	244,362	347,979	306,512	83,266	5.91
rance	22,960	331,175	474,970	567,818	554,328	22,960	1.63
ortugal.............	18,595	22,581	13,139	33,530	19,286	18,595	1.32
adeira Islands......	18,108	106,421	120,636	146,089	175,306	18,108	1.28
nited States........	7,699	20,610	41,837	10,244	13,378.	7,699	.55
aly.................	3,105	5,363	1,212	7,714	4,735	3,105	.22
anary Islands.......	3,012	1,060,863	1,266,784	1,696,087	2,051,385	3,012	.21
elgium..............	540	13,032	49,726	23,651	14,006	540	.04
Other................	6,239	2,054	3,543	1,742	3,971	6,239	.44
Total foreign countries.....	1,333,372	2,804,778	3,210,878	4,100,007	4,360,768	1,333,372	94.56
BRITISH POSSESSIONS.							
Channel Islands......	57,960	45,443	93,675	121,054	114,504	57,960	4.11
British West Indies...	10,453	16,235	61,488	8,818	18,322	10,453	.74
Malta and Gozo.......	569	438	2,861	219	....	569	.04
Canada...............	424	....	6,171	1,333	1,324	424	.03
Other d	7,290	8,069	7,918	5,884	5,733	7,290	.52
Total British possessions ...	76,696	70,185	172,113	137,308	139,883	76,696	5.44
Total	1,410,068	2,874,963	3,382,991	4,237,315	4,500,651	1,410,068	100.00

CURRANTS (DRIED).(a)

FOREIGN COUNTRIES.							
	Dollars.	Dollars.	Dollars.	Dollars.	Dollars.	Dollars.	
Greece...............	5,478,448	3,625,314	5,078,903	5,230,894	4,969,241	8,487,891	95.83
Netherlands..........	57,355	195	29,554	15,290	51,906	189,828	2.14
France	16,952	2,818	248	2,044	7,524	72,126	.82
Belgium.............	9,437	350	609	414	8,356	37,457	.42
Germany	7,546	1,426	20	....	107	36,178	.41
Turkey, Asiatic.......	10,901	7,932	23,612	10,322	1,363	11,276	.13
Russia...............	13,529	....	58,359	9,285	....	....	.....
Other e	5,653	813	2,341	2,978	2,584	19,549	.22
Total foreign countries.....	5,599,821	3,638,848	5,193,646	5,271,227	5,041,081	8,854,305	99.97
BRITISH POSSESSIONS.							
Total British possessions................	624	170	....	68	151	2,730	.03
Total	5,600,445	3,639,018	5,193,646	5,271,295	5,041,232	8,857,035	100.00

a For quantities, see page 189.
b Statistics for 1900 only.
c Including bananas, currants (fresh), gooseberries, and strawberries.
d Including imports from the Cape of Good Hope valued at $4,604 in 1896, $112 in 1898, and $4,117 in 1899, and from Natal, $63 in 1896.
e Including in 1900 imports from the United States valued at $6,774.

Value of the agricultural imports of the United Kingdom (vegetable matter), etc.—Cont'd.

FIGS AND FIG CAKE.(a)

Countries from which imported.	Annual average, 1896-1900.	Calendar years.					Per ct. in 1900.
		1896.	1897.	1898.	1899.	1900.	
FOREIGN COUNTRIES.							
	Dollars.	Dollars.	Dollars.	Dollars.	Dollars.	Dollars.	
Turkey, Asiatic.	865,838	871,814	967,251	391,301	886,009	1,212,815	91.
Portugal	57,668	33,462	36,499	89,943	64,505	63,931	4.86
Spain	48,714	19,841	18,697	121,010	55,916	28,104	2.13
Greece	8,229	6,940	341	16,784	10,361	6,721	.51
Italy	13,102	60,237	559	915	2,852	944	.07
France	4,926	5,003	1,192	13,719	3,995	720	.05
Belgium	2,469	832	501	7,129	3,660	224	.02
Other b	9,906	15,286	8,799	6,453	13,787	5,207	.40
Total foreign countries	1,010,852	1,013,415	1,033,839	647,254	1,041,085	1,318,666	99.99
BRITISH POSSESSIONS.							
Total British possessions	283	....	905	244	122	146	.01
Total	1,011,135	1,013,415	1,034,744	647,498	1,041,207	1,318,812	100.00

PRUNES.(a)

FOREIGN COUNTRIES.							
	Dollars.	Dollars.	Dollars.	Dollars.	Dollars.	Dollars.	
France	91,600	108,679	64,525	103,194	63,552	118,052	58.53
United States	61,122	27,554	58,958	58,349	91,140	69,610	34.51
Austria-Hungary	11,639	6,117	12,585	8,833	19,334	11,324	5.62
Germany	7,292	7,553	14,526	6,677	5,626	2,078	.03
Other	651	696	87	141	1,713	618	.31
Total	172,804	150,599	150,681	177,194	181,365	201,882	100.00

FRENCH PLUMS AND PRUNELLOES, DRIED.(a)

FOREIGN COUNTRIES.							
	Dollars.	Dollars.	Dollars.	Dollars.	Dollars.	Dollars.	
France	364,751	372,594	193,628	474,883	241,159	541,490	100.00
Other	1,645	1,981	365	....	5,874	5	
Total	366,396	374,575	193,993	474,883	247,033	541,495	100.00

PLUMS, DRIED OR PRESERVED, N. E. S., INCLUDING DRIED APRICOTS.(a)

FOREIGN COUNTRIES.							
	Dollars.	Dollars.	Dollars.	Dollars.	Dollars.	Dollars.	
United States	159,758	66,452	213,206	109,190	211,702	198,242	67.14
France	21,613	24,644	6,341	21,729	13,937	41,414	14.03
Germany	100,794	64,087	156,356	90,361	153,261	39,905	13.51
Austria-Hungary	44,827	36,051	65,898	51,341	60,340	10,507	3.56
Other	4,020	2,453	6,151	3,071	4,920	3,504	1.19
Total foreign countries	331,012	193,687	447,952	275,692	444,160	293,572	99.43
BRITISH POSSESSIONS.							
Australasia	3,295	297	277	11,670	2,560	1,669	.57
Total	334,307	193,984	448,229	287,362	446,720	295,241	100.00

a For quantities, see page 190.
b Including in 1900 imports from the United States valued at $2,691.

*'alue of the agricultural imports of the United Kingdom (vegetable matter), etc.—*Cont'd.

RAISINS.(a)

| om which ted. | Annual average, 1896–1900. | Calendar years. | | | | | Per ct. in 1900. |
		1896.	1897.	1898.	1899.	1900.	
FOREIGN COUNTRIES.							
	Dollars.	*Dollars.*	*Dollars.*	*Dollars.*	*Dollars.*	*Dollars.*	
pain................	2,454,538	2,106,241	2,275,332	1,934,526	2,191,098	3,765,493	58.71
urkey, Asiatic.......	2,330,873	1,962,947	2,452,911	2,162,069	2,778,874	2,297,562	35.83
reece...............	127,521	109,535	118,869	156,711	102,294	150,195	2.34
rance	19,790	44	2,010	9,378	16,867	70,652	1.10
ussia...............	12,538	....	594	7,475	12,702	41,920	.65
nited States	8,515	112	6,428	1,027	7,217	27,792	.43
ermany.............	8,740	5,538	8,453	6,307	4,419	18,984	.30
etherlands.........	9,425	44	35,540	2,020	102	9,417	.15
aly................	8,557	35,087	10	....	63	7,626	.12
ther...............	13,029	3,017	7,553	14,453	16,283	23,836	.37
Total foreign countries.....	4,993,526	4,222,565	4,907,700	4,293,966	5,129,919	6,413,477	100.00
BRITISH POSSESSIONS.							
otal British possessions................	55	170	29	....	34	44	......
Total	4,993,581	4,222,735	4,907,729	4,293,966	5,129,953	6,413,521	100.00

DRIED FRUITS NOT ELSEWHERE SPECIFIED.(a)

	Annual average, 1896–1900.	1896.	1897.	1898.	1899.	1900.	Per ct. in 1900.
FOREIGN COUNTRIES.							
	Dollars.	*Dollars.*	*Dollars.*	*Dollars.*	*Dollars.*	*Dollars.*	
Turkey, Asiatic	1,074,719	770,722	1,416,356	641,196	1,027,498	1,517,822	72.76
United States........	231,910	214,666	166,955	263,560	236,264	278,106	13.33
France	89,916	73,270	74,683	74,394	113,326	113,954.	5.46
Egypt	48,401	9,504	64,277	40,650	68,219	59,352	2.85
Persia	28,773	32,649	70,846	12,288	14,064	14,020	.67
Morocco.............	10,415	15,373	15,626	10,721	2,331	8,025	.39
Italy	6,909	8,877	9,042	6,297	3,353	6,974	.33
Germany............	3,046	229	637	6,881	4,414	3,071	.15
Belgium.............	3,509	25	263	13,714	3,494	49	} .38
Other b	4,878	1,908	2,380	7,932	4,268	7,903	
Total foreign countries.....	1,502,476	1,127,223	1,821,015	1,077,633	1,477,231	2,009,276	96.32
BRITISH POSSESSIONS.							
British East Indies:							
Bombay	47,220	34,372	74,876	45,818	42,991	38,046	
Madras	81	....	....	....	....	404	} 1.85
Bengal	616	....	2,803	97	34	146	
Ceylon	5	24	....	....	....	....	
Gibraltar.............	39,710	33,272	43,944	52,758	47,896	20,678	.99
Canada..............	8,341	10,113	9,991	6,862	4,302	10,439	.50
Malta and Gozo	2,652	764	5,947	2,029	3,776.	744	.03
Other...............	5,724	253	920	2,516	18,517	6,414	.31
Total British possessions ...	104,349	78,798	138,481	110,080	117,516	76,871	3.68
Total	1,606,825	1,206,021	1,959,496	1,187,713	1,594,747	2,086,147	100.00

a For quantities, see page 191.
b Including imports from China valued at $292 in 1896, $861 in 1897, and $3,913 in 1898.

Value of the agricultural imports of the United Kingdom (vegetable matter), etc.—Cont'd.

FRUITS, OTHER THAN PLUMS, PRESERVED WITHOUT SUGAR.(*a*)

Countries from which imported.	Annual average, 1896–1900.	Calendar years.					Per ct. in 1900.
		1896.	1897.	1898.	1899.	1900.	
FOREIGN COUNTRIES.							
	Dollars.	*Dollars.*	*Dollars.*	*Dollars.*	*Dollars.*	*Dollars.*	
United States	1,279,375	878,661	766,026	936,246	1,441,277	2,374,662	52.14
Spain................	549,049	603,339	566,037	665,328	407,219	503,323	11.05
Italy	425,205	373,903	416,212	469,812	439,158	426,938	9.38
France	222,439	200,646	207,128	199,293	169,773	335,355	7.37
Portugal.............	26,489	19,130	21,632	24,727	36,353	30,005	.67
Greece................	50,914	46,295	95,237	50,485	43,901	18,649	.41
Belgium.............	11,294	2,954	21,267	3,562	10,487	18,201	.40
Turkey, Asiatic	8,478	453	11,699	22,892	107	7,241	.16
Russia..............	10,382	5,295	8,229	7,383	25,865	5,129	.11
Madeira Islands......	3,875	5,606	5,017	4,273	822	3,655.	.08
Austria-Hungary.....	5,874	745	11,451	8,536	5,300	3,338	.07
Sweden	2,951	2,355	2,316	4,482	2,900	2,701	.06
Other *b*	15,190	8,127	10,478	18,488	11,967	26,892	.59
Total foreign countries	2,611,515	2,147,509	2,142,729	2,415,507	2,595,129	3,756,699	82.49
BRITISH POSSESSIONS.							
British East Indies:							
Straits Settlements	569,641	377,086	368,832	486,285	948,369	667,635	
Bombay	1,376	19	....	....	....	6,862	}14.81
Ceylon..........	722	....	3,611	....	....	....	
Bengal	23	....	117	....	....	....	
Canada..............	77,448	43,920	60,311	141,615	57,328	84,064	1.85
Australasia *c*.........	17,400	10,327	2,058	7,713	29,335	37,565	.82
Other................	2,636	2,608	4,380	3,660	1,197	1,333	.03
Total British possessions ...	669,246	433,960	439,309	639,273	1,036,229	797,459	17.51
Total	3,280,761	2,581,469	2,582,038	3,054,780	3,631,358	4,554,158	100.00

ALMONDS. (*a*)

FOREIGN COUNTRIES.							
	Dollars.	*Dollars.*	*Dollars.*	*Dollars.*	*Dollars.*	*Dollars.*	
Spain................	1,241,297	1,218,367	1,229,770	1,340,283	1,365,628	1,052,439	37
Morocco.............	374,204	121,190	173,213	417,171	338,382	821,066	29
Italy	323,144	368,579	333,939	339,828	332,513	240.862	8
Portugal.............	188,918	144,589	171,992	260,913	130,437	236,658	8
France	172,285	164,137	120,397	179,696	230.916	166,279	6
Canary Islands.......	70,544	27,588	57,590	87,071	45,988	134,481	4
Persia	10,910	4,492	....	944	1,990	47,122	1.
Turkey, Asiatic.......	4,581	253	3,796	1,679	292	16,887	.
Germany.............	17,229	11,451	15,699	21,140	25,559	12,298	.95
Austria-Hungary.....	4,963	735	1,178	18,828	3,032	1,041	.04
Turkey, European....	4,101	20,503	....	....	....	....	......
Other................	2,998	170	10,560	2,107	1,703	448	.02
Total foreign countries.....	2,415,174	2,082,054	2,118,134	2,669,660	2,476,440	2,729,581	98.42
BRITISH POSSESSIONS.							
Gibraltar.............	15,642	5,163	5,743	16,059	25,053	26,191	.95
Other................	5,585	2,789	....	7,553	....	17,583	.63
Total British possessions ...	21,227	7,952	5,743	23.612	25,053	43,774	1.58
Total	2,436,401	2,090,006	2,123,877	2,693,272	2,501,493	2,773,355	100.00

a For quantities, see page 192.
b Including imports from the Canary Islands valued at $1,742 in 1896, $1,718 in 1897, and $599 in 1898.
c Including imports from Victoria valued at $4,210 in 1896, $1,460 in 1897, $5,071 in 1898, $10,512 in 1899, and $20,600 in 1900, and from Tasmania $5,971 in 1896, $506 in 1898, and $983 in 1900.

Value of the agricultural imports of the United Kingdom (vegetable matter), etc.—Cont'd.

NUTS FOR FOOD, OTHER THAN ALMONDS. (a)

Countries from which imported.	Annual average, 1896–1900.	Calendar years.					Per ct. in 1900.
		1896.	1897.	1898.	1899.	1900.	
FOREIGN COUNTRIES.							
	Dollars.	*Dollars.*	*Dollars.*	*Dollars.*	*Dollars.*	*Dollars.*	
France	994,097	937,200	800,622	896,867	1,037,294	1,298,504	44.31
Spain	700,334	771,890	624,766	727,255	727,182	650,578	22.20
Brazil	373,128	401,584	351,634	378,891	507,668	225,864	7.71
Italy	101,663	56,860	74,540	145,873	97,481	133,561	4.56
Persia	9,219	278	380		487	44,952	1.53
Turkey, Asiatic	34,940	26,620	25,169	61,805	22,975	38,129	1.30
Netherlands	26,713	28,216	40,455	16,215	18,191	30,489	1.04
Germany	9,075	3,562	6,497	9,027	3,445	22,843	.78
United States	32,184	24,931	51,478	32,708	32,041	19,763	.67
Turkey, European	13,002	1,484	4,312	37,248	7,207	14,760	.50
Belgium	41,352	88,011	45,195	38,406	25,262	9,884	.34
Chile	15,001		4,205	56,880	8,721	5,197	.18
Egypt	4,567	16,546	973	1,995	58	3,261	.11
Other	15,149	11,514	12,351	14,278	29,214	8,390	.29
Total foreign countries	2,370,424	2,368,696	2,042,577	2,417,448	2,517,226	2,506,175	85.52
BRITISH POSSESSIONS.							
British East Indies:							
Ceylon	248,262	257,073	235,597	195,200	246,649	306,794	⎫
Bombay	1,322	2,224	949	2,073	657	705	
Bengal	3,242	4,331	5,275	5,465	555	584	
Straits Settlements	2,229	4,098	5,100	1,947			⎬10.51
Madras	1,546	6,039		472	1,217		
Burma	1,281	477	2,419	2,453	1,056		⎭
British West Indies	149,996	186,586	131,454	172,323	144,272	115,346	3.93
British Honduras	3,101	3,397	11,261	384	384	78	⎫ .04
Other	2,435	1,397	5,217	3,261	1,329	973	⎭
Total British possessions	413,414	465,622	397,272	383,578	396,119	424,480	14.48
Total	2,783,838	2,834,318	2,439,849	2,801,026	2,913,345	2,930,655	100.00

OIL NUTS. (a)

	Annual average, 1896–1900.	1896.	1897.	1898.	1899.	1900.	Per ct. in 1900.
FOREIGN COUNTRIES.							
	Dollars.	*Dollars.*	*Dollars.*	*Dollars.*	*Dollars.*	*Dollars.*	
Pacific islands	321,289	400,138	326,717	86,405	440,988	352,198	10.13
Philippine Islands b	204,818	283,678	222,404	73,095	124,397	320,517	9.21
German West Africa	33,250	939	195	22,362	905	141,849	4.08
Portuguese West Africa	25,777		214	6,725	7,563	114,382	3.29
French West Africa	50,326	11,378	34,664	64,004	41,307	100,279	2.88
France	34,435	28,318	2,920	33,676	42,363	64,900	1.87
Liberia	c 16,300	(d)	12,249	10,132	7,421	35,399	1.02
West Africa, n. e. s	c 9,566	1,956	2,341	1,547	7,280	27,097	.78
Argentina	6,035		12,010			18,167	.52
Spain	18,198	13,529	24,756	15,947	20,157	16,600	.48
Germany	20,384	21,495	19,043	22,469	27,194	11,718	.34
United States	12,402	5,562	12,974	14,298	21,789	7,436	.21
Netherlands	3,533	44	6,132	1,776	4,901	4,813	.14
Turkey, Asiatic	5,168	9,456	8,847	2,954	1,990	2,594	.07
Japan	8,802	22,843	17,276		3,650	243	⎫ .01
Java	1,794		8,896			73	⎭
German New Guinea	9,835	49,176					
China	6,025	3,407	243	5,694	20,780		
Other e	15,550	3,329	6,351	8,215	18,687	41,166	1.18
Total foreign countries	798,706	855,248	718,232	369,299	791,322	1,259,431	36.21

a For quantities, see page 193.
b Including the Ladrone Islands.
c Annual average, 1897–1900.
d Included in "West Africa, n. e. s."
e Including imports from Portugal valued at $1,650 in 1896, $988 in 1897, $248 in 1898, and $19 in 1899; from the Kongo Free State, $73 in 1896, $68 in 1897, and $910 in 1898; from Belgium, $141 in 1898 and $764 in 1899; and from Portuguese East Africa, $399 in 1896.

Value of the agricultural imports of the United Kingdom (vegetable matter), etc.—Cont'd.

OIL NUTS—Continued.

Countries from which imported.	Annual average, 1896–1900.	Calendar years.					Per ct. in 1900.
		1896.	1897.	1898.	1899.	1900.	
BRITISH POSSESSIONS.							
	Dollars.	*Dollars.*	*Dollars.*	*Dollars.*	*Dollars.*	*Dollars.*	
Niger Protectorate ...	302,130	127,405	239,004	354,729	207,089	582,423	16.75
British East Indies:							
Madras..........	100,624	32,790	38,650	180,343	41,239	210,101	
Ceylon	154,780	63,187	67,143	280,345	154,331	208,895	
Bengal	4,411	10,200	58	3,893	....	7,903	}12.56
StraitsSettlements	43,636	29,822	38,450	72,005	72,156	5,747	
Bombay	7,794	3,772	10,015	15,806	5,008	4,370	
Australasia:							
New South Wales.	443,845	558,859	439,319	482,548	409,146	329,355	
Fiji Islands.......	31,551	....	43,799	....	28,664	85,290	
New Zealand.....	49,005	123,040	70,525	18,931	18,502	14,025	}12.36
Queensland	3,222	1,168	1,241	11,811	574	1,314	
Victoria	19	....	....	....	....	98	
Sierra Leone	288,086	252,323	234,098	229,966	370,433	353,361	10.16
Lagos................	849,629	1,115,120	912,654	838,639	1,116,103	265,628	7.64
Gold Coast	26,389	14,780	8,015	16,809	26,590	65,751	1.89
Gambia..............	48,125	37,783	53,444	59,975	57,804	31,618	.91
Hongkong...........	7,638	9,212	141	....	....	28,839	.83
Other *a*	9,186	248	209	6,034	15,490	23,948	.69
Total British possessions ...	2,370,020	2,379,709	2,156,765	2,571,834	2,523,129	2,218,661	63.79
Total	3,168,726	3,234,957	2,874,997	2,941,133	3,314,451	3,478,092	100.00

NUTS NOT ELSEWHERE SPECIFIED.

FOREIGN COUNTRIES.							
	Dollars.	*Dollars.*	*Dollars.*	*Dollars.*	*Dollars.*	*Dollars.*	
Italy.................	7,413	6,507	4,730	6,526	12,585	6,716	1.40
Spain ,...............	2,308	1,372	1,698	1,212	1,046	6,214	1.30
France	9,888	10,225	4,808	16,892	12,083	5,431	1.14
Germany.............	3,926	4,102	14,828	574	....	127	.03
United States........	4,000	2,287	6,945	8,366	2,365	34	} .01
West Africa, n. e. s	296	1,475	....	....	....	5	
Belgium.............	969	....	886	350	3,611	....	
Other *b*..............	4,844	7,392	4,847	5,854	3,441	2,686	.56
Total foreign countries	33,644	33,360	38,742	39,774	35,131	21,213	4.44
BRITISH POSSESSIONS.							
British East Indies:							
Ceylon	504,168	527,723	504,860	520,044	515,956	452,258	
Bombay	1,298	842	....	453	2,769	2,428	
Bengal	2,603	6,808	5,285	....	730	190	
Burma	2,583	2,920	6,278	3,577	15	122	}95.20
Madras	482	....	2,409	....	....	....	
Straits Settlements	84	....	....	418	....	....	
Sierra Leone........	6,732	14,619	10,132	4,185	3,572	1,153	.24
Gold Coast	5,830	14,843	7,061	6,964	229	54	.01
Other..............	2,480	6,983	1,543	2,458	905	511	.11
Total British possessions ...	526,260	574,738	537,568	538,099	524,176	456,716	95.56
Total	559,904	608,098	576,310	577,873	559,307	477,929	100.00

a Comprising in 1896 imports from the British West Indies valued at $248.
b Including imports from Asiatic Turkey valued at $521 in 1896, $146 in 1897, and $414 in 1898.

ilue of the agricultural imports of the United Kingdom (vegetable matter), etc.—Cont'd.

FRUITS AND VEGETABLES, PRESERVED IN SUGAR. (a)

| | Annual average, 1896-1900. | Calendar years. | | | | | Per ct. in 1900. |
		1896.	1897.	1898.	1899.	1900.	
)REIGN COUNTRIES.							
	Dollars.	*Dollars.*	*Dollars.*	*Dollars.*	*Dollars.*	*Dollars.*	
ince	450,875	435,026	438,379	418,042	442,793	520,136	46.73
ited States........	355,074	210,564	251,398	418,183	825,227	69,995	6.29
lgium.............	34,632	28,917	32,411	34,226	35,949	41,657	3.74
therlands..........	22,911	17,909	16,585	14,989	24,517	40,557	3.64
rtugal	36,678	24,235	24,615	47,249	53,931	33,360	3.00
ly	57,969	64,355	48,714	54,816	91,315	30,644	2.75
ina	23,486	4,248	32,708	15,417	43,789	21,267	1.91
ain...............	23,280	5,650	30,016	36,474	31,306	12,955	1.16
rmany	9,305	6,107	5,446	8,278	19,062	7,681	.69
pan	3,951	209	5,932	6,404	1,552	5,660	.51
her...............	6,231	2,360	6,205	9,787	5,621	7,183	.65
Total foreign countries.....	1,024,392	799,580	892,409	1,063,865	1,575,062	791,045	71.07
RITISH POSSESSIONS.							
ngkong............	240,623	261,978	289,829	209,094	200,388	241,826	21.73
itish East Indies:							
Straits Settlements	169,817	115,969	114,504	398,635	175,160	44,816	⎫
Bengal	5,796	5,407	3,324	3,309	9,597	7,343	
Bombay	1,047	555	419	175	497	3,591	⎬ 5.13
Madras...........	865	268	526	871	1,776	886	
Ceylon	1,078	540	642	3,154	608	443	⎭
nada..............	16,036	12,366	9,485	34,542	12,551	11,237	1.01
itish West Indies...	15,929	21,271	19,855	16,595	12,716	9,207	.83
istralasia..........	4,518	1,796	2,978	2,832	13,373	1,611	.14
her...............	1,520	1,484	720	2,672	1,684	1,037.	.09
Total British possessions ...	457,229	421,634	442,282	671,879	428,350	ʙ321,997	28.93
Total	1,481,621	1,221,214	1,334,691	1,735,744	2,003,412	1,113,042	100.00

GLUCOSE AND GRAPE SUGAR. (a)

	Annual average, 1896-1900.	1896.	1897.	1898.	1899.	1900.	Per ct. in 1900.
'OREIGN COUNTRIES.							
	Dollars.	*Dollars.*	*Dollars.*	*Dollars.*	*Dollars.*	*Dollars.*	
nited States........	3,038,878	2,843,895	2,608,040	3,205,379	3,149,638	3,387,439	93.36
ermany	105,951	141,425	102,654	99,145	97,646	88,882	2.45
etherlands;........	12,117	16,867	11,884	11,022	9,188	11,621	.32
rance	28,695	28,221	28,922	32,056	44,475	9,801	.27
elgium.............	3,916	78	15,801	452	2,623	628	.02
ther...............	866	....	1,217	....	3,115	....	
Total foreign countries.....	3,190,423	3,030,486	2,768,518	3,348,054	3,306,685	3,498,371	96.42
RITISH POSSESSIONS.							
anada	114,687	....	59,892	212,895	170,868	129,780	⎫ 3.58
ther b	124	185	....	....	233	204	⎭
Total British possessions ...	114,811	185	59,892	212,895	171,101	129,984	3.58
Total	3,305,234	3,030,671	2,828,410	3,560,949	3,477,786	3,628,355	100.00

a For quantities, see page 194.
b Comprising in 1896 imports from Victoria valued at $185.

Value of the agricultural imports of the United Kingdom (vegetable matter), etc.—Cont'd.

HAY. (a)

Countries from which imported.	Annual average, 1896–1900.	Calendar years.					Per ct. in 1900.
		1896.	1897.	1898.	1899.	1900.	
FOREIGN COUNTRIES.	Dollars.	Dollars.	Dollars.	Dollars.	Dollars.	Dollars.	
United States.........	562,113	99,651	471,832	731,396	684,629	823,056	42.54
Netherlands..........	526,773	633,794	563,837	418,865	532,424	484,942	25.06
France	325,770	325,199	356,296	421,950	307,986	217,416	11.24
Belgium	111,453	169,296	124,826	101,282	88,415	73,445	3.79
Germany	61,864	166,249	65,727	11,918	30,386	35,039	1.81
Algeria	66,202	90,916	99,612	49,745	59,780	30,956	1.60
Argentina	24,418	35,603	42,874	15,957	21,481	6,176	.32
Denmark	24,868	49,351	33,803	12,512	22,800	5,874	.30
Chile	20,320	15,052	56,466	16,098	12,507	1,479	.08
Norway...............	29,183	77,504	67,206	599	214	394	.02
Russia	1,884	9,154	219	....	....	49	.01
Other b	2,646	12,833	292	..........:.	15	92	
Total foreign countries.....	1,757,494	1,684,602	1,882,990	1,780,322	1,760,637	1,678,918	86.77
BRITISH POSSESSIONS.							
Canada...............	175,584	44,577	113,199	146,287	330,907	242,950	12.56
Other c	2,791	103	122	681	73	12,979	.67
Total British possessions ...	178,375	44,680	113,321	146,968	330,980	255,929	13.23
Total.	1,935,869	1,729,282	1,996,311	1,927,290	2,091,617	1,934,847	100.00

HOPS. (a)

FOREIGN COUNTRIES.	Dollars.	Dollars.	Dollars.	Dollars.	Dollars.	Dollars.	
United States.........	2,589,225	1,795,086	1,364,824	4,078,487	2,858,368	2,849,360	73.60
Belgium..............	551,917	482,718	559,049	505,537	552,241	660,039	17.05
Germany	218,082	241,972	249,209	160,843	208,121	230,268	5.95
Netherlands..........	219,273	302,570	307,237	161,991	237,466	87,101	2.25
France	41,108	42,592	54,840	34,425	49,049	24,634	.64
Russia	17,805	4,448	195	64,924	8,847	10,609	.27
Other................	156	....	....	779	....	....	
Total foreign countries.....	3,637,566	2,869,386	2,535,354	5,006,986	3,914,092	3,862,011	99.76
BRITISH POSSESSIONS.							
Canada...............	9,138	9,548	16,137	5,465	5,548	8,993	.23
Australasia..........	4,475	....	....	725	21,456	195	.01
Total British possessions ...	13,613	9,548	16,137	6,190	27,004	9,188	.24
Total	3,651,179	2,878,934	2,551,491	5,013,176	3,941,096	3,871,199	100.00

INDIGO. (d)

FOREIGN COUNTRIES.	Dollars.	Dollars.	Dollars.	Dollars.	Dollars.	Dollars.	
Netherlands..........	136,325	43,662	90,225	158,463	252,464	136,812	5.19
Salvador	217,811	310,322	261,020	233,237	171,739	112,737	4.27
France	22,333	25,676	18,940	12,989	2,900	51,162	1.94
Germany	25,071	12,298	33,180	6,954	51,604	21,320	.81
United States........	25,137	6,521	1,290	88,638	10,074	19,164	.73
Belgium	6,844	8,872	5,523	6,433	6,375	7,017	.27
Austria-Hungary	2,087	5,937	808	....	1,484	2,205	.08
Italy................	4,319	14,113	....	4,477	910	2,093	.08
Nicaragua	5,875	4,136	19,714	925	4,390	209	.01
Colombia	25,920	21,413	14,648	....	93,539	....	
Guatemala	9,200	....	2,020	43,979	....	....	
Ecuador..............	8,760	....	....	43,798	....	....	
Spain	1,591	2,433	....	....	5,524	....	
French India........	1,061	5,304	....	....	....	....	
Other e	13,556	3,407	4,832	2,813	8,327	48,402	1.83
Total foreign countries.....	505,890	464,094	452,200	602,706	609,330	401,121	15.21

a For quantities, see page 195.
b Comprising in 1897 imports from Asiatic Turkey valued at $292.
c Comprising in 1896 imports from Malta and Gozo valued at $105.
d For quantities, see page 196.
e Including imports from the Philippine Islands valued at $1,071 in 1896 and $876 in 1897, and from Egypt, $852 in 1896 and $594 in 1897.

*?alue of the agricultural imports of the United Kingdom (vegetable matter), etc.—*Cont'd.

INDIGO—Continued.

es from which nported.	Annual average, 1896–1900.	Calendar years.					Per ct. in 1900.
		1896.	1897.	1898.	1899.	1900.	
;RITISH POSSESSIONS.							
rjtish East Indies:	*Dollars.*	*Dollars.*	*Dollars.*	*Dollars.*	*Dollars.*	*Dollars.*	
Bengal	3,718,368	4,589,329	5,660,503	3,000,407	3,509,744	1,831,858	
Madras	893,643	2,026,415	906,240	711,551	540,829	283,177	
Bombay	143,097	364,559	113,029	19,529	110,679	107,686	} 84.44
Straits Settlements	2,530	....	....	....	7,786	4,866	
Ceylon	8,117	19,369	20,561	657	....		
ther *a*	6,831	92	4,015	243	20,439	9,368	.35
Total British possessions ...	4,772,586	6,999,764	6,704,348	3,732,387	4,189,477	2,236,955	84.79
Total	5,278,476	7,463,858	7,156,548	4,335,093	4,798,807	2,638,076	100.00

TITUTES. (*b*)

	Annual average, 1896–1900.	1896.	1897.	1898.	1899.	1900.	Per ct. in 1900.
?OREIGN COUNTRIES.	*Dollars.*	*Dollars.*	*Dollars.*	*Dollars.*	*Dollars.*	*Dollars.*	
nited States........	340,612	223,786	161,130	428,841	424,797	464,507	96.78
ther................	2,804	331	243	4,136	9,310	....	......
Total foreign countries.....	343,416	224,117	161,373	432,977	434,107	464,507	96.78
BRITISH POSSESSIONS.							
Canada..............	5,268	7,217	....	127	3,859	15,135	3.15
Other...............	108	....	....	136	68	336	.07
Total British possessions ...	5,376	7,217	....	263	3,927	15,471	3.22
Total	348,792	231,334	161,373	433,240	438,034	479,978	100.00

MADDER, MADDER ROOT, GARANCIN, AND MUNJEET. (*b*)

	Annual average, 1896–1900.	1896.	1897.	1898.	1899.	1900.	Per ct. in 1900.
FOREIGN COUNTRIES.	*Dollars.c*	*Dollars.*	*Dollars.*	*Dollars.*	*Dollars.*	*Dollars.*	
Netherlands....:......	19,864	27,826	20,099	17,865	13,665		*e*86.29
France	2,479	4,351	1,742	2,078	1,747	} (*d*)	*e*11.03
Turkey, Asiatic	1,752	4,020	1,825	876	287		*e*1.81
Other	526	1,197	233	535	137		*e*.87
Total..........	24,621	37,394	23,899	21,354	15,836	(*d*)	*e*100.00

MALT. (*f*)

	Annual average, 1896–1900.	1896.	1897.	1898.	1899.	1900.	Per ct. in 1900.
FOREIGN COUNTRIES.	*Dollars,*	*Dollars.*	*Dollars.*	*Dollars.*	*Dollars.*	*Dollars.*	
Germany	3,217	2,385	2,156	1,946	584	9,013	90.61
United States........	8,343	26,707	8,263	2,409	3,655	681	6.85
Other *g*	790	443	....	2,628	628	253	2.54
Total foreign countries	12,350	29,535	10,419	6,983	4,867	9,947	100.00
BRITISH POSSESSIONS.							
Total British possessions..............	116	....	....	....	579	....	......
Total	12,466	29,535	10,419	6,983	5,446	9,947	100.00

a Comprising in 1896 imports from the Niger Protectorate valued at $92.
b For quantities, see page 196.
c Annual average, 1896–1899.
d Not stated.
e Per cent in 1899.
f For quantities, see page 197.
g Including imports from Belgium valued at $219 in 1896 and $628 in 1899.

Value of the agricultural imports of the United Kingdom (vegetable matter), etc.—Cont'd.

MALT LIQUORS.(a)

Countries from which imported.	Annual average, 1896–1900.	Calendar years.					Per ct. in 1900.
		1896.	1897.	1898.	1899.	1900.	
FOREIGN COUNTRIES.							
	Dollars.	Dollars.	Dollars.	Dollars.	Dollars.	Dollars.	
Netherlands.........	314,353	278,943	289,878	286,350	320,449	396,148	52.84
Germany.............	220,137	213,055	212,671	205,512	229,947	239,500	31.94
Denmark............	38,693	21,894	25,214	35,993	51,531	58,831	7.85
Belgium.............	30,891	29,656	28,469	32,927	27,686	35,715	4.76
Other b	10,777	7,378	10,779	9,786	9,748	16,196	2.16
Total foreign countries.....	614,851	550,926	567,011	570,568	639,361	746,390	99.55
BRITISH POSSESSIONS.							
Channel Islands......	787	1,144	1,007	672	652	457	.06
Other................	1,536	725	555	608	2,857	2,935	.39
Total British possessions ...	2,323	1,869	1,562	1,280	3,509	3,392	.45
Total	617,174	552,795	568,573	571,848	642,870	749,782	100.00

NURSERY STOCK (PLANTS, SHRUBS, TREES, AND FLOWER ROOTS).

FOREIGN COUNTRIES.							
	Dollars.	Dollars.	Dollars.	Dollars.	Dollars.	Dollars.	
Netherlands....	1,063,699	989,797	1,039,791	1,079,356	1,037,562	1,171,990	54.03
Belgium.............	234,049	195,979	217,922	242,702	251,311	262,334	12.09
France	238,200	225,012	202,403	241,904	267,215	254,469	11.73
Germany............	203,892	192,056	204,490	213,586	232,302	177,024	8.16
Japan	88,288	58,885	92,240	88,312	103,457	98,547	4.54
United States........	79,245	92,084	89,217	65,187	75,455	74,282	3.42
Brazil	23,765	24,342	18,079	30,460	31,554	14,390	.66
Colombia............	37,229	48,159	43,837	50,733	35,725	7,689	.35
Mexico	5,880	8,838	10,726	1,552	5,558	2,725	.13
Azores..............	2,192	2,886	2,881	1,139	2,307	1,747	.08
Venezuela...........	2,269	3,275	2,779	613	3,445	1,231	.06
Other...............	14,617	13,874	16,760	14,843	13,587	14,020	.65
Total foreign countries.....	1,993,325	1,855,187	1,941,125	2,030,387	2,059,478	2,080,448	95.90
BRITISH POSSESSIONS.							
Channel Islands......	52,923	36,212	50,398	50,432	71,202	56,369	2.60
British East Indies c ..	22,543	35,360	23,291	23,676	14,706	15,680	.72
Canada..............	5,447	3,358	5,898	5,601	4,531	7,845	.36
British West Indies...	3,027	3,041	4,594	2,642	2,375	2,482	.12
Natal...............	3,116	1,212	5,752	2,501	3,703	2,414	.11
Hongkong...........	3,895	1,981	14,517	847	1,455	672	.03
Australasia..........	2,831	2,365	4,239	3,796	3,329	428	.02
Bermuda............	1,144	637	3,635	730	720	....	....
Other d	2,853	2,604	2,589	4,175	1,981	2,968	.14
Total British possessions ...	97,789	86,770	114,913	94,400	104,002	88,858	4.10
Total	2,091,114	1,941,957	2,056,038	2,124,787	2,163,480	2,169,306	100.00

a For quantities, see page 197.
b Including in 1900 imports from the United States valued at $2,657.
c Including imports from Burma valued at $15,149 in 1896, $10,628 in 1897, $14,449 in 1898, $8,064 in 1899, and $5,480 in 1900.
d Including imports from the Cape of Good Hope valued at $1,893 in 1896, $1,543 in 1897, $1,479 in 1898, and $1,148 in 1899.

lue of the agricultural imports of the United Kingdom (vegetable matter), etc.—Cont'd.

COTTON-SEED OIL CAKE.(a)

	Annual average, 1896–1900.	Calendar years.					Per ct. in 1900.
		1896.	1897.	1898.	1899.	1900.	
REIGN COUNTRIES.							
	Dollars.	Dollars.	Dollars.	Dollars.	Dollars.	Dollars.	
ted States.........	2,576,674	1,427,009	1,759,892	2,518,677	3,449,507	3,728,284	72.86
'pt	749,998	387,033	586,481	763,860	1,046,721	965,893	18.88
xico	101,679	8,356	73,129	115,088	79,387	232,434	4.54
nce	128,148	74,423	88,196	218,593	144,345	115,185	2.25
u.................	36,354	19,758	30,771	32,372	51,546	47,322	.92
lgium.............	5,808	1,557	10,589	3,518	6,750	6,628	.13
zil ....·..........	5,372	13,787	219	6,614	156	6,083	} .12
rmany............	3,495	4,015	4,380	6,609	2,375	97	
ssia...............	177	....	886	....	....	....	
1er................	9,112	4,594	1,635	11,037	12,959	15,335	.30
Total foreign countries....	3,616,817	1,940,532	2,556,178	3,676,368	4,793,746	5,117,261	100 00
ITISH POSSESSIONS.							
itish East Indies:							
Burma	10,279	12,507	6,307	32,581	....	....	......
Bengal	193	....	....	....	963	....	......
Ceylon	14	....	68	....	....	....	......
nada.............	5,688	3,148	....	17,812	7,480	....	......
her b	2,097	6,935	341	....	3,212	....	......
Total British possessions ...	18,271	22,590	6,716	50,393	11,655	....	......
Total	3,635,088	1,963,122	2,562,894	3,726,761	4,805,401	5,117,261	100.00

	Annual average, 1896–1900.	1896.	1897.	1898.	1899.	1900.	Per ct. in 1900.
'OREIGN COUNTRIES.							
	Dollars.	Dollars.	Dollars.	Dollars.	Dollars.	Dollars.	
ermany	1,851,778	1,013,960	1,607,789	1,946,883	2,375,528	2,314,780	34.07
ussia................	2,276,000	1,482,258	2,018,590	2,888,774	3,006,509	1,983,868	29.20
nited States.........	1,911,668	2,611,403	1,959,462	1,602,524	1,566,901	1,818,047	26.76
)ain.................	87,573	78,141	89,325	86,366	108,494	75,538	1.11
rgentina	53,834	27,832	45,993	62,092	61,425	71,830	1.06
ustria-Hungary.....	36,546	....	63,201	28,737	39,779	51,015	.75
enmark.............	28,984	....	14,780	24,493	60,184	45,463	.67
rance	47,992	80,706	62,904	14,312	40,236	41,803	.62
elgium..............	20,154	11,144	13,943	33,905	18,556	23,174	.34
ruguay.............	5,466	8,151	3,412	1,455	3,611	10,701	.16
etherlands..........	3,822	2,205	6,404	1,504	1,178	7,820	.12
ortugal.............	9,781	9,207	11,358	14,687	6,910	6,745	.10
hile	6,089	6,667	5,757	12,254	4,925	842	.01
weden..............	4,489	16,434	....	6,010	....	....	......
orway	4,345	12,969	....	3,450	5,305	....	......
oumania............	3,373	12,483	4,380	....	....	....	......
aly	287	....	....	1,436	....	....	......
ther d	1,522	4,234	....	3,377	....	....	......
Total foreign countries.....	6,353,693	5,377,794	5,907,298	6,732,209	7,299,541	6,451,626	94.97
RITISH POSSESSIONS.							
ritish East Indies:							
Bengal	112,050	94,401	96,843	89,471	130,777	148,759	}
Bombay	91,618	81,791	103,944	132,821	103,379	36,153	
Straits Settlements	316	....	....	....	....	1,581	} 2.77
Madras	302	....	....	....	....	1,509	
anada..............	150,768	103,564	122,904	178,474	203,074	145,825	2.15
ther e	1,837	1,411	....	....	....	7,772	.11
Total British possessions ...	356,891	281,167	323,691	400,766	437,230	341,599	5.03
Total	6,710,584	5,658,961	6,230,989	7,132,975	7,736,771	6,793,225	100.00

a For quantities, see page 197.
b Including in 1896 imports from British Honduras valued at $6,570.
c For quantities, see page 198.
d Including in 1896 imports from Egypt valued at $730.
e Comprising in 1896 imports from New Zealand valued at $1,411.

Value of the agricultural imports of the United Kingdom (vegetable matter), etc.—Cont'd.

OIL CAKE NOT ELSEWHERE SPECIFIED.(a)

Countries from which imported.	Annual average, 1896–1900.	Calendar years.					Per ct. in 1900.
		1896.	1897.	1898.	1899.	1900.	
FOREIGN COUNTRIES.							
	Dollars.	*Dollars.*	*Dollars.*	*Dollars.*	*Dollars.*	*Dollars.*	
United States	54,798	17,281	16,181	57,8.4	26,479	156,234	32.07
Russia	50,261	5,017	17,918	45,570	104,527	78,273	16.07
France	41,014	23,486	26,216	42,699	59,045	53,624	11.01
Germany	13,270	10,448	6,560	1,942	17,315	30,085	6.18
Netherlands	9,640	8,195	5,801	12,103	5,884	16,215	3.33
Belgium	10,203	12,853	21,685	7,129	3,124	6,224	1.28
Other	7,613	4,696	68	6,176	9,037	18,089	3.71
Total foreign countries	186,799	81,976	94,429	173,433	225,411	358,744	73.65
BRITISH POSSESSIONS.							
British East Indies:							
Ceylon	34,449	14,312	19,291	44,529	34,655	59,459	} 25.38
Madras	29,140	9,641	16,999	27,106	53,196	38,757	
Burma	2,112			1,460		9,100	
Straits Settlements	2,187		642	1,460	243	8,589	
Bombay	3,679	2,716	886	1,718	7,154	5,922	
Bengal	5,716	3,153	1,995	5,051	16,585	1,796	
Australasia	3,310			214	12,093	4,244	.87
Canada	569		341	1,533	462	511	.10
Other b	118	29	243	34	282		
Total British possessions	81,280	29,851	40,397	83,105	124,670	128,378	26.35
Total	268,079	111,827	134,826	256,538	350,081	487,122	100.00

VEGETABLE OILS, ESSENTIAL OR PERFUMED. (c)

Countries from which imported.	Annual average, 1896–1900.	1896.	1897.	1898.	1899.	1900.	Per ct. in 1900.
FOREIGN COUNTRIES.							
	Dollars.	*Dollars.*	*Dollars.*	*Dollars.*	*Dollars.*	*Dollars.*	
Italy	375,964	323,948	362,330	368,302	429,503	395,739	33.04
Belgium	160,737	138,145	160,040	166,926	134,384	204,189	17.05
France	220,064	286,578	222,263	232,604	169,792	189,083	15.79
United States	150,689	208,656	204,412	160,488	114,494	65,396	5.46
Germany	56,428	67,070	86,478	48,548	33,389	46,655	3.89
Netherlands	24,709	38,095	28,484	15,709	23,087	18,172	1.52
Japan	13,209	17,004	24,147	9,655	6,039	9,198	.77
China	12,047	10,215	38,465	5,986	2,224	3,343	.28
Austria-Hungary	3,851	3,032	9,840	2,647	1,659	2,078	.17
Turkey, European	3,362	12,283	2,462	1,406	657		
Other	6,143	7,840	6,604	3,119	6,210	6,944	.58
Total foreign countries	1,027,203	1,112,866	1,145,525	1,015,390	921,438	940,797	78.55
BRITISH POSSESSIONS.							
British East Indies:							
Ceylon	195,818	300,215	184,640	198,680	141,591	153,961	} 14.96
Bombay	10,298	9,446	9,655	14,653	7,621	10,113	
Madras	38,182	31,627	37,662	90,084	22,254	9,285	
Straits Settlements	14,185	13,587	22,308	16,390	13,115	5,524	
Burma	44					219	
Bengal	5,307	26,508		29			
British West Indies	25,072	16,259	22,303	19,719	27,759	39,321	3.28
Hongkong	57,279	77,158	101,540	28,562	42,363	36,771	3.07
Other d	2,168	696	2,832	4,005	1,630	1,679	.14
Total British possessions	348,353	475,496	380,940	372,122	256,333	256,873	21.45
Total	1,375,556	1,588,362	1,526,465	1,387,512	1,177,771	1,197,670	100.00

a For quantities, see page 198.
b Comprising in 1896 imports from Hongkong valued at $29.
c For quantities, see page 199.
d Including imports from Australasia valued at $696 in 1896, $34 in 1897, and $297 in 1898.

Value of the agricultural imports of the United Kingdom (vegetable matter), etc.—Cont'd.

CASTOR OIL. (a)

Countries from which imported.	Annual average, 1896–1900.	Calendar years.					Per ct. in 1900.
		1896.	1897.	1898.	1899.	1900.	
FOREIGN COUNTRIES.							
	Dollars.	*Dollars.*	*Dollars.*	*Dollars.*	*Dollars.*	*Dollars.*	
France	340,816	456,327	345,239	369,878	388,512	144,126	37.56
Belgium..............	118,020	155,207	88,293	152,112	135,046	59,444	15.49
Italy	35,604	39,785	28,031	41,322	46,305	22,625	5.90
Netherlands..........	1,455	6,137	....	....	287	852	.22
Other b	2,514	3,392	900	2,677	1,382	4,219	1.10
Total foreign countries.....	498,409	660,798	462,463	565,989	571,532	231,266	60.27
BRITISH POSSESSIONS.							
British East Indies:							
Bengal	183,008	218,885	178,148	216,374	152,526	149,105	
Madras...........	34,359	52,816	35,939	45,969	33,734	3,338	
Bombay	3,843	2,205	2,823	9,149	5,037	....	39.73
Ceylon	285	....	1,426	....	....	....	
Total British possessions ...	221,495	273,906	218,336	271,492	191,297	152,443	39.73
Total	719,904	934,704	680,799	837,481	762,829	383,709	100.00

COCOANUT OIL. (c)

	Annual average, 1896–1900.	1896.	1897.	1898.	1899.	1900.	Per ct. in 1900.
FOREIGN COUNTRIES.							
	Dollars.	*Dollars.*	*Dollars.*	*Dollars.*	*Dollars.*	*Dollars.*	
Belgium..............	282,064	304,779	255,170	193,984	287,552	368,837	11.36
France ...:..........	111,883	114,426	145,056	52,972	157,227	89,733	2.76
Germany..............	2,814	5,343	6,375	1,187	1,134	29	
United States........	2,690	12,619	78	754	....	....	......
Other d	8,856	6,833	6,346	4,930	4,063	22,109	.68
Total foreign countries.....	408,307	444,000	413,025	253,827	449,976	480,708	14.80
BRITISH POSSESSIONS.							
British East Indies:							
Ceylon	908,032	572,130	514,009	679,247	1,052,858	1,721,914	
Madras...........	363,051	182,791	214,286	323,510	535,578	559,088	
Straits Settlements	3,275	4,190	....	....	5,596	6,589	70.51
Bengal	6,715	4,136	12,896	175	15,441	925	
Bombay	1,810	7,592	....	706	....	754	
Burma	316	....	1,582	....	....	....	
Australasia:							
New South Wales.	313,663	....	136,554	405,331	576,452	449,976	13.86
Victoria	104	....	521	....	....	....	
Mauritius...:........	11,628	....	....	11,680	19,466	26,994	.83
Other................	25	....	....	126	....	....	
Total British possessions ...	1,608,619	770,839	879,848	1,420,775	2,205,391	2,766,240	85.20
Total	2,016,926	1,214,839	1,292,873	1,674,602	2,655,367	3,246,948	100.00

a For quantities, see page 199.
b Including imports from the United States valued at $1,460 in 1900 and from Russia, $891 in 1898.
c For quantities, see page 200.
d Including imports from Russia valued at $4,088 in 1898, and from the Netherlands, $161 in 1896, $1,217 in 1897, and $1,504 in 1899.

Value of the agricultural imports of the United Kingdom (vegetable matter), etc.—Cont'd.

OLIVE OIL. (a)

Countries from which imported.	Annual average, 1896–1900.	Calendar years.					Per ct. in 1900.
		1896.	1897.	1898.	1899.	1900.	
FOREIGN COUNTRIES.							
	Dollars.	*Dollars.*	*Dollars.*	*Dollars.*	*Dollars.*	*Dollars.*	
Spain	909,870	973,388	37,151	1,678,232	699,044	1,161,536	51.77
Italy	1,066,188	1,389,113	1,446,124	831,106	1,052,215	612,381	27.29
France	225,748	247,092	144,919	189,974	280,782	265,974	11.85
Morocco	24,106	9,042	83	1,046	47,259	63,099	2.81
Greece	52,307	7,879	117,604	32,800	58,962	44,290	1.98
Portugal	17,916	4,501	7,183	29,316	8,633	39,949	1.78
Crete	b 107,190	(c)	(c)	(c)	190,047	24,333	1.09
Turkey, Asiatic	134,237	31,569	277,605	116,275	232,025	13,709	.61
Austria-Hungary	31,868	30,167	28,099	33,944	57,658	9,470	.42
Turkey, European	b 22,172	282,588	439,601	28,002	42,280	2,063	.09
Other d	18,021	6,750	9,879	18,668	22,790	7,017	.31
Total foreign countries	2,677,043	2,982,089	2,508,248	2,959,363	2,691,695	2,243,821	100.00
BRITISH POSSESSIONS.							
Total British possessions	407	472	584	63	871	44	......
Total	2,677,450	2,982,561	2,508,832	2,959,426	2,692,566	2,243,865	100.00

PALM OIL. (e)

	Annual average, 1896–1900.	1896.	1897.	1898.	1899.	1900.	Per ct. in 1900.
FOREIGN COUNTRIES.							
	Dollars.	*Dollars.*	*Dollars.*	*Dollars.*	*Dollars.*	*Dollars.*	
Germany	799,761	1,329,022	668,175	658,540	748,487	594,579	11.24
German West Africa	56,418	28,552	53,439	22,731	7,339	170,031	3.21
Portuguese West Africa	20,505	13,334	4,205	2,530	7,013	75,445	1.43
French West Africa	53,659	60,418	46,650	54,184	39,029	68,014	1.29
Liberia	f 27,109	(g)	15,938	15,553	10,731	66,214	1.25
West Africa, n. e. s.	f 14,022	32,659	10,589	8,891	10,804	25,802	.49
Kongo Free State	9,710	9,222	6,059	4,419	4,784	24,065	.45
Spanish West Africa	8,785	1,401	3,260	11,203	5,523	22,537	.43
Belgium	16,689	11,242	813	20,376	50,845	170	
France	1,821	6,039	2,453	263	277	73	} .18
Other h	5,597	6,618	4,448	6,073	1,674	9,174	
Total foreign countries	1,012,382	1,498,507	816,029	804,763	886,506	1,056,104	19.97
BRITISH POSSESSIONS.							
Niger Protectorate	1,212,719	802,140	803,907	730,690	741,158	2,985,700	56.47
Lagos	2,749,385	3,406,813	3,171,663	3,149,000	3,328,121	691,325	13.07
Gold Coast	152,462	77,212	45,750	43,638	72,190	523,518	9.90
Sierra Leone	36,585	77,664	35,730	18,824	19,758	30,951	} .59
Other	110	234	78	....	117	122	
Total British possessions	4,151,261	4,364,063	4,057,128	3,942,152	4,161,344	4,231,616	80.03
Total	5,163,643	5,862,570	4,873,157	4,746,915	5,047,850	5,287,720	100.00

a For quantities, see page 200.
b Annual average, 1899–1900.
c Included in European Turkey.
d Including in 1900 imports from the United States valued at $156.
e For quantities, see page 201.
f Annual average 1897–1900.
g Included in "West Africa, n. e. s."
h Including in 1900 imports from the United States valued at $2,015.

lue of the agricultural imports of the United Kingdom (vegetable matter), etc.—Cont'd.

SEED OIL (COTTON-SEED, LINSEED, ETC.). (a)

itries from which imported.	Annual average, 1896–1900.	Calendar years.					Per ct. in 1900.
		1896.	1897.	1898.	1899.	1900.	
.EIGN COUNTRIES.							
	Dollars.	*Dollars.*	*Dollars.*	*Dollars.*	*Dollars.*	*Dollars.*	
ed States........	1,180,298	778,664	737,547	1,179,377	1,793,660	1,412,243	27.94
ium.............	1,056,238	755,257	1,259,801	1,103,746	1,037,290	1,125,096	22.26
ierlands.........	441,145	283,201	228,662	229,183	400,941	1,063,739	21.05
nany............	507,701	785,224	277,415	295,431	419,132	761,301	15.06
ice	624,354	736,783	826,848	509,255	540,186	508,695	10.07
n	12,438	....	19,495	39	....	42,655	.84
il	6,880			97		34,304	.68
nark...........	14,210	12,556	2,745	5,908	27,467	22,376	.44
r^b..............	15,265	14,585	12,049	15,398	6,434	27,861	.55
Total foreign countries.....	3,858,529	3,366,270	3,364,562	3,338,434	4,225,110	4,998,270	98.89
TISH POSSESSIONS.							
ada..............	19,294	146	11,008	8,630	35,506	46,178	.92
ish East Indies ...	14,463	14,823	21,948	15,500	10,872	9,174	.18
er................	2,236	954	2,676	....	6,998	550	.01
Total ·British possessions ...	35,993	15,923	35,632	19,130	53,376	55,902	1.11
Total	3,894,522	3,382,193	3,400,194	3,357,564	4,278,486	5,054,172	100.00

	Annual average, 1896–1900.	Calendar years.					Per ct. in 1900.
		1896.	1897.	1898.	1899.	1900.	
REIGN COUNTRIES.							
	Dollars.	*Dollars.*	*Dollars.*	*Dollars.*	*Dollars.*	*Dollars.*	
ited States........	524,036	860,865	717,045	491,361	347,113	203,794	38.19
ina	19,778	316	3,202	3,801	14,478	77,095	14.45
ince	158,224	145,766	186,805	222,579	170,527	65,440	12.26
rmany	72,194	59,381	63,162	85,762	90,955	61,712	11.56
lgium............	76,035	82,969	81,621	76,019	99,929	39,638	7.43
therlands.........	63,365	119,492	70,900	52,325	51,828	22,279	4.17
)an	5,937	39	3,212	4,565	14,682	7,188	1.35
ssia..............	14,643	26,868	32,265	....	12,711	1,372	.26
ly................	21,557	13,018	12,244	14,040	67,177	1,304	.24
her...............	9,153	4,122	4,429	4,954	18,191	14,069	2.64
Total foreign countries.....	964,922	1,312,836	1,174,885	955,406	887,591	493,891	92.55
RITISH POSSESSIONS.							
itish East Indies ...	7,788	5,061	5,723	5,270	7,971	14,916	2.79
stralasia:							
New South Wales.	25,016	54,398	30,956	27,447	4,492	7,786	
Victoria	35,526	34,932	33,608	51,298	57,795	....	
Queensland	17,382	14,989	12,113	32,557	27,252	....	} 1.46
South Australia...	6,818	4,574	11,821	5,499	12,196	....	
New Zealand.....	6,758	9,728	9,694	11,821	2,545	....	
her c...............	7,585	2,681	4,112	8,531	5,519	17,082	3.20
Total British possessions ...	106,873	126,363	108,027	142,423	117,770	39,784	7.45
Total	1,071,795	1,439,199	1,282,912	1,097,829	1,005,361	533,675	100.00

For quantities, see page 201.
Including imports from Austria-Hungary valued at $414 in 1896, and from Spain $414 in 1897.
Including imports from the Niger Protectorate valued at $175 in 1896, $297 in 1897, and $321 in '8, and from the British West Indies $29 in 1896.

Value of the agricultural imports of the United Kingdom (vegetable matter), etc.—Cont'd.

OPIUM. (a)

Countries from which imported.	Annual average, 1896–1900.	Calendar years.					Per ct. in 1900.
		1896.	1897.	1898.	1899.	1900.	
FOREIGN COUNTRIES.							
	Dollars.	Dollars.	Dollars.	Dollars.	Dollars.	Dollars.	
Turkey, European	629,768	545,350	582,671	559,506	528,151	933,161	44.93
Turkey, Asiatic........	357,295	359,138	222,657	166,892	453,762	584,029	28.12
Persia	140,428	204,724	140,150	183,345	67,615	106,304	5.12
France	60,610	....	13,519	49,536	142,613	97,384	4.69
United States........	21,501	4,443	608	....	56,120	46,334	2.23
Netherlands..........	9,924	8,375	5,124	12,999	3,699	19,422	.93
Belgium..............	8,931	....	3,290	13,183	16,016	12,166	.59
China	143	715	....	....	....	....	....
Other b	9,020	3,621	4,643	10,191	8,940	17,704	.85
Total foreign countries	1,237,620	1,126,366	972,662	995,652	1,276,916	1,816,504	87.46
BRITISH POSSESSIONS.							
British East Indies:							
Bengal	90,727	12,006	2,175	28,279	161,913	249,262	} 12.12
Straits Settlements	496	....	....	....	....	2,477	
Bombay...........	25,711	25,603	31,267	53,531	18,152	....	
Hongkong...........	14,133	44,877	14,507	3,076	....	8,706	.42
Australasia: New South Wales........	1,314	6,229	341	....	....	....	......
Other................	25	....	127	....	....	....	......
Total British possessions ...	132,406	88,215	48,417	84,886	180,065	260,445	12.54
Total	1,370,026	1,214,581	1,021,079	1,080,538	1,456,981	2,076,949	100.00

RICE, RICE MEAL, AND RICE FLOUR. (a)

FOREIGN COUNTRIES.							
	Dollars.	Dollars.(c)	Dollars.(c)	Dollars.(c)	Dollars. (c)	Dollars.	
Netherlands..........	1,334,819	1,180,707	1,124,458	1,356,026	1,365,866	1,697,041	14.48
French Indo-China...	647,892	....	1,659,452	148,647	656,165	775,199	6.61
Germany.............	591,626	592,307	642,076	571,955	494,256	657,537	5.61
Turkey, Asiatic	53,514	18,313	19,077	....	95,393	134,788	1.15
Italy	30,618	14,103	13,738	44,558	19,748	60,943	.52
France	13,428	15,665	550	219	4,920	45,784	.39
Japan	426,006	469,408	607,841	16,167	999,000	37,613	.32
United States........	33,429	29,248	22,347	47,813	31,817	35,920	.31
Java.................	14,116	1,324	1,961	19,471	13,962	33,861	.29
Belgium..............	24,400	22,603	28,849	41,852	18,585	10,049	.09
Siam	130,807	2,628	633,292	....	9,247	8,867	.07
Denmark	9,139	31,369	3,110	7,567	3,635	15	} .51
Other	18,347	165	496	16,668	15,140	59,264	
Total foreign countries	3,328,141	2,327,900	4,757,247	2,270,943	3,727,734	3,556,881	30.35
BRITISH POSSESSIONS.							
British East Indies:							
Burma.............	4,898,922	4,209,055	3,686,194	5,696,681	5,307,916	5,594,767	} 69.29
Bengal	2,044,790	1,623,581	1,448,913	1,721,778	3,118,580	2,311,096	
Straits Settlements..........	144,075	49,561	401,676	41,740	18,181	209,216	
Bombay...........	4,148	161	764	7,319	8,117	4,380	
Madras...........	633	....	....	....	3,163	....	
Ceylon	3	....	....	....	15	....	
Natal................	2,819	....	....	14,093	....	....	......
Other d..............	12,311	5,859	574	7,796	4,949	42,528	.36
Total British possessions ...	7,107,731	5,888,217	5,538,121	7,489,407	8,460,921	8,161,987	69.65
Total	10,435,872	8,216,117	10,295,368	9,760,350	12,188,655	11,718,868	100.00

a For quantities, see page 202.
b Including imports from Egypt valued at $3,484 in 1896, $2,316 in 1897, $2,482 in 1898, and $3,898 in 1899.
c Exclusive of rice meal and rice flour, classed with "Breadstuffs not elsewhere specified, and preparations of," prior to 1900.
d Including in 1896 imports from Aden valued at $1,275.

`alue of the agricultural imports of the United Kingdom (vegetable matter), etc.—Cont'd.

SAFFLOWER. (a)

ountries from which imported.	Annual average, 1896–1900.	Calendar years.					Per ct. in 1900.
		1896.	1897.	1898.	1899.	1900.	
IR:TISH POSSESSIONS.	Dollars.	Dollars.	Dollars.	Dollars.	Dollars.	Dollars.	
ritish East Indies b..	c 3,611	9,261	4,297	584	302	(d)	e100.00

GARDEN SEEDS. (a)

FOREIGN COUNTRIES.	Dollars.	Dollars.	Dollars.	Dollars.	Dollars.	Dollars.	
rance	141,018	232,366	140,471	111,282	101,807	119,161	37.70
ermany..............	128,014	76,643	194,733	187,574	95,252	85,865	27.17
etherlands..........	42,862	49,740	36,416	36,363	46,178	45,614	14.43
:aly.................	16,919	13,850	13,247	15,738	18,571	23,189	7.34
nited States........	10,940	10,706	11,378	10,945	10,877	10,794	3.41
anary Islands	5,968	4,755	3,202	11,412	7,635	2,837	.90
elgium	2,570	4,344	1,041	925	3,694	2,248	.71
ther f................	4,954	3,494	5,918	3,737	5,494	6,127	1.94
Total foreign countries.....	353,245	396,498	406,406	377,976	289,508	295,835	93.60
BRITISH POSSESSIONS.							
Australasia g	18,645	6,687	24,805	14,400	28,046	19,286	6.10
ritish East Indics h..	2,332	8,818	326	2,020	345	151	.05
anada...............	571	....	1,927	642	287	....	
ther.................	392	180	180	346	477	778	.25
Total British possessions ...	21,940	15,685	27,238	17,408	29,155	20,215	6.40
Total	375,185	412,183	433,644	395,384	318,663	316,050	100.00

GRASS SEED, INCLUDING CLOVER SEED. (a)

FOREIGN COUNTRIES.	Dollars.	Dollars.	Dollars.	Dollars.	Dollars.	Dollars.	
United States........	1,221,678	972,336	1,176,676	1,472,437	1,361,681	1,125,261	45.44
Germany	619,940	1,088,125	667,878	541,296	377,475	424,923	17.16
France	571,182	1,051,140	490,066	559,380	481,311	274,013	11.06
Netherlands..........	101,441	106,387	98,430	115,472	90,517	96,401	3.89
Chile	32,876	7,285	20,897	31,949	33,666	70,584	2.85
Belgium..............	73,564	116,047	86,039	81,913	46,602	37,229	1.50
Italy	10,972	7,757	3,446	18,186	8,385	17,086	.69
Denmark.............	8,447	7,358	10,200	8,492	6,181	10,006	.41
Other................	7,009	7,139	243	3,407	3,197	21,057	.85
Total foreign countries.....	2,647,109	3,363,574	2,553,866	2,832,532	2,409,015	2,076,560	83.85
BRITISH POSSESSIONS.							
Australasia:							
New Zealand.....	284,735	385,330	203,371	239,110	236,049	359,814	} 14.67
New South Wales.	1,771	29	93	....	6,575	2,161	
Victoria	926	....	....	....	3,324	1,304	
Canada...............	64,653	87,660	61,571	116,942	20,308	36,786	1.48
Other i...............	188	827	58	....	53	....	
Total British possessions ...	352,273	473,846	265,093	356,052	266,309	400,065	16.15
Total	2,999,382	3,837,420	2,818,959	3,188,584	2,675,324	2,476,625	100.00

a For quantities, see page 203.
b Comprising in 1896 imports from Bengal valued at $7,217 and from Madras, $2,044, and in 1897 from Bengal, $4,297.
c Annual average, 1896–1899.
d Not stated.
e Per cent in 1899.
f Including imports from Denmark valued at $117 in 1896, $691 in 1897, and $287 in 1898.
g Including imports from New South Wales valued at $2,988 in 1896, $20,186 in 1897, $8,663 in 1898, $18,366 in 1899, and $11,373 in 1900.
h Including in 1896 imports from Bombay valued at $8,395.
i Comprising in 1896 imports from Bombay valued at $827.

Value of the agricultural imports of the United Kingdom (vegetable matter), etc.—Cont'd.

COTTON SEED. (a)

Countries from which imported.	Annual average, 1896–1900.	Calendar years.					Per ct. in 1900.
		1896.	1897.	1898.	1899.	1900.	
FOREIGN COUNTRIES.	*Dollars.*	*Dollars.*	*Dollars.*	*Dollars.*	*Dollars.*	*Dollars.*	
Egypt	9,221,522	7,739,823	8,764,951	9,357,978	8,953,975	11,290,883	88.40
Brazil	286,289	132,860	173,612	300,905	262,032	562,037	4.40
United States	341,376	281,999	213,119	239,451	448,312	524,000	4.10
Turkey, Asiatic	147,071	171,958	148,477	67,922	115,540	231,456	1.81
Peru	54,836	52,534	38,441	63,075	36,124	84,006	.66
Chile	11,238	5,003	9,436	9,772	5,183	26,795	.21
Colombia	11,151	10,492	3,888	14,332	11,538	15,505	.12
Germany	7,481	7,718	3,436	3,382	10,147	12,721	.10
France	13,283	2,628	3,752	3,246	44,548	12,239	.10
Pacific islands	2,914	3,893	2,832	3,762	2,531	1,552	} .02
Other	2,609	1,635	3,426	623	6,813	550	
Total foreign countries	10,099,770	8,410,543	9,365,370	10,064,448	9,896,743	12,761,744	99.92
BRITISH POSSESSIONS.							
British West Indies	5,889	6,079	3,436	4,793	6,434	8,701	.07
British East Indies	1,922	34	355	88	7,694	1,441	.01
Other	112		560				
Total British possessions	7,923	6,113	4,351	4,881	14,128	10,142	.08
Total	10,107,693	8,416,656	9,369,721	10,069,329	9,910,871	12,771,886	100.00

FLAXSEED, OR LINSEED. (a)

FOREIGN COUNTRIES.	*Dollars.*	*Dollars.*	*Dollars.*	*Dollars.*	*Dollars.*	*Dollars.*	
Russia	4,075,884	5,161,449	5,537,026	2,118,991	2,706,971	4,854,986	23.97
Argentina	3,456,340	5,683,707	3,135,866	2,158,619	2,983,963	3,319,547	16.39
Germany	448,451	422,690	354,773	219,066	350,456	895,270	4.42
United States	923,071	1,838,213	777,477	316,994	895,290	787,380	3.89
Turkey, European	126,480	222,521	61,201	55,731	40,445	252,503	1.25
Netherlands	136,931	221,562	102,269	87,616	55,532	217,674	1.07
France	35,761	44,640	623	876	1,820	130,846	.64
Turkey, Asiatic	42,072	70,676	25,768	25,165	10,984	77,767	.38
Italy	20,218	20,245	34,937	21,987	6,920	17,003	.08
Cyprus	4,028	8,638	5,494			6,010	.03
Belgium	14,402	19,875	7,747	9,723	30,844	3,820	.02
Uruguay	5,395	5,207	9,490	243	11,042	993	} .01
Chile	3,948	4,112	14,575	49	331	672	
Roumania	71,300	26,226	285,143	45,132			
Other	14,845	10,609	4,740	31,077	14,069	13,728	.07
Total foreign countries	9,379,126	13,760,370	10,357,129	5,091,269	7,108,667	10,578,199	52.22
BRITISH POSSESSIONS.							
British East Indies:							
Bengal	6,944,242	5,019,527	3,949,033	8,209,099	8,215,003	9,328,545	} 47.08
Bombay	285,711	758,322	35,842	148,750	311,081	174,562	
Madras	6,686	336				33,092	
Canada	387,223	32,031	198,650	762,796	830,249	112,450	.56
Gibraltar	3,791	5,747	2,896	1,411	3,051	5,850	.03
Other	4,481	20				22,386	.11
Total British possessions	7,632,134	5,815,983	4,186,421	9,121,996	9,359,384	9,676,885	47.78
Total	17,011,260	19,576,353	14,543,550	14,213,265	16,468,051	20,255,084	100.00

a For quantities, see page 204.

Value of the agricultural imports of the United Kingdom (vegetable matter), etc.—Cont'd.

RAPE SEED. (a)

	Annual average, 1896–1900.	Calendar years.					Per ct. in 1900.
		1896.	1897.	1898.	1899.	1900.	
FOREIGN COUNTRIES.							
	Dollars.	*Dollars.*	*Dollars.*	*Dollars.*	*Dollars.*	*Dollars.*	
Russia	400,961	460,639	331,730	373,514	478,494	360,427	30.03
Belgium	32,978	....	33,462	2,501	43,394	85,534	7.13
Netherlands	44,359	6,837	22,512	55,838	71,893	64,715	5.39
Roumania	176,707	98,488	251,841	357,907	112,090	63,211	5.27
Germany	38,992	82,760	20,858	38,757	23,486	29,097	2.42
France	5,761	5,572	3,168	6,901	6,424	6,740	.56
Argentina	3,125	4,964	4,317	165	....	6,180	.51
United States	2,227	....	1,285	9,339	511	....	......
Greece	1,548	6,813	....	925	....	....	......
Other	406	....	....	1,625	87	316	.03
Total foreign countries	707,064	666,073	669,173	847,472	736,379	616,220	51.34
BRITISH POSSESSIONS.							
British East Indies:							
Bengal	361,350	61,702	417,964	511,347	437,927	377,811	
Bombay	199,382	122,728	169,354	317,753	188,523	198,553	}48.54
Madras	70,339	101,029	....	113,015	131,444	6,205	
Other	317	....	200	....	....	1,887	.12
Total British possessions	631,388	285,459	587,518	942,115	757,894	583,956	48.66
Total	1,338,452	951,532	1,256,691	1,789,587	1,494,273	1,200,176	100.00

OILSEEDS NOT ELSEWHERE SPECIFIED. (a)

	Annual average, 1896–1900.	1896.	1897.	1898.	1899.	1900.	Per ct. in 1900.
FOREIGN COUNTRIES.							
	Dollars.	*Dollars.*	*Dollars.*	*Dollars.*	*Dollars.*	*Dollars.*	
Brazil	77,898	97	10,862	91,398	50,894	236,239	12.54
Netherlands	137,922	123,264	95,807	109,000	130,519	231,018	12.26
Russia	138,506	129,488	102,474	83,470	175,272	201,824	10.71
Germany	125,170	79,611	141,557	103,418	182,318	118,947	6.31
Turkey, Asiatic	13,141	9,460	8,550	12,809	11,889	22,999	1.22
France	14,057	10,443	18,809	6,784	12,327	21,924	1.16
Morocco	13,244	16,400	6,906	13,013	9,636	20,264	1.08
China	6,666	....	87	49	19,597	13,597	.72
Belgium	5,563	978	11,052	2,141	2,701	10,945	.58
Austria-Hungary	9,360	1,197	5,042	24,201	7,991	8,370	.45
Argentina	3,760	195	14,468	3,504	487	146	.01
Egypt	1,129	4,964	....	97	438	146	.01
Chile	4,859	19,675	4,594	....	24	....	......
Other	11,115	4,901	8,054	6,209	19,768	16,643	.88
Total foreign countries	562,390	400,673	428,262	456,093	623,861	903,062	47.93
BRITISH POSSESSIONS.							
British East Indies:							
Bombay	587,118	236,999	852,324	568,096	699,209	578,963	
Madras	290,313	49,473	450,740	456,804	296,005	198,543	}51.71
Bengal	156,747	105,900	222,676	160,740	99,900	194,519	
Ceylon	3,604	5,275	6,292	1,942	2,355	2,156	
Niger Protectorate	2,902	4,842	219	1,732	4,399	3,319	.18
Sierra Leone	2,230	4,594	258	1,820	2,263	2,214	.12
Lagos	1,651	535	4,317	2,935	453	14	} .06
Other	1,416	2,195	248	2,545	876	1,217	
Total British possessions	1,045,981	409,813	1,537,074	1,196,614	1,105,460	980,945	52.07
Total	1,608,371	810,486	1,965,336	1,652,707	1,729,321	1,884,007	100.00

a For quantities, see page 205.

Value of the agricultural imports of the United Kingdom (vegetable matter), etc.—Cont'd.

SEEDS NOT ELSEWHERE SPECIFIED. (a)

Countries from which imported.	Annual average, 1896–1900.	Calendar years.					Per ct. in 1900.
		1896.	1897.	1898.	1899.	1900.	
FOREIGN COUNTRIES.							
	Dollars.	*Dollars.*	*Dollars.*	*Dollars.*	*Dollars.*	*Dollars.*	
Turkey, Asiatic.......	246,182	305,830	268,606	185,117	173,379	297,976	27.25
Netherlands..........	104,658	89,772	118,085	67,985	107,165	140,282	12.83
Germany.............	99,274	76,496	100,070	92,614	111,365	115,827	10.59
Morocco.............	71,433	23,004	25,053	99,077	115,059	94,970	8.68
France	73,802	63,956	60,773	90,653	59,357	94,269	8.62
Russia..............	46,747	43,935	30,980	33,569	49,370	75,883	6.94
Turkey, European	119,171	163,797	194,120	102,990	67,712	67,235	6.15
United States........	31,324	7,061	38,680	31,433	34,421	45,073	4.12
Spain...............	54,575	40,728	61,508	81,207	44,733	44,699	4.09
Egypt	20,425	12,687	11,801	31,038	10,429	36,172	3.31
Austria-Hungary.....	8,983	3,767	3,149	7,475	6,025	24,498	2.24
Italy	17,812	19,232	17,758	16,483	11,159	24,430	2.23
Argentina...........	7,200	27,535	2,078	292	1,416	4,677	.43
Tripoli	5,447	....	....	4,589	18,298	4,346	.40
Belgium.............	4,158	6,521	4,370	5,227	1,066	3,606	.33
Roumania...........	60,583	....	38,236	148,618	114,854	959	.09
Bulgaria	1,716	....	....	8,580	....	....	.....
Portugal	1,159	4,015	....	341	1,441	....	.....
Other b	4,958	7,446	2,482	1,737	9,694	3,431	.31
Total foreign countries.....	979,557	895,782	977,699	1,009,025	936,943	1,078,333	98.61
BRITISH POSSESSIONS.							
British East Indies:							
Bombay..........	67,179	33,146	8,857	151,796	1,07	8,589	
Madras...........	2,927	3,713	1,679	3,202	696	1,348	
Bengal	2,030	1,168	3,227	3,431	33,027	1,299	1.11
Ceylon	621	934	311	905	66	891	
Straits Settlements	5	....	....	24	....	....	
Gibraltar	743	487	170	2,930	49	78	.01
Other c..............	3,690	3,002	5,120	1,767	5,553	3,008	.27
Total British possessions ...	77,195	42,450	19,364	164,055	144,895	15,213	1.39
Total	1,056,752	938,232	997,063	1,173,080	1,081,838	1,093,546	100.00

CINNAMON.(a)

	Annual average, 1896–1900.	1896.	1897.	1898.	1899.	1900.	Per ct. in 1900.
FOREIGN COUNTRIES.							
	Dollars.	*Dollars.*	*Dollars.*	*Dollars.*	*Dollars.*	*Dollars.*	
Germany.............	1,440	205	146	886	608	5,353	2.70
France	609	1,849	97	....	195	905	.45
Japan	35	....	....	....	....	175	.09
Other d	1,625	6,263	657	243	594	370	.19
Total foreign countries.....	3,709	8,317	900	1,129	1,397	6,803	3.43
BRITISH POSSESSIONS.							
British East Indies:							
Ceylon	265,262	202,286	257,287	306,351	371,513	188,874	
Madras...........	645	....	....	1,168	....	2,058	
Bengal	3,112	....	....	4,867	10,317	375	
Bombay..........	1,056	876	681	389	3,334	....	96.57
Straits Settlements	950	....	4,750	....	....	....	
Burma	487	....	....	2,433	....	....	
Other.............	81	....	10	394	....	....	
Total British possessions ...	271,593	203,162	262,728	315,602	385,164	191,307	96.57
Total	275,302	211,479	263,628	316,731	386,561	198,110	100.00

a For quantities, see page 206.
b Including imports from Cyprus valued at $1,830 in 1896, $1,129 in 1897, and $97 in 1898; from Persia, $876 in 1896 and $560 in 1899; and from the Canary Islands, $243 in 1896 and $258 in 1898.
c Including imports from Malta and Gozo valued at $341 in 1896, $3,747 in 1897, $399 in 1898, and $876 in 1899.
d Including imports from the Netherlands valued at $6,069 in 1896 and $555 in 1897.

Value of the agricultural imports of the United Kingdom (vegetable matter), etc.—Cont'd.

GINGER. (a)

Countries from which imported.	Annual average, 1896–1900.	Calendar years.					Per ct. in 1900.
		1896.	1897.	1898.	1899.	1900.	
FOREIGN COUNTRIES.							
	Dollars.	*Dollars.*	*Dollars.*	*Dollars.*	*Dollars.*	*Dollars.*	
United States..........	48,201	28,382	32,907	49,643	48,650	81,426	12.86
Japan	25,637	37,511	57,882	14,040	876	17,875	2.82
Germany.............	13,362	23,700	15,456	3,202	13,325	11,125	1.76
France	1,271	4,983	681	691	....	......	......
West Africa, n. e. s....	647	3,236	....	....	....	......	......
Other................	4,294	423	8,006	3,767	2,394	6,881	1.09
Total foreign countries....	93,412	98,235	114,932	71,343	65,245	117,307	18.53
BRITISH POSSESSIONS.							
British West Indies..:	172,819	176,746	191,351	113,399	180,532	202,067	31.91
British East Indies:							
Bombay	219,330	237,242	169,495	242,551	289,892	157,470	
Madras	108,657	135,931	214,763	127,862	28,294	36,436	
Bengal	25,102	89,266	28,148	6,288	1,304	506	}30.70
Straits Settlements	2,383	....	3,475	8,176	263	....	
Ceylon	280	....	....	438	964	....	
Sierra Leone.........	91,147	108,674	109,209	73,436	67,484	96,931	15.31
Canada...............	26,537	....	....	74,910	57,264	511	.08
Other b	9,203	7,660	3,431	3,056	9,923	21,943	3.47
Total British possessions ...	655,458	755,519	719,872	650,116	635,920	515,864	81.47
Total	748,870	853,754	834,804	721,459	701,165	633,171	100.00

PEPPER. (a)

	Annual average, 1896–1900.	1896.	1897.	1898.	1899.	1900.	Per ct. in 1900.
FOREIGN COUNTRIES.							
	Dollars.	*Dollars.*	*Dollars.*	*Dollars.*	*Dollars.*	*Dollars.*	
Java..................	114,875	14,244	65,834	141,060	204,310	148,929	5.00
Netherlands.........	91,066	27,457	181,410	96,786	65,834	133,892	4.50
France	36,942	7,091	10,449	38,290	34,484	94,395	3.17
Japan	23,506	15,889	12,536	31,540	20,809	36,757	1.23
Germany.............	14,568	5,519	22,250	24,303	3,217	17,549	.59
United States........	4,829	....	973	8,550	6,010	8,614	.29
Spain................	3,909	5,071	2,068	2,078	1,932	8,395	.28
Siam	2,764	5,645	4,477	....	....	3,698	}.12
Belgium.............	3,537	311	....	17,320	39	15	
Denmark.............	15,666	....	....	5,947	72,385	....	......
Other c	3,005	1,411	8,864	3,261	2,146	4,341	.15
Total foreign countries	314,667	82,638	253,861	369,085	411,166	456,585	15.33
BRITISH POSSESSIONS.							
British East Indies:							
Straits Settlements	1,943,638	1,291,793	1,682,315	2,441,893	2,192,782	2,109,404	
Madras...........	122,492	39,034	140,345	51,230	161,081	220,769	
Bombay	94,221	15,106	50,884	57,361	189,399	158,356	}84.16
Bengal	4,500	438	1,178	628	7,611	12,643	
Ceylon	3,979	2,472	297	652	11,393	5,080	
Zanzibar and Pemba..	9,240	18,259	10,244	5,786	6,584	5,329	.18
Niger Protectorate...	8,101	12,410	8,098	8,954	7,256	3,786	.13
Sierra Leone.........	6,522	6,473	9,241	11,821	2,219	2,857	.10
Natal................	1,329	569	983	540	2,579	1,976	.07
Other................	680	209	2,088	10	39	1,056	.03
Total British possessions ...	2,194,702	1,386,763	1,905,673	2,578,875	2,580,943	2,521,256	84.67
Total	2,509,369	1,469,401	2,159,534	2,947,960	2,992,109	2,977,841	100.00

a For quantities, see page 207.
b Including in 1896 imports from Hongkong valued at $4,959.
c Including imports from China valued at $141 in 1896 and $102 in 1897.

11820—No. 26—02——9

Value of the agricultural imports of the United Kingdom (vegetable matter), etc.—Cont'd.

SPICES NOT ELSEWHERE SPECIFIED. (a)

Countries from which imported.	Annual average, 1896–1900.	Calendar years.					Per ct. in 1900.
		1896.	1897.	1898.	1899.	1900.	
FOREIGN COUNTRIES.							
	Dollars.	*Dollars.*	*Dollars.*	*Dollars.*	*Dollars.*	*Dollars.*	
Netherlands..........	77,934	46,300	53,619	58,525	97,296	133,931	12.
Germany..............	64,509	48,290	87,879	47,755	43,112	95,510	8.
France	23,982	8,891	1,377	23,802	45,677	40,163	3.
United States........	31,942	42,621	8,575	24,011	46,319	38,183	3.
Japan	15,917	3,090	13,578	12,906	29,851	20,157	1.
China	11,980	12,570	9,782	11,402	6,497	19,646	1.60
Spain................	8,027	14,313	7,601	8,195	3,110	6,915	.58
Ecuador.............	5,352	25,019	526	....	1,217	....	
Colombia............	2,146	8,906	....	1,825	....	....	
Other b............	4,801	4,837	8,093	6,083	2,448	2,545	.24
Total foreign countries....	246,590	214,837	191,030	194,504	275,527	357,050	33.58
BRITISH POSSESSIONS.							
British West Indies...	380,239	345,259	322,620	361,601	478,275	393,442	37.00
British East Indies:							
Straits Settlements	295,619	439,975	369,922	268,256	251,136	148,808	⎫
Bombay	21,595	23,894	19,461	31,817	12,113	20,688	⎪
Ceylon	6,682	978	3,032	5,344	19,884	4,171	⎬16.63
Madras	1,059	594	263	185	1,056	3,197	⎪
Bengal	211	107	949	....	....	....	⎭
Hongkong...........	40,777	2,044	27,851	72,710	24,308	76,973	7.24
Zanzibar and Pemba..	76,838	89,495	119,239	41,380	75,129	58,948	5.55
Aden	4,661	19	....	23,286	....	....	......
Canada.............	4,481	560	146	17,558	4,141	....	......
Other...............	189	44	121	720	34	24	......
Total British possessions ...	832,351	902,969	863,604	799,571	889,362	706,251	66.42
Total	1,078,941	1,117,806	1,054,634	994,075	1,164,889	1,063,301	100.00

BRANDY. (a)

Countries from which imported.	Annual average, 1896–1900.	Calendar years.					Per ct. in 1900.
		1896.	1897.	1898.	1899.	1900.	
FOREIGN COUNTRIES.							
	Dollars.	*Dollars.*	*Dollars.*	*Dollars.*	*Dollars.*	*Dollars.*	
France	5,663,270	5,816,825	6,327,336	5,258,467	5,307,293	5,606,427	95.54
Germany.............	78,593	67,571	75,971	122,646	58,388	68,389	1.17
Spain................	75,636	94,707	63,873	82,935	75,850	60,817	1.04
Netherlands.........	64,996	82,512	79,981	51,059	64,257	47,171	.80
United States........	17,082	28,104	37,087	3,830	6,302	10,088	.17
Cyprus	1,884	2,886	146	....	355	6,034	.10
Greece..............	2,068	3,752	895	1,411	175	4,107	.07
Norway	1,380	2,570	88	5	292	3,947	.07
Egypt	2,227	1,411	560	1,952	4,258	2,954	.05
Denmark.............	9,960	4,560	28,167	6,448	9,222	1,402	.02
Other................	6,281	4,672	7,923	7,183	3,743	7,884	.14
Total foreign countries.	5,923,377	6,109,570	6,622,027	5,535,936	5,530,135	5,819,220	99.17
BRITISH POSSESSIONS.							
Australasia:							
Victoria	39,122	28,216	60,851	49,945	12,726	43,871	⎫
South Australia ..	2,008	63	4,063	2,204	1,518	2,190	⎬ .78
New South Wales.	828	983	2,409	....	740	10	⎭
Other................	3,507	1,718	3,859	5,149	4,039	2,769	.05
Total British possessions ...	45,465	30,980	71,182	57,298	19,023	48,840	.83
Total	5,968,842	6,140,550	6,693,209	5,593,234	5,549,158	5,868,060	100.00

a For quantities, see page 208.
b Including in 1896 imports from Java valued at $131 and from the other Dutch East Indies, $1,723, and in 1897 from Java $112.

alue of the agricultural imports of the United Kingdom (vegetable matter), etc.—Cont'd.

GIN. (a)

ountries from which imported.	Annual average, 1896–1900.	Calendar years.					Per ct. in 1900.
		1896.	1897.	1898.	1899.	1900.	
OREIGN COUNTRIES.							
	Dollars.	*Dollars.*	*Dollars.*	*Dollars.*	*Dollars.*	*Dollars.*	
etherlands............	309,136	294,262	300,453	303,490	327,613	319,860	99.08
elgium...............	2,772	3,358	3,660	2,535	2,307	2,000	.62
ermany..............	393	263	671	165	272	594	.18
nited States.........	4	....	....	10	10	....	......
her..................	176	39	355	78	63	346	.11
Total foreign countries.....	312,481	297,922	305,139	306,278	330,265	322,800	99.99
RITISH POSSESSIONS.							
otal British possessions	90	161	161	107	5	19	.01
Total	312,571	298,083	305,300	306,385	330,270	322,819	100.00

RUM. (a)

OREIGN COUNTRIES.							
	Dollars.	*Dollars.*	*Dollars.*	*Dollars.*	*Dollars.*	*Dollars.*	
nited States.........	228,476	242,868	186,480	253,919	80,064	379,047	16.14
etherlands..........	42,219	46,407	10,268	8,040	34,971	111,409	4.75
ance...............	41,770	1,299	1,227	34	150,209	56,082	2.39
atch Guiana	14,625	16,205	23,101	12,298	11,534	9,986	.43
ermany..............	9,231	8,711	....	1,703	29,335	6,404	.27
zores...............	5,051	....	25,257	....	....	....	......
iba and Porto Rico b	4,591	....	24	....	22,931	....	......
astria-Hungary	1,703	7,446	97	973	....	....	......
ain..................	2	5	....	5	....	....	......
her..................	1,786	68	511	715	5,674	1,961	.08
Total foreign countries.....	349,454	323,009	246,965	277,687	334,718	564,889	24.06
ITISH POSSESSIONS.							
tish Guiana	713,427	607,724	538,303	660,029	615,831	1,145,248	48.77
tish West Indies...	645,202	744,871	774,528	516,934	676,288	513,391	21.86
uritius.............	42,592	....	6,132	16,347	75,163	115,316	4.91
tralasia:							
Queensland	1,901	....	78	5	3,942	5,480	} .24
Victoria	18	....	....	....	....	88	
New South Wales.	605	199	....	2,823	....	5	
itish East Indies:							
Madras	1,236	....	....	365	2,925	2,891	}.13
Bengal	38	....	....	19	58	112	
Straits Settlements	30	....	49	....	....	102	
Burma	1	....	....	....	....	5	
Bombay	15	....	5	63	5	....	
nada................	62,873	....	24,342	209,128	80,385	511	.02
her..................	861	443	29	....	3,650	185	.01
Total British possessions ...	1,468,799	1,353,237	1,343,466	1,405,713	1,458,247	1,783,334	75.94
Total	1,818,253	1,676,246	1,590,431	1,683,400	1,792,965	2,348,223	100.00

a For quantities, see page 209.
b In 1899 the entire imports were credited to Cuba.

Value of the agricultural imports of the United Kingdom (vegetable matter, etc.)—Cont'd.

IMITATION RUM.(*a*)

Countries from which imported.	Annual average, 1896–1900.	Calendar years.					Per ct. in 1900.
		1896.	1897.	1898.	1899.	1900.	
FOREIGN COUNTRIES.							
	Dollars.	*Dollars.*	*Dollars.*	*Dollars.*	*Dollars.*	*Dollars.*	
Germany	9,582	6,064	7,081	4,482	15,145	15,135	89.
United States	195	....	97	10	87	783	4.
Netherlands	162	160	54	58	102	438	2.
Other	1,076	764	1,129	1,689	1,314	482	2.64
Total foreign countries	11,015	6,988	8,361	6,239	16,648	16,838	99.71
BRITISH POSSESSIONS.							
Total British possessions	21	25	....	34	....	49	.29
Total	11,036	7,013	8,361	6,273	16,648	16,887	100.00

DISTILLED SPIRITS, N. E. S., NOT SWEETENED OR MIXED. (*a*)

	Annual average, 1896–1900.	1896.	1897.	1898.	1899.	1900.	Per ct. in 1900.
FOREIGN COUNTRIES.							
	Dollars.	*Dollars.*	*Dollars.*	*Dollars.*	*Dollars.*	*Dollars.*	
Germany	227,052	201,541	190,231	201,176	270,704	271,609	69.92
United States	22,881	13,466	18,215	7,139	37,448	38,139	9.82
Belgium	8,577	1,601	998	3,859	4,550	31,876	8.21
France	28,347	17,096	33,486	32,946	39,263	18,945	4.88
Netherlands	9,137	7,553	7,305	10,629	9,266	10,930	2.81
Denmark	13,167	20,702	19,067	5,616	11,329	9,120	2.35
Norway	2,006	3,888	1,645	1,991	1,757	750	.19
Russia	9,776	16,979	28,114	3,596	160	29	.01
Other	3,358	3,168	3,241	3,640	3,645	3,095	.80
Total foreign countries	324,301	285,994	302,302	270,592	378,122	384,493	98.99
BRITISH POSSESSIONS.							
Canada	12,540	21,875	9,884	23,890	4,754	2,297	.59
Australasia	3,574	127	2,827	3,309	10,906	701	.18
Channel Islands	370	418	404	423	321	282	.07
Other	1,348	2,448	1,212	1,397	1,032	652	.17
Total British possessions	17,832	24,868	14,327	29,019	17,013	3,932	1.01
Total	342,133	310,862	316,629	299,611	395,135	388,425	100.00

a For quantities, see page 210.

*Value of the agricultural imports of the United Kingdom (vegetable matter), etc.—*Cont'd.

DISTILLED SPIRITS, SWEETENED OR MIXED (TESTED).(a)

Countries from which imported.	Annual average, 1896-1900.	Calendar years.					Per ct. in 1900.
		1896.	1897.	1898.	1899.	1900.	
FOREIGN COUNTRIES.							
	Dollars.	Dollars.	Dollars.	Dollars.	Dollars.	Dollars.	
United States............	324,275	265,546	340,480	267,288	349,935	398,128	40.25
France	332,318	257,034	304,137	381,271	401,185	317,963	32.14
Germany.............	55,354	48,636	50,539	55,760	53,162	68,676	6.94
Netherlands..........	51,412	43,857	49,964	54,607	51,809	56,821	5.74
Austria-Hungary.....	28,734	25,379	32,260	27,024	29,637	29,369	2.97
Denmark............	26,253	28,532	28,133	25,364	26,303	22,931	2.32
Russia..............	27,745	24,376	26,376	32,737	33,457	21,778	2.20
Belgium.............	5,544	1,523	4,059	6,832	8,876	6,429	.65
Italy..:.............	2,606	1,080	1,499	2,380	2,292	5,781	.59
Sweden..............	1,319	881	822	2,983	881	1,027	.10
Norway	272	423	229	268	263	175	.02
Other..............	3,080	3,665	1,956	4,642	2,813	2,326	.24
Total foreign countries.....	858,912	700,932	840,454	861,156	960,613	931,404	94.16
BRITISH POSSESSIONS.							
British West Indies...	62,405	58,958	62,413	66,141	68,360	56,150	5.67
Other................	2,281	613	2,477	2,652	4,005	1,659	.17
Total British possessions ...	64,686	59,571	64,890	68,793	72,365	57,809	5.84
Total	923,598	760,503	905,344	929,949	1,032,978	989,213	100.00

LIQUEURS, CORDIALS, ETC. (NOT TESTED).(b)

FOREIGN COUNTRIES.							
	Dollars.	Dollars.	Dollars.	Dollars.	Dollars.	Dollars.	
France	70,061	70,778	69,800	65,999	71,966	71,761	63.09
United States........	18,339	19,481	19,335	16,799	15,052	21,028	18.49
Netherlands:.........	6,549	6,472	7,387	6,078	7,655	5,154	4.53
Germany.............	5,179	5,407	5,553	5,480	5,134	4,322	3.80
Belgium.............	3,473	6,468	5,767	1,241	1,222	2,667	2.35
Denmark.............	1,193	1,849	1,231	1,616	1,017	253	.22
Russia..............	710	818	769	584	1,226	151	.13
Other...............	1,539	1,956	1,075	1,825	847	1,995	1.75
Total foreign countries.....	107,043	113,229	110,917	99,622	104,119	107,331	94.36
BRITISH POSSESSIONS.							
British West Indies...	1,777	1,056	492	1,460	482	5,392	4.74
Other................:	1,517	1,202	613	3,815	934	1,022	.90
Total British possessions....	3,294	2,258	1,105	5,275	1,416	6,414	5.64
Total	110,337	115,487	112,022	104,897	105,535	113,745	100.00

a For quantities, see page 210.   b For quantities, see page 211.

Value of the agricultural imports of the United Kingdom (vegetable matter), etc.—Cont'd.

DISTILLED SPIRITS, PERFUMED.(a)

Countries from which imported.	Annual average, 1896–1900.	Calendar years.					Per ct. in 1900.
		1896.	1897.	1898.	1899.	1900.	
FOREIGN COUNTRIES.	*Dollars.*	*Dollars.*	*Dollars.*	*Dollars.*	*Dollars.*	*Dollars.*	
France	372,122	348,821	368,788	380,444	388,687	373,869	59.36
Netherlands..........	175,966	186,883	179,413	180,450	174,999	158,084	25.10
Belgium..............	62,077	55,371	58,700	59,892	60,199	76,224	12.10
United States........	11,427	9,018	12,045	11,597	13,947	10,526	1.67
Germany.............	6,487	7,986	8,881	5,241	5,616	4,711	.75
Other...............	499	589	667	68	200	973	.15
Total foreign countries.....	628,578	608,668	628,494	637,692	643,648	624,387	99.13
BRITISH POSSESSIONS.							
Channel Islands......	9,034	9,927	9,674	10,429	9,835	5,304	.84
Other...............	947	1,173	1,173	423	1,806	161	.03
Total British possessions ...	9,981	11,100	10,847	10,852	11,641	5,465	.87
Total	638,559	619,768	639,341	648,544	655,289	629,852	100.00

STRAW.(a)

FOREIGN COUNTRIES.	*Dollars.*	*Dollars.*	*Dollars.*	*Dollars.*	*Dollars.*	*Dollars.*	
France	616,316	600,035	768,002	668,944	586,082	458,517	73.85
Netherlands..........	98,496	133,556	137,571	58,534	62,929	99,890	16.09
Germany.............	39,039	42,032	50,217	28,620	31,418	42,908	6.91
Belgium...............	34,271	42,694	52,549	32,425	25,160	18,527	2.98
United States........	1,596	268	6,662	88	63	900	.15
Denmark.............	4,843	13,806	8,453	1,290	531	136	.02
Other b	970	603	3,981	258	5	....	.....
Total	795,531	832,994	1,027,435	790,159	706,188	620,878	100.00

MOLASSES.(c)

FOREIGN COUNTRIES.	*Dollars.*	*Dollars.*	*Dollars.*	*Dollars.*	*Dollars.*	*Dollars.*	
United States........	1,286,360	640,894	1,090,704	1,506,702	1,710,351	1,483,149	87.54
Egypt	89,881	123,327	72,219	46,144	111,491	96,225	5.68
Netherlands..........	27,930	652	243	45,658	16,736	76,360	4.51
Germany.............	26,333	27,393	10,147	59,303	22,303	12,517	.74
Belgium..............	3,380	16,804	15	83	....	....	.....
Other d	3,457	2,448	3,392	6,964	2,677	1,801	.11
Total foreign countries.....	1,437,341	811,518	1,176,720	1,664,854	1,863,558	1,670,052	98.58
BRITISH POSSESSIONS.							
British West Indies...	19,834	11,222	19,914	15,412	28,883	23,739	1.40
British Guiana	1,670	....	681	7,495	151	24	} .02
Other...............	914	1,076	1,022	511	1,601	360	
Total British possessions ...	22,418	12,298	21,617	23,418	30,635	24,123	1.42
Total	1,459,759	823,816	1,198,337	1,688,272	1,894,193	1,694,175	100.00

a For quantities, see page 211.
b Including in 1896 imports from Algeria valued at $496.
c For quantities, see page 212.
d Including imports from Sweden valued at $219 in 1896, $1,470 in 1897, and $394 in 1898.

Value of the agricultural imports of the United Kingdom (vegetable matter), etc.—Continued.

BEET SUGAR, UNREFINED.(a)

Countries from which imported.	Annual average, 1896–1900.	Calendar years.					Per ct. in 1900.
		1896.	1897.	1898.	1899.	1900.	
FOREIGN COUNTRIES.							
	Dollars.	Dollars.	Dollars.	Dollars.	Dollars.	Dollars.	
France	5,915,797	3,831,239	6,229,402	4,426,359	4,252,587	10,839,447	43.50
Germany	10,811,115	12,426,535	9,258,331	12,470,134	12,275,225	7,625,353	30.60
Belgium	3,539,606	2,687,919	2,410,100	3,357,831	4,394,153	4,848,027	19.45
Netherlands	620,792	229,480	398,766	655,002	844,343	976,371	3.92
Austria-Hungary	376,136	207,658	115,964	313,583	784,086	459,388	1.84
Denmark	163,980	264,762	192,159	122,820	119,998	120,154	.48
Russia	247,698	638,334	265,297	218,676	66,106	50,076	.20
Egypt	332	....	....	....	....	1,659	.01
Other	271	....	....	....	1,353	....	.....
Total	21,675,727	20,285,927	18,870,019	21,564,415	22,737,801	24,920,475	100.00

SUGAR, CANE, ETC., UNREFINED.(a)

	Annual average, 1896–1900.	1896.	1897.	1898.	1899.	1900.	Per ct. in 1900.
FOREIGN COUNTRIES.							
	Dollars.	Dollars.	Dollars.	Dollars.	Dollars.	Dollars.	
France	683,307	30,352	155,986	568,325	1,260,204	1,401,669	16.03
Peru	1,686,638	2,326,085	2,071,479	2,496,875	909,257	629,496	7.20
Argentina	742,459	487,799	786,349	683,807	1,230,879	523,460	5.99
Philippine Islands b	1,602,477	3,150,426	1,512,703	1,942,001	928,149	479,107	5.48
Java	1,315,184	3,298,270	1,062,011	1,359,447	423,001	432,943	4.95
Brazil	644,601	925,161	696,309	1,021,147	310,721	269,667	3.09
Chile	147,237	147,596	30,795	190,704	175,690	191,399	2.19
Egypt	405,479	1,076,212	461,485	204,485	138,160	147,056	1.68
Dutch Guiana	90,961	87,193	63,518	95,894	112,942	95,257	1.09
French West Indies	20,068	....	....	....	7,942	92,400	1.06
Germany	99,673	126,096	88,054	95,831	108,615	79,767	.91
Netherlands	49,333	24,201	30,138	60,055	80,434	51,833	.59
Colombia	8,087	....	....	18,006	34	22,143	.25
United States	54,096	288,602	5,971	10,093	19,948	866	} .01
Denmark	1,246	....	....	584	5,596	49	
Danish West Indies	46,517	32,100	91,067	109,418	....	....	
Cuba and Porto Rico c	30,698	55,410	53,755	39,458	4,866	....	
Ecuador	14,077	8,190	....	62,194	....	....	
Spain	12,264	23,573	11,242	4,467	22,036	....	
Mexico	8,917	39,039	5,548	....	....	....	
Belgium	6,486	1,387	27,247	608	3,188	....	
Russia	2,769	....	....	7,665	6,180	....	
Other	3,662	....	307	14,210	3,553	239	
Total foreign countries	7,676,136	12,072,692	7,153,964	8,985,277	5,751,395	4,417,351	50.52
BRITISH POSSESSIONS.							
British West Indies	1,857,556	2,715,419	1,628,847	1,115,455	2,043,726	1,784,336	20.41
British Guiana	1,546,861	2,285,693	1,546,491	1,630,579	1,039,455	1,232,086	14.09
British East Indies:							
Madras	1,130,283	2,573,566	738,229	560,806	1,156,329	622,484	}
Straits Settlements	301,060	412,110	239,612	298,122	268,713	286,744	}10.40
Bengal	24,024	120,120	....	....	....	....	
Ceylon	1,703	....	....	8,516	....	....	
Mauritius	213,071	81,421	101,739	154,244	328,401	399,550	} 4.57
Australasia:							
Queensland	14,393	48	3,406	....	68,511	....	.....
New South Wales	7,389	....	....	73	36,873	....	.....
Natal	3,039	11,704	....	3,479	10	....	.....
Other d	1,292	467	1,781	3,037	487	686	.01
Total British possessions	5,100,671	8,200,548	4,260,105	3,774,311	4,942,505	4,325,886	49.48
Total	12,776,807	20,273,240	11,414,069	12,759,588	10,693,900	8,743,237	100.00

a For quantities, see page 212.
b Including the Ladrone Islands.
c In 1899 the entire imports were credited to Porto Rico.
d Including imports from Canada valued at $467 in 1896, $1,148 in 1897, and $3,022 in 1898.

Value of the agricultural imports of the United Kingdom (vegetable matter), etc.—Cont'd.

UNREFINED SUGAR (TOTAL). (a)

Countries from which imported.	Annual average, 1896–1900.	Calendar years.					Per ct. in 1900.
		1896.	1897.	1898.	1899.	1900.	
FOREIGN COUNTRIES.							
	Dollars.	*Dollars.*	*Dollars.*	*Dollars.*	*Dollars.*	*Dollars.*	
France	6,599,104	3,861,591	6,385,388	4,994,684	5,512,741	12,241,116	36.36
Germany.............	10,910,788	12,552,631	9,346,385	12,565,965	12,383,840	7,705,120	22.89
Belgium.............	3,546,092	2,689,306	2,437,347	3,358,439	4,397,341	4,848,027	14.40
Netherlands.........	670,125	253,681	428,904	715,060	924,777	1,028,204	3.05
Peru.................	1,686,638	2,326,085	2,071,479	2,496,875	909,257	629,496	1.87
Argentina...........	742,459	487,799	786,349	683,807	1,230,879	523,460	1.56
Philippine Islands b..	1,602,477	3,150,426	1,512,703	1,942,001	928,149	479,107	1.42
Austria-Hungary.....	376,136	207,658	115,964	313,583	784,086	459,388	1.37
Java.................	1,315,134	3,298,270	1,062,011	1,359,447	423,001	432,943	1.29
Brazil .....~........	644,601	925,161	696,309	1,021,147	310,721	269,667	.80
Chile	147,237	147,596	30,795	190,704	175,690	191,399	.57
Egypt ....‥	405,811	1,076,212	461,485	204,485	138,160	148,715	.44
Denmark............	165,226	264,762	192,159	123,414	125,594	120,208	.36
Dutch Guiana........	90,961	87,193	63,518	95,894	112,942	95,257	.28
French West Indies ..	20,068	....	....	....	7,942	92,400	.27
Russia	250,467	638,334	265,297	226,341	72,286	50,076	.15
Colombia.............	8,037	....	....	18,006	34	22,143	} .07
United States....‥....	54,096	233,602	5,971	10,093	19,948	866	
Danish West Indies .	46,517	32,100	91,067	109,418	....	....	......
Cuba and Porto Rico c	30,698	55,410	53,755	39,458	4,866	....	......
Ecuador..............	14,077	8,190	....	62,194	....	....	......
Spain................	12,264	23,573	11,242	4,467	22,036	....	......
Mexico...............	8,917	39,039	5,548	....	....	....	......
Other...............	8,933	....	307	14,210	4,906	239	......
Total foreign countries.....	29,351,863	32,358,619	26,023,983	30,549,692	28,489,196	29,337,826	87.15
BRITISH POSSESSIONS.							
British West Indies ..	1,857,556	2,715,419	1,628,847	1,115,455	2,043,726	1,784,336	5.30
British Guiana	1,546,861	2,285,693	1,546,491	1,630,579	1,039,455	1,252,086	3.66
British East Indies:							
Madras...........	1,130,283	2,573,566	.738,229	560,806	1,156,329	622,484	
Straits Settle‑ments	301,060	412,110	239,612	298,122	268,713	286,744	} 2.70
Bengal	24,024	120,120	....	....	....	....	
Ceylon	1,703	....	....	8,516	....	....	
Mauritius............	213,071	81,421	101,739	154,244	328,401	399,550	1.19
Australasia:							
Queensland	14,393	48	3,406.	....	68,511	....	......
New South Wales.	7,389	....	....	73	36,873	....	......
Natal................	3,039	11,704	....	3,479	10	....	......
Other d	1,292	467	1,781	3,037	487	686	......
Total British possessions ...	5,100,671	8,200,548	4,260,105	3,774,311	4,942,505	4,325,886	12.85
Total	34,452,534	40,559,167	30,284,088	34,324,003	33,431,701	33,663,712	100.00

a For quantities, see page 213.
b Including the Ladrone Islands.
c In 1899 the entire imports were credited to Porto Rico.
d Including imports from Canada valued at $467 in 1896, $1,148 in 1897, and $3,022 in 1898.

lue of the agricultural imports of the United Kingdom (vegetable matter), etc.—Cont'd.

REFINED SUGAR. (a)

ntries from which imported.	Annual average, 1896–1900.	Calendar years.					Per ct. in 1900.
		1896.	1897.	1898.	1899.	1900.	
REIGN COUNTRIES.							
	Dollars.	*Dollars.*	*Dollars.*	*Dollars.*	*Dollars.*	*Dollars.*	
rmany	33,827,551	32,679,545	29,898,866	33,851,807	35,813,260	36,894,275	61,44
ınce	8,797,560	4,956,676	9,359,866	6,765,253	9,474,662	13,431,340	22.37
therlands	6,925,864	7,068,966	5,646,999	7,220,421	7,419,232	7,273,704	12.11
lgium	1,818,015	2,106,606	2,272,135	1,422,410	1,388,490	1,900,432	3.17
stria-Hungary	76,682	....	5,110	....	38,689	339,609	.57
ssia	506,945	1,934,774	84,059	123,784	227,592	164,517	.27
ypt	11,000	....	788	....	·25,160	29,053	.05
ited States	45,668	63,036	69,129	39,964	46,655	9,558	} .02
nmark	6,762	19,305	2,998	7,042	2,180	2,287	
rtugal	5,262	2,258	195	21,135	2,720	....	......
her	4,902	3,836	885	12,409	5,917	1,465	......
Total foreign countries	52,026,211	48,835,002	47,341,030	49,464,225	54,444,557	60,046,240	100.00
ITISH POSSESSIONS.							
nada	3,010	1,090	·54	1,888	10,609	1,411	......
itish West Indies	3,937	....	....	19,685	....	....	......
her	426	535	97	1,066	336	97	......
Total British possessions	7,373	1,625	151	22,639	10,945	1,508	......
Total	52,033,584	48,836,627	47,341,181	49,486,864	54,455,502	60,047,748	100.00

TEA. (a)

	Annual average, 1896–1900.	1896.	1897.	1898.	1899.	1900.	Per ct. in 1900.
OREIGN COUNTRIES.							
	Dollars.	*Dollars.*	*Dollars.*	*Dollars.*	*Dollars.*	*Dollars.*	
hina	4,281,113	5,450,344	4,286,837	4,172,406	4,505,221	2,990,756	5.75
etherlands	814,366	845,326	581,931	·627,633	906,386	1,110,555	2.14
nited States	153,860	18,741	72,920	238,731	259,954	178,951	·.34
ıva	190,811	179,764	249,423	209,751	215,309	99,807	.19
rance	128,077	247,656	188,085	·76,428	51,084	77,134	.15
ermany	28,069	4,745	5,811	21,836	57,327	50,626	.10
elgium	6,293	1,071	1,041	1,732	452	27,170	.05
ıpan	22,346	25,714	19,953	26,386	·22,113	17,563	.03
ıacao	45,479	85,460	69,026	26,401	29,744	16,765	.03
enmark	992	1,187	53	5	2,745	·969	} .03
ther	12,048	2,375	3,421	25,539	16,400	12,507	
Total foreign countries	5,683,454	6,862,383	5,478,501	5,426,848	6,066,735	4,582,803	8.81
ßRITISH POSSESSIONS.							
ritish East Indies:							
Bengal	25,966,103	25,063,930	25,979,985	25,899,771	26,287,627	26,599,199	
Ceylon	18,540,540	18,491,303	18,143,120	17,977,450	18,156,600	19,934,225	
Madras	363,745	332,961	354,403	366,603	338,090	426,666	
Bombay	175,883	104,411	186,173	207,274	249,442	132,116	}90.52
Straits Settlements	7,042	·477	964	10,161	17,685	5,932	
Burma	2,979	3,139	3,465	4,613	2,798	881	
ĺongkong	451,300	522,433	448,900	393,315	549,121	342,733	.66
hannel Islands	4,627	6,244	5,032	5,251	4,136	2,472	
anada	5,400	4,351	1,032	8,643	11,383	1,591	
ustralasia	6,332	8,886	18,118	2,229	1,674	754	.01
atal	4,938	920	15,821	6,059	1,183	706	
ther	1,809	2,297	837	1,431	2,443	2,039	
Total British possessions	45,530,698	44,541,352	45,157,840	44,882,800	45,622,182	47,449,314	91.19
Total	51,214,152	51,403,735	50,636,341	50,309,648	51,688,917	52,032,117	100.00

a For quantities, see page 214.

Value of the agricultural imports of the United Kingdom (vegetable matter), etc.—Cont'd.

TOBACCO. (a)

Countries from which imported.	Annual average, 1896–1900.	Calendar years.					Per ct. in 1900.
		1896.	1897.	1898.	1899.	1900.	
FOREIGN COUNTRIES.							
	Dollars.	*Dollars.*	*Dollars.*	*Dollars.*	*Dollars.*	*Dollars.*	
United States.........	11,051,712	9,659,881	9,052,863	9,624,560	14,865,133	12,056,126	84.42
Netherlands..........	1,376,626	1,163,736	1,419,524	1,460,495	1,528,728	1,310,646	9.18
Germany.............	234,021	257,306	214,301	215,897	241,894	240,707	1.68
France	184,595	104,362	114,129	110,800	354,043	239,641	1.68
Turkey, European....	92,680	112,737	101,384	97,174	24,323	127,780	.89
Turkey, Asiatic.......	147,805	183,199	102,620	181,248	162,298	109,662	.77
Belgium.............	57,572	54,646	41,662	63,912	65,182	62,456	.44
China	34,689	13,300	24,527	28,007	59,162	48,451	.34
Japan	56,850	99,987	100,060	45,633	6,828	31,744	.22
Austria-Hungary.....	2,579	5,450				7,446	.05
Greece..............	4,025	14,950	1,747	1,110	584	1,732	} .01
Italy	3,810	18,712	19		107	214	
Philippine Islands b ..	45,398	49	226,940	....	....	......	
Colombia............	2,256	10,833	39	68	340	......	
Argentina............	401	1,616	....	389	....	......	
Other................	9,059	1,786	11,957	22,800	3,635	5,115	.04
Total foreign countries.....	13,304,078	11,702,550	11,411,772	11,852,093	17,312,257	14,241,720	99.72
BRITISH POSSESSIONS.							
Australasia...........	13,528	17,110	438	1,674	21,286	27,131	.19
Canada..............	2,995	6,098	1,655	1,100	107	6,015	.05
British East Indies ...	2,731	4,935	1,212	4,939	934	1,635	.01
Hongkong............	450	696	1,290	....	117	146	} .03
Other................	3,443	1,494	160	7,256	3,923	4,384	
Total British possessions ...	23,147	30,333	4,755	14,969	26,367	39,311	.28
Total	13,327,225	11,732,883	11,416,527	11,867,062	17,338,624	14,281,031	100.00

ONIONS. (a)

FOREIGN COUNTRIES.							
	Dollars.	*Dollars.*	*Dollars.*	*Dollars.*	*Dollars.*	*Dollars.*	
Spain	1,260,747	1,066,372	1,206,216	1,125,062	1,404,292	1,501,792	36.20
Egypt	881,761	637,473	853,696	994,352	899,845	1,023,440	24.67
Netherlands	799,570	713,288	825,354	766,751	867,206	825,251	19.89
France	269,216	241,899	200,558	300,930	350,612	252,080	6.08
Belgium	168,685	138,486	188,236	170,551	136,982	209,172	5.04
Portugal............	224,419	185,978	194,898	270,057	307,451	163,709	3.95
Germany.............	175,755	280,724	182,430	149,372	134,140	132,111	3.18
Italy...............	5,934	7,563	2,803	4,915	4,326	10,064	.24
Canary Islands.......	5,853	58	....	27,681	68	1,460	.04
Austria-Hungary	1,070	170	4,098	39	1,022	.19	} .06
Turkey, European....	1,448	657	3,747	2,832	....	5	
Other c	1,960	4,891	419	1,329	516	2,643	
Total foreign countries.....	3,796,418	3,277,559	3,662,455	3,813,871	4,106,460	4,121,746	99.35
BRITISH POSSESSIONS.							
Malta and Gozo	30,356	39,457	37,010	41,302	8,959	25,053	.60
Other d..............	1,863	1,689	1,800	3,519	433	1,873	.05
Total British possessions ...	32,219	41,146	38,810	44,821	9,392	26,926	.65
Total	3,828,637	3,318,705	3,701,265	3,858,692	4,115,852	4,148,672	100.00

a For quantities, see page 215.
b Including the Ladrone Islands.
c Including imports from the United States valued at $1,124 in 1896 and $2,589 in 1900, and from Asiatic Turkey $2,628 in 1896, $39 in 1897, and $151 in 1899.
d Comprising in 1896 imports from the Channel Islands valued at $1,689.

lue of the agricultural imports of the United Kingdom (vegetable matter), etc.—Cont'd.

POTATOES. (a)

ntries from which imported.	Annual average, 1896-1900.	Calendar years.					Per ct. in 1900.
		1896.	1897.	1898.	1899.	1900.	
REIGN COUNTRIES.							
	Dollars.	Dollars.	Dollars.	Dollars.	Dollars.	Dollars.	
nce	2,089,218	1,165,911	1,590,241	2,226,813	2,462,347	3,000,781	27.59
gium	906,705	5,407	495,497	1,011,210	597,431	2,423,979	22.29
many	867,864	15,612	330,469	2,046,319	751,164	1,195,758	11.00
herlands	506,635	57,157	513,932	680,979	331,876	949,230	8.73
tugal	184,096	46,567	141,532	254,625	227,222	250,532	2.30
ary Islands	228,829	273,609	170,936	215,479	284,860	199,264	1.83
in	26,645	9,071	51,268	2,195	27,116	43,575	.40
eria	12,512	7,864	3,475	5,100	10,458	35,662	.33
pt	5,316	7,650	10,366	5,163	715	2,686	.03
way	6,132	....	613	28,849	302	895	.01
er b	13,100	1,947	6,448	23,963	4,735	28,406	.26
Total foreign countries	4,847,052	1,590,795	3,314,777	6,500,695	4,698,226	8,130,768	74.77
ITISH POSSESSIONS.							
annel Islands	2,680,166	2,742,574	2,445,567	2,663,708	2,926,845	2,622,133	24.11
lta and Gozo	97,588	85,135	80,166	149,445	52,378	120,816	1.11
her	523	156	886	205	555	813	.01
Total British possessions	2,778,277	2,827,865	2,526,619	2,813,358	2,979,778	2,743,762	25.23
Total	7,625,329	4,418,660	5,841,396	9,314,053	7,678,004	10,874,530	100.00

ountries from which imported.	Calendar year 1900	Per cent.	Countries from which imported.	Calendar year 1900	Per cent.
FOREIGN COUNTRIES.			**BRITISH POSSESSIONS.**		
	Dollars.			Dollars.	
nary Islands	1,001,531	25.98	Channel Islands	1,397,401	36.24
rance	529,169	13.72	Other	3,645	.09
ain	428,617	11.12			
aly	205,055	5.32	Total British possessions	1,401,046	36.33
nited States	194,660	5.05			
rtugal	70,564	1.83	Total	3,855,918	100.00
enmark	12,828	.33			
etherlands	53	.32			
ther d	12,395				
Total foreign countries	2,454,872	63.67			

a For quantities, see page 216.
b Including in 1900 imports from the United States valued at $453.
c Prior to 1900 included in "Fresh vegetables not elsewhere specified."
d Including imports, for which the corresponding quantities are not stated, as follows: From Germany $11,383 and from Belgium $107.

Value of the agricultural imports of the United Kingdom (vegetable matter), etc.—Cont'd.

FRESH VEGETABLES NOT ELSEWHERE SPECIFIED.

Countries from which imported.	Annual average, 1896–1900.	Calendar years.					Per ct. in 1900.
		1896.	1897.	1898.	1899.	1900.	
FOREIGN COUNTRIES.	Dollars. (a)	Dollars. (b)	Dollars. (b)	Dollars. (b)	Dollars. (b)	Dollars.	
France	1,784,696	1,934,078	2,358,223	2,398,868	2,246,230	1,784,696	47.85
Netherlands..........	670,185	590,156	694,712	580,797	672,506	670,185	17.97
Germany	276,860	125,249	174,415	191,370	192,324	276,860	7.42
Italy.................	197,945	208,598	196,801	285,805	299,144	197,945	5.31
Belgium..............	146,029	41,336	42,786	67,479	93,164	146,029	3.92
United States........	108,231	316,347	452,147	527,830	486,777	108,231	2.90
Roumania............	80,925	....	....	11,680	6,180	80,925	2.17
Austria-Hungary	69,455	21,695	6,151	74,871	67,552	69,455	1.86
Chile	57,303	360	....	6,020	52,690	57,303	1.54
Madeira Islands......	20,726	29,875	29,209	31,642	13,286	20,726	.56
Portugal.............	17,247	60,291	82,181	123,517	109,886	17,247	.46
Spain................	15,427	482,465	458,619	569,473	470,211	15,427	.41
Denmark.............	5,621	36,027	34,343	6,049	13,621	5,621	.15
Canary Islands.......	774	799,488	1,026,720	1,208,688	1,463,089	774	.02
Other................	43,944	8,346	10,930	22,089	15,149	43,944	1.18
Total foreign countries	3,495,368	4,654,311	5,567,237	6,106,178	6,201,809	3,495,368	93.72
BRITISH POSSESSIONS.							
Channel Islands......:	220,282	1,497,792	1,466,588	1,979,561	2,230,731	220,282	5.91
Canada	13,130	94,711	50,757	92,400	54,432	13,130	.35
Other c	876	5,436	4,453	1,406	2,920	876	.02
Total British possessions ...	234,288	1,597,939	1,521,798	2,073,367	2,288,083	234,288	6.28
Total	3,729,656	6,252,250	7,089,035	8,179,545	8,489,892	3,729,656	100.00

BEANS, DRIED. (d) (e)

FOREIGN COUNTRIES.	Dollars.	Dollars. (f)	Dollars. (f)	Dollars. (f)	Dollars.	Dollars.	
Egypt	1,172,054	1,666,961	1,108,180	719,419	1,582,318	783,390	29.98
Morocco	320,183	436,481	90,313	247,087	196,913	630,119	24.12
Turkey, Asiatic.......	671,290	746,365	1,021,921	755,495	277,648	555,019	21.24
Germany	416,996	466,473	414,134	475,180	433,114	296,078	11.33
Russia	128,779	83,806	126,067	176,070	149,703	108,250	4.14
Turkey, European....	41,292	40,616	56,082	35,701	20,215	53,848	2.06
Netherlands..........	33,309	55,775	30,240	13,816	29,194	37,521	1.44
Italy.................	113,679	85,787	287,956	156,497	13,836	24,318	.93
Austria-Hungary	6,505	1,767	652	6,647	7,183	16,274	.62
Sweden...............	16,875	28,664	16,244	19,758	9,704	10,005	.38
Cyprus	197,159	322,848	353,736	309,212	....	....	......
Portugal.............	111,849	89,865	158,317	311,062	....	....	......
Mexico	7,311	....	....	....	36,557	....	......
Algeria	2,044	....	....	10,220	....	....	......
Other g	18,363	6,015	19,437	18,035	21,564	26,766	1.03
Total foreign countries	3,257,688	4,031,423	3,683,279	3,254,199	2,777,949	2,541,588	97.27
BRITISH POSSESSIONS.							
Australasia:							
New Zealand.....	25,637	22,766	20,123	813	13,646	70,837	} 2.71
New South Wales.	229	....	....	....	1,144	....	
Canada	5,845	21,101	6,117	2,010	....	....	......
Other................	978	....	92	4,307	102	389	.02
Total British possessions ...	32,689	43,867	26,332	7,130	14,892	71,226	2.73
Total	3,290,377	4,075,290	3,709,611	3,261,329	2,792,841	2,612,814	100.00

a Statistics for 1900 only.
b Including tomatoes.
c Including imports from the Cape of Good Hope valued at $2,716 in 1896 and $404 in 1898.
d For quantities, see page 217.
e Exclusive of kidney, haricot, and French beans.
f Including carob beans.
g Including imports from Spain valued at $730 in 1896 and $10,502 in 1898, and from the United States $599 in 1900.

lue of the agricultural imports of the United Kingdom (vegetable matter), etc.—Cont'd.

PEAS, DRIED.(a)

ıntries from which imported.	Annual average, 1896–1900.	Calendar years.					Per ct. in 1900.
		1896.	1897.	1898.	1899.	1900.	
)REIGN COUNTRIES.							
	Dollars.	*Dollars.*	*Dollars.*	*Dollars.*	*Dollars.*	*Dollars.*	
ited States.........	797,081	555,272	821,485	846,265	789,891	972,492	25.62
therlands.........	308,760	209,547	183,010	237,986	413,482	474,771	12.51
ssia...............	710,691	1,254,939	1,109,795	436,437	405,895	346,388	9.12
rmany.............	151,787	144,769	82,161	145,504	209,897	176,605	4.65
rocco.............	19,389	2,968	49	1,689	27,277	64,963	1.71
ile	8,383	15,490	2,010	....	15,875	8,541	.22
lombia...........	2,944	....	....	....	14,721	....	......
her...............	13,521	12,974	6,993	5,986	26,883	14,770	.39
Total foreign countries.....	2,007,556	2,195,959	2,205,503	1,673,867	1,903,921	2,058,530	54.22
RITISH POSSESSIONS.							
nada...............	1,380,228	1,479,655	1,399,099	1,505,160.	1,171,123	1,346,103	35.46
itish East Indies:							
Bengal	439,337	395,067	104,279	156,818	1,244,773	295,747	⎫
Bombay	5,367	8,098	341	4,837	13,349	209	⎬ 7.79
Ceylon	109	....	545	....	....	....	⎭
ustralasia:							
New Zealand.....	38,001	39,759	40,562	16,079	40,372	53,235	
Victoria	7,040	2,239	813	....	467	31,681	
Tasmania	2,141	....	....	....	....	10,706	⎬ 2.53
New South Wales.	197	....	....	....	740	243	
South Australia ..	5,797	28,566	418	....	....	88	
ther...............	173	....	779	....	....	....	
Total British possessions ...	1,878,390	1,953,384	1,546,836	1,682,894	2,470,824	1,738,012	45.78
Total	3,885,946	4,149,343	3,752,339	3,356,761	4,374,745	3,796,542	100.00

VETCHES AND LENTILS.(b)

	Annual average, 1896–1900.	1896.	1897.	1898.	1899.	1900.	Per ct. in 1900.
FOREIGN COUNTRIES.	*Dollars.*	*Dollars.*	*Dollars.*	*Dollars.*	*Dollars.*	*Dollars.*	
iermany.............	118,785	92,892	100,016	85,412	125,97ย	189,628	53.56
Egypt	45,715	15,972	60,899	46,684	46,578	58,442	16.51
tussia...............	52,080	50,913	33,920	50,266	77,095	48,208	13.62
urkey, Asiatic.......	5,448	8,594	7,071	6,526	273	4,779	1.35
hile	7,880	10,312	8,570	15,480	1,197	3,840	1.08
iweden.............	4,369	6,409	4,691	4,794	2,657	3,295	.93
urkey, European....	1,288	1,314	3,066	131	....	1,927	.54
rance	2,098	419	5,402	818	2,769	1,680	.31
)enmark...........	1,253	618	2,915	1,898	....	832	.23
)ther..............	2,163	3,903	1,095	803	2,141	2,871	.81
Total foreign countries.....	241,079	191,346	227,645	212,812	258,689	314,902	88.94
BRITISH POSSESSIONS.							
iritish East Indies:							
Bombay	78,039	103,189	27,593	134,442	94,712	30,260	⎫10.40
Bengal	14,496	40,757	....	102	25,067	6,555	⎬
)ther c	798	1,426	234	....	....	2,331	.66
Total British possessions ...	93,333	145,372	27,827	134,544	119,779	39,146	11.06
Total	334,412	336,718	255,472	347,356	378,468	354,048	100.00

a For quantities, see page 217.
b For quantities, see page 218.
c Comprising in 1896 imports from New Zealand valued at $1,426.

Value of the agricultural imports of the United Kingdom (vegetable matter), etc.—Cont'd.

VEGETABLES, PRESERVED IN SALT OR VINEGAR, INCLUDING PICKLES. (a)

Countries from which imported.	Annual average, 1896–1900.	Calendar years.					Per ct. in 1900.
		1896.	1897.	1898.	1899.	1900.	
FOREIGN COUNTRIES.							
	Dollars.	Dollars.	Dollars.	Dollars.	Dollars.	Dollars.	
France	358,693	339,949	362,335	334,105	381,509	375,567	43.61
Netherlands..........	273,430	243,412	233,383	243,967	313,627	332,762	38.64
United States........	81,036	29,316	30,868	93,320	160,911	90,765	10.54
Belgium..............	29,424	30,849	12,857	32,391	45,531	25,491	2.96
Italy	17,142	16,264	18,386	10,950	18,016	22,094	2.57
Germany.............	7,146	8,716	7,962	6,580	4,818	7,655	.89
Other................	1,414	1,343	1,742	2,336	569	1,080	.13
Total foreign countries.....	768,285	669,849	667,533	723,649	924,981	855,414	99.34
BRITISH POSSESSIONS.							
Total British possessions	9,049	8,186	9,290	14,020	8,044	5,703	.66
Total	777,334	678,035	676,823	737,669	933,025	861,117	100.00

SAUCES AND CONDIMENTS. (a) (b)

	Annual average, 1896–1900.	1896.	1897.	1898.	1899.	1900.	Per ct. in 1900.
FOREIGN COUNTRIES.	Dollars.	Dollars.	Dollars.	Dollars.	Dollars.	Dollars.	
United States........	55,784	42,543	65,975	68,243	61,084	41,078	12.08
Germany.............	27,061	24,746	26,016	27,885	27,900	28,756	8.46
France	21,846	21,062	22,021	25,622	18,804	21,719	6.39
Italy.................	22,532	12,969	24,649	30,985	22,863	21,194	6.23
Russia	16,125	24,897	16,424	11,845	18,940	8,521	2.51
Netherlands..........	4,867	1,348	1,888	6,497	6,200	8,400	2.47
Japan	4,136	5,280	3,046	827	5,674	5,854	1.72
Belgium..............	4,899	4,424	5,728	6,643	5,256	2,443	.72
China	1,751	1,586	1,460	4,540	1,168	....	
Other................	1,800	842	2,784	2,419	2,025	930	.27
Total foreign countries.....	160,801	139,697	169,991	185,506	169,914	138,895	40.85
BRITISH POSSESSIONS.							
British East Indies:							
Bombay	67,837	58,890	61,956	82,439	67,805	68,097	
Madras	35,599	27,963	40,927	36,012	31,973	41,122	
Bengal	23,818	17,388	22,454	28,274	22,590	28,386	41.60
Straits Settlements	1,367	443	1,139	....	1,479	3,772	
Burma	18	....	....	15	39	34	
Ceylon	211	141	414	287	199	15	
Hongkong...........	35,332	26,216	24,994	28,727	37,745	58,977	17.35
Other...............	1,025	856	355	1,844	1,392	676	.20
Total British possessions ...	165,207	131,897	152,239	177,598	163,222	201,079	59.15
Total	326,008	271,594	322,230	363,104	333,136	339,974	100.00

•a For quantities, see page 218.   b Including table salt.

lue of the agricultural imports of the United Kingdom (vegetable matter), etc.—Cont'd.

VINEGAR. (a)

untries from which imported.	Annual average, 1896-1900.	Calendar years.					Per ct. in 1900.
		1896.	1897.	1898.	1899.	1900.	
OREIGN COUNTRIES.	Dollars.	Dollars.	Dollars.	Dollars.	Dollars.	Dollars.	
:therlands.........	14,858	11,529	12,059	13,062	14,681	22,960	36.40
ance	19,101	17,110	17,471	17,529	22,960	20,434	32.40
lgium..............	16,347	15,972	17,962	15,558	16,885	15,357	24.35
rmany	3,652	3,324	4,823	2,122	5,899	2,093	3.32
her b	1,141	652	185	1,489	1,149	2,229	3.53
Total foreign countries.....	55,099	48,587	52,500	49,760	61,574	63,073	100.00
RITISH POSSESSIONS.							
otal British possessions.................	110	....	....	92	457	....	......
Total	55,209	48,587	52,500	49,852	62,031	63,073	100.00

AND OTHER SPARKLING WINES. (a)

	Annual average, 1896-1900.	1896.	1897.	1898.	1899.	1900.	Per ct. in 1900.
OREIGN COUNTRIES.	Dollars.	Dollars.	Dollars.	Dollars.	Dollars.	Dollars.	
rance	11,347,588	11,205,700	12,986,275	12,834,581	9,917,611	9,793,773	96.50
etherlands..........	416,428	402,012	440,170	457,018	466,108	316,829	3.12
elgium...........:..	7,788	8,784	11,130	5,450	4,171	9,407	.09
ermany	6,173	11,198	4,083	5,076	5,519	4,988	.05
:aly.................	1,766	1,747	1,698	1,358	2,151	1,878	.02
ortugal.............	335	160	365	263	589	297	
pain................	530	268	389	1,849	107	39	.03
ther c	26,828	111,837	6,594	11,383	1,338	2,988	
Total foreign countries.....	11,807,436	11,741,706	13,450,704	13,316,978	10,397,594	10,130,199	99.81
BRITISH POSSESSIONS.							
Australasia	5,500	1,966	5,042	1,888	7,465	11,139	.11
Cape of Good Hope...	956	224	292	545	1,961	1,757	.02
Natal...............	310	....	....	351	793	404	
)ther	5,974	4,769	5,499	9,397	4,249	5,957	.06
Total British possessions ...	12,740	6,959	10,833	12,181	14,468	19,257	.19
Total	11,820,176	11,748,665	13,461,537	13,329,159	10,412,062	10,149,456	100.00

a For quantities, see page 219.
b Including in 1900 imports from the United States valued at $346.
c Including in 1900 imports from the United States valued at $185.

Value of the agricultural imports of the United Kingdom (vegetable matter), etc.—Cont'd.

STILL WINES, BOTTLED. (a)

Countries from which imported.	Annual average, 1896–1900.	Calendar years.					Per ct. in 1900.
		1896.	1897.	1898.	1899.	1900.	
FOREIGN COUNTRIES.							
	Dollars.	*Dollars.*	*Dollars.*	*Dollars.*	*Dollars.*	*Dollars.*	
Netherlands	920,830	995,272	1,080,193	1,162,947	802,520	563,219	43.62
France	1,027,098	1,353,792	1,427,486	977,719	855,467	521,027	40.35
Germany	36,601	40,368	33,048	35,024	20,975	53,590	4.15
Belgium	40,728	41,059	43,735	37,165	32,172	49,507	3.83
Italy	43,891	60,481	41,365	49,872	36,304	31,433	2.43
Portugal	41,185	47,550	48,816	51,147	34,567	23,846	1.85
Spain b	17,195	18,653	17,806	26,878	11,772	10,867	.84
Other c	20,357	18,634	18,673	25,092	22,401	16,984	1.32
Total foreign countries	2,147,885	2,575,809	2,711,122	2,365,844	1,816,178	1,270,473	98.39
BRITISH POSSESSIONS.							
Australasia	7,960	12,449	5,835	6,453	9,358	5,704	.44
Cape of Good Hope	6,164	7,966	6,434	5,874	5,348	5,197	.40
Channel Islands	10,471	8,789	11,646	11,329	15,646	4,949	.38
Natal	365	472	438	351	564		
Other	6,386	6,857	4,501	9,655	5,923	4,993	.39
Total British possessions	31,346	36,533	28,854	33,662	36,839	20,843	1.61
Total	2,179,231	2,612,342	2,739,976	2,399,506	1,853,017	1,291,316	100.00

STILL WINES, UNBOTTLED. (a)

	Annual average, 1896–1900.	1896.	1897.	1898.	1899.	1900.	Per ct. in 1900.
FOREIGN COUNTRIES.							
	Dollars.	*Dollars.*	*Dollars.*	*Dollars.*	*Dollars.*	*Dollars.*	
Portugal	5,716,687	5,105,139	5,506,922	6,875,810	5,715,982	5,379,580	38.90
Spain d	3,656,071	3,356,586	3,911,065	3,856,477	3,750,597	3,405,630	24.62
France	3,703,275	4,289,372	3,844,194	3,705,971	3,650,045	3,026,793	21.88
Netherlands	374,074	293,659	313,515	334,791	472,863	455,543	3.29
Italy	316,386	336,290	321,077	321,442	328,708	274,412	1.98
Germany	242,216	220,978	236,011	237,179	245,135	271,775	1.97
Madeira Islands	118,161	106,975	182,348	97,710	87,719	116,051	.84
United States	143,776	162,332	123,643	162,385	160,439	110,080	.80
Belgium	33,971	35,598	35,039	37,472	25,189	36,557	.26
Cyprus	4,567	3,241	2,355	1,221	4,949	11,071	.08
Turkey, Asiatic	3,605	803	998	1,548	6,818	7,859	.06
Canary Islands	35,637	60,753	36,236	51,828	25,846	3,519	.03
Turkey, European	5,310	13,748	4,404	6,185	1,217	998	.01
Other	18,437	13,446	19,592	19,291	17,276	22,581	.16
Total foreign countries	14,372,173	13,998,920	14,537,399	15,709,310	14,492,783	13,122,449	94.88
BRITISH POSSESSIONS.							
Australasia:							
South Australia	308,182	252,284	300,224	320,513	330,591	337,297	
Victoria	260,978	272,534	235,616	209,508	250,016	337,219	
New South Wales	19,302	20,863	9,480	8,604	38,694	18,867	5.02
New Zealand	53	151	58			54	
Queensland	470	2,336	15				
Tasmania	52	258					
Cape of Good Hope	9,144	10,088	12,030	6,088	8,891	8,624	.06
Natal	93	15	97	24	112	219	.04
Other	14,277	19,193	14,308	17,889	14,205	5,791	
Total British possessions	612,551	577,722	571,828	562,626	642,509	708,071	5.12
Total	14,984,724	14,576,642	15,109,227	16,271,936	15,135,292	13,830,520	100.00

a For quantities, see page 220.
b The imports from Spain comprised red wine to the value of $7,665 in 1896, $10,395 in 1897, $14,551 in 1898, $6,925 in 1899, and $4,122 in 1900, and white wine, $10,988 in 1896, $7,411 in 1897, $12,327 in 1898, $4,847 in 1899, and $6,745 in 1900.
c Including in 1900 imports from the United States valued at $4,419.
d The imports from Spain comprised red wine to the value of $1,099,858 in 1896, $1,467,255 in 1897, $1,460,320 in 1898, $1,559,246 in 1899, and $1,451,497 in 1900, and white wine $2,256,728 in 1896, $2,443,810 in 1897, $2,396,157 in 1898, $2,191,351 in 1899, and $1,954,133 in 1900.

Value of the agricultural imports of the United Kingdom (vegetable matter), etc.—Cont'd.

WINES (TOTAL). (a)

Countries from which imported.	Annual average, 1896-1900.	Calendar years.					Per ct. in 1900.
		1896.	1897.	1898.	1899.	1900.	
FOREIGN COUNTRIES.	Dollars.	Dollars.	Dollars.	Dollars.	Dollars.	Dollars.	
France	16,077,961	16,848,864	18,257,955	17,518,271	14,423,123	13,341,593	52.79
Portugal	5,758,207	5,152,849	5,556,108	6,927,220	5,751,138	5,403,723	21.38
Spain	3,673,796	3,375,507	3,929,260	3,885,204	3,762,476	3,416,536	13.52
Netherlands	1,711,332	1,690,943	1,833,878	1,954,756	1,741,491	1,335,591	5.29
Germany	284,990	272,544	273,142	277,279	271,629	330,353	1.31
Italy	362,043	398,518	364,140	372,672	367,163	307,723	1.22
Madeira Islands	121,617	110,270	185,083	100,897	90,454	121,380	.48
United States	172,551	275,458	131,648	173,228	167,738	114,684	.45
Belgium	82,487	85,441	89,904	80,087	61,532	95,471	.38
Cyprus	4,646	3,416	2,550	1,221	4,974	11,071	.04
Austria-Hungary	6,552	1,698	7,514	7,052	6,833	9,665	.04
Turkey, Asiatic	6,294	2,385	2,735	11,076	7,052	8,220	.03
Greece	5,566	6,831	7,270	4,501	4,818	4,910	.02
Canary Islands	36,220	61,556	36,796	52,792	26,274	3,679	.02
Turkey, European	6,296	16,420	5,324	7,086	1,479	1,173	} .07
Other	16,936	14,235	15,923	18,790	18,381	17,349	
Total foreign countries	28,327,494	28,316,435	30,699,225	31,392,132	26,706,555	24,523,121	97.04
BRITISH POSSESSIONS.							
Australasia:							
Victoria	265,840	275,152	237,543	211,518	262,689	342,295	
South Australia	310,061	255,491	302,015	322,406	331,472	338,922	
New South Wales	24,608	25,374	15,432	12,536	40,976	28,722	} 2.81
New Zealand	866	1,640	1,246	311	866	268	
Queensland	1,069	4,925	29	195	121	73	
Tasmania	53	258	5				
Cape of Good Hope	16,264	18,278	18,756	12,507	16,200	15,578	.06
Channel Islands	13,075	10,711	14,746	15,490	17,632	6,798	.03
Malta and Gozo	4,211	4,813	4,360	4,584	4,409	2,891	.01
Gibraltar	3,468	4,419	6,550	2,881	1,626	1,864	.01
Natal	768	487	535	726	1,469	623	} .04
Other	16,354	19,666	10,298	25,315	16,356	10,137	
Total British possessions	656,637	621,214	611,515	608,469	693,816	748,171	2.96
Total	28,984,131	28,937,649	31,310,740	32,000,601	27,400,371	25,271,292	100.00

YEAST. (a)

	Annual average	1896.	1897.	1898.	1899.	1900.	Per ct. in 1900.
FOREIGN COUNTRIES.	Dollars.	Dollars.	Dollars.	Dollars.	Dollars.	Dollars.	
Netherlands	998,381	1,065,856	1,069,798	1,010,933	958,316	887,002	53.50
France	593,405	665,017	557,701	579,512	540,668	624,129	37.65
Germany	196,195	320,371	227,416	175,890	146,146	111,151	6.70
Denmark	17,800	20,780	18,269	17,933	16,181	15,835	.96
Other b	6,529	5,835	4,302	3,913	6,842	11,753	.71
Total foreign countries	1,812,310	2,077,859	1,877,486	1,788,181	1,668,153	1,649,870	99.52
BRITISH POSSESSIONS.							
Canada	4,103	974	1,363	6,136	4,015	8,030	.48
Total	1,816,413	2,078,833	1,878,849	1,794,317	1,672,168	1,657,900	100.00

a For quantities, see page 221.
b Including in 1900 imports from the United States valued at $10,925.

11820—No. 26—02——10

Quantity of the agricultural imports of the United Kingdom (animal matter), by articles and countries, during the five calendar years 1896–1900.

CATTLE. (a)

Countries from which imported.	Annual average, 1896–1900.	Calendar years.					Per ct. in 1900.
		1896.	1897.	1898.	1899.	1900.	
FOREIGN COUNTRIES.							
	Number.	Number.	Number.	Number.	Number.	Number.	
United States........	370,067	393,119	416,299	369,478	321,229	350,209	70.66
Argentina............	70,570	65,699	73,852	89,369	85,365	38,562	7.78
Uruguay	220	332	42	....	518	209	} .04
Other b	7	36	....	....	....	....	
Total foreign countries....	440,864	459,186	490,193	458,847	407,112	388,980	78.48
BRITISH POSSESSIONS.							
Canada..............	107,198	101,591	126,495	108,405	94,660	104,839	21.15
Channel Islands.....	1,745	1,719	1,633	1,814	1,732	1,826	.37
Other c	11	57	....	....	....	....	......
Total British possessions ..	108,954	103,367	128,128	110,219	96,392	106,665	21.52
Total	549,818	562,553	618,321	569,066	503,504	495,645	100.00

HORSES. (d)

	Annual average, 1896–1900.	1896.	1897.	1898.	1899.	1900.	Per ct. in 1900.
FOREIGN COUNTRIES.							
	Number.	Number.	Number.	Number.	Number.	Number.	
United States........	25,065	17,980	26,520	25,328	25,169	30,380	58.
Russia	6,651	3,201	5,662	5,413	7,198	11,779	22.
Denmark............	2,890	2,567	2,637	2,545	3,597	3,102	5.
Netherlands.........	1,045	923	989	1,175	1,112	1,028	1.
France	454	242	186	316	503	1,022	1.
Germany	1,497	3,025	1,645	1,091	1,043	679	1.
Argentina...........	340	558	251	227	177	487	
Belgium.............	186	179	186	202	199	166	} .99
Other...............	61	106	56	42	45	57	
Total foreign countries	38,189	28,731	38,132	36,339	39,043	48,700	94.04
BRITISH POSSESSIONS.							
Canada..............	7,445	11,852	11,247	6,359	4,792	2,976	5.75
Australasia:							
Victoria.........	10	6	1	7	....	36	
New South Wales	32	10	48	87	6	10	
New Zealand	5	7	4	7	6	3	} .09
South Australia..	1	4	....	....	2	....	
Queensland	....	1	....	....	....	....	
Channel Islands.....	26	31	24	23	22	27	.05
British East Indies e.	17	17	17	20	12	17	.03
Cape of Good Hope..	13	3	11	35	7	8	.02
Malta and Gozo	7	4	31	1	....	1	} .02
Other...............	15	11	4	43	9	8	
Total British possessions ..	7,571	11,946	11,387	6,582	4,856	3,086	5.96
Total	45,760	40,677	49,519	42,921	43,899	51,786	100.00

a For values, see page 64.
b In 1896 including 4 cows from Norway.
c In 1896 including 32 oxen and bulls from Queensland.
d For values, see page 65.
e Including stallions and mares, as follows: From Bombay, 13 in 1896 and 3 in 1897; from Madras, 1 in 1896 and 1 in 1897; and from Bengal, 1 in 1896 and 5 in 1897.

uantity of the agricultural imports of the United Kingdom (animal matter), etc.—Cont'd.

SHEEP. (a)

	Annual average, 1896-1900.	Calendar years.					Per ct. in 1900.
		1896.	1897.	1898.	1899.	1900.	
OREIGN COUNTRIES.	*Number.*	*Number.*	*Number.*	*Number.*	*Number.*	*Number.*	
rgentina............	335,144	339,381	345,217	430,073	382,080	178,969	46.75
nited States........	172,894	266,760	186,755	147,021	121,030	142,906	37.33
enmark.............	30,208	63,293	12,797	28,086	22,650	24,217	6.32
ruguay.............	2,319	3,090	2,972	....	4,463	1,068	.28
hile	3,761	897	....	4,304	13,602	....	......
orway	2,375	11,874	....	....	....	....	......
Total foreign countries....	546,701	685,295	547,741	609,484	543,825	347,160	90.68
RITISH POSSESSIONS.							
anada..............	57,840	83,767	63,761	42,070	63,930	35,673	9.32
alkland Islands....	2,438	....	....	12,193	....	....	......
ustralasia..........	104	518	....	....	....	....	......
ther................	3	12	2	....	....	....	......
Total British possessions ..	60.385	84,297	63,763	54,263	63,930	35,673	9.32
Total	607,086	769,592	611,504	663,747	607,755	382,833	100.00

SWINE. (b)

OREIGN COUNTRIES.	*Number.*	*Number.*	*Number.*	*Number.*	*Number.*	*Number.*
nited States........	90	....	....	450	....	....
ther................	1	4	....	....	....	....
Total	91	4	....	450	....	....

BONES FOR FERTILIZERS. (c)

OREIGN COUNTRIES.	*Tons.* (d)	*Tons.* (d)	*Tons.* (d)	*Tons.* (d)	*Tons.* (d)	*Tons.* (d)	
rgentina............	9,355	13,219	10,440	11,574	7,397	4,143	6.08
ruguay	2,645	4,190	3,348	719	907	4,063	5.96
etherlands.........	2,130	2,001	2,296	2,689	2,112	1,550	2.28
ermany.............	956	467	1,191	1,196	1,409	519	.76
razil	2,266	2,382	2,184	1,851	4,449	463	.68
pain...............	543	496	789	860	214	356	.52
enmark............	461	380	479	581	534	332	.49
gypt	1,218	1.334	949	1,953	1,532	320	.47
urkey, Asiatic	526	577	276	506	991	281	.41
hile	269	302	305	98	360	279	.41
rance	454	109	1,216	394	307	246	.36
elgium.............	497	156	935	665	574	156	.23
orway	139	....	49	315	267	64	.09
nited States........	85	188	80	31	109	15	.02
urkey, European...	186	10	....	22	883	13	.02
ussia..............	1,189	179	325	2,120	3,322	....	......
orocco.............	624	1,164	5	1,301	650	....	......
ther e	150	182	151	217	87	112	.17
Total foreign countries....	23,693	27,336	25,018	27,092	26,104	12,912	18.95

a For values, see page 65.
b For values, see page 66.
c For values, see page 67.
d Tons of 2,240 pounds.
e In 1896 including 81 tons from Cyprus.

Quantity of the agricultural imports of the United Kingdom (animal matter), etc.—Cont'd.

BONES FOR FERTILIZERS—Continued.

Countries from which imported.	Annual average, 1896–1900.	Calendar years.					Per ct. in 1900.
		1896.	1897.	1898.	1899.	1900.	
BRITISH POSSESSIONS.							
British East Indies:	*Tons.* (a)	*Tons.* (a)	*Tons.* (a)	*Tons.* (a)	*Tons.* (a)	*Tons.* (a)	
Bombay	30,741	27,633	23,315	24,289	32,778	45,691	
Bengal	9,355	10,062	10,381	7,463	9,705	9,165	80.73
Burma	194	399	151	161	110	149	
Madras	4				18		
Cape of Good Hope..	71	76	24	100	61	94	.14
Channel Islands.....	90	109	103	80	81	79	.11
Australasia b	256	986	109	117	18	47	.07
Gibraltar	54	80	85	104			
Other	16		42		40		
Total British possessions ..	40,781	39,345	34,210	32,314	42,811	55,225	81.05
Total	64,474	66,681	59,228	59,406	68,915	68,137	100.00

BONES (EXCEPT FOR FERTILIZERS), INCLUDING ANIMAL CHARCOAL. (c)

	Annual average	1896.	1897.	1898.	1899.	1900.	Per ct. in 1900.
FOREIGN COUNTRIES.	*Tons.*(a)	*Tons.*(a)	*Tons.*(a)	*Tons.*(a)	*Tons.*(a)	*Tons.*(a)	
Argentina	1,413	773	911	956	188	4,237	35.73
Brazil	2,391	2,099	2,917	3,358	1,317	2,265	19.10
Uruguay	851	1,319		633	60	2,245	18.93
Germany	147	90	10	42	52	540	4.55
Netherlands	166	90	58	120	228	333	2.81
United States	211	386	132	176	161	200	1.69
France	235	230	34	284	510	115	.97
Belgium	144	214	149	135	139	83	.70
Other d	191	170	39	115	400	231	1.95
Total foreign countries	5,749	5,371	4,250	5,819	3,055	10,249	86.43
BRITISH POSSESSIONS.							
Australasia:							
New South Wales	522	887	392	331	571	428	
Queensland	162	246	195	165	67	138	
Victoria	139	147	179	126	134	109	
South Australia .	22	44	4	40	9	12	5.87
New Zealand....	10	13	8	11	12	9	
West Australia ..	1	6					
Tasmania		2					
British East Indies ..	256	369	250		63	597	.03
Other	91	13	18	27	80	316	5.87
Total British possessions ..	1,203	1,727	1,046	700	936	1,609	13.57
Total	6,952	7,098	5,296	6,519	3,991	11,858	100.00

a Tons of 2,240 pounds.
b In 1896 including 117 tons from Victoria and 590 tons from Queensland.
c For values, see page 67.
d Including imports from Colombia amounting to 19 tons in 1896 and 2 tons in 1898.

Quantity of the agricultural imports of the United Kingdom (animal matter), etc.—Cont'd.

BRISTLES. (a)

ountries from which imported.	Annual average, 1896–1900.	Calendar years.					Per ct. in 1900.
		1896.	1897,	1898.	1899.	1900.	
FOREIGN COUNTRIES.	*Pounds.*	*Pounds.*	*Pounds.*	*Pounds.*	*Pounds.*	*Pounds.*	
China	1,527,557	1,628,398	1,600,994	1,570,126	1,743,024	1,095,244	29.32
Russia	855,301	810,668	853,222	813,302	1,147,550	651,763	17.45
Germany	537,680	664,525	470,769	432,083	542,440	578,582	15.49
Netherlands	388,473	310,390	337,820	307,297	519,517	467,340	12.51
France	147,083	106,704	102,543	122,290	163,493	240,387	6.44
Belgium	32,353	27,235	23,023	29,305	25,616	56,587	1.52
United States	16,085	23,579	8,404	10,665	22,453	15,322	.41
Japan	14,300	10,730	9,560	18,568	24,130	8,512	.23
Italy	11,188	....	....	18,180	33,010	4,500	.12
Other *b*	3,500	2,355	4,830	7,760	1,249	1,306	.03
Total foreign countries	3,533,470	3,584,584	3,411,165	3,329,576	4,222,482	3,119,543	83.52
BRITISH POSSESSIONS.							
British East Indies:							
Bengal	239,437	230,345	327,938	128,325	159,428	351,148	} 9.53
Ceylon	660	....	....	....	....	3,300	
Bombay	9,382	3,670	21,510	8,400	11,859	1,470	
Hongkong	246,882	237,680	240,360	312,448	184,479	259,445	6.94
Other	1,394	....	6,720	....	....	250	.01
Total British possessions	497,755	471,695	596,528	449,173	355,766	615,613	16.48
Total	4,031,225	4,056,279	4,007,693	3,778,749	4,578,248	3,735,156	100.00

BUTTER. (a)

	Annual average, 1896–1900.	1896.	1897,	1898.	1899.	1900.	Per ct. in 1900.
FOREIGN COUNTRIES.	*Pounds.*	*Pounds.*	*Pounds.*	*Pounds.*	*Pounds.*	*Pounds.*	
Denmark	155,566,521	137,623,808	149,489,312	164,083,360	160,165,824	166,470,304	44.00
France	44,991,318	52,371,424	50,190,336	46,683,952	39,641,504	36,069,376	9.53
Netherlands	30,240,874	26,260,528	31,206,672	30,164,288	31,898,720	31,674,160	8.37
Russia	19,700,890	17,002,160	22,253,280	20,197,296	15,561,056	23,490,656	6.21
Sweden	30,456,048	36,268,848	33,511,968	33,035,744	27,507,088	21,956,592	5.80
Belgium	5,506,749	4,270,784	3,418,016	4,075,008	6,947,584	8,822,352	2.33
United States	12,939,226	15,853,936	17,269,952	7,471,744	17,823,344	6,277,152	1.66
Germany	6,133,389	12,076,400	5,797,232	4,617,872	4,138,736	4,036,704	1.07
Argentina	1,983,990	1,765,456	1,216,320	1,649,648	2,253,552	3,034,976	.80
Norway	2,900,240	1,912,400	3,159,744	3,039,456	3,468,080	2,921,520	.77
Italy	86,419	152,208	151,088	32,816	....	95,984	} .03
Other	25,402	8,176	2,688	87,248	21,840	7,056	
Total foreign countries	310,531,066	305,566,128	317,666,608	315,138,432	309,427,328	304,856,832	80.57
BRITISH POSSESSIONS.							
Australasia:							
Victoria	20,709,024	17,344,880	18,936,400	13,912,976	23,715,328	29,635,536	} 15.30
New Zealand	10,715,130	6,313,776	8,570,464	7,884,288	12,503,568	18,353,552	
New South Wales	4,278,400	871,024	2,669,520	3,851,792	4,878,832	9,120,832	
South Australia	346,371	126,896	18,256	179,424	792,064	615,216	
Queensland	261,766	....	143,360	782,768	200,704	182,000	
Canada	16,643,648	9,895,984	12,253,024	17,568,880	26,004,296	15,491,056	4.09
British East Indies	92,109	63,840	92,736	110,096	76,832	117,040	.03
Channel Islands	28,784	40,544	41,888	28,112	15,568	17,808	} .01
Other *c*	13,798	1,344	1,568	18,368	43,792	3,920	
Total British possessions	53,089,030	34,658,288	42,727,216	44,286,704	70,235,984	73,536,960	19.43
Total	363,620,096	340,224,416	360,393,824	359,425,136	379,663,312	378,393,792	100.00

a For values, see page 68.
b Including imports from Denmark amounting to 560 pounds in 1896, 2,370 pounds in 1897, and 7,010 pounds in 1898.
c Including imports from Newfoundland and Labrador amounting to 2,240 pounds in 1898 and 5,040 pounds in 1899.

Quantity of the agricultural imports of the United Kingdom (animal matter), etc.—Cont'd.

CHEESE. (a)

Countries from which imported.	Annual average, 1896–1900.	Calendar years.					Per ct. in 1900.
		1896.	1897.	1898.	1899.	1900.	
FOREIGN COUNTRIES.							
	Pounds.	*Pounds.*	*Pounds.*	*Pounds.*	*Pounds.*	*Pounds.*	
United States........	66,530,643	65,092,944	70,740,992	54,431,440	66,162,544	76,225,296	25.15
Netherlands.........	34,483,456	32,814,656	33,331,648	32,807,600	36,796,592	36,666,784	12.10
Belgium.............	5,339,981	3,504,144	4,370,240	5,460,224	6,414,688	6,950,608	2.29
France	4,133,629	5,115,712	4,072,096	3,705,632	3,842,384	3,932,320	1.30
Italy................	254,800	148,736	211,904	62,272	125,664	725,424	.24
Germany............	64,982	57,344	71,792	63,056	58,352	74,368	.03
Other b	58,442	69,664	44,800	57,456	57,456	62,832	.02
Total foreign countries....	110,865,933	106,803,200	112,843,472	96,587,680	113,457,680	124,637,632	41.13
BRITISH POSSESSIONS.							
Canada..............	157,745,549	138,241,264	170,986,368	160,404,272	149,766,176	169,329,664	55.87
Australasia:							
New Zealand....	6,218,285	6,170,640	7,644,336	4,977,168	3,606,176	8,693,104	} 2.99
Victoria	74,659	5,040	24,640	18,480	8,960	316,176	
New South Wales	16,442	1,008	15,904	448	1,792	63,056	
Newfoundland and Labrador..........	79,497	157,920	39,200	16,912	169,680	13,776	} .01
Other................	6,720	7,728	2,016	13,664	5,264	4,928	
Total British possessions ..	164,141,152	144,583,600	178,712,464	165,430,944	153,558,048	178,420,704	58.87
Total	275,007,085	251,386,800	291,555,936	262,018,624	267,015,728	303,058,336	100.00

CONDENSED MILK. (a)

FOREIGN COUNTRIES.							
	Pounds.	*Pounds.*	*Pounds.*	*Pounds.*	*Pounds.*	*Pounds.*	
Netherlands.........	35,358,758	24,403,792	31,853,472	37,642,304	38,449,376	44,444,848	40.
France	36,465,184	33,653,872	36,233,120	34,602,848	34,693,792	43,142,288	39.
Norway	9,768,640	5,226,704	8,632,064	11,972,576	11,205,376	11,806,480	10.
United States........	3,295,174	1,562,736	4,411,568	3,228,512	3,094,784	4,178,272	3.
Belgium.............	2,822,781	2,441,824	2,557,744	2,677,808	2,613,632	3,822,896	3.
Germany	1,039,965	870,464	666,064	761,376	1,240,176	1,661,744	1.20
Italy................	618,778	210,224	148,848	410,480	987,840	1,336,496	1.16
Denmark............	51,946	11,648	142,240	87,808	9,744	8,288	} .01
Other................	19,107	6,272	6,496	75,712	3,808	3,248	
Total foreign countries	89,440,333	68,387,536	84,651,616	91,459,424	92,298,528	110,404,560	99.87
BRITISH POSSESSIONS.							
Total British possessions.............	80,237	81,984	47,600	75,264	56,560	139,776	.13
Total	89,520,570	68,469,520	84,699,216	91,534,688	92,355,088	110,544,336	100.00

a For values, see page 69.
b Including imports from Russia amounting to 40,992 pounds in 1896, 29,792 pounds in 1897, 25,424 pounds in 1898, and 34,720 pounds in 1899.

uantity of the agricultural imports of the United Kingdom (animal matter), etc.—Cont'd.

MILK, OTHER THAN CONDENSED.(a)

	Annual average, 1896–1900.	Calendar years.					Per ct. in 1900.
		1896.	1897.	1898.	1899.	1900.	
ꓷREIGN COUNTRIES.	*Pounds.(b)*	*Gallons.(c)*	*Pounds.*	*Pounds.*	*Pounds.*	*Pounds.*	
rance	752,444	31	704,144	820,960	280,560	1,204,112	68.75
etherlands.........	100,912	792	10,976	43,008	91,952	257,712	14.71
enmark...........	196,784	6,726	88,032	144,368	323,456	231,280	13.20
nited States........	33,712	....	134,736	....	....	112	.01
weden...:........	83,804	19,261	146,720	134,848	53,648	....	
ther..............	57,820	24	35,952	41,216	95,872	58,240	3.33
Total foreign countries	1,225,476	26,834	1,120,560	1,184,400	845,488	1,751,456	100.00
RITISH POSSESSIONS.							
otal British possessions d	11,956	504	112	12,992	34,720	....	......
Total	1,237,432	27,338	1,120,672	1,197,392	880,208	1,751,456	100.00

EGGS. (e)

FOREIGN COUNTRIES.	*Dozens.*	*Dozens.*	*Dozens.*	*Dozens.*	*Dozens.*	*Dozens.*	
Russia..............	35,055,434	24,061,680	31,323,330	36,459,030	43,186,010	40,247,120	23.84
Germany...........	31,384,868	29,304,860	29,718,460	28,211,280	34,549,860	35,139,880	20.82
Denmark...........	20,079,638	15,666,230	17,488,000	20,195,080	22,660,300	24,388,580	14.45
Belgium............	23,783,188	22,439,090	24,641,820	23,499,620	24,575,580	23,759,830	14.07
France	25,263,894	32,757,760	26,756,670	21,150,960	22,885,580	22,768,500	13.49
Egypt	1,865,764	107,930	546,840	1,493,840	2,547,780	4,632,430	2.74
United States.......	1,855,808	477,030	1,155,090	1,941,050	1,447,240	4,258,630	2.52
Morocco...........	1,098,000	527,800	380,440	788,820	1,079,460	2,713,480	1.61
Netherlands.........	712,564	321,230	528,830	607,190	1,087,460	1,018,110	.60
Spain.:............	742,712	753,620	490,500	1,260,270	380,260	828,910	.49
Portugal	631,906	538,060	557,070	1,007,000	408,160	649,240	.38
Sweden	109,912	194,450	118,270	66,160	104,120	66,560	.04
Austria-Hungary....	42,640	....	182,600	....	3,600	27,000	.02
Italy	44,186	6,220	195,300	16,720	170	2,520	} .01
Other..............	49,764	21,670	100,710	21,860	86,460	18,120	
Total foreign countries.:	142,720,278	127,177,630	134,183,930	136,718,880	155,002,040	160,518,910	95.08
BRITISH POSSESSIONS.							
Canada.............	6,538,020	5,003,170	5,687,690	7,453,550	6,468,670	8,077,020	4.78
Gibraltar...........	52,226	16,540	58,800	18,500	67,460	99,830	.06
Channel Islands.....	173,418	231,750	345,660	55,080	141,260	93,340	.06
Malta and Gozo.....	14,794	14,540	38,100	....	730	20,600	.01
Australasia	10,076	3,680	....	....	46,700	....	
Other..............	7,588	2,800	3,360	....	20,700	11,080	.01
Total British possessions ..	6,796,122	5,272,480	6,133,610	7,527,130	6,745,520	8,301,870	4.92
Total	149,516,400	132,450,110	140,317,540	144,246,010	161,747,560	168,820,780	100.00

a For values, see page 69.
b Annual average, 1897–1900.
c United States standard gallons

d In 1896 comprising 504 gallons from Victoria.
e For values, see page 70.

Quantity of the agricultural imports of the United Kingdom (animal matter), etc.—Cont'd.

FEATHERS AND DOWNS FOR BEDS. (a) (b)

Countries from which imported.	Annual average, 1896–1900.	Calendar years.					Per ct. in 1900.
		1896.	1897.	1898.	1899.	1900.	
FOREIGN COUNTRIES.	*Pounds.*	*Pounds.*	*Pounds.*	*Pounds.*	*Pounds.*	*Pounds.*	
France	978,387	798,448	1,063,888	1,055,712	1,104,992	868,896	18.99
United States.......	348,947	219,856	301,616	51,184	307,664	864,416	18.90
China	666,826	418,096	251,888	1,214,976	699,776	749,392	16.38
Germany	729,523	927,584	768,656	651,056	642,880	657,440	14.37
Japan	218,557	111,216	172,704	152,544	335,216	321,104	7.02
Netherlands........	95,446	79,744	97,328	101,136	70,000	129,024	2.82
Belgium............	67,648	52,864	53,536	141,904	54,656	35,280	.77
Russia.............	33,018	78,064	20,160	41,552	15,904	9,408	.21
Other c	67,738	54,992	33,152	35,616	85,456	129,472	2.83
Total foreign countries	3,206,090	2,740,864	2,762,928	3,445,680	3,316,544	3,764,432	82.29
BRITISH POSSESSIONS.							
Hongkong..........	801,270	200,816	1,176,784	922,992	929,040	776,720	16.98
Other...............	43,613	41,664	85,232	21,616	35,952	33,600	.73
Total British possessions ..	844,883	242,480	1,262,016	944,608	964,992	810,320	17.71
Total	4,050,973	2,983,344	4,024,944	4,390,288	4,281,536	4,574,752	100.00

FEATHERS AND DOWNS FOR ORNAMENT. (d)

FOREIGN COUNTRIES.	*Pounds.*	*Pounds.*	*Pounds.*	*Pounds.*	*Pounds.*	*Pounds.*	
France	416,359	419,808	450,444	438,169	452,587	320,787	27.27
Netherlands........	216,602	162,400	169,471	180,714	321,335	249,089	21.17
Germany...........	42,000	4,105	2,994	90,542	62,527	49,831	4.23
United States.......	43,664	50,646	34,848	63,047	43,811	25,967	2.21
Egypt	6,784	4,184	4,922	7,154	9,360	8,301	.70
Tripoli	2,331	4,250	1,110	1,008	1,872	3,416	.29
China	9,659	1,559	2,957	15,707	24,707	3,364	.29
Dutch East Indies, n. e. s..............	3,268	860	1,210	7,541	4,160	2,568	.22
Japan	2,157	130	1,385	2,602	4,318	2,352	.20
Turkey, Asiatic	2,142	33	364	6,590	1,400	2,326	.20
Belgium............	3,968	2,798	5,056	6,011	3,865	2,110	.18
Brazil	2,009	2,069	2,413	1,553	2,039	1,969	.17
Colombia...........	1,412	3,825	685	1,343	673	535	.04
Venezuela..........	745	1,048	930	722	576	447	} .04
Argentina..........	118	173	160	28	208	20	
Portuguese East Africa	1,030	5,150	....	....	....	....	
Morocco............	522	7	774	790	1,040	....	
Uruguay...........	128	20	133	326	160	....	
Other...............	5,344	2,116	1,458	15,796	5,857	1,493	.13
Total foreign countries	760,242	665,181	681,314	839,643	940,495	674,575	57.34
BRITISH POSSESSIONS.							
Cape of Good Hope..	367,231	333,186	370,873	372,000	381,686	378,413	32.16
British East Indies:							
Bombay........	68,506	83,232	68,126	109,517	29,960	51,694	}
Bengal	53,118	67,720	76,104	40,077	30,868	50,820	
Straits Settlements	2,244	3,960	796	3,410	661	2,392	} 9.03
Madras..........	451	50	290	340	273	1,300	
Ceylon	218	460	300	180	112	40	
Hongkong..........	12,683	1,586	9,690	18,744	24,692	8,705	.74
Malta and Gozo	4,484	2,477	3,988	5,366	6,410	4,180	.36
British West Indies..	1,891	712	2,624	3,360	584	2,174	.18
Australasia.........	1,836	1,774	2,252	1,384	2,409	1,360	.12
Aden	2,093	1,964	2,489	4,445	1,066	502	.04
Natal..............	1,013	4,200	86	25	750	2	} .03
Other..............	150	10	32	183	207	320	
Total British possessions ..	515,918	501,331	537,650	559,031	479,678	501,902	42.66
Total	1,276,160	1,166,512	1,218,964	1,398,674	1,420,173	1,176,477	100.00

a For values, see page 70.
b Including feather beds.
c Including imports from Portugal amounting to 29,120 pounds in 1896, 15,008 pounds in 1897, 11,872 pounds in 1898, and 63,840 pounds in 1899, and from European Turkey 8,960 pounds in 1896 and 5,488 pounds in 1897.
d For values, see page 71.

Quantity of the agricultural imports of the United Kingdom (animal matter), etc.—Cont'd.

SILK, RAW. (a)

Countries from which imported.	Annual average, 1896–1900.	Calendar years.					Per ct. in 1900.
		1896.	1897.	1898.	1899.	1900.	
FOREIGN COUNTRIES.							
	Pounds.	*Pounds.*	*Pounds.*	*Pounds.*	*Pounds.*	*Pounds.*	
China	772,758	571,580	628,442	838,914	1,193,953	630,901	.44.64
France	686,297	658,068	773,433	882,908	756,573	360,500	25.51
Japan	48,334	87,662	12,900	38,480	51,240	51,385	3.64
Italy	30,289	28,050	40,111	27,210	28,510	27,562	1.95
United States........	993	....	3,024	....	....	1,942	.14
Turkey, European...	5,612	8,852	8,728	3,108	5,744	1,630	.11
Greece...............	1,322	....	2,595	2,460	....	1,556	.11
Turkey, Asiatic......	1,071	3,446	220	220	....	1,470	.10
Belgium..............	1,332	250	558	5,200	482	171	.01
Other................	1,610	200	....	2,620	1,700	3,550	.25
Total foreign countries....	1,549,618	1,358,108	1,470,011	1,801,120	2,038,202	1,080,647	76.46
BRITISH POSSESSIONS.							
British East Indies:							
Bengal	236,589	198,170	268,687	278,552	195,980	241,555	
Ceylon	3,550	900	1,500	110	1,000	14,240	18.10
Bombay	494	2,300	170	....	....	....	
Hongkong...........	69,237	138,190	65,240	32,300	33,580	76,878	5.44
Other................	5,366	....	....	26,830	....	....	
Total British possessions ..	315,236	339,560	335,597	337,792	230,560	332,673	23.54
Total	1,864,854	1,697,668	1,805,608	2,138,912	2,268,762	1,413,320	100.00

SILK WASTE. (b)

FOREIGN COUNTRIES.							
	Pounds.	*Pounds.*	*Pounds.*	*Pounds.*	*Pounds.*	*Pounds.*	
China	3,088,736	2,646,336	2,332,960	3,838,016	3,723,664	2,902,704	42.68
France	547,994	542,640	392,224	521,808	598,600	689,696	10.14
Belgium..............	508,704	567,504	537,264	530,768	520,240	387,744	5.70
Japan	593,667	838,096	369,488	898,016	590,800	271,936	4.00
Germany.............	88,167	4,032	58,912	45,584	104,384	227,920	3.35
Netherlands........	21,347	3,584	6,496	4,816	30,128	61,712	.91
Turkey, European...	43,904	29,792	68,544	54,768	29,232	37,184	.55
Russia..............	10,774	17,360	2,240	1,904	25,760	6,608	.10
United States........	23,005	15,008	27,888	10,864	55,776	5,488	.08
Spain............	11,200	18,816	11,648	6,608	14,672	4,256	.06
Macao	2,016	....	....	6,608	3,472	....	
Other c	34,832	45,360	27,776	32,928	45,472	22,624	.33
Total foreign countries....	4,974,346	4,728,528	3,835,440	5,952,688	5,737,200	4,617,872	67.90
BRITISH POSSESSIONS.							
Hongkong...........	1,715,235	1,726,256	1,372,000	1,365,168	2,335,424	1,777,328	26.14
British East Indies:							
Bengal	307,754	87,696	373,632	419,552	401,072	256,816	
Bombay	98,784	138,432	30,912	65,632	128,800	130,144	
Madras	18,323	12,320	40,096	21,504	7,504	10,192	
Burma	5,667	5,936	....	4,144	9,968	8,288	5.96
Ceylon	187,130	346,752	482,608	103,264	3,024	....	
Straits Settlements	5,600	....	....	....	28,000	....	
Other................	627	1,456	....	....	1,680	....	
Total British possessions ..	2,339,120	2,318,848	2,299,248	1,979,264	2,915,472	2,182,768	32.10
Total	7,313,466	7,047,376	6,134,688	7,931,952	8,652,672	6,800,640	100.00

a For values, see page 71.   b For values, see page 72.   c In 1896 including 33,600 pounds from Italy.

Quantity of the agricultural imports of the United Kingdom (animal matter), etc.—Cont'd.

MOHAIR. (a)

Countries from which imported.	Annual average, 1896–1900.	Calendar years.					Per ct. in 1900.
		1896.	1897.	1898.	1899.	1900.	
FOREIGN COUNTRIES.							
	Pounds.	*Pounds.*	*Pounds.*	*Pounds.*	*Pounds.*	*Pounds.*	
Turkey, European...	8,796,805	4,224,730	9,958,920	9,491,139	12,283,242	8,025,994	44.48
Turkey, Asiatic......	519,672	604,680	742,470	670,730	68,100	512,380	2.84
France	22,920	15,390	15,770	45,460	15,220	22,760	.12
Germany	16,891	43,400	140	200	19,406	21,310	.12
Russia	56,518	1,560	....	263,560	17,470	....	....
China	34,478	27,300	....	....	145,090	....	....
Italy............	13,788	12,600	56,340	....	....	....	....
Other b	37,797	32,920	48,320	40,696	41,920	25,130	.14
Total foreign countries....	9,498,869	4,962,580	10,821,960	10,511,785	12,590,448	8,607,574	47.70
BRITISH POSSESSIONS.							
Cape of Good Hope..	10,356,655	9,240,035	10,889,380	9,881,057	12,948,574	8,824,229	48.90
British East Indies:							
Madras	144,520	....	....	112,200	214,930	395,470	} 2.19
Bombay	784	3,920	....	....	....	....	
Natal	749,110	775,644	1,166,010	692,473	895,880	215,543	1.20
Other c	2,401	4,800	3,100	1,000	1,020	2,082	.01
Total British possessions ..	11,253,470	10,024,399	12,058,490	10,686,730	14,060,404	9,437,324	52.30
Total	20,752,339	14,986,979	22,880,450	21,198,515	26,650,852	18,044,898	100.00

GOATS' HAIR, OTHER THAN MOHAIR. (d)

Countries	Annual average	1896.	1897.	1898.	1899.	1900.	Per ct.
FOREIGN COUNTRIES.							
	Pounds.	*Pounds.*	*Pounds.*	*Pounds.*	*Pounds.*	*Pounds.*	
China	461,134	584,530	496,450•	428,920	297,130	498,640	12.95
Germany	53,327	11,600	31,540	224	42,622	180,650	4.69
France	107,565	24,900	145,520	123,936	74,260	169,208	4.39
United States........	43,471	37,700	1,000	51,160	....	127,495	3.31
Belgium............	193,411	150,190	393,926	192,833	138,699	91,403	2.37
Turkey, European...	833	....	3,000	....	....	266	.01
Turkey, Asiatic......	2,240	....	6,300	280	4,420	200	.01
Russia	60,760	....	276,300	27,500	....	....	....
Italy............	14,216	8,740	....	55,140	7,200	....	....
Other............	107,314	5,145	65,480	83,620	177,684	204,642	5.31
Total foreign countries....	1,044,271	822,805	1,419,516	963,613	742,915	1,272,504	33.04
BRITISH POSSESSIONS.							
British East Indies:							
Bombay	1,654,088	1,300,828	1,805,600	2,308,732	1,377,580	1,477,700	} 66.92
Madras	314,671	4,000	200	291,000	191,000	1,087,156	
Ceylon..........	2,576	....	....	•	....	12,880	
Bengal	3,748	5,000	340	13,400	....	....	
Natal	22,680	....	32,700	80,700	....	....	
Other............	28,778	23,600	700	6,560	111,500	1,530	.04
Total British possessions ..	2,026,541	1,333,428	1,839,540	2,700,392	1,680,080	2,579,266	66.96
Total	3,070,812	2,156,233	3,259,056	3,664,005	2,422,995	3,851,770	100.00

HAIR OF THE ALPACA, VICUÑA, AND LLAMA. (d)

Countries	Annual average	1896.	1897.	1898.	1899.	1900.	Per ct.
FOREIGN COUNTRIES.							
	Pounds.	*Pounds.*	*Pounds.*	*Pounds.*	*Pounds.*	*Pounds.*	
Peru	4,108,821	3,635,440	4,550,463	3,887,534	4,234,100	4,236,566	73.10
Chile	906,198	842,840	465,508	889,610	1,184,338	1,148,694	19.82
Germany	164,480	207,610	84,720	75,780	47,060	407,232	7.02
United States........	57,576	276,190	11,692	....	....	....	....
Other............	2,627	....	9,160	670	....	3,304	.06
Total	5,239,702	4,962,080	5,121,543	4,853,594	5,465,498	5,795,796	100.00

a For values, see page 72.
b In 1900 including 13,360 pounds from the United States.
c The statistics for 1896 and 1900 here given differ somewhat from those published in the trade reports of the United Kingdom, owing to the correction of two obvious errors in the British returns.
d For values, see page 73.

Quantity of the agricultural imports of the United Kingdom (animal matter), etc.—Cont'd.

SHEEP'S WOOL. (a)

Countries from which imported.	Annual average, 1896–1900.	Calendar years.					Per ct. in 1900.
		1896.	1897.	1898.	1899.	1900.	
FOREIGN COUNTRIES.							
	Pounds.	*Pounds.*	*Pounds.*	*Pounds.*	*Pounds.*	*Pounds.*	
France	21,972,714	20,280,339	23,338,713	20,318,094	26,261,321	19,665,106	3.56
Turkey, Asiatic	14,174,485	14,645,740	22,635,270	11,824,198	8,341,680	13,425,539	2.43
Chile	10,384,907	6,324,690	7,529,166	12,105,028	13,514,585	12,451,065	2.25
Argentina	11,782,052	7,239,648	12,338,050	17,580,717	10,823,289	10,928,557	1.98
Russia	10,187,850	10,009,260	11,811,600	11,168,038	8,270,433	9,679,918	1.75
Belgium	9,644,467	11,391,012	9,606,619	10,742,655	9,347,166	7,134,882	1.29
Germany	3,943,348	3,105,128	6,114,680	3,074,242	2,397,193	5,025,495	.91
Uruguay	2,660,122	1,963,320	3,244,730	2,631,216	612,210	4,849,135	.88
Turkey, European	2,353,823	1,897,170	3,092,192	2,269,900	1,557,764	2,952,091	.53
Egypt	2,573,204	3,145,630	2,701,805	2,442,722	2,283,764	2,292,100	.41
Peru	2,236,173	2,698,128	2,753,912	1,694,424	2,064,334	1,970,065	.36
Italy	1,335,944	559,550	770,484	1,498,154	2,564,005	1,287,527	.23
Portugal	1,917,684	2,363,900	3,052,270	1,402,150	1,505,187	1,264,912	.23
China	1,804,348	2,187,000	1,603,860	3,667,020	596,710	967,150	.17
Denmark	1,464,904	1,120,832	1,822,208	1,232,619	2,188,346	960,517	.17
Morocco	1,083,653	557,272	1,858,600	1,438,650	617,790	945,953	.17
Netherlands	1,183,543	1,184,702	1,651,406	1,096,508	1,045,997	939,102	.17
United States	3,040,962	4,236,920	675,909	943,232	8,647,440	701,309	.13
Persia	988,960	416,200	1,984,200	1,538,100	418,900	587,400	.11
Portuguese East Africa	206,576	33,500	302,600	143,500	31,260	522,020	.09
Spain	993,068	851,332	2,415,704	754,695	577,616	365,994	.07
Austria-Hungary	83,948	110,050	203,200	71,980	29,636	4,872	
Brazil	30,440	59,100			90,900	2,200	
Tripoli	61,329		306,643				
Roumania	50,454	184,470	67,800				
Pacific islands	32,754		163,770				
Canary Islands	18,388	91,380		560			
Other b	51,499	23,436	95,670	63,615	51,897	22,878	
Total foreign countries	106,261,599	96,679,709	122,141,061	109,702,017	103,839,423	98,945,787	17.89
BRITISH POSSESSIONS.							
Australasia:							
New Zealand	129,718,469	117,648,300	127,672,688	135,857,500	131,188,675	136,225,180	
New South Wales	148,440,747	163,717,080	165,843,338	152,658,462	146,184,762	113,800,092	
Victoria	76,110,291	82,370,220	84,456,615	74,662,506	71,813,542	67,248,570	69.85
Queensland	46,177,539	50,044,200	62,195,616	46,572,700	38,377,157	33,698,020	
South Australia	31,673,135	46,675,270	36,688,010	24,960,500	26,748,020	23,293,875	
West Australia	9,485,824	11,550,190	9,486,272	8,539,680	8,830,040	9,022,940	
Tasmania	4,401,425	5,639,920	4,968,300	4,336,200	3,984,266	3,078,440	
British East Indies:							
Bombay	34,145,188	40,056,340	35,172,330	34,525,584	32,980,210	28,041,477	
Bengal	2,587,449	2,612,440	3,248,250	2,580,830	1,957,340	2,288,384	
Madras	410,862	545,280	321,230	609,300	177,990	400,510	5.56
Straits Settlements	444,594	139,300	595,780	715,650	750,700	21,540	
Ceylon	4,616		11,400	8,400	3,280		
Cape of Good Hope	60,049,578	70,476,150	59,215,070	70,833,183	71,083,962	28,639,525	5.18
Falkland Islands	4,491,034	4,091,200	4,142,450	4,788,800	4,780,730	4,651,991	.84
Natal	17,377,744	21,228,250	19,164,710	22,520,000	20,395,913	3,579,844	.64
Hongkong	22,467					112,336	.02
Canada	63,544	23,500		32,200	203,550	58,470	.01
British West Indies	175,048	42,980	31,870	716,306	44,055	40,031	
St. Helena	2,150		1,400	7,100		2,250	.01
Gibraltar	26,162	11,220	84,900	33,796		896	
Malta and Gozo	37,392	2,200	173,600	3,360	7,800		
Other	25,262	21,424	12,530	37,380	50,402	4,574	
Total British possessions	565,820,520	616,895,464	613,486,359	584,999,437	559,512,394	454,208,945	82.11
Total	672,082,119	713,575,173	735,627,420	694,701,454	663,351,817	553,154,732	100.00

a For values, see page 73.
b Including imports from Greece amounting to 8,320 pounds in 1896, 4,480 pounds in 1897, 9,000 pounds in 1898, and 7,280 pounds in 1899.

Quantity of the agricultural imports of the United Kingdom (animal matter), etc.—Cont'd.

WOOL, ETC., NOT ELSEWHERE SPECIFIED, INCLUDING FLOCKS. (a)

Countries from which imported.	Annual average, 1896–1900.	Calendar years.					Per ct. in 1900.
		1896.	1897.	1898.	1899.	1900.	
FOREIGN COUNTRIES.							
	Pounds.	*Pounds.*	*Pounds.*	*Pounds.*	*Pounds.*	*Pounds.*	
France	1,142,986	664,858	1,620,597	774,137	1,204,470	1,450,868	50.17
Belgium.............	398,850	346,845	284,945	341,060	406,755	614,643	21.25
Germany.............	397,754	374,058	454,020	190,430	431,601	538,662	18.63
Netherlands........	104,329	75,897	71,294	97,098	136,671	140,686	4.86
United States........	71,172	86,560	34,602	103,242	43,363	88,094	3.05
Other...............	73,959	75,694	142,900	14,738	80,855	55,608	1.92
Total foreign countries....	2,189,050	1,623,912	2,608,358	1,520,705	2,303,715	2,888,561	99.88
BRITISH POSSESSIONS.							
Total British possessions..............	16,650	36,705	10,450	17,290	15,219	3,585	.12
Total..........	2,205,700	1,660,617	2,618,808	1,537,995	2,318,934	2,892,146	100.00

GLUE, SIZE, AND GELATIN. (b) (c)

Countries from which imported.	Calendar year 1900.	Per cent.	Countries from which imported.	Calendar year 1900.	Per cent.
FOREIGN COUNTRIES.			FOREIGN COUNTRIES—cont'd.		
	Pounds.			*Pounds.*	
France .....:........	8,120,448	34.01	Other	384,608	1.61
Germany..................	5,806,304	24.32	Total foreign countries.	23,839,872	99.86
Netherlands..............	2,767,520	11.59			
Belgium..................	2,709,056	11.35	BRITISH POSSESSIONS.		
United States..	2,272,256	9.52			
Austria-Hungary	1,291,248	5.41	Total British possessions.....	34,384	.14
Russia..........:........	488,432	2.05	Total...................	23,874,256	100.00

GLUE STOCK. (b)(c)

FOREIGN COUNTRIES.			BRITISH POSSESSIONS—cont'd.		
	Pounds.		Australasia:	*Pounds.*	
France ....:....	2,387,056	14.13	New South Wales........	1,436,512	
Belgium....................:....	1,304,016	7.72	Victoria....................	394,912	
Germany ....:....	1,199,968	7.10	Queensland..............	216,384	12.60
Argentina	843,472	5.00	New Zealand	43,344	
United States...:...........	89,040	.53	South Australia..........	30,912	
Other.......................	1,073,632	6.36	West Australia...........	6,272	
Total foreign countries.	6,897,184	40.84	Other	43,120	.25
BRITISH POSSESSIONS.			Total British possessions..........	9,992,640	59.16
British East Indies:			Total..............	16,889,824	100.00
Madras	4,645,984				
Bengal	2,531,536				
Bombay	629,440	46.31			
Straits Settlements	10,080				
Burma	4,144				

a For values, see page 74.   *b* For values, see page 75.   *c* Prior to 1900 not stated by countries.

uantity of the agricultural imports of the United Kingdom (animal matter), etc.—Cont'd.

CATTLE HAIR. (a)(b)

	Annual average, 1896–1900.	Calendar years.					Per ct. in 1900.
		1896.	1897.	1898.	1899.	1900.	
ꓛREIGN COUNTRIES.							
	Pounds.	*Pounds.*	*Pounds.*	*Pounds.*	*Pounds.*	*Pounds.*	
rance	2,391,894	2,672,544	2,697,520	2,188,032	2,561,104	1,840,272	26.47
ermany	1,817,446	1,347,360	2,317,280	1,719,984	1,901,648	1,800,960	25.90
etherlands	1,216,096	1,782,816	1,209,376	927,360	1,215,200	945,728	13.60
nited States	514,797	299,376	119,952	454,160	763,168	937,328	13.48
ussia	380,778	66,304	1,164,352	45,136	323,680	304,416	4.38
elgium	391,104	472,976	110,880	489,104	582,960	299,600	4.31
aly	246,131	93,632	215,376	215,600	421,232	284,816	4.10
ꝑain	57,501	112,000	58,464	....	31,920	85,120	1.22
rgentina	45,942	31,136	17,136	78,848	79,744	22,848	.33
ruguay	28,426	91,392	784	23,968	14,560	11,424	.17
ther	206,349	82,432	251,104	198,800	303,296	196,112	2.82
Total foreign countries	7,296,464	7,051,968	8,162,224	6,340,992	8,198,512	6,728,624	96.78
BRITISH POSSESSIONS.							
Australasia:							
New South Wales	78,109	68,320	74,368	86,688	94,080	67,088	
South Australia	14,022	3,808	7,056	14,560	18,816	25,872	
New Zealand	11,715	12,544	11,760	6,832	14,112	13,328	
Victoria	10,730	10,304	4,816	13,104	19,936	5,488	1.66
Queensland	7,078	12,320	8,960	8,400	3,248	2,464	
West Australia	493			1,008		1,456	
Tasmania	493	1,232	....	784	448	....	
British East Indies	56,112	32,144	40,320	67,200	47,824	93,072	1.34
Other	6,966	3,024	6,160	2,688	7,504	15,456	.22
Total British possessions	185,718	143,696	153,440	201,264	205,968	224,224	3.22
Total	7,482,182	7,195,664	8,315,664	6,542,256	8,404,480	6,952,848	100.00

HORSEHAIR. (c)

FOREIGN COUNTRIES.							
	Pounds.	*Pounds.*	*Pounds.*	*Pounds.*	*Pounds.*	*Pounds.*	
Russia	1,000,294	654,976	1,139,040	1,156,848	1,335,488	715,120	21.35
China	708,042	773,472	805,504	565,376	870,128	525,728	15.70
France	356,742	236,656	569,632	287,168	278,768	411,488	12.29
Belgium	296,016	249,984	196,560	254,800	371,504	407,232	12.16
Germany	396,973	287,392	633,696	471,520	293,888	298,368	8.91
Argentina	205,050	196,448	333,536	133,952	149,408	211,904	6.33
United States	89,712	82,096	25,760	50,960	86,800	202,944	6.06
Uruguay	63,325	11,872	55,440	65,632	81,424	102,256	3.05
Italy	30,845	448	22,400	48,384	36,624	46,368	1.38
Brazil	35,123	52,976	37,296	19,824	43,680	21,840	.65
Netherlands	39,760	29,120	88,480	54,768	12,880	13,552	.41
Other d	27,462	10,640	19,824	15,568	66,304	24,976	.75
Total foreign countries	3,249,344	2,586,080	3,927,168	3,124,800	3,626,896	2,981,776	89.04
BRITISH POSSESSIONS.							
Australasia:							
New South Wales	149,968	128,800	192,416	146,496	120,624	161,504	
Victoria	72,263	72,688	98,112	74,368	65,184	50,960	
New Zealand	32,301	29,120	44,128	29,008	31,696	27,552	
South Australia	19,712	32,704	23,072	15,792	13,328	13,664	7.66
Queensland	4,726	11,872	5,376	2,912	1,904	1,568	
Tasmania	381	....	....		896	1,008	
West Australia	403	672	....	560	448	336	
Canada	29,702	34,272	38,864	16,800	8,624	49,952	1.49
Hongkong	2,733	1,344	....	4,480	....	7,840	.23
Other	27,373	5,376	24,080	19,600	35,056	52,752	1.58
Total British possessions	339,562	316,848	426,048	310,016	277,760	367,136	10.96
Total	3,588,906	2,902,928	4,353,216	3,434,816	3,904,656	3,348,912	100.00

a For values, see page 75.
b Including elk hair.
c For values, see page 76.
d Including imports from Denmark amounting to 1,232 pounds in 1896 and 672 pounds in 1897.

Quantity of the agricultural imports of the United Kingdom (animal matter), etc.—Cont'd.

HIDES. (a)

Countries from which imported.	Annual average, 1896–1900.	Calendar years.					Per ct. in 1900.
		1896.	1897.	1898.	1899.	1900.	
FOREIGN COUNTRIES.	*Pounds.*	*Pounds.*	*Pounds.*	*Pounds.*	*Pounds.*	*Pounds.*	
Belgium	12,688,570	14,690,704	11,457,376	10,266,032	13,864,032	13,164,704	8.49
Germany	12,360,230	8,258,096	13,283,424	13,432,944	14,851,536	11,975,152	7.73
Italy	9,703,411	8,853,376	7,475,552	9,562,784	11,200,448	11,424,896	7.37
Netherlands	10,532,054	8,981,504	10,417,344	11,643,856	12,206,768	9,410,800	6.07
France	9,212,717	7,109,536	8,179,696	9,196,880	12,702,368	8,875,104	5.73
Denmark	4,818,666	1,028,720	3,375,904	7,068,656	7,313,376	5,306,672	3.42
Russia	2,396,442	492,800	1,150,128	2,386,384	3,888,752	4,064,144	2.62
Brazil	2,247,997	1,390,592	1,414,000	2,516,304	8,340,624	2,578,464	1.66
Portugal	2,440,211	1,871,856	2,534,560	3,000,480	2,652,832	2,141,328	1.38
China	1,480,640	1,173,648	894,544	1,467,760	2,421,664	1,445,584	.93
Sweden	1,520,602	547,792	834,960	2,476,208	2,407,776	1,336,272	.86
Norway	841,165	529,536	307,552	586,880	1,775,200	1,006,656	.65
Argentina	2,316,384	3,120,320	3,908,352	2,155,664	1,458,576	939,008	.61
Colombia	535,763	442,736	166,544	579,600	813,904	676,032	.44
Egypt	348,410	237,888	119,280	52,080	695,184	637,616	.41
United States	1,912,803	6,356,336	1,008,000	606,816	1,116,640	476,224	.31
Uruguay	1,728,541	1,459,920	3,346,000	2,924,096	481,824	430,864	.28
French West Africa	109,402		3,584	185,024	167,888	190,512	.12
French Indo-China	626,371	595,392	652,512	1,129,408	574,672	179,872	.12
Chile	391,798	561,568	429,968	361,760	426,272	179,424	.12
Austria-Hungary	102,032	49,056	148,960	82,096	54,768	175,280	.11
Spain	124,118	71,120	123,312	87,808	177,184	161,168	.10
Ecuador	58,554	49,616	10,640	35,952	75,152	121,408	.08
Japan	232,758	228,368	255,024	324,688	248,416	107,296	.07
Peru	66,394	84,784	47,488	59,360	43,232	97,104	.06
Madagascar	272,182	559,216	430,528	77,168	229,824	64,176	.04
Dutch Guiana	94,864	82,208	140,224	84,336	127,232	40,320	.03
Portuguese East Africa	488,365	878,976	1,465,744	85,232	1,792	10,080	.01
Morocco	67,962	96,656	54,320	178,640	6,944	3,248	.21
Other b	178,214	49,392	110,544	186,704	219,520	324,912	
Northern whale fisheries	44,419	10,640	2,016	51,968	94,416	63,056	.04
Total foreign countries	79,942,039	69,862,352	73,748,080	82,853,568	95,638,816	77,607,376	50.07
BRITISH POSSESSIONS.							
British East Indies:							
Bombay	7,990,461	934,752	2,198,448	1,563,632	4,002,432	31,253,040	
Bengal	16,272,032	10,801,504	22,448,944	11,539,136	12,059,152	24,511,424	
Straits Settlements	7,024,281	6,364,064	9,377,200	5,997,264	6,774,880	6,608,000	42.02
Burma	1,799,213	1,873,648	2,616,768	1,257,424	1,744,848	1,503,376	
Madras	827,008	619,136	1,042,944	688,800	611,632	1,172,528	
Ceylon	65,856	49,616	110,096	44,800	33,600	91,168	
Australasia:							
New South Wales	6,797,728	7,340,144	6,700,960	5,884,256	6,832,224	7,231,056	
Queensland	998,995	1,227,072	1,015,952	1,272,208	753,424	726,320	
New Zealand	68,790	13,328	123,760	18,032	8,512	180,320	5.36
Victoria	398,541	381,248	823,088	524,160	122,752	141,456	
South Australia	53,357	88,928	62,272	43,456	44,128	28,000	
West Australia	2,285	1,904	224			9,296	
British West Indies	819,056	737,744	856,576	723,632	812,224	965,104	.62
Natal	3,548,182	2,370,032	2,358,272	9,541,840	2,674,112	796,656	.51
Cape of Good Hope	6,625,002	5,546,128	9,422,336	15,613,024	1,827,728	715,792	.46
Gibraltar	392,090	107,408	215,488	474,208	578,480	584,864	.38
Malta and Gozo	100,867	4,256	8,848	25,648	302,176	163,408	.11
Channel Islands	148,803	163,408	165,984	126,672	146,832	141,120	.09
Falkland Islands	41,978	56,560	28,224	19,936	32,032	73,136	.05
Aden	85,120	72,352	87,472	85,344	121,408	59,024	.04
Zanzibar and Pemba	43,702	92,624	19,264	46,256	19,824	40,544	.03
Mauritius	47,242	36,960	63,504	9,072	91,504	35,168	.02
Sierra Leone	128,934	269,584	258,496	54,880	32,480	29,232	.02
Gambia	16,979	15,904	15,344	15,904	19,376	18,368	.01
St. Helena	6,832		12,320	7,504	5,376	8,960	.01
Hongkong	37,072	6,944	66,304	56,112	56,000		
Other c	143,136	27,664	77,392	98,224	204,624	307,776	.20
Total British possessions	54,483,542	39,202,912	60,176,480	55,731,424	39,911,760	77,395,136	49.93
Total	134,425,581	109,065,264	133,924,560	138,584,992	135,550,576	155,002,512	100.00

a For values, see page 77.
b Including dry hides from Asiatic Turkey amounting to 54,320 pounds in 1897, 71,904 pounds in 1898, 53,424 pounds in 1899, and 164,864 pounds in 1900.
c Including wet hides from Canada amounting to 4,144 pounds in 1896, 14,000 pounds in 1897, 36,512 pounds in 1898, 26,544 pounds in 1899, and 121,968 pounds in 1900, and from Newfoundland and Labrador 112 pounds in 1896 and 6,048 pounds in 1899.

uantity of the agricultural imports of the United Kingdom (animal matter), etc.—Cont'd.

GOATSKINS. (a)

rom which rted.	Annual average, 1896–1900.	Calendar years.					Per ct. in 1900.
		1896.	1897.	1898.	1899.	1900.	
ÐREIGN COUNTRIES.							
	Number.	*Number.*	*Number.*	*Number.*	*Number.*	*Number.*	
ussia	1,764,989	1,356,360	1,658,360	1,705,550	2,120,370	1,984,805	13.34
rance	1,504,436	972,119	1,374,714	1,158,771	2,550,160	1,471,418	9.89
[orocco	776,333	235,040	568,466	1,179,232	1,061,018	837,910	5.63
hina	675,915	865,790	899,586	655,730	364,610	593,858	3.99
urkey, Asiatic	211,655	117,080	269,930	377,520	67,840	225,905	1.52
gypt	88,266	53,390	35,840	67,550	99,300	185,250	1.24
etherlands	410,129	306,536	492,486	628,038	460,434	163,151	1.10
ermany	196,288	285,792	183,940	104,486	272,381	134,840	.91
aly	56,944	54,470	83,320	22,340	10,218	114,370	.77
elgium	83,810	129,682	108,415	34,700	85,242	61,013	.41
urkey, European	65,436	97,720	2,800	52,060	120,860	53,741	.36
razil	11,407	504		270	9,000	47,260	.32
nited States	76,327	211,754	20,382	52,140	62,061	35,300	.24
Cyprus	18,285	9,716	36,970	16,920	12,448	15,370	.10
Algeria	85,043	12,600	261,360	74,810	61,220	15,224	.10
Norway	13,780	18,075	9,420	18,250	12,930	10,226	.07
Spain	21,635	44,982	42,398	10,350	3,600	6,844	.05
Portuguese West Africa	6,704		12,072	11,700	3,370	6,380	.04
Tripoli	17,653	60,000			24,424	3,840	.02
Austria-Hungary	11,087	36,430	16,416	190		2,400	.02
Greece	7,417	36,360				726	} .01
Chile	13,332	31,519	17,517	17,442		181	
Japan	13,790	26,020			42,930		
Madagascar	4,114	2,890	17,680				
Other *b*	83,177	30,190	3,450	28,678	48,120	55,445	.37
Total foreign countries	6,167,952	4,995,019	6,115,522	6,211,727	7,492,536	6,024,957	40.50
BRITISH POSSESSIONS.							
British East Indies:							
Bengal	5,598,786	2,783,545	5,506,559	5,999,016	8,144,650	5,560,161	}
Madras	565,922	38,940	60,000	55,090	744,560	1,931,020	
Bombay	63,736	56,820	117,252	23,525	4,950	116,131	51.20
Burma	3,737			40	10,340	8,307	
Straits Settlements	44,945	113,770	28,550	17,420	63,735	1,250	
Cape of Good Hope	1,188,902	1,328,970	1,163,288	1,236,875	1,198,670	1,021,707	6.87
Aden	540,503	616,023	502,785	974,469	432,210	177,027	1.19
Natal	23,722	41,305	19,700	39,990	10,057	7,555	.05
Zanzibar and Pemba	2,341	3,892	5,300	2,514			
Other	22,642	3,770	4,100	8,994	68,673	27,675	.19
Total British possessions	8,055,236	4,987,035	7,407,534	8,357,933	10,672,845	8,850,833	59.50
Total	14,223,188	9,982,054	13,523,056	14,569,660	18,165,381	14,875,790	100.00

RABBIT SKINS. (a)

FOREIGN COUNTRIES.							
	Number.	*Number.*	*Number.*	*Number.*	*Number.*	*Number.*	
Belgium	4,428,071	957,610	3,942,180	5,571,434	5,357,196	6,311,936	18.89
France	2,581,591	2,212,244	2,049,500	3,726,745	2,491,796	2,427,672	7.27
Germany	510,233	865,232	503,480	165,500	221,300	795,653	2.38
Netherlands	220,542	475,400	344,620	19,350	124,740	138,598	.41
United States	56,505	170,350	31,520	74,552	4,000	2,104	.01
Japan	3,600	18,000					
Chile	5	25					
Other	33,283	6,125				160,290	.48
Total foreign countries	7,833,830	4,704,986	6,871,300	9,557,581	8,199,032	9,836,253	29.44

a For values, see page 78.
b Including imports from Argentina amounting to 650 in 1896 and 5,400 in 1898, and from Peru 450 in 1896, 950 in 1897, and 1,066 in 1898.

Quantity of the agricultural imports of the United Kingdom (animal matter), etc.—Cont'd.

RABBIT SKINS—Continued.

Countries from which imported.	Annual average, 1896–1900.	Calendar years.					Per ct. in 1900.
		1896.	1897.	1898.	1899.	1900.	
BRITISH POSSESSIONS.							
Australasia:	*Number.*	*Number.*	*Number.*	*Number.*	*Number.*	*Number.*	
Victoria	10,294,700	11,305,020	9,667,354	6,881,370	10,581,624	13,038,130	
New Zealand	6,187,475	8,233,120	8,017,027	3,955,660	6,433,142	4,298,425	
South Australia	2,041,596	1,861,190	941,240	890,980	2,228,890	4,285,680	
New South Wales	2,302,494	3,059,455	3,592,800	1,510,550	2,061,990	1,287,676	70.43
Tasmania	792,860	896,975	980,670	712,660	759,400	614,596	
Queensland	1,000					5,000	
West Australia	900					4,500	
Other	94,452	96,870	143,580	118,110	68,710	44,988	.13
Total British possessions	21,715,477	25,452,630	23,342,671	14,069,330	22,133,756	23,578,995	70.56
Total	29,549,307	30,157,616	30,213,971	23,626,911	30,332,788	33,415,248	100.00

SHEEPSKINS. (a)

Countries from which imported.	Annual average, 1896–1900.	Calendar years.					Per ct. in 1900.
		1896.	1897.	1898.	1899.	1900.	
FOREIGN COUNTRIES.	*Number.*	*Number.*	*Number.*	*Number.*	*Number.*	*Number.*	
Argentina	1,354,123	606,314	1,375,813	1,321,813	2,047,830	1,418,843	9.42
France	329,867	56,950	92,410	207,172	703,223	589,579	3.91
Germany	299,274	148,426	396,831	248,948	302,776	399,388	2.65
Spain	281,590	182,660	175,558	259,502	415,377	374,854	2.49
Turkey, Asiatic	207,471	188,709	206,660	246,180	144,260	251,545	1.67
Chile	130,246	70,600	82,631	119,047	138,207	240,745	1.60
Russia	226,221	170,730	242,420	237,660	260,300	219,994	1.46
Uruguay	79,300	93,338	43,305	123,594	20,216	116,048	.77
Denmark	79,702	78,846	65,633	77,054	66,113	110,866	.74
Egypt	79,577	71,190	115,433	65,160	36,420	109,680	.73
China	35,751	31,140	18,440	10,740	20,530	97,905	.65
Brazil	76,964		438	187,400	105,800	91,184	.60
Belgium	43,737	25,550	41,334	36,227	24,960	90,614	.60
Netherlands	93,374	54,166	130,963	123,894	81,957	75,891	.50
United States	43,149	84,261	42,488	8,548	7,306	73,140	.49
Turkey, European	14,268	20,380	9,105	650	8,275	32,930	.22
Morocco	31,224	18,140	23,450	65,890	33,830	14,810	.10
Portuguese East Africa	103,043	230,480	262,390	12,226		10,120	.07
Persia	20,960	9,900	40,890	31,500	22,210	300	
Madagascar	5,586	16,550	11,110			270	1.45
Other	89,744	38,197	42,665	68,455	82,297	217,104	
Total foreign countries	3,625,171	2,196,527	3,419,967	3,451,660	4,521,889	4,535,810	30.12
BRITISH POSSESSIONS.							
Australasia:							
New Zealand	4,002,773	2,999,972	3,711,542	4,422,341	4,459,896	4,420,114	
Victoria	700,431	681,242	754,240	670,538	593,780	802,355	
South Australia	915,834	1,061,035	1,071,200	970,980	686,999	788,955	
New South Wales	530,549	673,263	518,150	419,610	639,857	401,865	44.95
West Australia	172,902	114,775	90,970	142,575	257,940	258,251	
Queensland	160,759	489,815	173,290	57,450	13,210	70,032	
Tasmania	27,826	15,855	27,020	37,320	31,978	26,958	
Cape of Good Hope	3,443,846	4,168,192	3,766,053	3,617,973	2,985,575	2,681,434	17.81
Aden	556,362	610,200	608,258	557,750	486,520	519,081	3.45
British East Indies b	202,256	70,730	148,980	236,055	226,214	329,301	2.19
Natal	294,492	243,720	149,168	459,223	499,343	121,006	.80
Falkland Islands	63,887	35,850	91,380	27,630	67,525	97,050	.64
St. Helena	455		1,100	420		150	
Hongkong	300				1,500		
Other	5,672	3,458	7,738	5,547	5,986	5,633	.04
Total British possessions	11,078,344	11,168,107	11,119,089	11,625,412	10,956,927	10,522,185	69.88
Total	14,703,515	13,364,634	14,539,056	15,077,072	15,478,816	15,057,995	100.00

a For values, see page 79.
b Including imports from Bengal amounting to 28,210 in 1896, 38,850 in 1897, 96,110 in 1898, 157,020 in 1899, and 202,291 in 1900.

uantity of the agricultural imports of the United Kingdom (animal matter), etc.—Cont'd.

SKINS NOT ELSEWHERE SPECIFIED. (a)

ich	Annual average, 1896–1900.	Calendar years.					Per ct. in 1900.
		1896.	1897.	1898.	1899.	1900.	
ꓛREIGN COUNTRIES.	Number. (b)	Number.	Number.	Number.	Number.	Number. (c)	
hina	4,696	214	14,730	2,790	1,050	70,578	22.36
rance	6,429	1,932	5,084	10,131	8,569	36,760	11.65
ermany	13,810	10,606	6,628	23,900	14,105	20,194	6.40
etherlands	656	8	300	1,550	766	6,107	1.93
nited States	11,456	8,563	5,378	10,434	21,448	3,017	.95
ussia	3,227	1,862	7,062	14	3,970	1,297	.41
hile	2,794	205	136	10,829	8	115	.04
ther d	8,484	8,428	9,594	8,077	7,839	109,353	34.65
Total foreign countries	51,552	31,818	48,912	67,725	57,755	247,421	78.39
RITISH POSSESSIONS.							
ustralasia:							
New South Wales	85,534	40,546	151,520	76,800	73,270	37,390	
Victoria	22,791	25,204	12,400	50,170	3,390	1,670	
Queensland	1,362		3,248	2,200		160	
South Australia	5,305	18,670	2,550				12.42
West Australia	432		1,580	200			
Tasmania	70		140		140		
New Zealand	2				6		
ritish East Indies:							
Madras	7,168	4,086	2,970	7,890	13,125	13,752	
Straits Settlements	15,757	24,204	7,304	13,930	17,590	10,093	
Burma	13				50	1,817	8.22
Bengal	825	1,890	3	1,107	300	208	
Bombay	525		250		1,852	60	
Ceylon	47		190			5	
ongkong						1,260	.40
anada	1,463	2,625	1,394	88	1,744		
ther	8,523	14,390	9,150	6,752	3,799	1,794	.57
Total British possessions	149,817	132,215	192,649	159,137	115,266	68,209	21.61
Total	201,369	164,083	241,561	226,862	173,021	315,630	100.00

HONEY. (a)

FOREIGN COUNTRIES.	Pounds.	Pounds.	Pounds.	Pounds.	Pounds.	Pounds.	
Chile	576,285	691,824	402,752	714,336	492,240	580,272	27.45
United States	556,439	793,744	443,632	618,352	388,640	537,824	25.44
Peru	178,931	205,744	182,784	218,176	52,640	235,312	11.13
France	121,408	128,912	123,312	99,680	122,080	133,056	6.30
Italy	64,109	60,928	59,024	77,280	68,880	54,432	2.58
Germany	25,670	44,352	8,960	4,704	35,504	34,832	1.65
Cuba and Porto Rico	21,078	49,392	56,000				
Haiti and Santo Domingo	11,827	6,720	52,416				
Other	21,325	30,352	28,336	24,192	11,200	12,544	.59
Total foreign countries	1,577,072	2,011,968	1,357,216	1,756,720	1,171,184	1,588,272	75.14
BRITISH POSSESSIONS.							
British West Indies	276,617	138,096	205,408	253,344	402,416	383,824	18.16
Australasia:							
New South Wales	71,568	13,888	51,744	146,160	111,440	34,608	
Queensland	22,042	6,832	12,656	45,696	18,368	26,656	
New Zealand	32,816	51,744	39,424	27,888	26,432	18,592	3.89
Victoria	1,837	6,048	336	336	224	2,240	
South Australia	4,458	672	20,608	112	672	224	
Canada	60,681	7,840	4,592	103,152	131,824	56,000	2.65
Other	1,411	112		3,360	224	3,360	.16
Total British possessions	471,430	225,232	334,768	580,048	691,600	525,504	24.86
Total	2,048,502	2,237,200	1,691,984	2,336,768	1,862,784	2,113,776	100.00

a For values, see page 80.
b Annual average, 1896–1899.
c Including "Skins in any way dressed (not leather)."
d Including imports from Argentina amounting to 500 in 1897, 36 in 1898, and 102,900 in 1900 (the figures for the last two years including dressed skins); from Brazil 3,780 in 1896 and 30 in 1897; and from Asiatic Turkey 50 in 1896.

Quantity of the agricultural imports of the United Kingdom (animal matter), etc.—Cont'd.

HORNS, HORN TIPS, HORN STRIPS, AND HOOFS.(a)

Countries from which imported.	Annual average, 1896–1900.	Calendar years.					Per ct. in 1900.
		1896.	1897.	1898.	1899.	1900.	
FOREIGN COUNTRIES.							
	Tons. (b)	Tons. (b)	Tons. (b)	Tons. (b)	Tons. (b)	Tons. (b)	
France	587	373	456	624	898	585	9.37
Germany	322	141	250	307	470	443	7.10
Argentina	432	305	683	492	296	384	6.15
Netherlands	243	459	138	196	116	306	4.90
United States	384	508	549	324	283	256	4.10
Belgium	206	300	249	160	141	179	2.87
Brazil	82	57	77	64	133	77	1.23
Chile	104	164	117	89	81	72	1.15
Peru	49	76	36	43	37	53	.85
Portugal	17	18	8	7	11	43	.69
Norway	32	21	26	57	22	35	.56
Egypt	49	50	29	59	72	34	.55
Sweden	24	10	25	18	36	31	.50
China	31	84	39	(c)	26	6	.10
Uruguay	38	54	55	55	25	....	......
Portuguese East Africa	19	34	61	1	....	....	......
Other	79	63	54	67	97	112	1.80
Total foreign countries	2,698	2,717	2,852	2,563	2,744	2,616	41.92
BRITISH POSSESSIONS.							
British East Indies:							
Bombay	729	485	532	502	775	1,354	
Bengal	856	1,026	836	731	978	711	
Madras	324	141	343	369	427	341	
Burma	161	180	108	197	183	138	42.40
Ceylon	97	108	66	85	138	87	
Straits Settlements	22	49	21	13	13	15	
Australasia:							
New South Wales	569	766	635	453	506	483	
Victoria	223	230	209	240	212	224	
Queensland	144	236	236	96	77	73	
South Australia	53	46	68	46	78	26	13.33
New Zealand	20	32	24	17	8	19	
West Australia	2	....	(c)	2	....	7	
Tasmania	3	5	....	5	5	....	
Cape of Good Hope	212	236	222	412	125	67	1.07
Natal	137	94	88	350	119	34	.54
Hongkong	6	12	1	5	6	5	.08
Other	43	22	26	46	78	41	.66
Total British possessions	3,601	3,668	3,415	3,569	3,728	3,625	58.08
Total	6,299	6,385	6,267	6,132	6,472	6,241	100.00

FRESH BEEF. (a)

FOREIGN COUNTRIES.	Pounds.	Pounds.	Pounds.	Pounds.	Pounds.	Pounds.	
United States	274,228,841	232,360,128	251,111,056	257,819,072	308,723,296	321,130,656	69.46
Argentina	18,047,366	5,610,640	9,483,376	12,128,256	16,841,216	46,173,344	9.99
Denmark	4,168,282	190,512	3,801,616	4,106,256	5,014,800	7,728,224	1.67
Netherlands	689,114	2,912	619,136	171,696	1,745,968	905,856	.19
Belgium	117,040	....	264,880	320,320	....	....	
Sweden	55,059	....	....	273,616	1,680	....	
France	41,709	....	199,584	....	8,960	....	
Other	118,227	38,864	448	125,328	191,856	234,640	.05
Total foreign countries	297,465,638	238,203,056	265,480,096	274,944,544	332,527,776	376,172,720	81.36

a For values, see page 81.   b Tons of 2240 pounds.   c Less than one-half ton.

antity of the agricultural imports of the United Kingdom (animal matter), etc.—Cont'd.

FRESH BEEF—Continued.

ntries from which imported.	Annual average, 1896–1900.	Calendar years.					Per ct. in 1900.
		1896.	1897.	1898.	1899.	1900.	
ITISH POSSESSIONS.							
stralasia:	*Pounds.*	*Pounds.*	*Pounds.*	*Pounds.*	*Pounds.*	*Pounds.*	
Queensland	52,265,853	50,394,512	55,672,960	54,099,584	57,481,200	43,681,008	
New Zealand	14,337,770	3,225,936	8,223,712	10,388,672	15,055,824	34,794,704	
New South Wales	5,663,168	5,033,392	6,659,408	5,427,408	9,334,752	1,860,880	} 17.55
Victoria	431,782	9,296	480,480	17,920	826,112	825,104	
South Australia..	118,026	....	....	....	590,128	....	
nada...............	3,840,435	1,020,208	646,688	2,412,816	10,106,656	5,015,808	} 1.09
her.................	582	....	....	1,008	1,568	336	
Total British possessions ..	76,657,616	59,683,344	71,683,248	72,347,408	93,396,240	86,177,840	18.64
Total	374,123,254	297,886,400	337,163,344	347,291,952	425,924,016	462,350,560	100.00

BEEF, SALTED OR PICKLED.(a)

REIGN COUNTRIES.							
	Pounds.	*Pounds.*	*Pounds.*	*Pounds.*	*Pounds.*	*Pounds.*	
nited States........	21,876,512	26,950,560	19,260,640	22,808,240	19,606,272	20,756,848	96.06
ther b	238,179	95,984	194,544	416,192	230,160	254,016	1.17
Total foreign countries....	22,114,691	27,046,544	19,455,184	23,224,432	19,836,432	21,010,864	97.23
RITISH POSSESSIONS.							
anada...............	324,778	671,888	75,936	172,144	112,224	591,696	2.74
ther c	17,293	5,600	61,712	5,264	7,840	6,048	.03
Total British possessions ..	342,071	677,488	137,648	177,408	120,064	597,744	2.77
Total	22,456,762	27,724,032	19,592,832	23,401,840	19,956,496	21,608,608	100.00

BEEF, CURED, NOT ELSEWHERE SPECIFIED.(a)

FOREIGN COUNTRIES.							
	Pounds.	*Pounds.*	*Pounds.*	*Pounds.*	*Pounds.*	*Pounds.*	
Jnited States...	21,792,781	23,495,808	17,092,432	15,268,176	20,727,616	32,379,872	55.81
Argentina...........	1,958,007	1,366,288	1,333,248	1,439,312	1,954,624	3,696,560	6.37
Belgium.............	1,102,663	733,488	1,225,280	918,512	1,097,264	1,538,768	2.65
Jruguay ....'...	490,134	174,384	115,360	835,296	98,112	1,227,520	2.12
Jermany	200,368	70,336	120,064	180,880	233,744	396,816	.69
'rance	58,061	56,560	38,640	10,416	39,424	145,264	.25
Vetherlands.........	45,606	80,864	7,952	44,128	60,144	34,944	.06
Brazil	15,971	7,280	38,304	25,088	1,456	7,728	.01
Vorway	15,478	48,048	12,656	3,248	6,272	7,168	.01
apan	17,315	86,576	....	....	....	....	......
Jther...............	13,910	8,624	14,784	26,096	15,792	4,256	.01
Total foreign countries	25,710,294	26,128,256	19,998,720	18,751,152	24,234,448	39,438,896	67.98
IRITISH POSSESSIONS.							
Australasia:							
Queensland	9,594,010	11,089,344	13,738,368	7,064,400	7,788,480	8,289,456	
New South Wales	6,065,226	4,554,256	5,987,968	4,164,048	7,396,480	8,223,376	
New Zealand	414,960	231,280	254,688	371,056	398,048	819,728	} 30.07
South Australia .	36,512	224	560	64,288	9,072	108,416	
Victoria	45,898	34,944	87,360	42,896	59,920	4,368	
'anada	1,580,678	2,981,328	1,648,976	1,052,240	1,102,752	1,118,096	1.92
Jther...............	16,710	....	24,304	448	41,888	16,912	.03
Total British possessions ..	17,753,994	18,891,376	21,742,224	12,759,376	16,796,640	18,580,352	32.02
Total ..'.........	43,464,288	45,019,632	41,740,944	31,510,528	41,031,088	58,019,248	100.00

a For values, see page 82.
b Including imports from Argentina amounting to 42,560 pounds in 1896, 24,640 pounds in 1897, 05,840 pounds in 1898, and 66,752 pounds in 1899, and from Germany 22,512 pounds in 1896, 32,032 pounds in 1897, 22,624 pounds in 1898, and 30,352 pounds in 1899.
c Including imports from South Australia amounting to 5,600 pounds in 1896: from New South Wales 53,760 pounds in 1897; from New Zealand 7,280 pounds in 1897: from Queensland 672 pounds in 897; and from total Australasia 5,264 pounds in 1898 and 4,816 pounds in 1899.

Quantity of the agricultural imports of the United Kingdom (animal matter), etc.—Cont'd.

TALLOW AND STEARIN. (a)

Countries from which imported.	Annual average, 1896–1900.	Calendar years.					Per ct. in 1900.
		1896.	1897.	1898.	1899.	1900.	
FOREIGN COUNTRIES.	*Pounds.*	*Pounds.*	*Pounds.*	*Pounds.*	*Pounds.*	*Pounds.*	
United States........	53,352,880	45,977,568	30,411,696	64,059,408	62,405,392	63,910,336	26.20
Argentina...........	15,825,107	14,558,544	12,054,000	18,372,144	14,174,720	19,966,128	8.18
France	6,997,827	5,409,936	5,682,208	8,834,336	8,895,600	6,167,056	2.53
Belgium............	4,133,158	3,366,272	3,576,272	4,354,784	4,387,600	4,980,864	2.04
Germany...........	1,844,349	849,632	1,633,744	1,599,920	2,020,144	3,118,304	1.28
Uruguay............	3,639,328	5,937,120	4,044,656	4,717,104	1,120,000	2,377,760	.97
Netherlands........	2,103,763	1,819,888	1,852,816	1,898,288	2,626,064	2,321,760	.95
China..............	868,045	1,533,840	1,195,264	697,984	239,904	673,232	.28
Chile	156,979	442,288	147,392	76,160	....	119,056	.05
Russia.............	69,082	293,776	22,400	1,282	9,744	18,256	.01
Turkey, European...	49,616	220,640	4,368	22,400	....	672	} .14
Other b	402,506	317,520	365,904	457,714	542,528	328,832	
Total foreign countries	89,442,640	80,727,024	60,990,720	105,091,504	96,421,696	103,982,256	42.63
BRITISH POSSESSIONS.							
Australasia:							
New South Wales	64,221,248	74,477,984	77,892,976	56,444,192	63,400,960	48,890,128	}
New Zealand	32,583,689	21,819,504	33,585,888	34,187,440	32,789,680	40,535,936	
Victoria	20,702,483	22,498,448	26,232,192	14,814,016	16,581,712	23,386,048	55.84
Queensland	18,750,122	24,619,392	16,432,752	13,287,904	16,405,536	23,005,024	
South Australia..	1,354,326	3,218,208	1,973,104	....	1,180,592	399,728	
Tasmania........	2,979	14,896					
Canada.............	1,683,898	492,464	152,096	2,186,128	3,062,640	2,526,160	1.03
Falkland Islands	426,675	827,232	83,440	117,376	487,648	617,680	.25
British East Indies c.	555,582	810,320	923,216	189,504	474,432	380,688	.16
Channel Islands.....	47,130	26,432	101,696	93,072	10,416	4,032	} .09
Other d	92,221	39,984	135,520	46,256	32,032	207,312	
Total British possessions ..	140,420,403	148,844,864	157,512,880	121,365,888	134,425,648	139,952,736	57.37
Total	229,863,043	229,571,888	218,503,600	226,457,392	230,847,344	243,934,992	100.00

BACON. (a)

FOREIGN COUNTRIES.	*Pounds.*	*Pounds.*	*Pounds.*	*Pounds.*	*Pounds.*	*Pounds.*	
United States........	413,876,176	308,170,016	402,375,120	457,787,568	457,917,152	443,131,024	70.14
Denmark............	124,799,898	136,876,768	114,973,824	113,962,240	135,588,544	122,598,112	19.40
Netherlands.........	2,498,854	2,536,912	1,988,112	1,957,872	2,242,128	3,769,248	.60
Sweden	4,616,551	8,547,504	5,474,448	4,531,072	3,271,408	1,258,320	.20
Russia.............	1,410,819	2,128,112	3,103,856	1,128,064	60,704	633,360	.10
Other e	338,150	102,032	50,288	278,432	177,520	1,082,480	.17
Total foreign countries	547,540,448	458,361,344	527,965,648	579,645,248	599,257,456	572,472,544	90.61
BRITISH POSSESSIONS.							
Canada.............	50,770,093	51,152,976	32,511,696	60,018,448	50,822,576	59,344,768	9.39
Newfoundland and Labrador.........	24,528	28,000	63,280	....	31,360	....	......
Other...............	4,413	4,592	9,856	4,368	1,904	1,344	......
Total British possessions ..	50,799,034	51,185,568	32,584,832	60,022,816	50,855,840	59,346,112	9.39
Total ....:..	598,339,482	509,546,912	560,550,480	639,668,064	650,113,296	631,818,656	100.00

a For values, see page 83.
b In 1896 including 116,480 pounds from Asiatic Turkey.
c Including imports from the Straits Settlements amounting to 792,400 pounds in 1896, 795,200 pounds in 1897, 112,000 pounds in 1898, 314,720 pounds in 1899, and 293,328 pounds in 1900.
d In 1896 including 39,984 pounds from Newfoundland and Labrador.
e Including imports from Germany amounting to 57,344 pounds in 1896 and 5,040 pounds in 1897.

antity of the agricultural imports of the United Kingdom (animal matter), etc.—Cont'd.

HAMS. (a)

untries from which imported.	Annual average, 1896–1900.	Calendar years.					Per ct. in 1900.
		1896.	1897.	1898.	1899.	1900.	
REIGN COUNTRIES.							
	Pounds.	*Pounds.*	*Pounds.*	*Pounds.*	*Pounds.*	*Pounds.*	
ited States........	182,950,813	144,029,312	179,595,696	207,370,240	204,284,080	179,474,736	88.89
rmany...........	143,226	140,224	155,344	126,000	136,416	158,144	.08
nmark..........	138,432	218,064	110,096	101,696	170,352	91,952	.05
ain..............	22,758	18,368	22,736	22,848	27,776	22,064	.01
her b............	105,280	86,464	69,328	124,320	99,680	146,608	.07
Total foreign countries....	183,360,509	144,492,432	179,953,200	207,745,104	204,718,304	179,893,504	89.10
ITISH POSSESSIONS.							
nada..............	16,860,861	18,958,912	13,342,896	13,151,936	16,878,176	21,972,384	10.88
her................	9,587	2,800	1,904	448	9,632	33,152	.02
Total British possessions ..	16,870,448	18,961,712	13,344,800	13,152,384	16,887,808	22,005,536	10.90
Total	200,230,957	163,454,144	193,298,000	220,897,488	221,606,112	201,899,040	100.00

OREIGN COUNTRIES.	*Pounds.*	*Pounds.*	*Pounds.*	*Pounds.*	*Pounds.*	*Pounds.*	
etherlands.........	31,959,447	27,366,528	25,336,080	24,939,264	38,566,752	43,588,608	55.97
nited States.......	19,302,147	967,456	6,855,856	31,004,848	31,006,528	26,676,048	34.25
elgium............	4,435,447	4,391,296	4,125,184	3,931,424	3,958,304	5,771,024	7.41
enmark...........	506,934	242,368	156,688	115,472	817,488	1,202,656	1.54
rgentina..........	92,624	83,216	95,648	135,072	83,664	65,520	.08
rance	795,379	407,904	2,328,032	1,189,552	1,232	50,176	} .07
ther..............	2,262	3,584	6,272	1,232	....	224	
Total foreign countries....	57,094,240	33,462,352	38,903,760	61,316,864	74,433,968	77,354,256	99.32
RITISH POSSESSIONS.							
anada..............	401,319	....	10,080	1,128,400	484,512	383,600	.49
ustralasia..........	46,592	71,008	14,000	8,920	3,584	140,448	.18
ther..............	3,382	672	5,264	2,240	2,800	5,936	.01
Total British possessions ..	451,293	71,680	29,344	1,134,560	490,896	529,984	.68
Total	57,545,533	33,534,032	38,933,104	62,451,424	74,924,864	77,884,240	100.00

PORK, SALTED OR PICKLED.(a)

OREIGN COUNTRIES.	*Pounds.*	*Pounds.*	*Pounds.*	*Pounds.*	*Pounds.*	*Pounds.*	
nited States........	16,722,608	15,419,376	15,839,936	19,600,000	18,372,704	14,381,024	51.63
enmark...........	8,809,830	9,863,840	7,403,645	7,946,288	9,587,536	9,247,840	33.20
ermany...........	1,399,082	912,688	1,208,144	1,250,816	1,727,264	1,896,496	6.81
etherlands.......	116,278	152,432	84,560	69,104	82,320	192,976	.69
rance	39,424	45,472	58,016	33,152	15,568	44,912	.16
weden............	73,427	303,296	33,600	30,240	....	....	
ther..............	35,728	36,848	114,352	3,808	6,048	17,584	.06
Total foreign countries....	27,196,377	26,733,952	24,742,256	28,933,408	29,791,440	25,780,832	92.55
RITISH POSSESSIONS.							
anada..............	1,966,317	1,864,016	1,824,592	1,977,808	2,094,176	2,070,992	7.43
ther c.............	1,792	....	224	....	3,024	5,712	.02
Total British possessions ..	1,968,109	1,864,016	1,824,816	1,977,808	2,097,200	2,076,704	7.45
Total	29,164,486	28,597,968	26,567,072	30,911,216	31,888,640	27,857,536	100.00

a For values, see page 84.
b Including imports from Belgium amounting to 49,392 pounds in 1896, 37,856 pounds in 1897, 47,040 ounds in 1898, and 42,448 pounds in 1899.
c In 1897 comprising 224 pounds from Australasia.

Quantity of the agricultural imports of the United Kingdom (animal matter), etc.—Cont'd.

LARD. (a)

Countries from which imported.	Annual average, 1896–1900.	Calendar years.					Per ct. in 1900.
		1896.	1897.	1898.	1899.	1900.	
FOREIGN COUNTRIES.							
	Pounds.	*Pounds.*	*Pounds.*	*Pounds.*	*Pounds.*	*Pounds.*	
United States	206,127,331	180,109,104	188,733,328	229,009,424	232,014,384	200,770,416	93.01
Germany	443,654		137,760	186,032	131,376	1,141,056	622,048	.29
Denmark	594,250	1,458,688	179,872	319,872	428,736	584,080	.27
Netherlands	619,965	366,464	682,080	289,744	1,344,336	417,200	.19
Belgium	507,203	124,320	579,264	1,115,632	448,560	268,240	.12
France	75,981	184,576	2,240	42,336	99,456	51,296	}.03
Other b	30,643	115,920	5,824	26,096	3,472	1,904	
Total foreign countries	208,399,027	182,496,832	190,368,640	230,934,480	235,480,000	202,715,184	93.91
BRITISH POSSESSIONS.							
Canada	8,852,055	12,308,800	4,516,512	5,035,072	9,308,096	13,091,792	6.07
Newfoundland and Labrador	54,678	....	....	....	273,392	....	
Other c	21,840	14,224	47,264	....	....	47,712	.02
Total British possessions	8,928,573	12,323,024	4,563,776	5,035,072	9,581,488	13,139,504	6.09
Total	217,327,600	194,819,856	194,932,416	235,969,552	245,061,488	215,854,688	100.00

FRESH MUTTON. (a)

	Annual average, 1896–1900.	1896.	1897.	1898.	1899.	1900.	Per ct. in 1900.
FOREIGN COUNTRIES.							
	Pounds.	*Pounds.*	*Pounds.*	*Pounds.*	*Pounds.*	*Pounds.*	
Argentina	113,625,344	89,794,096	101,765,776	123,894,512	127,815,296	124,857,040	32
Netherlands	30,364,377	25,679,696	29,886,304	29,740,816	31,907,232	37,107,840	9
Denmark	724,617	661,024	472,640	483,392	1,419,040	586,992	
United States	176,848	38,080	149,408	70,000	282,016	344,736	
Belgium	68,096	15,008	10,416	83,664	....	231,392	.
France	123,917	....	74,592	63,616	276,864	204,512	
Germany	201,645	404,320	259,952	142,240	68,096	133,616	;.04
Other	36,042	112,672	9,408	50,176	7,952	....	
Total foreign countries	145,820,886	116,704,896	132,628,496	154,528,416	161,776,496	163,466,128	43.02
BRITISH POSSESSIONS.							
Australasia:							
New Zealand	149,161,085	120,860,208	145,861,296	147,237,328	165,280,528	166,566,064	
New South Wales	52,621,005	69,226,192	64,299,200	53,596,144	45,155,936	30,827,552	
Victoria	10,616,816	11,653,600	11,792,592	8,075,000	7,407,232	14,152,656	}56.98
South Australia	1,625,859	969,248	208,096	1,172,640	2,834,608	2,944,704	
Queensland	3,950,083	4,841,200	2,856,336	6,535,984	3,484,320	2,032,576	
Other d	9,543	2,352	896	19,600	15,344	9,520	
Total British possessions	217,984,391	207,552,800	225,018,416	216,639,696	224,177,968	216,533,072	56.98
Total	363,805,277	324,257,696	357,646,912	371,168,112	385,954,464	379,999,200	100.00

a For values, see page 85.
b Including imports from Russia amounting to 32,480 pounds in 1896 and 112 pounds in 1898.
c Comprising imports from Australasia amounting to 14,224 pounds in 1896 and 47,264 pounds in 1897.
d In 1898 including 448 pounds from the Falkland Islands.

uantity of the agricultural imports of the United Kingdom (animal matter), etc.—Cont'd.

MUTTON, CURED, OTHER THAN SALTED. (a)

	Annual average, 1896–1900.	Calendar years.					Per ct. in 1900.
		1896.	1897.	1898.	1899.	1900.	
REIGN COUNTRIES.							
	Pounds.	Pounds.	Pounds.	Pounds.	Pounds.	Pounds.	
nited States........	277,379	407,232	419,552	88,256	191,184	280,672	3.89
rgentina...........	233,520	270,368	430,192	256,032	63,392	147,616	}2.04
ermany............	4,973	1,008	896	1,008	21,840	112	
rance	7,191	35,952	....	....	....	....	......
ruguay	4,211	17,920	3,136	....	....	....	......
elgium.............	2,800	....	14,000	....	....	....	......
ther...............	918	1,232	1,680	336	672	672	.01
Total foreign countries....	530,992	733,712	869,456	345,632	277,088	429,072	5.94
RITISH POSSESSIONS.							
ustralasia:							
New South Wales	5,767,194	7,296,128	4,978,400	7,440,496	5,401,760	3,719,184	}
New Zealand....	2,922,797	2,212,448	3,150,000	4,374,720	2,794,512	2,082,304	
Queensland	1,010,531	2,600,192	1,014,384	418,320	710,416	309,344	}88.00
Victoria	490,112	649,376	733,712	472,976	352,128	242,368	
South Australia .	65,206	129,696	196,336	....	....	....	
anada..............	209,126	104,160	113,792	199,024	191,296	437,360	}6.06
ther...............	16,867	....	34,384	....	49,840	112	
Total British possessions ..	10,481,833	12,992,000	10,221,008	12,905,536	9,499,952	6,790,672	94.06
Total..........	11,012,825	13,725,712	11,090,464	13,251,168	9,777,040	7,219,744	100.00

OLEO OIL. (a)

	Annual average, 1896–1900.	1896.	1897.	1898.	1899.	1900.	Per ct. in 1900.
FOREIGN COUNTRIES.							
	Pounds.	Pounds.	Pounds.	Pounds.	Pounds.	Pounds.	
United States........	10,669,747	7,442,064	10,136,000	12,742,912	8,666,672	14,361,088	70.63
France..............	2,346,893	1,639,456	1,791,440	2,559,760	3,152,016	2,591,792	12.75
Netherlands.........	3,547,600	2,881,872	3,360,224	3,771,040	5,987,408	1,737,456	8.54
Germany............	252,403	275,296	569,072	275,520	142,128	....	......
Other b	146,474	11,760	....	....	47,040	673,568	3.31
Total foreign countries....	16,963,117	12,250,448	15,856,736	19,349,232	17,995,264	19,363,904	95.23
BRITISH POSSESSIONS.							
Canada..............	529,335	1,096,816	516,320	....	329,504	704,032	3.46
Australasia..........	228,614	136,080	356,720	96,320	287,840	266,112	1.31
Total British possessions ..	757,949	1,232,896	873,040	96,320	617,344	970,144	4.77
Total	17,721,066	13,483,344	16,729,776	19,445,552	18,612,608	20,334,048	100.00

OLEOMARGARIN (IMITATION BUTTER). (a)

	Annual average, 1896–1900.	1896.	1897.	1898.	1899.	1900.	Per ct. in 1900.
FOREIGN COUNTRIES.							
	Pounds.	Pounds.	Pounds.	Pounds.	Pounds.	Pounds.	
Netherlands.........	97,182,332	96,531,344	97,716,976	94,547,824	100,554,272	96,561,248	93.67
France	3,307,293	3,418,576	3,423,056	3,393,488	3,323,600	2,977,744	2.89
Germany............	1,779,156	2,243,584	1,646,960	1,565,088	1,367,296	2,074,352	2.01
Norway	1,034,208	1,137,696	1,212,624	949,424	927,136	944,160	.92
Belgium.............	453,309	312,256	721,728	365,120	471,296	396,144	.38
United States........	54,813	26,768	135,296	....	36,736	75,264	.07
Other...............	32,681	31,136	36,176	11,648	36,624	47,824	.05
Total foreign countries....	103,844,092	103,701,360	104,892,816	100,832,592	106,716,960	103,076,736	99.99
BRITISH POSSESSIONS.							
Total British possessions...	17,517	3,248	....	36,288	38,640	9,408	.01
Total	103,861,609	103,704,608	104,892,816	100,868,880	106,755,600	103,086,144	100.00

a For values, see page 86.　　　　b In 1896 comprising 11,760 pounds from Egypt.

Quantity of the agricultural imports of the United Kingdom (animal matter), etc.—Cont'd.

IMITATION CHEESE. (a)

Countries from which imported.	Annual average, 1896–1900.	Calendar years.					Per ct. in 1900.
		1896.	1897.	1898.	1899.	1900.	
FOREIGN COUNTRIES.	*Pounds.*	*Pounds.*	*Pounds.*	*Pounds.*	*Pounds.*	*Pounds.*	
United States........	799,971	....	1,202,656	1,034,544	475,664	1,286,992	94.72
Other b	84,672	24,416	128,464	103,936	166,208	336	.02
Total foreign countries....	884,643	24,416	1,331,120	1,138,480	641,872	1,287,328	94.74
BRITISH POSSESSIONS.							
Total British possessions c	18,839	22,736	....	....	....	71,456	5.26
Total	903,482	47,152	1,331,120	1,138,480	641,872	1,358,784	100.00

RABBITS (DEAD). (a)

FOREIGN COUNTRIES.	*Pounds.*	*Pounds.*	*Pounds.*	*Pounds.*	*Pounds.*	*Pounds.*	
Belgium............	8,968,669	10,258,640	9,456,160	9,464,560	9,070,096	6,593,888	12.44
Netherlands........	1,525,529	1,270,640	1,538,880	1,539,888	1,739,024	1,539,216	2.91
France	1,416,442	1,589,504	1,158,864	1,255,632	1,583,008	1,495,200	} 2.82
Other d	3,338	672	1,008	....	13,888	1,120	
Total foreign countries....	11,913,978	13,119,456	12,154,912	12,260,080	12,406,016	9,629,424	18.17
BRITISH POSSESSIONS.							
Australasia:							
New Zealand....	11,373,398	1,284,192	7,717,472	13,089,552	15,023,120	19,752,656	
Victoria	9,482,659	4,234,384	8,406,384	5,996,144	10,025,680	18,750,704	
South Australia .	1,033,626	....	192,976	1,210,160	823,872	2,941,120	} 81.83
New South Wales	2,271,494	499,744	2,391,648	2,610,496	3,980,144	1,875,440	
Queensland	38,170	....	99,904	46,144	....	44,800	
Total British possessions ..	24,199,347	6,018,320	18,808,384	22,952,496	29,852,816	43,364,720	81.83
Total	36,113,325	19,137,776	30,963,296	35,212,576	42,258,832	52,994,144	100.00

MEAT, FRESH OR SALTED, NOT ELSEWHERE SPECIFIED. (e)

FOREIGN COUNTRIES.	*Pounds.*	*Pounds.*	*Pounds.*	*Pounds.*	*Pounds.*	*Pounds.*	
Netherlands.........	25,945,114	18,287,024	25,159,120	27,993,168	28,448,112	29,838,144	50.20
United States........	8,458,554	6,788,320	8,523,424	10,126,144	1,121,904	15,732,976	26.47
Denmark............	2,920,826	1,880,032	2,216,928	2,231,936	3,476,032	4,799,200	8.07
Argentina	2,377,267	1,481,536	1,524,768	1,964,480	2,198,112	4,717,440	7.94
France	3,680,678	1,431,024	1,166,368	1,106,224	13,823,376	876,400	1.48
Belgium............	463,187	283,584	431,648	537,376	516,208	547,120	.92
Germany	272,451	174,944	242,032	270,816	280,112	394,352	.66
Other...............	32,480	6,832	39,872	36,624	63,280	15,792	.03
Total foreign countries....	44,150,557	30,333,296	39,304,160	44,266,768	49,927,136	56,921,424	95.77
BRITISH POSSESSIONS.							
Australasia:							
New Zealand....	924,000	407,680	963,424	972,384	1,041,936	1,234,576	
New South Wales	164,214	190,512	149,968	185,360	100,800	194,432	
Victoria	58,106	20,944	37,520	19,376	48,160	164,528	} 2.88
Queensland	236,589	58,576	184,464	300,608	532,448	106,848	
South Australia .	9,206	....	....	3,360	27,664	15,008	
Canada.............	~476,761	260,400	220,416	728,448	374,640	799,904	} 1.35
Other f	4,413	20,272	112	1,120	224	336	
Total British possessions ..	1,873,289	958,384	1,555,904	2,210,656	2,125,872	2,515,632	4.23
Total	46,023,846	31,291,680	40,860,064	46,477,424	52,053,008	59,437,056	100.00

a For values, see page 87.
b In 1896 comprising 24.416 pounds from the Netherlands.
c In 1896 comprising 22,736 pounds from Canada.
d In 1896 comprising 672 pounds from the United States.
e For values, see page 88.
f In 1896 comprising 20.272 pounds from Newfoundland and Labrador.

tantity of the agricultural imports of the United Kingdom (animal matter), etc.—Cont'd.

MEAT, CURED, NOT ELSEWHERE SPECIFIED. (a)

untries from which imported.	Annual average, 1896–1900.	Calendar years.					Per ct. in 1900.
		1896.	1897.	1898.	1899.	1900.-	
REIGN COUNTRIES.							
	Pounds.	*Pounds.*	*Pounds.*	*Pounds.*	*Pounds.*	*Pounds.*	
nited States........	11,137,549	8,458,464	9,325,568	11,582,144	11,957,456	14,364,112	57.39
uguay	1,066,486	771,456	1,332,800	943,712	1,105,104	1,179,360	4.71
lgium	712,992	454,160	428,624	637,056	929,040	1,116,080	4.46
gentina...........	1,006,790	1,371,104	1,202,656	797,888	810,768	851,536	3.40
ance	407,232	276,080	283,696	361,648	510,720	604,016	2.41
rmany	295,949	188,384	201,264	415,184	262,416	412,496	1.65
etherlands........	235,088	156,464	244,832	137,312	277,424	359,408	1.44
ssia..............	124,656	116,144	117,712	133,728	133,952	121,744	.49
rway	50,400	46,032	48,272	64,960	27,440	65,296	.26
her b..............	42,784	22,512	18,032	21,504	67,760	84,112	.34 •
Total foreign countries....	15,079,926	11,860,800	13,203,456	15,095,136	16,082,080	19,158,160	76.55
ITISH POSSESSIONS.							
ustralasia:							
Victoria.........	3,505,107	3,935,456	4,874,800	2,158,352	2,668,176	3,888,752	⎫
South Australia .	538,205	30,912	310,240	589,232	1,034,880	725,760	⎪
Queensland	382,906	632,912	290,304	281,568	396,256	313,488	⎬ 21.66
New Zealand....	942,614	1,761,760	1,574,496	377,888	717,696	281,232	⎪
New South Wales	540,736	494,816	967,456	518,672	513,296	209,440	⎪
West Australia ..	426	....	....	....	....	2,128	⎭
anada..............	793,027	1,132,432	940,688	602,672	849,408	439,936	1.76
ther................	6,003	1,568	11,760	7,728	1,232	7,728	.03
Total British possessions ..	6,709,024	7,989,856	8,969,744	4,536,112	6,180,944	5,868,464	23.45
Total........	21,788,950	19,850,656	22,173,200	19,631,248	22,263,024	25,026,624	100.00

ANIMAL OILS NOT ELSEWHERE SPECIFIED, EXCEPT WHALE AND FISH. (c)

FOREIGN COUNTRIES.							
	Pounds.	*Pounds.*	*Pounds.*	*Pounds.*	*Pounds.*	*Pounds.*	
nited States........	5,692,893	6,624,688	5,516,448	6,012,944	5,729,360	4,581,024	39.37
elgium.............	465,562	26,208	104,944	72,128	....	2,124,528	18.26
rance	273,952	2,240	5,600	5,040	4,816	1,352,064	11.62
etherlands.........	272,115	29,792	42,112	46,928	101,024	1,140,720	9.80
ermany	85,680	45,360	77,840	89,824	26,432	188,944	1.63
rgentina...........	86,643	48,384	82,208	114,016	105,728	82,880	.71
ther................	23,094	3,920	40,320	1,456	....	69,776	.60
Total foreign countries....	6,899,939	6,780,592	5,869,472	6,342,336	5,967,360	9,539,936	81.99
RITISH POSSESSIONS.							
ustralasia:							
Victoria.........	260,311	4,480	12,768	....	5,824	1,278,480	⎫
Queensland	76,294	17,360	24,528	....	224	339,360	⎪
South Australia..	33,645	....	31,360	....	....	136,864	⎬ 15.71
New Zealand....	16,195	10,640	....	2,016	....	68,320	⎪
New South Wales	17,002	13,216	46,032	....	20,720	5,040	⎭
anada..............	189,392	377,888	197,568	8,624	94,976	267,904	2.30
ther................	1,254	....	5,600	....	672	....	......
Total British possessions ..	594,093	423,584	317,856	10,640	122,416	2,095,968	18.01
Total..........	7,494,032	7,204,176	6,187,328	6,352,976	6,089,776	11,635,904	100.00

a For values, see page 88.
b Including imports from Italy amounting to 6,048 pounds in 1896 and 224 pounds in 1897.
c For values, see page 89.

Quantity of the agricultural imports of the United Kingdom (animal matter), etc.—Cont'd.

WAX (INCLUDING OZOKERITE AND EARTH WAX).(*a*)

Countries from which imported.	Annual average, 1896–1900.	Calendar years.					Per ct. in 1900.
		1896.	1897.	1898.	1899.	1900.	
FOREIGN COUNTRIES.							
	Pounds.	*Pounds.*	*Pounds.*	*Pounds.*	*Pounds.*	*Pounds.*	
Germany	1,837,002	1,496,544	1,473,920	1,965,152	2,144,016	2,105,376	36.42
Brazil	875,863	1,155,616	633,696	953,232	552,832	1,083,936	18.75
Japan	351,031	93,520	328,048	405,104	431,424	497,056	8.60
France	199,046	109,984	109,648	146,944	357,392	271,264	4.69
United States	407,210	518,784	376,096	307,328	591,920	241,920	4.18
Morocco	140,470	120,400	109,760	208,544	88,256	175,392	3.03
Italy	135,766	125,216	122,192	156,128	138,320	136,976	2.37
Chile	142,733	153,664	145,824	122,528	155,456	136,192	2.36
Portuguese East Africa	62,272	4,256	35,952	50,624	158,368	62,160	1.08
Netherlands	88,950	45,024	98,112	155,568	85,232	60,816	1.05
Spain	51,766	58,240	60,816	39,088	50,064	50,624	.88
Madagascar	172,189	243,488	341,152	165,872	61,040	49,392	.85
Belgium	33,734	57,232	49,840	6,944	17,472	37,184	.64
China	16,486	224	32,144	14,112	....	35,952	.62
French West Africa	21,818	11,648	16,352	39,536	24,752	16,800	.29
Peru	21,616	13,104	17,472	35,504	25,760	16,240	.28
Portugal	20,563	15,232	3,360	79,632	4,480	112	.28
Abyssinia	314	....	....	1,568	....	....	......
Other *b*	63,504	40,992	55,216	51,520	82,208	87,584	1.52
Total foreign countries	4,642,333	4,263,168	4,009,600	4,904,928	4,968,992	5,064,976	87.61
BRITISH POSSESSIONS.							
British East Indies:							
Bengal	155,568	145,712	189,280	114,912	157,920	170,016	
Bombay	47,600	30,240	28,112	20,720	65,968	92,960	
Madras	11,558	25,088	1,904	11,424	5,824	13,552	4.79
Straits Settlements	11,290	112	7,952	....	48,160	224	
Ceylon	2,755	....	224	12,320	1,232	....	
Burma	986	1,792	....	3,136	....	....	
Zanzibar and Pemba	125,597	56,448	124,432	143,136	147,168	156,800	2.71
British West Indies	99,097	93,072	133,280	91,280	104,496	73,360	1.27
Australasia:							
New South Wales	38,326	27,664	39,648	26,432	51,856	46,032	
Queensland	1,434	1,456	2,688	1,568	....	1,456	
South Australia	8,490	16,912	12,544	6,496	5,152	1,344	.86
Victoria	17,387	27,664	34,048	12,432	11,536	1,008	
New Zealand	896	2,464	672	....	1,344	....	
Tasmania	358	1,008	112	336	336	....	
Gambia	60,973	89,936	48,272	41,104	98,224	27,328	.47
Gibraltar	21,773	13,104	16,912	35,616	31,136	12,096	.21
Sierra Leone	5,600	12,544	6,720	336	8,400	(*c*)	......
Mauritius	6,698	3,360	10,528	1,456	18,144	....	......
Other *d*	43,344	23,072	18,032	30,352	25,424	119,840	2.08
Total British possessions	659,680	571,648	675,360	553,056	782,320	716,016	12.39
Total	5,302,013	4,834,816	4,684,960	5,457,984	5,751,312	5,780,992	100.00

a For values, see page 89.
b Including in 1896, 6,048 pounds from Portuguese West Africa and 224 pounds from the Canary Islands.
c Less than 56 pounds (one-half hundredweight).
d Including imports from Natal amounting to 8,176 pounds in 1896, 3,472 pounds in 1897, 3,920 pounds in 1898, and 9,632 pounds in 1899, and from the Cape of Good Hope, 2,016 pounds in 1896 and 9,968 pounds in 1897.

Quantity of the agricultural imports of the United Kingdom (vegetable matter), by articles and countries, during the five calendar years 1896–1900.

BARLEY. (a)

Countries from which imported.	Annual average, 1896–1900.	Calendar years.					Per ct. in 1900.
		1896.	1897.	1898.	1899.	1900.	
FOREIGN COUNTRIES.	*Bushels.(b)*	*Bushels.(b)*	*Bushels.(b)*	*Bushels.(b)*	*Bushels.(b)*	*Bushels.(b)*	
Russia	18,417,714	21,572,600	17,486,234	23,956,333	18,216,170	10,857,233	27.28
United States	7,098,686	7,564,434	7,825,067	5,583,200	4,540,830	9,979,900	25.08
Turkey, Asiatic	7,696,421	8,092,840	7,145,833	7,596,866	6,291,833	9,354,730	23.51
Roumania	6,440,976	6,942,367	7,642,134	11,047,773	3,094,770	3,477,833	8.74
France	726,861	467,600	176,493	1,177,867	855,213	957,133	2.41
Chile	1,334,867	2,586,500	1,220,263	784,140	1,144,033	939,400	2.36
Germany	655,755	958,141	329,723	633,101	444,775	913,033	2.29
Mexico	163,940	....	....	60,200	495,133	264,367	.66
Turkey, European	438,807	445,900	85,400	890,400	525,700	246,633	.62
Denmark	367,565	809,013	233,333	235,667	346,500	213,313	.54
Cyprus	167,300	49,700	120,400	381,267	78,867	206,267	.52
Netherlands	290,278	338,030	403,923	288,365	252,117	168,957	.43
Austria-Hungary	357,140	293,533	514,267	479,967	345,100	152,833	.38
Bulgaria	160,113	59,033	74,433	491,867	52,267	122,967	.31
Tripoli	601,114	1,525,767	630,233	376,367	364,000	109,200	.27
Egypt	312,657	301,933	110,880	429,893	651,980	68,600	.17
Argentina	31,080	31,033	12,367	12,600	32,200	67,200	.17
Algeria	201,026	....	....	358,330	591,733	55,067	.14
Tunis	276,593	....	....	761,133	570,267	51,567	.13
Morocco	12,600	....	....	....	38,500	24,500	.06
Persia	20,720	76,767	11,900	....	....	14,933	.04
Belgium	17,416	1,727	44,333	27,767	117	13,137	.03
Sweden	5,413	2,100	....	....	22,867	2,100	} .01
Spain	278,525	....	....	1,111,833	280,327	467	
Italy	10,827	45,500	....	8,633	....	....	
Other	3,654	....	11,200	1,167	5,903	....	
Total foreign countries	46,088,048	52,164,518	44,078,416	56,694,736	39,241,202	38,261,370	96.15
BRITISH POSSESSIONS.							
Canada	611,282	277,200	158,597	366,007	857,733	1,396,873	3.51
Australasia:							
New Zealand	27,720	....	....	....	3,967	184,633	
South Australia	117	467	....	....	....	117	
West Australia	23	....	....	....	....	117	} .34
New South Wales	1,214	4,900	....	....	1,167	....	
Other	2,380	....	....	5,600	4,433	1,867	
Total British possessions	642,736	282,567	158,597	371,607	867,300	1,533,607	3.85
Total	46,730,784	52,447,085	44,237,013	57,066,343	40,108,502	39,794,977	100.00

BUCKWHEAT. (c)

FOREIGN COUNTRIES.	*Bushels. (b)*	*Bushels. (b)*	*Bushels. (b)*	*Bushels. (b)*	*Bushels. (b)*	*Bushels. (b)*	
France	128,332	229,428	147,467	34,650	125,394	104,720	40.70
Russia	59,594	54,133	18,433	22,867	121,334	81,200	31.55
United States	63,597	47	51,520	199,896	56,443	10,080	3.92
Netherlands	3,945	4,433	15,293	....	....	....	
Other	4,643	11,597	2,777	747	7,303	793	.31
Total foreign countries	260,111	299,638	235,490	258,160	310,474	196,793	76.48
BRITISH POSSESSIONS.							
Canada	89,539	18,573	157,336	184,660	26,600	60,527	23.52
Channel Islands	994	420	4,457	....	93	....	
Total British possessions	90,533	18,993	161,793	184,660	26,693	60,527	23.52
Total	350,644	318,631	397,283	442,820	337,167	257,320	100.00

a For values, see page 90. b Bushels of 48 pounds. c For values, see page 91.

Quantity of the agricultural imports of the United Kingdom (vegetable matter), etc.—Cont'd.

CORN (MAIZE).(a)

Countries from which imported.	Annual average, 1896–1900.	Calendar years.					Per ct. in 1900.
		1896.	1897.	1898.	1899.	1900.	
FOREIGN COUNTRIES.							
	Bushels.(b)	Bushels.(b)	Bushels.(b)	Bushels.(b)	Bushels.(b)	Bushels.(b)	
United States........	72,968,340	54,854,600	79,290,200	74,932,200	78,920,800	76,843,900	70.95
Argentina..........	15,002,060	32,215,800	7,098,760	7,180,740	15,462,600	13,052,400	12.05
Roumania...........	9,512,560	7,636,000	9,871,800	10,695,200	14,806,600	4,553,200	4.20
Russia..............	3,932,800	2,571,000	2,560,800	5,471,800	5,281,400	3,779,000	3.49
Turkey, European...	39,720	10,200	3,800	14,400	17,600	152,600	.14
Morocco.............	44,220	....	3,200	27,080	63,420	127,400	.12
Uruguay.............	115,348	251,080	134,600	33,660	51,360	106,040	.10
Turkey, Asiatic......	26,640	2,400	54,000	....	....	76,800	.07
Germany............	23,400	37,200	30,800	27,800	10,400	10,800	.01
Egypt	35,440	127,200	....	4,800	44,600	600	
Bulgaria............	14,960	....	....	....	74,800	....	
Other..............	12,932	14,520	21,600	4,500	14,640	9,400	.01
Total foreign countries....	101,728,420	97,720,000	99,069,560	98,392,180	114,748,220	98,712,140	91.14
BRITISH POSSESSIONS.							
Canada...............	10,098,961	5,766,800	8,470,800	15,945,004	10,721,400	9,590,800	
British East Indies:							8.86
Bengal	2,416	....	....	....	11,880	200	
Bombay	10,560	51,600	....	....	1,200	....	
Natal................	6,080	....	....	30,400	....	....	
Other................	1,440	5,800	....	1,400	....	....	
Total British possessions ..	10,119,457	5,824,200	8,501,200	15,946,404	10,734,480	9,591,000	8.86
Total	111,847,877	103,544,200	107,570,760	114,338,584	125,482,700	108,303,140	100.00

OATS.(c)

	Annual average, 1896–1900.	1896.	1897.	1898.	1899.	1900.	Per ct. in 1900.
FOREIGN COUNTRIES.							
	Bushels.(d)	Bushels.(d)	Bushels.(d)	Bushels.(d)	Bushels.(d)	Bushels.(d)	
Russia..............	24,098,599	35,779,800	19,122,180	11,704,770	16,528,750	37,357,495	53.08
United States........	23,690,324	15,933,750	28,288,050	29,474,620	24,752,000	20,003,200	28.42
Germany............	2,500,736	1,491,700	819,210	1,292,900	3,015,950	5,883,920	8.36
Netherlands.........	561,239	763,875	726,600	556,745	263,375	495,600	.71
Sweden.............	1,460,746	2,822,400	603,750	1,008,630	2,451,750	417,200	.59
Turkey, Asiatic......	566,860	1,304,800	248,150	444,150	448,000	389,200	.55
Argentina	73,850	52,150	....	10,150	117,250	189,700	.27
Chile	37,520	53,900	6,300	....	36,400	91,000	.13
Roumania...........	275,800	88,200	65,800	665,700	479,850	79,450	.11
Turkey, European ...	310,681	185,500	215,250	521,570	572,635	58,450	.08
Denmark............	62,811	24,850	55,230	50,925	166,950	16,100	.02
France	18,480	9,520	490	48,020	34,370	....	
Cyprus.............	9,618	26,390	20,650	1,050	....	....	
Other e	7,763	4,270	350	9,695	19,600	4,900	.01
Total foreign countries	53,675,027	58,541,105	50,172,010	45,788,925	48,886,880	64,986,215	92.33
BRITISH POSSESSIONS.							
Canada..............	5,540,465	2,735,950	6,141,625	8,656,550	4,854,850	5,313,350	7.55
Australasia:							
New Zealand....	268,933	276,500	91,350	42,875	868,350	65,590	
Victoria	6,860	....	3,850	15,400	10,500	4,550	
West Australia...	21	....	....	....	....	105	.10
New South Wales	14,560	....	....	....	72,800	....	
South Australia .	35	....	....	....	175	....	
Other................	6,510	....	....	18,900	....	13,650	.02
Total British possessions ..	5,837,384	3,012,450	6,236,825	8,733,725	5,806,675	5,397,245	7.67
Total	59,512,411	61,553,555	56,408,835	54,522,650	54,693,555	70,383,460	100.00

a For values, see page 91.
b Bushels of 56 pounds.
c For values, see page 92.
d Bushels of 32 pounds.
e Including imports from Norway amounting to 1,820 bushels in 1896 and 350 bushels in 1897.

uantity of the agricultural imports of the United Kingdom (vegetable matter), etc.—Cont'd.

RYE.(*a*)

·untriesfrom which imported.	Annual average, 1896–1900.	Calendar years.					Per ct. in 1900.
		1896.	1897.	1898.	1899.	1900.	
REIGN COUNTRIES.	*Bushels.*(*b*)	*Bushels.*(*b*)	*Bushels.*(*b*)	*Bushels.*(*b*)	*Bushels.*(*b*)	*Bushels.* (*b*)	
ussia................	490,240	746,400	205,400	117,800	555,000	826,600	33.75
nited States........	861,180	524,000	972,200	1,051,500	936,800	821,400	33.54
ermany............	110,760	83,080	77,000	22,200	155,400	216,120	8.83
oumania...........	245,040	363,800	373,800	148,200	279,400	60,000	2.45
ther *c*	21,872	9,800	80	44,100	40,260	15,120	.62
Total foreign countries....	1,729,092	1,727,080	1,628,480	1,383,800	1,966,860	1,939,240	79.19
RITISH POSSESSIONS.							
anada..............	461,772	238,320	409,400	731,740	419,800	509,600	20.81
Total	2,190,864	1,965,400	2,037,880	2,115,540	2,386,660	2,448,840	100.00

OREIGN COUNTRIES.	*Bushels.* (*d*)	*Bushels.* (*d*)	*Bushels.* (*d*)	*Bushels.* (*d*)	*Bushels.* (*d*)	*Bushels.* (*d*)	
nited States...:....	63,613,169	57,297,147	64,592,640	70,663,040	64,681,209	60,831,811	47.46
rgentina...........	14,835,084	9,198,187	1,741,787	7,435,680	21,221,386	34,578,133	26.98
ussia..............	16,994,320	32,184,320	28,093,147	11,634,000	4,700,640	8,359,493	6.52
ermany............	2,005,558	1,928,099	2,489,014	1,327,928	869,923	3,412,826	2.66
oumania...........	2,835,295	10,082,427	2,279,835	342,906	59,920	1,411,387	1.10
ulgaria............	892,752	1,993,413	2,131,920	164,827	....	173,600	.14
yprus	56,709	20,347	5,600	145,787	....	111,813	.09
ruguay	132,122	8,773	118,907	237,813	188,347	106,773	.08
urkey, European...	960,766	2,287,787	2,324,933	93,483	1,120	96,507	.07
enmark	22,445	....	....	3,360	13,104	95,760	.07
Turkey, Asiatic......	559,111	1,295,280	1,146,208	267,643	49,840	36,587	.03
Persia	11,984	26,133	....	....	....	33,787	.03
Netherlands........	13,250	7,411	9,893	31,957	9,147	7,840	.01
Chile	1,504,720	3,614,053	1,902,693	1,506,960	495,227	4,667	
Belgium............	17,394	821	1,064	49,037	31,379	4,667	
France	25,779	4,872	5,843	114,763	19	3,397	.01
Egypt..............	62,265	56,000	50,363	154,747	49,093	1,120	
Greece.............	14,672	....	73,360	....	....	....	
Spain..............	13,231	392	65,333	....	429	....	
Brazil ..·.........	4,107	....	....	20,533	....	....	
Tripoli·............	2,763	....	13,813	....	....	....	
Other..............	1,889	....	1,045	8,400	....	....	
Total foreign countries....	104,579,335	120,005,462	107,047,398	94,202,864	92,370,783	109,270,168	85.25
BRITISH POSSESSIONS.							
Canada.............·...	9,349,958	6,753,414	8,998,266	9,355,789	9,812,134	11,830,187	9.23
Australasia:							
Victoria	1,423,460	12,133	....	340,331	3,848,357	2,916,480	
New Zealand....	689,547	....	....	8,960	1,317,120	2,121,654	
South Australia .	660,132	....	....	....	1,620,845	1,679,813	
New South Wales	80,155	....	....	45,733	94,640	260,400	5.51
Tasmania	19,488	....	....	....	5,413	92,027	
West Australia ..	187	....	....	....	....	933	
Queensland	5,189	....	....	....	25,947	....	
British East Indies:							
Bengal	1,941,266	135,333	37	5,202,587	4,357,360	11,013	.01
Bombay	5,682,910	3,808,821	1,069,115	12,601,494	10,934,747	373	
Other.............:	246	....	187	1,045	....	....	
Total British possessions ..	19,852,538	10,709,701	10,067,605	27,555,939	32,016,563	18,912,880	14.75
Total	124,431,873	130,715,163	117,115,003	121,758,803	124,387,346	128,183,048	100.00

a For values, see page 92.
b Bushels of 56 pounds.
c Including imports from France amounting to 4,400 bushels in 1896 and 80 bushels in 1897.
d Bushels of 60 pounds.

Quantity of the agricultural imports of the United Kingdom (vegetable matter), etc.—Cont'd.

CORN (MAIZE) MEAL. (a)

Countries from which imported.	Annual average, 1896–1900.	Calendar years. 1896.	1897.	1898.	1899.	1900.	Per ct. in 1900.
FOREIGN COUNTRIES.	Barrels.(b)	Barrels.(b)	Barrels.(b)	Barrels.(b)	Barrels.(b)	Barrels.(b)	
United States........	716,060	209,749	587,863	827,074	1,026,653	928,962	99.52
Other.................	1,912	240	269	1,469	4,198	3,383	.36
Total foreign countries....	717,972	209,989	588,132	828,543	1,030,851	932,345	99.88
BRITISH POSSESSIONS.							
Total British possessions c	1,968	354	40	2,200	6,158	1,086	.12
Total	719,940	210,343	588,172	830,743	1,037,009	933,431	100.00

OATMEAL AND GROATS. (a)

FOREIGN COUNTRIES.	Pounds.	Pounds.	Pounds.	Pounds.	Pounds.	Pounds.	
United States........	74,454,688	49,060,480	70,683,200	95,529,280	77,467,040	79,533,440	84.80
Other.................	825,328	408,800	679,280	504,000	1,221,920	1,312,640	1.40
Total foreign countries....	75,280,016	49,469,280	71,362,480	96,033,280	78,688,960	80,846,080	86.20
BRITISH POSSESSIONS.							
Canada..............	12,159,616	12,662,720	10,676,960	14,786,240	9,724,960	12,947,200	13.80
Other.................	9,408	....	....	2,240	44,800	....	......
Total British possessions ..	12,169,024	12,662,720	10,676,960	14,788,480	9,769,760	12,947,200	13.80
Total	87,449,040	62,132,000	82,039,440	110,821,760	88,458,720	93,793,280	100.00

WHEAT FLOUR. (d)

FOREIGN COUNTRIES.	Barrels.(b)	Barrels.(b)	Barrels.(b)	Barrels.(b)	Barrels.(b)	Barrels.(b)	
United States........	9,565,379	9,088,629	8,035,983	9,969,080	10,517,598	10,215,605	82.96
Austria-Hungary....	623,898	793,314	653,686	416,737	588,352	667,403	5.42
France	598,589	982,509	961,383	250,377	366,765	431,913	3.51
Argentina	43,329	33,429	3,771	15,429	63,217	100,800	.82
Belgium.............	45,870	37,251	30,766	52,246	64,407	44,682	.36
Germany.............	55,170	117,023	42,140	61,337	34,690	20,659	.17
Netherlands.........	15,133	7,691	10,514	23,714	17,168	16,577	.14
Russia...............	24,894	8,623	31,840	70,394	2,002	11,611	.09
Chile................	3,634	114	....	7,372	6,971	3,714	.03
Italy.................	1,350	1,051	1,457	377	1,720	2,143	.02
Denmark.............	8,323	5,777	19,691	11,114	3,554	1,480	.01
Roumania............	447	....	1,714	6	....	514	} .02
Other................	1,856	3,034	1,654	1,125	1,389	2,077	
Total foreign countries....	10,987,872	11,078,445	9,794,599	10,879,308	11,667,833	11,519,178	93.55
BRITISH POSSESSIONS.							
Canada..............	1,042,794	1,103,669	874,680	1,124,686	1,427,954	682,982	5.55
Australasia:							
New South Wales	11,020	....	....	1,829	3,200	50,069	
Victoria	12,337	....	....	3,543	8,828	49,314	
South Australia .	2,254	....	....	....	526	10,743	} .90
New Zealand....	286	....	....	....	629	800	
Tasmania	57	....	....	....	286	....	
Natal................	1,314	....	4,957	....	2,514	....	
Other................	559	857	1,332	411	63	132	......
Total British possessions ..	1,070,621	1,104,526	880,069	1,130,469	1,444,000	794,040	6.45
Total	12,058,493	12,182,971	10,674,668	12,009,777	13,111,833	12,313,218	100.00

a For values, see page 93.
b Barrels of 196 pounds.
c In 1896 comprising 354 barrels from Canada.
d For values, see page 94.

antity of the agricultural imports of the United Kingdom (vegetable matter), etc.—Cont'd.

GROUND CEREALS (a) NOT ELSEWHERE SPECIFIED. (b)

ntries from which imported.	Annual average, 1896-1900.	Calendar years.					Per ct. in 1900.
		1896.	1897.	1898.	1899.	1900.	
EIGN COUNTRIES.	*Pounds.*	*Pounds.*	*Pounds.*	*Pounds.*	*Pounds.*	*Pounds.*	
ile	10,764,096	9,984,800	9,045,120	6,768,160	14,750,400	13,272,000	35.94
ited States	26,836,007	21,514,080	70,273,280	5,279,904	31,358,208	5,754,560	15.58
gentina	5,210,912	12,007,520	4,488,960	574,560	4,738,720	4,244,800	11.49
rmany	4,792,368	6,615,168	3,427,648	5,166,784	5,335,120	3,417,120	9.25
ıssia	1,867,936	2,121,280	2,040,640	1,431,360	558,880	3,187,520	8.63
ance	2,440,099	3,058,720	1,366,400	2,194,080	2,969,456	2,611,840	7.07
nmark	412,496	470,400	236,320	428,960	422,800	504,000	1.37
lgium	407,008	112,000	224,000	539,840	1,080,800	78,400	.21
uguay	190,400	22,400	....	....	929,600	....	....
rkey, Asiatic	119,168	595,840	....	....	....	....	....
her c	684,096	369,600	415,520	577,920	344,960	1,712,480	4.64
Total foreign countries	53,724,586	56,871,808	91,517,888	22,961,568	62,488,944	34,782,720	94.18
ITISH POSSESSIONS.							
nada	3,104,035	3,197,936	5,922,560	515,200	4,641,280	1,243,200	3.37
itish East Indies:							
Bombay	863,520	....	....	571,200	2,850,400	596,000	} 2.42
Bengal	56,896	....	....	56,000	228,480	....	
her d	9,184	34,720	....	....	....	11,200	.03
Total British possessions ..	4,033,635	3,232,656	5,922,560	1,142,400	7,720,160	2,150,400	5.82
Total	57,758,221	60,104,464	97,440,448	24,103,968	70,209,104	36,933,120	100.00

SAGO, SAGO MEAL, AND SAGO FLOUR. (e)

	Annual average	Calendar years.					Per ct.
FOREIGN COUNTRIES.	*Pounds.*	*Pounds.*	*Pounds.*	*Pounds.*	*Pounds.*	*Pounds.*	
ava	89,376	....	....	....	110,880	336,000	0.67
íetherlands	110,678	2,240	....	386,512	101,920	62,720	.13
hilippine Islands f	163,520	817,600	....	....	....	....	....
pain	33,600	....	....	....	168,000	....	....
'ther	59,517	74,816	112,112	3,360	81,536	25,760	.05
Total foreign countries	456,691	894,656	112,112	389,872	462,336	424,480	.85
ıRITISH POSSESSIONS.							
ıritish East Indies:							
Straits Settlements	52,931,827	69,283,200	49,802,816	50,824,480	45,093,776	49,654,864	} 99.15
Bombay	11,424	....	....	....	57,120	....	
Total British possessions ..	52,943,251	69,283,200	49,802,816	50,824,480	45,150,896	49,654,864	99.15
Total	53,399,942	70,177,856	49,914,928	51,214,352	45,613,232	50,079,344	100.00

a Including ground beans and peas.
b For values, see page 94.
c Including imports from the Netherlands amounting to 145,600 pounds in 1896, 61,600 pounds in 1897, 06,400 pounds in 1898, and 42,560 pounds in 1899; from Austria-Hungary, 11,200 pounds in 1897 and 68,000 pounds in 1898; from Cyprus, 134,400 pounds in 1896; and from European Turkey, 89,600 pounds n 1897 and 33,600 pounds in 1898.
d In 1896 comprising 34,720 pounds from Australasia.
e For values, see page 95.
f Including the Ladrone Islands.

Quantity of the agricultural imports of the United Kingdom (vegetable matter), etc.—Cont'd.

CAROB BEANS (LOCUST BEANS).(a)

Countries from which imported.	Annual average, 1896-1900.	Calendar years. 1896.	1897.	1898.	1899.	1900.	Per ct. in 1900.
FOREIGN COUNTRIES.	Pounds. (b)	Pounds.	Pounds.	Pounds.	Pounds.	Pounds.	
Cyprus	23,784,320				21,468,944	26,099,696	33.23
Portugal	25,930,408				28,169,008	23,691,808	30.17
Algeria	6,962,928				5,292,000	8,633,856	10.99
Turkey, Asiatic	4,247,264				1,165,472	7,329,056	9.33
Italy	7,134,848	(c)	(c)	(c)	8,808,912	5,460,784	6.95
Morocco	1,740,480				....	3,480,960	4.43
Spain	3,830,624				6,947,248	714,000	.91
France	702,800				1,046,080	359,520	.46
Russia	1,881,600				3,763,200	....	......
Other	2,151,408				1,534,736	2,768,080	3.53
Total	78,366,680	(c)	(c)	(c)	78,195,600	78,537,760	100.00

CIDER AND PERRY.(a)

	Annual average, 1896-1900.	1896.	1897.	1898.	1899.	1900.	Per ct. in 1900.
FOREIGN COUNTRIES.	Gallons.(d)	Gallons.(d)	Gallons.(d)	Gallons.(d)	Gallons.(d)	Gallons.(d)	
United States	454,969	369,472	586,330	364,263	448,414	506,365	96.63
France	12,456	14,000	13,289	8,471	11,545	14,977	2.86
Netherlands	1,088	443	796	3,534	175	491	.09
Other	765	379	137	2,171	216	924	.17
Total foreign countries	469,278	384,294	600,552	378,439	460,350	522,757	99.75
BRITISH POSSESSIONS.							
Canada	18,333	....	120	91,546	....	....	......
Other e	660	1,022	389	219	383	1,284	.25
Total British possessions	18,993	1,022	509	91,765	383	1,284	.25
Total	488,271	385,316	601,061	470,204	460,733	524,041	100.00

COCOA, CRUDE. (a)

	Annual average, 1896-1900.	1896.	1897.	1898.	1899.	1900.	Per ct. in 1900.
FOREIGN COUNTRIES.	Pounds.	Pounds.	Pounds.	Pounds.	Pounds.	Pounds.	
Portugal	6,901,129	5,579,892	1,441,414	6,925,332	8,675,881	11,883,124	22.57
France	3,875,559	2,802,209	3,912,651	4,608,652	2,618,484	5,435,851	10.32
Brazil	2,553,805	1,522,435	3,320,850	1,795,960	2,862,288	3,267,494	6.21
Ecuador	3,398,050	3,326,648	2,073,786	4,362,893	4,107,303	3,119,619	5.92
Germany	2,640,343	2,282,801	2,326,833	2,885,902	2,812,002	2,894,176	5.50
Colombia	615,733	196,142	367,300	749,235	1,064,110	701,879	1.33
United States	379,759	378,633	496,674	342,786	196,273	484,429	.92
Netherlands	764,638	1,005,622	630,372	948,851	796,989	441,355	.84
Dutch Guiana	99,627	55,666	178,181	84,735	70,107	109,495	.21
Venezuela	61,972	79,011	42,784	98,615	43,029	46,419	.09
Spanish West Africa	34,202	3,016	7,741	105,302	41,414	13,539	} .03
Belgium	103,581	624	107,898	26,875	381,683	827	
Guatemala	27,911	....	5,956	16,108	117,492	....	......
Other	45,148	42,343	44,390	33,340	46,742	58,925	.11
Total foreign countries	21,501,467	17,275,042	14,956,830	22,984,586	23,833,747	28,457,132	54.05
BRITISH POSSESSIONS.							
British West Indies	16,807,229	17,409,013	15,772,460	15,274,518	15,114,192	20,465,964	38.88
British East Indies:							
Ceylon	3,603,738	3,274,199	3,443,468	4,062,142	4,058,393	3,180,740	}
Straits Settlements	6,742	1,394	22,522	4,436	1,096	4,260	
Bombay	6,907	4,034	1,066	21,776	6,174	1,487	} 6.05
Burma	2,260	....	....	11,302	....	....	
Bengal	2,039	....	10,070	126	....	....	
Madras	319	109	150	1,334	....	....	

a For values, see page 96.
b Annual average, 1899-1900.
c Included in "Beans, dried."
d United States standard gallons.
e In 1896 comprising 1,022 gallons from the Channel Islands.

uantity of the agricultural imports of the United Kingdom (vegetable matter), etc.—Cont'd.

COCOA, CRUDE—Continued.

hich	Annual average, 1896–1900.	Calendar years.					Per ct. in 1900.
		1896.	1897.	1898.	1899.	1900.	
RITISH POSSES-SIONS—continued.							
	Pounds.	*Pounds.*	*Pounds.*	*Pounds.*	*Pounds.*	*Pounds.*	
iger Protectorate ..	130,756	105,243	87,949	139,220	146,802	174,565	0.33
old Coast..........	77,640	28,159	8,277	85,031	120,730	146,001	.28
agos...............	74,282	61,033	55,579	52,391	95,877	106,531	.20
ritish Guiana	114,532	122,438	173,531	84,711	91,504	100,474	.19
ierra Leone	1,306	417	....	683	3,555	1,874	} .02
ther...............	24,710	722	1,629	111,737	1,171	8,290	
Total British possessions ..	20,852,510	21,006,761	19,576,701	19,849,407	19,639,494	24,190,186	45.95
Total	42,353,977	38,281,803	34,533,531	42,833,993	43,473,241	52,647,318	100.00

COCOA HUSKS AND SHELLS. (a)

OREIGN COUNTRIES.							
otal foreign countries b..............	*Pounds.* 476,000	*Pounds.* 264,992	*Pounds.* 434,448	*Pounds.* 1,088,304	*Pounds.* 343,392	*Pounds.* 248,864	100.00
RITISH POSSESSIONS.							
otal British possessions...............	1,008	2,016	448	1,120	1,456	....	....
Total	477,008	267,008	434,896	1,089,424	344,848	248,864	100.00

COCOA BUTTER. (a)

FOREIGN COUNTRIES.							
	Pounds.	*Pounds.*	*Pounds.*	*Pounds.*	*Pounds.*	*Pounds.*	
Netherlands.........	796,620	225,501	1,539,893	728,216	439,320	1,050,168	83.36
Germany	62,867	17,439	56,438	6,624	25,780	208,053	16.51
Belgium.............	2,059	....	4,360	202	4,135	1,600	.13
Other...............	5,433	....	441	2,508	24,217	....	
Total	866,979	242,940	1,601,132	737,550	493,452	1,259,821	100.00

COCOA, GROUND OR PREPARED, AND CHOCOLATE. (a)

FOREIGN COUNTRIES.							
	Pounds.	*Pounds.*	*Pounds.*	*Pounds.*	*Pounds.*	*Pounds.*	
Netherlands	5,094,042	2,992,621	7,627,909	6,843,152	3,364,736	4,641,791	59.86
France	712,043	204,494	241,788	411,746	845,584	1,856,601	23.94
Belgium	863,857	537,181	1,011,127	708,906	873,126	1,188,948	15.33
Germany	49,363	24,241	82,827	39,592	50,834	49,320	.64
United States........	18,304	20,754	21,810	18,205	14,978	15,773	.20
Other...............	3,432	3,835	6,590	3,645	2,002	1,087	.01
Total foreign countries	6,741,041	3,783,126	8,992,051	8,025,246	5,151,260	7,753,520	99.98
BRITISH POSSESSIONS.							
British Guiana	1,528	7,640	....	....	....	....	
Other...............	2,007	3,656	892,	2,749	1,380	1,359	.02
Total British possessions ..	3,535	11,296	892	2,749	1,380	1,359	.02
Total	6,744,576	3,794,422	8,992,943	8,027,995	5,152,640	7,754,879	100.00

a For values, see page 97.
b Including imports from Spain amounting to 237,664 pounds in 1896 and 127,232 pounds in 1897, and from the United States 8,736 pounds in 1900.

Quantity of the agricultural imports of the United Kingdom (vegetable matter), etc.—Cont'd.

COCOA AND CHOCOLATE, CONTAINING DISTILLED SPIRITS. (*a*)

Countries from which imported.	Annual average, 1896–1900.	Calendar years.					Per ct. in 1900.
		1896.	1897.	1898.	1899.	1900.	
FOREIGN COUNTRIES.							
	Pounds.	*Pounds.*	*Pounds.*	*Pounds.*	*Pounds.*	*Pounds.*	
Belgium	72,447	36,851	59,515	87,721	94,975	83,174	78.40
Germany	11,037	5,332	10,551	10,169	14,359	14,773	13.93
Netherlands	2,925	4,938	2,330	26	40	7,289	6.87
Other *b*	1,966	4,482	2,837	1,280	380	851	.80
Total	88,375	51,603	75,233	99,196	109,754	106,087	100.00

COFFEE, RAW.(*a*)

	Annual average, 1896–1900.	1896.	1897.	1898.	1899.	1900.	Per ct. in 1900.
FOREIGN COUNTRIES.							
	Pounds.	*Pounds.*	*Pounds.*	*Pounds.*	*Pounds.*	*Pounds.*	
Germany	8,515,002	2,589,104	5,010,208	11,485,488	9,817,136	13,673,072	16.08
United States	11,731,888	13,586,720	14,296,240	9,764,048	8,797,824	12,214,608	14.37
Costa Rica	9,809,520	6,440,000	7,608,720	16,351,328	7,715,568	10,931,984	12.86
France	8,476,966	5,766,880	8,708,448	10,375,344	11,870,656	5,663,504	6.66
Colombia	8,792,538	7,054,096	6,987,232	12,083,344	12,803,168	5,034,848	5.92
Brazil	6,950,518	4,657,520	6,467,328	9,362,640	9,353,568	4,911,536	5.78
Chile	2,192,400	116,480	77,728	38,192	6,385,344	4,344,256	5.11
Salvador	2,864,579	1,934,240	2,036,048	3,887,184	2,879,632	3,585,792	4.22
Guatemala	6,229,283	7,800,464	7,161,504	6,379,744	6,401,136	3,403,568	4.00
Nicaragua	1,603,571	669,872	2,433,760	1,804,096	1,107,008	2,003,120	2.36
Netherlands	1,897,638	5,710,992	1,177,120	1,158,528	552,048	889,504	1.05
Mexico	639,587	268,576	501,872	608,944	1,129,968	688,576	.81
Peru	515,446	332,416	631,008	493,584	503,552	616,672	.72
Ecuador	272,070	295,792	250,432	185,360	77,504	551,264	.65
Belgium	621,690	451,920	1,995,280	306,656	64,512	290,080	.34
Liberia	*c* 358,036	(*d*)	494,928	408,128	274,624	254,464	.30
Egypt	75,443	6,720	12,768	257,152	37,296	63,280	.07
Venezuela	56,470	11,648	126,560	83,776	29,232	31,136	.04
Portuguese East Africa	27,373	112,784	336		6,160	17,584	.02
Portugal	270,861	685,776	302,064	132,608	219,856	14,000	.02
Haiti	18,050	71,792	8,288		448	9,744	.01
Portuguese West Africa	121,139	182,336	149,632	185,472	84,784	3,472	
German West Africa	650				112	3,136	
West Africa, n. e. s	*c* 700	332,864				2,800	.01
Austria-Hungary	44,576	5,376	38,528	224	176,400	2,352	
French West Africa	470		560		1,680	112	
Honduras	66,595	75,040	3,248	254,688			
Java	17,920	16,464	70,112	3,024			
Kongo Free State	2,755	9,856	3,920				
Spanish West Africa	67	224	112				
Other	62,384	52,976	84,784	121,184	27,888	25,088	.03
Total foreign countries	72,231,018	59,238,928	66,638,768	85,730,736	80,317,104	69,229,552	81.43
BRITISH POSSESSIONS.							
British East Indies:							
Bombay	8,302,112	6,584,816	4,410,448	5,706,288	18,168,192	6,640,816	
Madras	5,895,008	7,954,464	7,323,568	6,024,816	3,994,816	4,177,376	
Ceylon	1,428,291	1,548,736	1,561,392	939,120	1,963,920	1,128,288	14.12
Straits Settlements	194,432	399,728	307,328	168,224	43,568	53,312	
Bengal	13,933	16,240	16,800	12,656	19,936	4,032	
British West Indies	2,027,088	1,725,584	2,297,344	2,228,576	2,372,944	1,510,992	1.
Natal	777,011	496,160	625,520	432,096	1,197,952	1,133,328	1.55
Aden	1,296,176	1,778,224	1,381,856	1,371,104	918,048	1,033,648	1.22
Niger Protectorate	43,030	48,048	48,720	53,200	37,296	27,888	.03
Gold Coast	24,573	34,496	32,592	20,720	26,768	8,288	.01
Other	186,928	82,992	81,648	586,320	118,272	65,408	.08
Total British possessions	20,188,582	20,669,488	18,087,216	17,543,120	28,859,712	15,783,376	18.57
Total	92,419,600	79,908,416	84,725,984	103,273,856	109,176,816	85,012,928	100.00

a For values, see page 98.
b In 1900 including 260 pounds from the United States.
c Annual average, 1897–1900.
d Included in "West Africa, n. e. s."

uantity of the agricultural imports of the United Kingdom (vegetable matter), etc.—Cont'd.

COFFEE, KILN-DRIED, ROASTED, OR GROUND. (*a*)

from which orted.	Annual average, 1896-1900.	Calendar years.					Per ct. in 1900.
		1896.	1897.	1898.	1899.	1900.	
REIGN COUNTRIES.	*Pounds.*	*Pounds.*	*Pounds.*	*Pounds.*	*Pounds.*	*Pounds.*	
ited States........	7,328	942	190	189	445	34,877	50.88
lgium.............	3,137	1,022	1,074	982	1,505	11,153	16.27
rmany	8,430	6,202	7,032	11,094	11,313	6,509	9.50
therlands.........	2,839	1,767	842	1,460	4,831	5,294	7.72
ance	1,914	2,338	1,445	1,508	1,401	2,877	4.20
her...............	1,184	1,211	740	1,215	1,752	1,002	1.46
Total foreign countries....	24,832	13,482	11,323	16,398	21,247	61,712	90.03
ITISH POSSESSIONS.							
tal British possessions..............	2,105	90	731	1,961	908	6,835	9.97
Total	26,937	13,572	12,054	18,359	22,155	68,547	100.00

CHICORY ROOT, RAW OR KILN-DRIED. (*a*)

OREIGN COUNTRIES.	*Pounds.*	*Pounds.*	*Pounds.*	*Pounds.*	*Pounds.*	*Pounds.*	
elgium..........	10,867,449	11,533,424	11,000,304	10,534,272	10,323,936	10,945,312	100.00
ermany	1,770	112	2,128	6,608	....	....	
ther.............	9,005	20,384	....	24,640	....	....	
Total	10,878,224	11,553,920	11,002,432	10,565,520	10,323,936	10,945,312	100.00

FOREIGN COUNTRIES.	*Pounds.*	*Pounds.*	*Pounds.*	*Pounds.*	*Pounds.*	*Pounds.*	
Belgium.............	77,008	113,725	108,367	60,365	36,040	66,542	63.79
Germany	18,475	18,224	19,222	21,558	15,563	17,809	17.07
Netherlands........	20,887	20,287	19,819	23,493	23,221	17,613	16.88
France	11,066	44,878	2,722	2,342	3,031	2,358	2.26
Other...............	1,245	5,386	....	339	501	....	
Total foreign countries ...	128,681	202,500	150,130	108,097	78,356	104,322	100.00
BRITISH POSSESSIONS.							
Channel Islands.....	38,230	152,509	38,528	112	....	....	
British West Indies..	246	....	....	560	668	....	
Total British possessions ..	38,476	152,509	38,528	672	668	....	
Total	167,157	355,009	188,658	108,769	79,024	104,322	100.00

CHICORY ROOT AND COFFEE (MIXED), ROASTED AND GROUND.(*a*)

FOREIGN COUNTRIES.	*Pounds.*	*Pounds.*	*Pounds.*	*Pounds.*	*Pounds.*	*Pounds.*	
Germany	1,107	1,209	738	1,835	534	1,221	62.11
Denmark.............	7,398	17,241	11,110	6,744	1,894	....	....
Other...............	163	239	56	....	518	....	
Total foreign countries....	8,668	18,689	11,904	8,579	2,946	1,221	62.11
BRITISH POSSESSIONS.							
Channel Islands.....	739	2,016	1,680	....	....	....	
Other...............	608	836	45	910	504	745	37.89
Total British possessions ..	1,347	2,852	1,725	910	504	745	37.89
Total	10,015	21,541	13,629	9,489	3,450	1,966	100.00

a For values, see page 99.

Quantity of the agricultural imports of the United Kingdom (vegetable matter), etc.—Cont'd.

COFFEE SUBSTITUTES, OTHER THAN CHICORY ROOT.(a)

Countries from which imported.	Annual average, 1896–1900.	Calendar years.					Per ct. in 1900.
		1896.	1897.	1898.	1899.	1900.	
FOREIGN COUNTRIES.	*Pounds.*	*Pounds.*	*Pounds.*	*Pounds.*	*Pounds.*	*Pounds.*	
Total	8,579	37,856	2,352	1,456	1,120	112	100.00

COTTON, RAW. (a)

	Annual average	1896.	1897.	1898.	1899.	1900.	Per ct. in 1900.
FOREIGN COUNTRIES.	*Pounds.*	*Pounds.*	*Pounds.*	*Pounds.*	*Pounds.*	*Pounds.*	
United States........	1,435,764,893	1,394,027,152	1,380,186,080	1,805,353,424	1,233,958,880	1,365,298,928	77.56
Egypt	295,676,931	273,056,224	274,132,992	275,929,584	342,816,992	312,448,864	17.75
Brazil	13,826,624	10,540,208	16,814,448	6,022,128	5,464,592	30,291,744	1.72
Peru................	8,526,963	7,332,192	7,852,208	9,834,496	9,585,184	8,030,736	.46
Chile	751,856	265,776	423,360	585,984	776,832	1,707,328	.10
China	436,016	625,520	60,816	560	57,792	1,435,392	.08
Turkey, Asiatic......	391,485	899,920	204,400	....	22,400	830,704	.05
Colombia............	446,611	262,080	200,144	585,760	515,984	669,088	.04
Germany............	392,605	56,560	558,432	531,104	415,856	401,072	.02
Netherlands.........	272,765	1,008	23,968	978,656	96,880	263,312	.01
France	255,382	274,512	170,800	112,448	528,752	190,400	.01
Belgium............	83,014	289,968	3,472	17,360	39,088	65,184	
Italy...............	89,869	259,280	100,800	36,624	....	52,640	} .01
Pacific islands	94,506	114,576	281,792	17,920	35,840	22,400	
Java................	28,874	....	....	144,368	....	....	
Russia	22,579	896	101,584	7,616	2,800	....	
Other b	333,984	222,768	71,792	62,048	166,208	1,147,104	.07
Total foreign countries	1,757,394,957	1,688,228,640	1,681,187,088	2,100,220,080	1,594,484,080	1,722,854,896	97.88
BRITISH POSSESSIONS.							
British East Indies:							
Madras..........	17,912,765	19,346,208	10,233,552	13,960,800	19,307,904	26,715,360	
Bombay	17,254,384	38,895,696	24,255,728	10,593,184	6,007,232	6,520,080	
Ceylon	396,951	2,016	....	159,264	....	1,823,472	
Bengal	5,043,584	7,759,584	7,567,504	2,598,288	5,601,792	1,690,752	} 2.09
Straits Settlements	71,590	173,152	39,312	38,192	24,640	82,656	
Burma	358	....	....	....	1,792	....	
British West Indies..	335,955	402,080	236,880	320,880	284,032	435,904	} .08
Canada	244,966	....	181,216	584,528	458,976	112	
Aden	84,000	....	420,000	....	....	....	
Other c	71,008	82,880	39,088	73,136	76,496	83,440	
Total British possessions ..	41,415,561	66,661,616	42,973,280	28,328,272	31,762,864	37,351,776	2.12
Total	1,798,810,518	1,754,890,256	1,724,160,368	2,128,548,352	1,626,246,944	1,760,206,672	100.00

WASTE COTTON.(a)(d)

	Annual average	1896.	1897.	1898.	1899.	1900.	Per ct. in 1900.
FOREIGN COUNTRIES.	*Pounds.*	*Pounds.*	*Pounds.*	*Pounds.*	*Pounds.*	*Pounds.*	
United States........	4,643,057	3,493,034	6,793,957	2,394,134	2,284,006	8,250,153	44.59
France	1,910,644	2,151,067	2,942,968	1,667,256	1,129,804	1,662,126	8.98
Portugal............	736,773	537,660	701,280	786,140	473,756	1,185,028	6.41
Belgium............	1,068,582	1,052,690	1,184,441	715,259	1,413,434	977,085	5.28
Netherlands.........	393,717	296,070	538,621	168,582	230,113	735,249	3.98
Italy	924,673	1,989,100	936,390	1,139,320	77,432	481,126	2.60
Germany...........	111,193	153,416	173,846	77,665	32,522	118,515	.64
Sweden.............	164,002	368,386	218,264	128,016	75,148	30,195	.16
Other e	626,008	508,820	513,628	560,760	797,067	749,766	4.05
Total foreign countries	10,578,649	10,550,243	14,003,395	7,637,082	6,513,282	14,189,243	76.69

a For values, see page 100.
b Including imports from Cyprus amounting to 21,280 pounds in 1896, 50,176 pounds in 1897, 6,720 pounds in 1898, and 11,872 pounds in 1899.
c Including imports from Australasia amounting to 59,360 pounds in 1896, 34,608 pounds in 1897, 16,576 pounds in 1898, and 27,104 pounds in 1899.
d This item probably includes cop and mill waste as well as the waste of raw cotton.
e In 1896 including 185,200 pounds from Spain.

ıantity of the agricultural imports of the United Kingdom (vegetable matter), etc.—Cont'd.

WASTE COTTON—Continued.

ıtries from which imported.	Annual average, 1896–1900.	Calendar years.					Per ct. in 1900.
		1896.	1897.	1898.	1899.	1900.	
ITISH POSSESSIONS.							
·itish East Indies:	*Pounds.*	*Pounds.*	*Pounds.*	*Pounds.*	*Pounds.*	*Pounds.*	
Bombay	6,564,866	8,622,896	6,727,790	6,006,880	7,437,522	4,029,244	} 22.95
Bengal	165,918	306,220	232,580	....	77,300	213,490	
Madras	770	....	....	....	....	3,850	
ther...............	18,507	23,690	2,240	460	....	66,143	.36
Total British possessions ..	·6,750,061	8,952,806	6,962,610	6,007,340	7,514,822	4,312,727	23.31
Total ....:	17,328,710	19,503,049	20,966,005	13,644,422	14,028,104	18,501,970	100.00

ESPARTO AND OTHER VEGETABLE FIBERS FOR PAPER MAKING.(a)

OREIGN COUNTRIES.							
	Tons.(b)	*Tons.(b)*	*Tons.(b)*	*Tons.(b)*	*Tons.(b)*	*Tons.(b)*	
lgeria..............	82,222	70,251	81,486	83,701	84,806	90,869	45.37
pain...............	58,520	67,715	61,828	55,612	56,926	50,520	25.23
ripoli	39,620	33,662	43,596	32,376	49,266	39,198	19.57
unis...............	18,939	·15,604	17,499	25,532	16,490	19,568	9.77
ther...............	106	36	155	100	116	125	.06
Total foreign countries	199,407	187,268	204,564	197,321	207,604	200,280	100.00
RITISH POSSESSIONS.							
otal British possessions c	9	10	15	20	....	....	....
Total	199,416	187,278	204,579	197,341	207,604	200,280	100.00

FLAX (EXCEPT TOW).(a)

FOREIGN COUNTRIES.							
	Tons.(b)	*Tons.(b)*	*Tons.(b)*	*Tons.(b)*	*Tons.(b)*	*Tons.(b)·*	
Russia..:.............	58,767	57,095	62,659	66,217	65,022	42,841	73.31
Belgium.............	12,887	14,834	14,218	12,443	11,980	10,960	18.75
Netherlands....... ..	2,460	2,381	2,344	2,562	2,525	2,491	4.26
Germany	.859	1,103	500	579	660	1,452	2.48
France	239	169	303	170	362	193	.33
Turkey, European...	56	127	93	26	....	32	.05
Turkey, Asiatic......	37	94	55	21	....	15	.03
United States........	35	140	16	14	4	....	....
Other d	13	4	....	27	3	33	.06
Total foreign countries	75,353	.75,947	80,188	82,059	80,556	58,017	99.27
BRITISH POSSESSIONS.							
Australasia:							
New Zealand	197	152	....	9	423	·400	} .73
New South Wales	5	....	....	....	....	24	
Victoria	....	....	....	....	....	1	
Other...............	..	....	....	1	....	....	....
Total British possessions ..	202	152	....	10	423	425	.73
Total	75,555	76,099	80,188	82,069	80,979	58,442	100.00

a For values, see page 101.
b Tons of 2,240 pounds.

c In 1896 comprising 10 tons from Malta and Gozo.
d In 1896 comprising 4 tons from Brazil.

Quantity of the agricultural imports of the United Kingdom (vegetable matter), etc.—Cont'd.

FLAX, TOW OF. (a)

Countries from which imported.	Annual average, 1896–1900.	Calendar years.					Per ct. in 1900.
		1896.	1897.	1898.	1899.	1900.	
FOREIGN COUNTRIES.							
	Tons. (b)	Tons. (b)	Tons. (b)	Tons. (b)	Tons. (b)	Tons. (b)	
Russia..............	10,449	10,132	10,720	9,597	13,315	8,480	64.52
Belgium.............	5,034	7,436	6,497	4,334	3,582	3,320	25.26
France	590	650	614	548	493	646	4.91
Germany	464	340	447	485	549	498	3.79
Netherlands........	246	373	316	220	134	190	1.44
Other c	10	20	20	....	....	10	.08
Total foreign countries....	16,793	18,951	18,614	15,184	18,073	13,144	100.00
BRITISH POSSESSIONS.							
New Zealand	30	149	....	....	....	....	....
Total	16,823	19,100	18,614	15,184	18,073	13,144	100.00

HEMP (d) (EXCEPT TOW). (a)

	Annual average, 1896–1900.	1896.	1897.	1898.	1899.	1900.	Per ct. in 1900.
FOREIGN COUNTRIES.	Tons.(b)	Tons.(b)	Tons.(b)	Tons.(b)	Tons.(b)	Tons.(b)	
Philippine Islands e .	38,382	39,319	44,578	41,604	28,361	38,046	37.97
Italy.................	11,626	10,644	14,389	11,030	10,904	11,165	11.14
Russia	6,711	8,665	5,592	6,014	5,811	7,475	7.46
Germany	7,746	7,045	6,600	7,307	10,486	7,291	7.28
United States.......	933	569	406	1,652	1,440	597	.60
France	367	18	65	386	911	456	.46
Mexico	395	195	233	151	974	421	.42
Austria-Hungary	179	349	96	74	136	238	.24
Spain...............	377	727	189	129	685	155	.15
China	75	21	155	(f)	76	125	.12
Egypt	24	20	6	....	45	47	.05
Denmark............	118	275	84	96	98	38	.04
Belgium	69	91	33	106	87	28	.03
Netherlands........	67	32	11	130	142	19	.02
Japan	159	497	263	....	35	....	....
Madagascar	10	....	49	....	....	....	....
Other g	56	24	43	145	29	41	.04
Total foreign countries ...	67,294	68,491	72,792	68,824	60,220	66,142	66.02
BRITISH POSSESSIONS.							
Australasia:							
New Zealand....	4,692	1,167	1,399	2,309	6,533	12,054	} 13.04
New South Wales	203	....	....	....	....	1,016	
Hongkong..........	9,196	10,527	2,848	10,411	10,751	11,440	11.42
British East Indies:							
Bengal	3,273	1,966	4,446	3,078	3,193	3,682	}
Bombay..........	2,053	2,559	2,127	2,275	1,486	1,816	
Straits Settlements	516	100	1	758	750	972	} 6.89
Madras	515	920	164	711	425	354	
Ceylon	102	4	46	51	335	75	
Mauritius	1,298	767	580	1,142	1,791	2,211	2.21
British Borneo	7	....	....	34	....	....	....
Other..............	104	17	10	7	59	426	.42
Total British possessions ..	21,959	18,027	11,621	20,776	25,323	34,046	33.98
Total	89,253	86,518	84,413	89,600	85,543	100,188	100.00

a For values, see page 102.
b Tons of 2,240 pounds.
c In 1900 comprising 10 tons from the United States.
d Including Manila hemp, New Zealand flax, sisal grass, sunn, etc.
e Including the Ladrone Islands.
f Less than one-half ton.
g Including imports from European Turkey amounting to 4 tons in 1896, 13 tons in 1897, and 1 ton in 1899, and from Asiatic Turkey, 10 tons in 1898.

antity of the agricultural imports of the United Kingdom (vegetable matter), etc.—Cont'd.

HEMP, TOW OF. (a)

tries from which imported.	Annual average, 1896–1900.	Calendar years.					Per ct. in 1900.
		1896.	1897.	1898.	1899.	1900.	
EIGN COUNTRIES.	Tons.(b)	Tons.(b)	Tons.(b)	Tons.(b)	Tons.(b)	Tons.(b)	
many	1,923	2,277	1,885	1,498	1,562	2,394	47.51
sia	2,599	2,406	1,940	2,782	4,078	1,792	35.56
y	478	381	586	300	471	653	12.96
er c	120	116	102	153	185	42	.83
Total foreign countries....	5,120	5,180	4,513	4,733	6,296	4,881	96.86
ITISH POSSESSIONS.							
itish East Indies d.	68	20	93	109	95	22	.44
her................	35	....	....	....	39	136	2.70
Total British possessions ..	103	20	93	109	134	158	3.14
Total	5,223	5,200	4,606	4,842	6,430	5,039	100.00

JUTE. (a)

REIGN COUNTRIES.	Tons.(b)	Tons.(b)	Tons.(b)	Tons.(b)	Tons.(b)	Tons.(b)	
hina	350	6	58	344	295	1,044	0.37
ermany	1,897	1,734	1,647	757	4,527	818	.29
etherlands.........	173	12	312	37	354	149	.05
rance	47	1	7	7	121	101	.04
elgium	63	13	9	21	185	88	.03
nited States.......	65	180	....	2	90	55	.02
ther................	69	19	3	22	55	244	.09
Total foreign countries....	2,664	1,965	2,036	1,190	5,627	2,499	.89
BRITISH POSSESSIONS.							
British East Indies:							
Bengal	318,352	338,238	334,636	360,702	280,429	277,752	
Madras..........	293	37	244	47	575	561	
Ceylon	53	....	....	163	....	104	99.11
Bombay	98	409	3	....	75	3	
Straits Settlements	24	....	....	7	115	....	
Hongkong...........	9	....	....	28	18	....	
Total British possessions ..	318,829	338,684	334,883	360,947	281,212	278,420	99.11
Total	321,493	340,649	336,919	362,137	286,839	280,919	100.00

PIASSAVA AND OTHER VEGETABLE FIBERS FOR BRUSH MAKING. (a) (e)

Countries from which imported.	Calendar year 1900.	Per cent.	Countries from which imported.	Calendar year 1900.	Per cent.
FOREIGN COUNTRIES.			BRITISH POSSESSIONS.		
	Tons.(b)		British East Indies:	Tons.(b)	
Brazil	1,296	15.79	Ceylon	2,146	
Liberia	1,262	15.37	Bombay...................	662	
Germany	454	5.53	Madras..................	418	39.63
United States.................	320	3.90	Straits Settlements.......	26	
France	283	3.45	Burma	1	
West Africa, n. e. s	258	3.14	Niger Protectorate	203	2.47
Belgium	232	2.83	Other	116	1.41
Italy........................	153	1.86			
French West Africa	119	1.45	Total British possessions	3,572	43.51
Other........................	260	3.17			
Total foreign countries.	4,637	56.49	Total	8,209	100.00

a For values, see page 103.
b Tons of 2,240 pounds.
c Including imports from France amounting to 29 tons in 1896, 5 tons in 1897, 12 tons in 1898, and 31 tons in 1899.
d Including imports from Bengal amounting to 20 tons in 1896, 78 tons in 1897, 71 tons in 1898, 95 tons in 1899, and 20 tons in 1900, and from Ceylon 7 tons in 1898.
e Prior to 1900 not stated by countries.

*Quantity of the agricultural imports of the United Kingdom (vegetable matter), etc.—*Cont'd.

VEGETABLE FIBERS NOT ELSEWHERE SPECIFIED. (a)

Countries from which imported.	Annual average, 1896–1900.	Calendar years.					Per ct. in 1900.
		1896.	1897.	1898.	1899.	1900.	
FOREIGN COUNTRIES.							
	Tons.(b)	*Tons.(b)*	*Tons.(b)*	*Tons.(b)*	*Tons.(b)*	*Tons.(b)*	
France	194	207	63	110	184	408	6.29
Madagascar	374	579	500	93	316	382	5.89
China	157	119	256	135	65	209	3.22
Germany.............	101	67	100	93	39	206	3.18
Mexico...............	698	1,955	802	369	168	195	3.01
Belgium.............	114	43	97	147	113	169	2.61
United States........	583	1,265	833	278	439	102	1.57
Algeria..............	94	175	110	69	60	56	.86
Japan	43	....	40	169	6	1	.02
Russia...............	26	127	2	....	....	....	
Other...............	43	19	63	64	27	43	.66
Total foreign countries....	2,427	4,556	2,866	1,527	1,417	1,771	27.31
BRITISH POSSESSIONS.							
British East Indies:							
Ceylon	2,043	1,211	1,633	2,668	1,687	3,015	
Bombay	405	210	286	582	455	492	
Madras..........	345	142	843	348	153	.238	
Bengal	151	178	135	351	72	20	58.17
Burma	17	52	....	18	8	7	
Straits Settlements	5	5	....	17	....	(c)	
Mauritius	222	47	84	62	232	685	10.57
Hongkong...........	4	5	....	2	....	14	.22
Other d	107	38	51	45	159	242	3.73
Total British possessions ..	3,299	1,888	3,032	4,093	2,766	4,713	72.69
Total	5,726	6,444	5,898	5,620	4,183	6,484	100.00

FRUIT JUICES, NONALCOHOLIC. (a) (e)

Countries from which imported.	Calendar year 1900.	Per cent.	Countries from which imported.	Calendar year 1900.	Per cent.
FOREIGN COUNTRIES.			BRITISH POSSESSIONS—cont'd.		
	Gallons.(f)			*Gallons.(f)*	
Italy.....................	321,888	26.29	Canada	201,670	16.48
United States...............	50,939	4.16	Other	3,324	.27
Other....................	23,238	1.90			
Total foreign countries.	396,065	32.35	Total British possessions	828,073	67.65
BRITISH POSSESSIONS.			Total...................	1,224,138	100.00
British West Indies..........	623,079	50.90			

a For values, see page 104.
b Tons of 2,240 pounds.
c Less than one-half ton.
d Including imports from Natal amounting to 1 ton in 1896 and less than one-half ton in 1897.
e Prior to 1900 not stated by countries.
f United States standard gallons.

*ιntity of the agricultural imports of the United Kingdom (vegetable matter), etc.—*Coɴт d.

APPLES, FRESH. (*a*)

ιntries from which imported.	Annual average, 1896–1900.	Calendar years.					Per ct. in 1900.
		1896.	1897.	1898.	1899.	1900.	
REIGN COUNTRIES.	*Pounds. (b)*	*Bushels. (c)*	*Bushels. (c)*	*Bushels. (c)*	*Bushels. (c)*	*Pounds.*	
ited States	100,653,168	2,696,742	1,865,071	1,289,373	1,287,728	100,653,168	42.22
lgium	17,742,704	321,228	394,975	181,962	285,691	17,742,704	7.44
ιnce	7,132,384	223,593	178,430	170,770	241,796	7,132,384	2.99
therlands	5,965,568	53,643	398,857	91,806	107,210	5,965,568	2.50
rtugal	3,855,824	150,611	150,531	123,049	209,640	3,855,824	1.62
rmany	1,754,480	14,926	27,807	28,819	13,996	1,754,480	.74
ιin	147,392	5,428	60,677	18,726	14,010	147,392	.06
deira Islands	1,904	89	2,849	945	757	1,904	}
ly		627	4,271	162	418		
ιerd	211,232	1,690	1,970	751	14,344	211,232	.09
Total foreign countries	137,464,656	3,468,577	3,085,438	1,906,363	2,175,590	137,464,656	57.66
ITISH POSSESSIONS.							
ɴada	90,007,456	2,725,396	1,053,088	1,488,389	1,598,774	90,007,456	37.76
stralasia:							
Tasmania	8,874,544	157,272	139,763	133,845	159,586	8,874,544	}
South Australia	531,664	1,002	10,367	2,978	8,372	531,664	
Victoria	418,992	6,378	21,146	1,894	5,370	418,992	4.12
New South Wales	2,576	203	179	2,396	2,874	2,576	
New Zealand		87		6	1,599		
ιannel Islands	891,744	12,489	22,283	27,029	26,379	891,744	.37
ther	204,960	126	6	4,766	4,255	204,960	.09
Total British possessions	100,931,936	2,902,953	1,246,832	1,661,303	1,807,209	100,931,936	42.34
Total	238,396,592	6,371,530	4,332,270	3,567,666	3,982,799	238,396,592	100.00

APRICOTS AND PEACHES, FRESH. (*a*) (*e*)

Countries from which imported.	Calendar year 1900.	Per cent.	Countries from which imported.	Calendar year 1900.	Per cent.
FOREIGN COUNTRIES.	*Pounds.*		BRITISH POSSESSIONS.	*Pounds.*	
ʹrance	1,362,816	88.89	Total British possessions	14,336	0.94
ʃnited States	146,944	9.58			
ʃther	9,072	.59	Total	1,533,168	100.00
Total foreign countries	1,518,832	99.06			

BANANAS. (*a*) (*f*)

FOREIGN COUNTRIES.	*Bunches.*		BRITISH POSSESSIONS.	*Bunches.*	
ʹanary Islands	1,243,562	96.59	British West Indies	1,337	} 0.11
ʃadeira Islands	41,981	3.26	Other	18	
ʃnited States	21	} .04			
ʃther	523		Total British possessions	1,355	.11
Total foreign countries.	1,286,087	99.89	Total	1,287,442	100.00

a For values, see page 105.
b Statistics for 1900 only.
c Winchester bushels.
d Including imports from Denmark amounting to 1,029 bushels in 1896 and 992 bushels in 1897.
e Prior to 1900 included in "Plums, fresh."
f Prior to 1900 included in "Fresh fruits not elsewhere specified."

Quantity of the agricultural imports of the United Kingdom (vegetable matter), etc.—Cont'd.

CHERRIES.(a)

Countries from which imported.	Annual average, 1896–1900.	Calendar years.					Per ct. in 1900.
		1896.	1897.	1898.	1899.	1900.	
FOREIGN COUNTRIES.	*Pounds.(b)*	*Bushels.(c)*	*Bushels.(c)*	*Bushels.(c)*	*Bushels.(c)*	*Pounds.*	
France	18,920,272	88,600	198,755	266,218	202,053	18,920,272	69.65
Germany	3,491,824	42,023	59,016	43,790	32,144	3,491,824	12.86
Netherlands.........	2,716,672	67,433	41,676	61,523	29,934	2,716,672	10.00
Belgium.............	2,028,208	28,221	22,225	42,936	25,918	2,028,208	7.47
Other................	3,920	....	459	....	46	3,920	.01
Total foreign countries....	27,160,896	226,277	322,131	414,467	290,095	27,160,896	99.99
BRITISH POSSESSIONS.							
Total British possessions	1,904	....	....	....	....	1,904	.01
Total	27,162,800	226,277	322,131	414,467	290,095	27,162,800	100.00

CURRANTS (FRESH). (a) (d)

Countries from which imported.	Calendar year 1900.	Per cent.	Countries from which imported.	Calendar year 1900.	Per cent.
FOREIGN COUNTRIES.	*Pounds.*		FOREIGN COUNTRIES—cont'd.	*Pounds.*	
France	3,974,208	55.05	Germany	315,952	4.38
Netherlands.................	2,484,384	34.41	Other	11,200	.15
Belgium...................	434,000	6.01	Total...................	7,219,744	100.00

GOOSEBERRIES. (a) (d)

FOREIGN COUNTRIES.	*Pounds.*		FOREIGN COUNTRIES—cont'd.	*Pounds.*	
Netherlands..................	2,727,088	93.49	Other	59,248	2.03
France	130,704	4.48	Total...................	2,917,040	100.00

GRAPES. (a)

Countries from which imported.	Annual average, 1896–1900.	Calendar years.					Per ct. in 1900.
		1896.	1897.	1898.	1899.	1900.	
FOREIGN COUNTRIES.	*Pounds.(b)*	*Bushels.(c)*	*Bushels.(c)*	*Bushels.(c)*	*Bushels.(c)*	*Pounds.*	
Spain	53,008,928	698,528	812,389	872,273	920,690	53,008,928	79.83
Portugal.............	9,080,960	130,095	125,434	194,402	192,840	9,080,960	13.68
Belgium.............	472,080	12,926	17,230	16,617	15,589	472,080	.71
France	250,320	4,566	6,691	32,939	9,175	250,320	.38
Italy................	85,792	659	6,710	....	583	85,792	.13
Netherlands.........	1,792	2,279	242	73	101	1,792	} .10
Other e	66,080	946	2,610	1,823	1,536	66,080	
Total foreign countries	62,965,952	849,999	971,306	1,118,127	1,140,514	62,965,952	94.83
BRITISH POSSESSIONS.							
Channel Islands.....	3,069,472	50,946	44,743	50,771	50,225	3,069,472	4.62
Cape of Good Hope..	296,464	4,455	3,841	1,899	2,410	296,464	.45
Canada.............	50,960	....	3,143	280	264	50,960	.08
Other f	17,136	5,666	1,982	458	700	17,136	.02
Total British possessions ..	3,434,032	61,067	53,709	53,408	53,599	3,434,032	5.17
Total	66,399,984	911,066	1,025,015	1,171,535	1,194,113	66,399,984	100.00

a For values, see page 106.
b Statistics for 1900 only.
c Winchester bushels.
d Prior to 1900 included in "Fresh fruits not elsewhere specified."
e In 1900 including 3,248 pounds from the United States.
f In 1896 including 4,369 bushels from the British West Indies.

intity of the agricultural imports of the United Kingdom (vegetable matter), etc.—Cont'd.

LEMONS, LIMES, AND CITRONS. (a)

:rom which ›rted.	Annual average, 1896–1900.	Calendar years.					Per ct. in 1900.
		1896.	1897.	1898.	1899.	1900.	
EIGN COUNTRIES.	Pounds. (b)	Bushels. (c)	Bushels. (c)	Bushels. (c)	Bushels. (c)	Pounds.	
y	91,701,904	1,539,763	1,381,043	1,487,143	1,537,527	91,701,904	86.38
in	12,130,048	141,945	178,667	160,002	175,389	12,130,048	11.43
many	744,912	6,843	6,280	9,981	8,996	744,912	.70
tugal	518,672	13,380	9,469	9,480	11,905	518,672	.49
·key, Asiatic	480,928	1,650	7,976	1,460	5,155	480,928	.45
nce	318,528	384		8,270	14	318,528	.30
ited States	6,720	186	12,031	2,677	287	6,720	.01
›er	193,536	1,287	358	2,536	2,007	193,536	..18
Total foreign countries	106,095,248	1,705,438	1,595,824	1,681,549	1,741,280	106,095,248	99.94
ITISH POSSESSIONS.							
tal British possesions	68,544	7,281	1,885	1,492	411	68,544	.06
Total	106,163,792	1,712,719	1,597,709	1,683,041	1,741,691	106,163,792	100.00

ORANGES. (a)

REIGN COUNTRIES.	Pounds. (b)	Bushels. (c)	Bushels. (c)	Bushels. (c)	Bushels. (c)	Pounds.	
ain	494,021,360	6,464,652	8,152,156	6,411,891	7,880,201	494,021,360	86.65
rkey, Asiatic	24,061,520	196,337	246,962	279,922	261,651	24,061,520	4.22
·ly	23,146,928	318,879	295,978	317,540	350,183	23,146,928	4.06
rtugal	17,370,192	200,355	112,895	161,272	124,982	17,370,192	3.05
gypt	5,320,448	108,078	88,013	77,736	78,910	5,320,448	.93
rance	2,128,560	46,664	22,345	42,338	25,181	2,128,560	.37
·ermany	1,060,976	465	11,199	8,507	29,490	1,060,976	.19
anary Islands	888,720	11,755	16,524	12,559	10,405	888,720	.16
·nited States	425,824	28,409	22,644	23,016	7,369	425,824	.07
.zores	210,112	49,698	74,044	102,672	26,830	210,112	.04
·razil	9,408	2,411	9,776	9,465	4,250	9,408	} .03
·ther	144,256	956	627	1,362	5,508	144,256	
Total foreign countries	568,788,304	7,428,659	9,053,163	7,448,280	8,804,960	568,788,304	99.77
RITISH POSSESSIONS.							
·ritish West Indies	827,680	16,807	9,089	11,167	11,159	827,680	.14
[alta and Gozo	317,520	8,580	4,857	5,083	4,982	317,520	.06
.ustralasia:							
South Australia	138,208	268	2,924	281	1,440	138,208	
New South Wales	31,248	3,041	3,809	24,455	318	31,248	
West Australia	672	5				672	
Victoria		30	103	6,655	45		} .03
Tasmania		8		5,785	74		
New Zealand			12				
Queensland			5				
·ther	19,600	833	353	1,747	177	19,600	
Total British possessions	1,334,928	29,572	21,152	55,173	18,195	1,334,928	.23
Total	570,123,232	7,458,231	9,074,315	7,503,453	8,823,155	570,123,232	100.00

a For values, see page 107.　　*b* Statistics for 1900 only.　　*c* Winchester bushels.

Quantity of the agricultural imports of the United Kingdom (vegetable matter), etc.—Cont'd.

PEARS, FRESH. (a)

Countries from which imported.	Annual average, 1896–1900.	Calendar years.					Per ct. in 1900.
		1896.	1897.	1898.	1899.	1900.	
FOREIGN COUNTRIES.	Pounds.(b)	Bushels.(c)	Bushels.(c)	Bushels.(c)	Bushels.(c)	Pounds.	
France	33,775,840	246,833	277,620	300,741	279,563	33,775,840	63.24
Belgium	13,370,000	148,019	545,762	83,280	124,549	13,370,000	25.03
United States	2,823,968	38,900	89,598	47.115	79,860	2,823,968	5.29
Netherlands	1,562,288	49,220	138,704	23,423	47,184	1,562,288	2.92
Germany	643,216	2,594	23,718	9,500	27,848	643,216	1.20
Other	68,880	1,206	1,473	1,518	12,513	68,880	.13
Total foreign countries....	52,244,192	486,772	1,076,875	465,577	571,517	52,244,192	97.81
BRITISH POSSESSIONS.							
Channel Islands	943,152	11,602	4,901	10,961	11,464	943,152	1.77
Canada	211,008	16	2,737	30,423	5,140	211,008	.39
Other	14,560	673	498	196	1,724	14,560	.03
Total British possessions ..	1,168,720	12,291	8,136	41,580	18,328	1,168,720	2.19
Total	53,412,912	499,063	1,085,011	507,157	589,845	53,412,912	100.00

PLUMS, FRESH. (a) (d)

FOREIGN COUNTRIES.	Pounds.(b)	Bushels.(c)	Bushels.(c)	Bushels.(c)	Bushels.(c)	Pounds.	
France	29,381,968	254,546	525,997	551,107	325,552	29,381,968	62.02
Germany	8,427,328	159,491	295,942	263,255	197,038	8,427,328	17.79
Belgium	4,748,240	81,046	92,732	60,969	3,451	4,748,240	10.02
Netherlands	4,233,936	78,966	154,212	67,490	35,589	4,233,936	8.94
United States	518,560	2,815	5,521	3,453	9,141	518,560	1.09
Other	9,184	41	1,441	489	211	9,184	.02
Total foreign countries....	47,319,216	576,905	1,075,845	946,763	570,982	47,319,216	99.88
BRITISH POSSESSIONS.							
Cape of Good Hope..	40,992	988	379	718	590	40,992	.08
Other	17,920	....	475	3,818	4,287	17,920	.04
Total British possessions ..	58,912	988	854	4,536	4,877	58,912	.12
Total	47,378,128	577,893	1,076,699	951,299	575,859	47,378,128	100.00

STRAWBERRIES. (a) (e)

Countries from which imported.	Calendar year 1900.	Per cent.	Countries from which imported.	Calendar year 1900.	Per cent.
FOREIGN COUNTRIES.	Pounds.		BRITISH POSSESSIONS.	Pounds.	
France	5,055,232	86.43	Total British possessions.....	672	0.01
Netherlands	793,296 }	13.56	Total..................	5,849,200	100.00
Other	(f)				
Total foreign countries.	5,848,528	99.99			

a For values, see page 108.
b Statistics for 1900 only.
c Winchester bushels.
d Prior to 1900 including fresh apricots and peaches.
e Prior to 1900 included in "Fresh fruits not elsewhere specified."
f Less than 56 pounds (one-half hundredweight).

tantity of the agricultural imports of the United Kingdom (vegetable matter), etc.—Cont'd.

FRESH FRUITS NOT ELSEWHERE SPECIFIED. (a) (b)

rom which rted.	Annual average, 1896–1900.	Calendar years.					Per ct. in 1900.
		1896.	1897.	1898.	1899.	1900.	
REIGN COUNTRIES.	Pounds. (c)	Bushels. (d)	Bushels. (d)	Bushels. (d)	Bushels. (d)	Pounds.	
ain..............	41,347,712	439,252	550,683	775,395	725,749	41,347,712	74.62
ores......	5,176,640	65,158	55,524	66,695	81,882	5,176,640	9.34
rmany...........	4,007,136	140,221	113,102	118,596	104,127	4,007,136	7.23
therlands........	2,075,584	135,291	152,723	217,014	178,966	2,075,584	3.75
rtugal	680,064	12,519	8,932	13,532	11,686	680,064	1.23
ance	455,392	92,664	137,613	183,770	158,935	455,392	.82
.ly...............	276,976	4,234	818	6,323	3,314	276,976	.50
deira Islands....	211,568	45,481	74,188	77,582	83,043	211,568	.38
ited States.......	143,024	8,208	17,070	2,843	4,561	143,024	.26
nary Islands.....	111,552	500,751	587,245	743,313	933,104	111,552	.20
lgium...........	13,328	10,034	30,613	14,176	6,143	13,328	.02
her..............	175,056	1,308	1,531	853	2,348	175,056	.32
Total foreign countries	54,674,032	1,455,121	1,730,042	2,220,092	2,293,858	54,674,032	98.67
RITISH POSSESSIONS.							
hannel Islands.....	396,144	6,804	11,676	18,994	14,122	396,144	.72
ritish West Indies..	179,984	7,751	28,320	4,298	9,279	179,984	.33
alta and Gozo	21,504	400	2,469	178	....	21,504	.04
anada..............	7,616	....	3,042	733	646	7,616	.01
ther e..............	129,584	1,983	3,908	1,417	685	129,584	.23
Total British possessions ..	734,832	16,938	49,415	25,620	24,732	734,832	1.33
Total..........	55,408,864	1,472,059	1,779,457	2,245,712	2,318,590	55,408,864	100.00

CURRANTS (DRIED). (a)

FOREIGN COUNTRIES.	Pounds.	Pounds.	Pounds.	Pounds.	Pounds.	Pounds.	
Greece...............	118,136,435	110,164,208	126,165,536	137,902,352	129,194,800	87,255,280	94.49
Netherlands........	1,068,816	5,152	616,784	441,840	1,422,064	2,858,240	3.10
France	235,066	73,696	9,632	54,656	206,192	831,152	.90
Belgium.............	151,939	9,072	11,872	10,416	202,496	525,840	.57
Germany............	112,426	48,048	336	....	1,680	512,064	.55
Turkey, Asiatic	249,782	185,696	603,232	297,696	37,520	124,768	.13
Russia...............	377,239	....	1,625,456	260,736			
Other f :..............	96,342	11,536	119,056	70,336	77,504	203,280	.22
Total foreign countries	120,428,045	110,497,408	129,151,904	139,038,032	131,142,256	92,310,624	99.96
BRITISH POSSESSIONS.							
Total British possessions	9,744	8,176	....	1,792	2,352	36,400	.04
Total	120,437,789	110,505,584	129,151,904	139,039,824	131,144,608	92,347,024	100.00

a For values, see page 109.
b Prior to 1900 including bananas, currants (fresh), gooseberries, and strawberries.
c Statistics for 1900 only.
d Winchester bushels.
e Including imports from the Cape of Good Hope amounting to 1,263 bushels in 1896, 45 bushels in 1898, and 347 bushels in 1899, and from Natal 14 bushels in 1896.
f In 1900 including 97,664 pounds from the United States.

Quantity of the agricultural imports of the United Kingdom (vegetable matter), etc.—Cont'd.

FIGS AND FIG CAKE. (*a*)

Countries from which imported.	Annual average, 1896–1900.	Calendar years.					Per ct. in 1900.
		1896.	1897.	1898.	1899.	1900.	
FOREIGN COUNTRIES.							
	Pounds.	*Pounds.*	*Pounds.*	*Pounds.*	*Pounds.*	*Pounds.*	
Turkey, Asiatic......	11,192,451	12,829,600	13,911,408	3,284,400	11,626,048	14,310,800	7
Portugal.............	2,284,397	1,236,256	1,626,688	3,618,048	2,376,752	2,564,240	1.0
Spain................	1,341,424	606,592	515,088	3,309,600	1,439,312	836,528	4.
Greece..............	182,470	117,712	8,624	373,184	247,184	165,648	.
Italy................	201,287	888,272	7,728	15,680	74,928	19,824	.
France	103,578	159,152	32,256	235,760	79,072	11,648	.66
Belgium.............	70,112	20,160	18,032	244,720	60,592	7,056	.04
Other *b*	146,966	196,224	183,792	111,664	173,824	69,328	.39
Total foreign countries....	15,522,685	16,053,968	16,303,616	11,193,056	16,077,712	17,985,072	99.98
BRITISH POSSESSIONS.							
Total British possessions...............	9,385	....	35,056	7,952	896	3,024	.02
Total..........	15,532,070	16,053,968	16,338,672	11,201,008	16,078,608	17,988,096	100.00

PRUNES. (*a*)

FOREIGN COUNTRIES.							
	Pounds.	*Pounds.*	*Pounds.*	*Pounds.*	*Pounds.*	*Pounds.*	
France	1,589,504	2,153,200	1,140,272	1,762,320	897,008	1,994,720	62.31
United States........	768,790	278,544	733,936	675,024	1,161,440	995,008	31.08
Austria-Hungary....	209,866	112,112	238,896	155,792	376,544	165,984	5.19
Germany............	126,224	139,328	244,944	113,904	98,000	34,944	1.09
Other................	10,618	11,760	896	2,240	27,664	10,528	.33
Total..........	2,705,002	2,694,944	2,358,944	2,709,280	2,560,656	3,201,184	100.00

FRENCH PLUMS AND PRUNELLOES, DRIED. (*a*)

FOREIGN COUNTRIES.							
	Pounds.	*Pounds.*	*Pounds.*	*Pounds.*	*Pounds.*	*Pounds.*	
France	4,172,403	3,641,120	1,378,832	6,049,456	1,828,064	7,964,544	}100.00
Other................	24,080	30,576	2,800	....	86,912	112	
Total..........	4,196,483	3,671,696	1,381,632	6,049,456	1,914,976	7,964,656	100.00

PLUMS, DRIED OR PRESERVED, N. E. S.. INCLUDING DRIED APRICOTS. (*a*)

FOREIGN COUNTRIES.							
	Pounds.	*Pounds.*	*Pounds.*	*Pounds.*	*Pounds.*	*Pounds.*	
United States........	1,910,093	632,016	2,628,864	1,146,096	2,691,584	2,451,904	58.21
France	322,986	322,000	69,440	321,888	145,712	755,888	17.94
Germany............	1,877,075	1,293,600	2,663,024	1,872,640	2,812,432	743,680	17.66
Austria-Hungary....	863,273	674,352	1,147,664	1,041,712	1,225,280	227,360	5.40
Other................	32,122	9,296	60,480	18,032	51,520	21,280	.50
Total foreign countries....	5,005,549	2,931,264	6,569,472	4,400,368	6,926,528	4,200,112	99.71
BRITISH POSSESSIONS.							
Australasia..........	25,782	2,800	2,016	94,528	17,472	12,096	.29
Total..........	5,031,331	2,934,064	6,571,488	4,494,896	6,944,000	4,212,208	100.00

a For values, see page 110.   *b* In 1900 including 18,592 pounds from the United States.

uantity of the agricultural imports of the United Kingdom (vegetable matter), etc.—Cont'd.

RAISINS. (a)

ountries from which imported.	Annual average, 1896–1900.	Calendar years.					Per ct. in 1900.
		1896.	1897.	1898.	1899.	1900.	
ʼOREIGN COUNTRIES.							
	Pounds.	*Pounds.*	*Pounds.*	*Pounds.*	*Pounds.*	*Pounds.*	
pain	36,647,453	32;365,200	35,286,048	33,074,272	37,225,552	45,286,192	61.42
urkey, Asiatic	33,079,223	34,265,616	37,239,888	30,467,248	39,060,112	24,363,248	33.04
reece	1,886,797	1,943,872	1,897,168	2,355,136	1,583,008	1,654,800	2.25
rance	200,637	448	33,824	96,768	238,112	634,032	.86
ussia	172,704		9,968	151,984	176,400	525,168	.71
nited States	99,523	1,904	86,464	11,984	109,536	287,728	.39
ermany	113,254	35,616	128,800	81,984	84,672	235,200	.32
etherlands	124,208	448	428,736	25,536	2,240	164,080	.22
:aly	169,299	726,432	112		1,232	118,720	.16
ther	225,725	42,336	107,968	281,120	229,600	467,600	.63
Total foreign countries	72,718,823	69,381,872	75,218,976	66,546,032	78,710,464	73,736,768	100.00
RITISH POSSESSIONS.							
otal British possessions	560	1,344	448		224	784	
Total	72,719,383	69,383,216	75,219,424	66,546,032	78,710,688	73,737,552	100.00

DRIED FRUITS NOT ELSEWHERE SPECIFIED. (a)

FOREIGN COUNTRIES.							
	Pounds.	*Pounds.*	*Pounds.*	*Pounds.*	*Pounds.*	*Pounds.*	
Turkey, Asiatic	40,817,191	27,206,704	48,508,656	24,112,928	42,641,536	61,616,128	86.83
United States	2,975,123	3,168,592	2,343,376	3,176,992	2,573,088	3,613,568	5.09
France	1,048,925	837,312	880,768	853,776	1,326,864	1,345,904	1.90
Egypt	804,698	133,504	967,568	815,808	1,128,736	977,872	1.38
Persia	1,279,533	1,071,840	2,423,680	426,384	1,654,800	820,960	1.16
Italy	113,837	155,008	142,240	76,272	74,928	120,736	.17
Morocco	85,478	133,504	119,504	81,088	19,376	73,920	.10
Germany	38,998	2,688	7,168	98,784	49,056	37,296	.05
Belgium	46,435	672	4,704	182,224	41,888	2,688	} .17
Other b	68,275	27,888	22,064	125,776	47,600	118,048	
Total foreign countries	47,278,493	32,737,712	55,419,728	29,950,032	49,557,872	68,727,120	96.85
BRITISH POSSESSIONS.							
British East Indies:							
Bombay	1,899,184	1,544,704	2,907,632	1,704,864	1,598,576	1,740,144	} 2.49
Madras	4,301					21,504	
Bengal	23,677		100,800	5,824	2,912	8,848	
Ceylon	22	112					
Canada	149,744	142,912	163,632	94,192	124,096	223,888	.32
Gibraltar	278,185	221,536	309,680	380,800	344,960	133,952	.19
Malta and Gozo	30,867	10,304	45,472	25,200	60,704	12,656	.02
Other	50,109	1,792	3,584	33,600	119,280	92,288	.13
Total British possessions	2,436,089	1,921,360	3,530,800	2,244,480	2,250,528	2,233,280	3.15
Total	49,714,582	34,659,072	58,950,528	32,194,512	51,808,400	70,960,400	100.00

a For values, see page 111.
b Including imports from China amounting to 1,120 pounds in 1896, 3,808 pounds in 1897, and 36,736 pounds in 1898.

Quantity of the agricultural imports of the United Kingdom (vegetable matter), etc.—Cont'd.

FRUITS, OTHER THAN PLUMS, PRESERVED WITHOUT SUGAR. (*a*)

Countries from which imported.	Annual average, 1896–1900.	Calendar years.					Per ct. in 1900.
		1896.	1897.	1898.	1899.	1900.	
FOREIGN COUNTRIES.							
	Pounds.	*Pounds.*	*Pounds.*	*Pounds.*	*Pounds.*	*Pounds.*	
United States........	22,868,174	15,172,248	16,050,738	16,297,462	22,911,717	43,908,704	39.39
Italy	27,007,507	21,844,136	23,063,768	28,743,635	32,418,316	28,967,680	25.99
Spain................	8,097,239	7,210,943	7,845,145	8,109,048	7,441,875	9,879,184	8.86
France	4,164,264	3,653,463	4,098,268	3,770,167	2,931,884	6,367,536	5.71
Portugal	461,210	290,486	311,232	425,920	645,278	633,136	.57
Greece	1,352,500	1,062,938	2,174,262	1,531,890	1,405,410	588,000	.53
Belgium.............	235,552	38,510	490,416	49,372	160,756	438,704	.40
Russia..............	319,576	175,536	251,459	200,981	812,322	157,584	.14
Austria-Hungary....	201,453	24,500	381,714	230,270	226,860	143,920	.13
Turkey, Asiatic	218,723	6,628	246,306	700,270	3,212	137,200	.12
Madeira Islands.....	123,673	201,840	94,810	163,020	25,302	133,392	.12
Sweden	117,330	93,342	92,734	179,960	108,280	112,336	.10
Other *b*	376,338	184.108	312,760	489,635	284,788	610,400	.55
Total foreign countries	65,543,539	49,958,678	55,413,612	60,891,630	69,376,000	92,077,776	82.61
BRITISH POSSESSIONS.							
British East Indies: Straits Settlements	13,983,148	11,536,110	8,628,416	11,267,394	22,164,747	16,319,072	⎫
Bombay	15,779	160				78,736	⎪ 14.71
Ceylon	14,896	....	74,480	....	....	....	⎬
Bengal	660	....	3,300	....	....	....	⎪
Canada......	2,009,213	1,318,900	1,561,232	3,421,612	1,463,663	2,280,656	2.
Australasia *c*	319,624	152,650	57,790	185,590	529,754	672,336	.05
Other................	46,485	20,018	77,476	84,106	15,659	35,168	.06
Total British possessions ..	16,389,805	13,027,838	10,402,694	14,958,702	24,173,823	19,385,968	17.39
Total	81,933,344	62,986,516	65,816,306	75,850,332	93,549,823	111,463,744	100.00

ALMONDS. (*a*)

FOREIGN COUNTRIES.							
	Pounds.	*Pounds.*	*Pounds.*	*Pounds.*	*Pounds.*	*Pounds.*	
Spain................	7,993,709	7,608,160	9,625,504	8,619,744	8,187,536	5,927,600	37.71
Morocco.............	2,648,240	1,466,864	1,819,216	3,108,224	2,332,176	4,514,720	28.72
Italy................	2,446,595	3,375,680	2,765,840	2,628,528	2,130,912	1,332,016	8.47
Portugal	1,597,747	1,789,648	1,719,088	2,111,760	1,085,392	1,282,848	8.16
France	1,506,490	1,545,824	1,444,464	1,401,232	1,948,128	1,192,800	7.59
Canary Islands......	489,507	257,824	496,160	710,864	301,728	680,960	4.33
Persia	80,864	44,912	....	9,296	20,944	329,168	2.09
Turkey, Asiatic......	30,598	2,352	37,856	18,032	4,480	90,272	.58
Germany............	140,359	143,920	164,416	154,784	167,552	71,120	.45
Austria-Hungary	31,987	7,728	12,544	115,920	18,368	5,376	.04
Turkey, European...	47,712	238,560	....	....	....	....	
Other................	26,029	1,344	96,768	17,696	10,528	3,808	.02
Total foreign countries	17,039,837	16,482,816	18,181,856	18,896,080	16,207,744	15,430,688	98.16
BRITISH POSSESSIONS.							
Gibraltar	104,025	50,288	47,936	115,808	161,392	144,704	.92
Other................	47,466	33,712	....	58,800	....	144,816	.92
Total British possessions ..	151,491	84,000	47,936	174,608	161,392	289,520	1.84
Total	17,191,328	16,566,816	18,229,792	19,070,688	16,369,136	15,720,208	100.00

a For values, see page 112.
b Including imports from the Canary Islands amounting to 41,720 pounds in 1896, 38,420 pounds in 1897, and 17,520 pounds in 1898.
c Including imports from Victoria amounting to 57,490 pounds in 1896, 47,710 pounds in 1897, 103,300 pounds in 1898, 170,144 pounds in 1899, and 364,224 pounds in 1900, and from Tasmania, 90,900 pounds i 1896, 6,720 pounds in 1898, and 19,376 pounds in 1900.

ιantity of the agricultural imports of the United Kingdom (vegetable matter), etc.—Cont'd.

NUTS FOR FOOD, OTHER THAN ALMONDS.(a) (b)

	Calendar year 1900.	Per cent.	Countries from which imported.	Calendar year 1900.	Per cent.
FOREIGN COUNTRIES.			BRITISH POSSESSIONS.		
	Pounds.				
ance	33,883,472	39.63	British East Indies:	*Pounds.*	
ain	13,511,568	15.81	Ceylon	15,093,792	
azil	3,759,840	4.40	Bengal	39,200	} 17.72
ly	1,903,776	2.23	Bombay	11,648	
therlands	1,176,448	1.38	British West Indies	12,468,064	14.58
ited States	839,328	.98	British Honduras	3,360	}
rkey, Asiatic	769,664	.90	Other	55,664	} .07
lgium	505,568	.59			
rmany	490,336	.57	Total British possessions	27,671,728	32.37
rsia	383,376	.45			
rkey, European	234,080	.27			
ile	116,480	.14	Total	85,489,040	100.00
ypt	44,800	.05			
her	198,576	.23			
Total foreign countries.	57,817,312	67.63			

OIL NUTS.(a)

	Annual average, 1896-1900.	1896.	1897.	1898.	1899.	1900.	Per ct. in 1900.
OREIGN COUNTRIES.							
	Pounds.	*Pounds.*	*Pounds.*	*Pounds.*	*Pounds.*	*Pounds.*	
acific islands	10,157,056	13,478,080	11,464,320	2,710,400	12,799,360	10,333,120	8.14
hilippine Islands c .	6,961,024	10,514,560	8,252,160	2,195,200	3,897,600	9,945,600	7.84
erman West Africa.	1,422,848	31,360	8,960	952,000	35,840	6,086,080	4.79
ortuguese West Africa	1,102,080		11,200	264,320	291,200	4,943,680	3.89
rench West Africa..	2,244,928	573,440	1,682,240	2,938,880	1,805,440	4,224,640	3.33
rance	1,188,096	981,120	73,920	1,124,480	1,509,760	2,251,200	1.77
iberia	d 705,040	(e)	564,480	434,560	311,360	1,509,760	1.19
West Africa, n. e. s...	d 407,120	82,880	105,280	67,200	286,720	1,169,280	.92
rgentina	238,336		479,360			712,320	.56
Netherlands	350,336	2,240	237,440	53,760	815,360	642,880	.51
pain	786,688	456,960	1,155,840	752,640	947,520	620,480	.49
ermany	783,104	504,000	792,960	1,043,840	1,088,640	486,080	.38
nited States	386,176	203,840	575,680	658,560	268,800	224,000	.18
urkey, Asiatic	89,600	112,000	114,240	89,600	78,400	53,760	.04
apan	276,864	694,400	571,200		112,000	6,720	} .01
ava	65,856		327,040			2,240	}
erman New Guinea	308,672	1,543,360					
hina	188,608	112,000	8,960	201,600	620,480		
ther f	422,464	159,040	176,960	280,000	434,560	1,061,760	.84
Total foreign countries....	27,879,040	29,449,280	26,602,240	13,767,040	25,303,040	44,273,600	34.88
BRITISH POSSESSIONS.							
Niger Protectorate ..	13,353,088	6,758,080	11,712,960	15,368,640	8,839,040	24,086,720	18.98
Sierra Leone	12,925,696	11,858,560	11,708,480	10,498,880	16,186,240	14,376,320	11.33
Australasia:							
New South Wales	15,575,168	20,690,880	16,157,120	16,116,800	14,067,200	10,843,840	
Fiji Islands	1,033,984		1,792,000		851,200	2,526,720	
New Zealand....	1,776,768	4,495,680	2,728,320	611,520	571,200	477,120	} 10.95
Queensland	109,760	44,800	56,000	371,840	24,640	51,520	
Victoria	896					4,480	
British East Indies:							
Madras	3,212,160	1,039,360	1,691,200	5,360,320	1,270,080	6,699,840	
Ceylon	5,065,536	2,349,760	2,412,480	9,412,480	4,809,280	6,343,680	
Bengal	120,512	306,880	2,240	112,000		181,440	} 10.63
Straits Settlements	1,415,680	1,052,800	1,393,280	2,266,880	2.197,440	168,000	
Bombay	245,504	112,000	429,040	436,800	141,120	98,560	

a For values, see page 113.
b Quantities not stated prior to 1900.
c Including the Ladrone Islands.
d Annual average, 1897-1900.
e Included in "West Africa, n. e. s."
f Including imports from Portugal amounting to 89,600 pounds in 1896, 47,040 pounds in 1897, 8,960 pounds in 1898, and less than 1,120 pounds (one-half ton) in 1899; from the Kongo Free State, 4,480 pounds in 1896, 2,240 pounds in 1897, and 49,280 pounds in 1898; from Belgium, 6,720 pounds in 1898 and 22,400 pounds in 1899; and from Portuguese East Africa, 17,920 pounds in 1896.

*Quantity of the agricultural imports of the United Kingdom (vegetable matter), etc. —*Cont'd.

OIL NUTS—Continued.

Countries from which imported.	Annual average, 1896–1900.	Calendar years.					Per ct. in 1900.
		1896.	1897.	1898.	1899.	1900.	
BRITISH POSSESSIONS— continued.	*Pounds.*	*Pounds.*	*Pounds.*	*Pounds.*	*Pounds.*	*Pounds.*	
Lagos................	40,279,232	59,559,360	42,418,880	38,189,760	50,019,200	11,208,960	8.83
Gold Coast	1,116,864	629,440	324,800	705,600	1,117,760	2,806,720	2.21
Gambia..............	1,781,696	1,408,960	1,984,640	2,199,680	2,172,800	1,142,400	.90
Hongkong...........	239,680	302,400	4,480	....	....	891,520	.70
Other*a*..............	288,512	2,240	6,720	192,640	486,080	754,880	.59
Total British possessions ..	98,540,736	110,611,200	94,832,640	101,843,840	102,753,280	82,662,720	65.12
Total	126,419,776	140,060,480	121,434,880	115,610,880	128,056,320	126,936,320	100.00

FRUITS AND VEGETABLES, PRESERVED IN SUGAR. (*b*)

FOREIGN COUNTRIES.							
	Pounds.	*Pounds.*	*Pounds.*	*Pounds.*	*Pounds.*	*Pounds.*	
France	3,352,362	3,201,744	3,454,752	3,623,760	3,001,712	3,479,840	25.89
United States........	6,785,341	3,449,264	4,370,800	8,519,504	16,290,064	1,297,072	9.65
Belgium.............	409,965	316,512	359,296	435,120	416,080	522,816	3.89
Netherlands.........	236,566	142,464	152,320	137,088	232,176	518,784	3.86
China	401,610	50,736	559,776	298,368	604,464	494,704	3.68
Italy................	687,255	614,992	586,208	693,280	1,213,520	328,272	2.44
Portugal.............	327,622	142,464	345,856	387,520	472,640	289,632	2.16
Spain...............	451,158	84,224	725,984	709,072	549,360	187,152	1.39
Japan	64,086	3,136	88,816	107,296	35,952	85,232	.63
Germany	127,411	65,296	79,184	124,432	306,096	62,048	.46
Other...............	95,155	24,416	99,568	196,784	101,696	53,312	.40
Total foreign countries	12,938,531	8,095,248	10,822,560	15,232,224	23,223,760	7,318,864	54.45
BRITISH POSSESSIONS.							
Hongkong...........	4,166,781	4,301,360	4,972,016	3,810,352	3,566,304	4,183,872	31.13
British East Indies:							
Straits Settlements.	4,319,079	2,883,776	3,023,328	10,188,080	4,602,640	897,568	} 9.80
Bengal	239,568	198,800	136,528	115,248	418,096	329,168	
Bombay..........	17,136	6,272	4,256	2,800	27,104	45,248	
Madras..........	36,624	13,440	7,616	36,960	82,432	42,672	
Ceylon	14,806	4,592	6,720	55,216	4,816	2,688	
Canada..............	399,526	356,048	130,816	857,024	353,808	299,936	2.23
British West Indies..	491,456	786,352	490,112	485,296	407,680	287,840	2.14
Australasia	76,698	19,936	52,528	61,824	228,592	20,608	.16
Other...............	15,590	13,552	9,184	31,360	12,096	11,760	.09
Total British possessions ..	9,777,264	8,584,128	8,833,104	15,644,160	9,703,568	6,121,360	45.55
Total	22,715,795	16,679,376	19,655,664	30,876,384	32,927,328	13,440,224	100.00

GLUCOSE AND GRAPE SUGAR. (*b*)

FOREIGN COUNTRIES.							
	Pounds.	*Pounds.*	*Pounds.*	*Pounds.*	*Pounds.*	*Pounds.*	
United States........	181,559,773	164,485,440	169,558,816	192,374,448	186,986,016	194,394,144	94.20
Germany............	4,299,590	5,760,048	4,227,328	4,033,792	4,012,848	3,463,936	1.68
France	1,523,021	1,487,696	1,627,360	1,735,552	2,314,816	449,680	.22
Netherlands.........	448,202	634,032	464,128	408,576	339,248	395,024	.19
Belgium.............	174,518	4,480	709,072	16,800	108,640	33,600	.02
Other...............	43,456	....	67,200	....	150,080	....	....
Total foreign countries	188,048,560	172,371,696	176,653,904	198,569,168	193,911,648	198,736,384	96.31
BRITISH POSSESSIONS.							
Canada..............	6,922,496	....	3,678,976	12,779,984	10,543,120	7,610,400	} 3.69
Other *c*.............	7,482	10,528	....	....	13,440	13,440	
Total British possessions ..	6,929,978	10,528	3,678,976	12,779,984	10,556,560	7,623,840	3.69
Total	194,978,538	172,382,224	180,332,880	211,349,152	204,468,208	206,360,224	100.00

a In 1896 comprising 2,240 pounds from the British West Indies.
b For values, see page 115.
c In 1896 comprising 10,528 pounds from Victoria.

*uantity of the agricultural imports of the United Kingdom (vegetable matter), etc.—*Cont'd.

HAY. (a)

	Annual average, 1896–1900.	Calendar years.					Per ct. in 1900.
		1896.	1897.	1898.	1899.	1900.	
)REIGN COUNTRIES.	*Tons.(b)*	*Tons.(b)*	*Tons.(b)*	*Tons.(b)*	*Tons.(b)*	*Tons.(b)*	
nited States........	32,495	5,939	26,633	42,876	42,827	44,198	40.29
etherlands.........	33,640	40,127	36,432	27,297	34,465	29,880	27.24
rance	19,159	20,540	21,657	23,840	17,977	11,780	10.74
elgium.............	7,196	10,989	8,520	6,141	5,780	4,550	4.15
ermany............	3,661	10,205	3,626	765	1,774	1,937	1.77
lgeria.............	4,201	5,964	6,446	2,975	3,770	1,850	1.69
rgentina...........	1,728	2,440	3,117	1,153	1,517	412	.37
enmark...........	1,525	3,118	1,967	771	1,423	344	.31
hile	1,221	876	3,360	939	800	131	.12
orway	1,494	3,926	3,481	32	11	20	} .02
ussia	145	707	16	....	....	3	
ther c	171	841	13	....	1	2	
Total foreign countries....	106,636	105,672	115,268	106,789	110,345	95,107	86.70
RITISH POSSESSIONS.							
anada..............	10,475	2,308	6,265	9,278	21,196	13,327	12.15
ther d	265	7	8	40	5	1,264	1.15
Total British possessions ..	10,740	2,315	6,273	9,318	21,201	14,591	13.30
Total	117,376	107,987	121,541	116,107	131,546	109,698	100.00

HOPS. (a)

FOREIGN COUNTRIES.	*Pounds.*	*Pounds.*	*Pounds.*	*Pounds.*	*Pounds.*	*Pounds.*	
United States........	15,346,352	15,212,064	9,509,360	21,451,920	14,052,080	16,506,336	74.25
Belgium.............	3,512,522	3,694,208	4,120,144	3,376,912	2,735,376	3,635,968	16.36
Germany............	1,354,528	1,457,232	1,778,672	927,360	1,312,864	1,296,512	5.83
Netherlands.........	1,518,698	2,230,144	2,314,704	1,026,928	1,546,608	475,104	2.14
France	361,043	447,552	577,808	184,128	397,488	198,240	.89
Russia..............	102,099	52,752	1,568	342,608	39,648	73,920	.33
Other................	627	....	....	3,136	....	....	
Total foreign countries....	22,195,869	23,093,952	18,302,256	27,312,992	20,084,064	22,186,080	99.80
BRITISH POSSESSIONS.							
Canada..............	54,902	94,640	82,992	27,888	24,864	44,128	} .20
Australasia..........	16,128	....	....	2,352	77,168	1,120	
Total British possessions ..	71,030	94,640	82,992	30,240	102,032	45,248	.20
Total	22,266,899	23,188,592	18,385,248	27,343,232	20,186,096	22,231,328	100.00

a For values, see page 116.
b Tons of 2,240 pounds.
c In 1897 comprising 13 tons from Asiatic Turkey.
d In 1896 comprising 7 tons from Malta and Gozo.

Quantity of the agricultural imports of the United Kingdom (vegetable matter), etc.—Cont'd.

INDIGO. (a)

Countries from which imported.	Annual average, 1896–1900.	Calendar years.					Per ct. in 1900.
		1896.	1897.	1898.	1899.	1900.	
FOREIGN COUNTRIES.							
	Pounds.	*Pounds.*	*Pounds.*	*Pounds.*	*Pounds.*	*Pounds.*	
Netherlands.........	157,786	42,672	95,312	151,648	298,592	200,704	.29
Salvador	285,757	381,472	316,176	291,088	254,240	185,808	5.40
France	34,227	37,632	21,616	18,256	4,144	89,488	3.36
Germany............	38,326	17,136	55,776	12,768	70,896	35,056	2.92
United States........	35,280	8,064	2,688	117,040	17,248	31,360	.82
Belgium.............	8,579	7,728	8,512	10,640	8,176	7,840	.21
Austria-Hungary....	2,442	5,712	1,120	....	2,210	3,136	.08
Italy	6,227	23,296	....	3,360	1,568	2,912	.08
Nicaragua...........	8,490	7,056	26,880	1,792	6,272	448	.01
Colombia............	36,826	29,344	20,384	....	134,400	....	......
Guatemala	12,454	....	2,688	59,584	....	....	......
Ecuador.............	11,200	....	....	56,000	....	....	......
Spain	4,995	4,114	....	....	20,832	....	......
French India	1,904	9,520	....	....	....	....	......
Other b..............	21,870	6,048	10,192	10,752	14,336	65,520	1.73
Total foreign countries	665,863	579,824	561,344	732,928	832,944	622,272	16.40
BRITISH POSSESSIONS.							
British East Indies:							
Bengal	4,661,664	5,517,120	6,894,720	3,974,544	4,546,080	2,375,856	
Madras..........	1,528,733	3,389,568	1,545,936	1,286,544	943,936	477,680	
Bombay	251,910	542,416	199,360	34,384	217,056	266,336	82.72
Straits Settlements	10,550	....	....	....	34,048	18,704	
Ceylon	16,173	43,008	36,736	1,120	....	....	
Other c..............	14,269	1,456	4,816	336	31,360	33,376	.88
Total British possessions ..	6,483,299	9,493,568	8,681,568	5,296,928	5,772,480	3,171,952	83.60
Total	7,149,162	10,073,392	9,242,912	6,029,856	6,605,424	3,794,224	100.00

LARD SUBSTITUTES. (d)

FOREIGN COUNTRIES.							
	Pounds.	*Pounds.*	*Pounds.*	*Pounds.*	*Pounds.*	*Pounds.*	
United States........	6,672,355	4,287,024	3,466,176	9,376,528	8,481,984	7,750,064	97.01
Other................	59,046	5,376	4,480	75,040	210,336	....	......
Total foreign countries	6,731,401	4,292,400	3,470,656	9,451,568	8,692,320	7,750,064	97.01
BRITISH POSSESSIONS.							
Canada..............	91,907	149,856	....	2,800	73,696	233,184	2.92
Other................	2,375	....	....	4,480	1,456	5,936	.07
Total British possessions ..	94,282	149,856	....	7,280	75,152	239,120	2.99
Total	6,825,683	4,442,256	3,470,656	9,458,848	8,767,472	7,989,184	100.00

MADDER, MADDER ROOT, GARANCIN, AND MUNJEET. (d)

FOREIGN COUNTRIES.							
	Pounds.(e)	*Pounds.*	*Pounds.*	*Pounds.*	*Pounds.*	*Pounds.*	
Netherlands.........	318,388	415,072	359,856	264,320	234,304	(f)	g 81.87
France	43,148	82,096	21,392	38,416	30,688	(f)	g 11.12
Turkey, Asiatic	32,564	66,416	40,320	16,912	6,608	(f)	g 2.39
Other................	10,108	20,720	3,248	11,984	4,480	(f)	g 1.62
Total	404,208	584,304	424,816	331,632	276,080	(f)	g 100.00

a For values, see page 116.
b Including imports from the Philippine Islands amounting to 2,128 pounds in 1896 and 2,240 pounds in 1897, and from Egypt 1,456 pounds in 1896 and 1,904 pounds in 1897.
c In 1896 comprising 1,456 pounds from the Niger Protectorate.
d For values, see page 117.
e Annual average. 1896–1899.
f Not stated.
g Per cent in 1899.

uantity of the agricultural imports of the United Kingdom (vegetable matter), etc.—Cont'd.

MALT. (a)

	Annual average, 1896–1900.	Calendar years.					Per ct. in 1900.
		1896.	1897.	1898.	1899.	1900.	
OREIGN COUNTRIES.	*Bushels.(b)*	*Bushels.(b)*	*Bushels.(b)*	*Bushels.(b)*	*Bushels.(b)*	*Bushels.(b)*	
ermany..........	2,789	2,401	2,146	1,791	833	6,775	88.47
nited States.......	9,129	29,287	9,019	3,078	3,590	668	8.72
ther c	619	338	....	1,964	578	215	2.81
Total foreign countries	12,537	32,026	11,165	6,833	5,001	7,658	100.00
RITISH POSSESSIONS.							
Total British possessions ..	145	....	....	....	726	....	....
Total	12,682	32,026	11,165	6,833	5,727	7,658	100.00

FOREIGN COUNTRIES.	*Gallons.(e)*	*Gallons.(e)*	*Gallons.(e)*	*Gallons.(e)*	*Gallons.(e)*	*Gallons.(e)*	
Netherlands.........	1,141,626	1,039,916	1,108,621	1,127,418	1,192,753	1,239,421	53.89
Germany............	683,313	716,525	648,986	629,368	712,550	709,136	30.84
Denmark............	110,490	64,687	72,638	101,848	144,800	168,480	7.33
Belgium.............	124,240	107,984	124,102	140,911	109,021	139,182	6.05
Other f	24,354	16,377	35,001	19,575	18,494	32,322	1.41
Total foreign countries	2,084,023	1,945,489	1,989,348	2,019,120	2,177,618	2,288,541	99.52
BRITISH POSSESSIONS.							
Channel Islands.....	3,776	4,235	4,623	3,673	3,586	2,765	.12
Other...............	4,745	2,549	1,383	2,679	8,729	8,383	.36
Total British possessions ..	8,521	6,784	6,006	6,352	12,315	11,148	.48
Total	2,092,544	1,952,273	1,995,354	2,025,472	2,189,933	2,299,689	100.00

COTTON-SEED OIL CAKE. (g)

FOREIGN COUNTRIES.	*Pounds.*	*Pounds.*	*Pounds.*	*Pounds.*	*Pounds.*	*Pounds.*	
United States........	219,085,440	131,985,280	156,766,400	221,202,240	302,462,720	283,010,560	67.31
Egypt	81,386,816	51,266,880	69,630,400	87,351,040	101,716,160	96,969,600	23.07
Mexico	10,201,408	891,520	7,593,600	12,028,800	7,777,280	22,715,840	5.40
France	14,586,880	9,804,480	11,112,640	25,188,800	15,312,640	11,515,840	2.74
Peru...............	3,212,608	2,002,560	2,956,800	2,831,360	4,450,880	3,821,440	.91
Belgium............	557,312	136,640	1,030,400	358,400	616,000	645,120	.15
Brazil	631,232	2,065,280	31,360	539,840	17,920	501,760	} .12
Germany	279,552	369,600	369,600	439,040	212,800	6,720	
Russia	11,648	....	58,240	....	....	....	
Other	815,360	454,720	161,280	996,800	1,209,600	1,254,400	.30
Total foreign countries	330,768,256	198,976,960	249,710,720	350,936,320	433,776,000	420,441,280	100.00
BRITISH POSSESSIONS.							
British East Indies:							
Burma	933,184	940,800	725,760	2,999,360	....	....	
Bengal	20,160	....	....	....	100,800	....	
Ceylon	1,344	....	6,720	....	....	....	
Canada...........	498,176	374,080	....	1,189,600	627,200	....	
Other h	205,184	696,640	38,080	....	291,200	....	
Total British possessions ..	1,658,048	2,011,520	770,560	4,488,960	1,019,200	....	
Total	332,426,304	200,988,480	250,481,280	355,425,280	434,795,200	420,441,280	100.00

a For values, see page 117.
b Winchester bushels.
c Including imports from Belgium amounting to 124 bushels in 1896 and 578 bushels in 1899.
d For values, see page 118.
e United States standard gallons.
f In 1900 including 3,587 gallons from the United States.
g For values, see page 119.
h In 1896 including 672,000 pounds from British Honduras.

Quantity of the agricultural imports of the United Kingdom (vegetable matter), etc.—Cont'd.

OIL CAKE, FLAXSEED, OR LINSEED. (a)

Countries from which imported.	Annual average, 1896–1900.	Calendar years.					Per ct. in 1900.
		1896.	1897.	1898.	1899.	1900.	
FOREIGN COUNTRIES.	*Pounds.*	*Pounds.*	*Pounds.*	*Pounds.*	*Pounds.*	*Pounds.*	
Germany	126,249,088	84,313,600	120,151,360	129,429,440	156,439,360	140,911,680	33.56
Russia	159,179,328	123,282,880	152,602,240	198,300,480	202,677,440	119,033,600	28.35
United States	150,514,560	241,601,920	163,766,400	118,016,640	111,000,960	118,186,880	28.15
Argentina	3,840,256	2,573,760	3,637,760	4,318,720	4,130,560	4,540,480	1.08
Spain	5,978,112	6,594,560	6,292,160	5,481,280	7,044,800	4,477,760	1.07
Austria-Hungary	2,349,312	....	4,480,000	1,778,560	2,464,000	3,024,000	.72
Denmark	1,937,152	....	1,180,480	1,617,280	4,074,560	2,813,440	.67
France	3,635,520	4,641,280	6,348,160	1,171,520	3,561,600	2,455,040	.59
Belgium	1,488,256	1,068,480	974,400	2,392,320	1,417,920	1,588,160	.38
Uruguay	390,208	712,320	259,840	103,040	201,600	674,240	.16
Netherlands	435,456	349,440	687,680	331,520	190,400	618,240	.15
Portugal	722,176	833,280	819,840	992,320	421,120	544,320	.13
Chile	469,056	627,200	512,960	804,160	349,440	51,520	.01
Sweden	365,120	1,400,000	....	425,600	....	....	
Norway	320,768	996,800	....	226,240	380,800	....	
Roumania	299,712	1,072,960	425,600	....	....	....	
Other *b*	130,368	291,200	....	360,640	....	....	
Total foreign countries	458,304,448	470,359,680	462,138,880	465,749,760	494,354,560	398,919,360	95.02
BRITISH POSSESSIONS.							
British East Indies:							
Bengal	7,798,336	7,990,080	7,432,320	5,918,080	8,720,320	8,930,880	⎫
Bombay	6,664,000	7,087,360	8,406,720	8,886,080	6,749,120	2,190,720	⎬ 2.71
Madras	29,120	....	....	....	....	145,600	⎪
Straits Settlements	22,400	....	....	....	....	112,000	⎭
Canada	10,937,024	8,592,640	10,337,600	13,034,560	13,650,560	9,069,760	2.16
Other *c*	114,240	118,720	....	....	....	452,480	.11
Total British possessions	25,565,120	23,788,800	26,176,640	27,838,720	29,120,000	20,901,440	4.98
Total	483,869,568	494,148,480	488,315,520	493,588,480	523,474,560	419,820,800	100.00

OIL CAKE NOT ELSEWHERE SPECIFIED. (d)

Countries from which imported.	Annual average, 1896–1900.	1896.	1897.	1898.	1899.	1900.	Per ct. in 1900.
FOREIGN COUNTRIES.	*Pounds.*	*Pounds.*	*Pounds.*	*Pounds.*	*Pounds.*	*Pounds.*	
United States	4,521,216	2,208,640	1,462,720	4,600,960	2,096,640	12,237,120	27.63
Russia	5,341,952	533,120	2,464,000	5,261,760	10,077,760	8,373,120	18.90
France	4,763,136	2,770,880	2,880,640	4,921,280	6,431,040	6,811,840	15.38
Germany	1,440,320	1,330,640	1,028,160	300,160	1,498,560	3,044,160	6.87
Netherlands	1,944,320	2,085,440	1,352,960	2,423,680	1,131,200	2,728,320	6.16
Belgium	1,252,160	1,520,960	2,757,440	931,840	378,560	672,000	1.52
Other	765,184	499,520	6,720	761,600	893,760	1,664,320	3.76
Total foreign countries	20,028,288	10,949,120	11,952,640	19,201,280	22,507,520	35,530,880	80.22
BRITISH POSSESSIONS.							
British East Indies:							
Ceylon	2,192,512	575,680	1,693,440	3,393,600	2,058,560	3,241,280	⎫
Madras	2,502,080	714,560	1,886,080	2,696,960	4,343,360	2,869,440	⎪
Burma	228,480	....	....	224,000	....	918,400	⎪
Straits Settlements	168,000	....	58,240	134,400	11,200	636,160	⎬ 18.75
Bombay	377,664	331,520	78,400	159,040	815,360	504,000	⎪
Bengal	400,960	293,440	118,720	347,200	1,111,040	134,400	⎭
Australasia	230,272	....	....	15,680	728,000	407,680	.92
Canada	46,592	....	44,800	94,080	44,800	49,280	.11
Other *e*	14,784	2,240	22,400	6,720	42,560	....	
Total British possessions	6,161,344	1,917,440	3,902,080	7,071,680	9,154,880	8,760,640	19.78
Total	26,189,632	12,866,560	15,854,720	26,272,960	31,662,400	44,291,520	100.00

a For values, see page 119.
b Including imports from Italy amounting to 107,520 pounds in 1898 and from Egypt 67,200 pounds in 1896.
c In 1896 comprising 118,720 pounds from New Zealand.
d For values, see page 120.
e In 1896 comprising 2,240 pounds from Hongkong.

uantity of the agricultural imports of the United Kingdom (vegetable matter), etc.—Cont'd.

VEGETABLE OILS, ESSENTIAL OR PERFUMED. (a)

untries from which imported.	Annual average, 1896–1900.	Calendar years.					Per ct. in 1900.
		1896.	1897.	1898.	1899.	1900.	
)REIGN COUNTRIES.							
	Pounds.	*Pounds.*	*Pounds.*	*Pounds.*	*Pounds.*	*Pounds.*	
aly	380,530	286,536	384,383	379,639	434,180	417,912	23.77
rance	218,020	244,574	238,218	234,348	168,350	204,611	11.64
ermany	80,031	85,453	122,203	77,886	41,842	72,772	4.14
nited States	139,881	158,543	164,955	178,178	128,898	68,832	3.91
elgium	37,186	6,329	28,301	42,538	55,156	53,606	3.05
etherlands	23,724	25,820	17,615	12,438	30,137	32,607	1.85
ipan	13,300	26,463	19,996	5,290	7,030	7,720	.44
hina	8,577	6,290	26,132	4,669	1,990	3,803	.21
ustria-Hungary	11,156	4,214	41,030	4,782	2,620	3,134	.18
urkey, European	322	678	695	58	180	....	
ther	8,750	10,572	5,925	5,982	8,315	12,957	.74
Total foreign countries	921,477	855,472	1,049,453	945,808	878,698	877,954	49.93
RITISH POSSESSIONS.							
ritish East Indies:							
Ceylon	744,286	921,576	679,422	737,180	620,675	762,578	} 45.66
Madras	58,925	80,754	48,918	113,150	26,450	25,350	
Straits Settlements	17,293	14,165	16,970	31,142	14,650	9,537	
Bombay	9,712	13,955	9,184	14,020	6,147	5,255	
Burma	22	....	....	....	....	112	
Bengal	17,425	87,100	....	25	....	....	
Hongkong	46,042	49,867	65,970	29,104	45,630	39,640	2.25
British West Indies	22,652	12,891	18,150	20,268	25,224	36,726	2.09
Other b	1,912	2,544	369	2,708	2,760	1,179	.07
Total British possessions	918,269	1,182,852	838,983	947,597	741,536	880,377	50.07
Total	1,839,746	2,038,324	1,888,436	1,893,405	1,620,234	1,758,331	100.00

CASTOR OIL. (c)

	Annual average	1896.	1897.	1898.	1899.	1900.	Per ct.
FOREIGN COUNTRIES.							
	Pounds.	*Pounds.*	*Pounds.*	*Pounds.*	*Pounds.*	*Pounds.*	
France	6,079,427	9,504,544	6,053,824	6,117,440	6,524,672	2,196,656	36.77
Belgium	2,190,541	3,089,632	1,685,376	2,696,848	2,479,344	1,001,504	16.77
Italy	513,206	614,768	404,656	545,776	687,792	313,040	5.24
Netherlands	26,858	117,712	....	....	5,488	11,088	.19
Other d	39,334	62,720	13,440	44,128	24,192	52,192	.87
Total foreign countries	8,849,366	13,389,376	8,157,296	9,404,192	9,721,488	3,574,480	59.84
BRITISH POSSESSIONS.							
British East Indies:							
Bengal	3,116,377	4,126,080	2,958,480	3,496,192	2,680,496	2,320,640	} 40.16
Madras	767,021	1,121,568	862,624	1,044,736	727,776	78,400	
Bombay	66,394	43,904	51,520	144,480	92,064	....	
Ceylon	3,293	....	16,464	....	....	....	
Total British possessions	3,953,085	5,291,552	3,889,088	4,685,408	3,500,336	2,399,040	40.16
Total	12,802,451	18,680,928	12,046,384	14,089,600	13,221,824	5,973,520	100.00

a For values, see page 120.
b Including imports from Australasia amounting to 2,544 pounds in 1896, 14 pounds in 1897, and 264 pounds in 1898.
c For values, see page 121.
d Including imports from Russia amounting to 18,592 pounds in 1898 and from the United States 13,776 pounds in 1900.

Quantity of the agricultural imports of the United Kingdom (vegetable matter), etc.—Cont'd.

COCOANUT OIL. (a)

Countries from which imported.	Annual average, 1896–1900.	Calendar years.					Per ct. in 1900.
		1896.	1897.	1898.	1899.	1900.	
FOREIGN COUNTRIES.	*Pounds.*	*Pounds.*	*Pounds.*	*Pounds.*	*Pounds.*	*Pounds.*	
Belgium.............	5,614,605	6,011,152	5,372,752	3,922,240	5,710,544	7,056,336	11.40
France	2,237,715	2,321,872	3,102,176	1,158,976	2,979,536	1,626,016	} 2.63
Germany............	58,173	110,208	135,408	22,624	22,400	224	
United States.......	47,757	219,856	2,800	16,128	....	....	......
Other b	169,993	140,896	137,760	84,000	70,560	416,752	.67
Total foreign countries....	8,128,243	8,803,984	8,750,896	5,203,968	8,783,040	9,099,328	14.70
BRITISH POSSESSIONS.							
British East Indies:							
Ceylon	18,319,325	11,948,272	11,111,744	14,361,872	20,814,304	33,360,432	
Madras..........	6,575,699	3,492,384	3,909,920	5,999,840	9,486,736	9,989,616	
Straits Settlements	56,806	89,040	....	....	87,920	107,072	} 70.24
Bengal..........	132,496	82,096	281,680	3,696	281,904	13,104	
Bombay.........	31,539	134,400	....	11,760	....	11,536	
Burma..........	8,467	....	42,336	....	....	....	
Australasia:							
New South Wales	6,390,922	....	3,076,528	8,587,936	11,505,760	8,784,384	} 14.19
Victoria.........	2,554	....	12,768	....	....	....	
Mauritius	227,069	....	....	224,000	369,600	541,744	.87
Other...............	448	....	....	2,240	....	....	......
Total British possessions ..	31,745,325	15,746,192	18,434,976	29,191,344	42,546,224	52,807,888	85.30
Total	39,873,568	24,550,176	27,185,872	34,395,312	51,329,264	61,907,216	100.00

OLIVE OIL. (c)

FOREIGN COUNTRIES.	Gallons. (d)	Gallons. (d)	Gallons. (d)	Gallons. (d)	Gallons. (d)	Gallons. (d)	
Spain..............	1,767,186	2,117,937	71,384	3,348,712	1,247,108	2,050,787	56.29
Italy	1,790,779	2,401,659	2,557,132	1,318,493	1,797,010	879,600	24.15
France	351,054	434,658	217,480	294,612	451,899	356,619	9.79
Morocco............	46,702	18,149	302	1,815	102,842	110,404	3.03
Portugal	32,546	8,469	14,519	51,118	15,729	72,897	2.00
Greece	99,091	14,519	245,611	55,656	109,799	69,872	1.92
Crete	e 215,061	(f)	(f)	(f)	384,447	45,674	1.25
Turkey, Asiatic	276,282	68,057	585,594	231,999	473,072	22,686	.62
Austria-Hungary	62,007	62,915	56,865	63,822	109,799	16,636	.46
Turkey, European ..	e 44,011	560,791	899,564	53,236	83,786	4,235	.12
Other g	26,436	15,124	21,173	38,414	43,859	13,611	.37
Total foreign countries....	4,858,430	5,702,278	4,669,624	5,457,877	4,819,350	3,643,021	100.00
BRITISH POSSESSIONS.							
Total British possessions	544	302	605	(h)	1,815	(h)	......
Total	4,858,974	5,702,580	4,670,229	5,457,877	4,821,165	3,643,021	100.00

a For values, see page 121.
b Including imports from Russia amounting to 67,200 pounds in 1898, and from the Netherlands 2,688 pounds in 1896, 22,400 pounds in 1897, and 26,880 pounds in 1899.
c For values, see page 122.
d United States standard gallons.
e Annual average, 1899–1900.
f Included in European Turkey.
g In 1900 including less than 151 United States standard gallons (one-half tun) from the United States.
h Less than 151 United States standard gallons (one-half tun).

uantity of the agricultural imports of the United Kingdom (vegetable matter), etc.—Cont'd.

PALM OIL (a).

FOREIGN COUNTRIES.	Annual average, 1896–1900.	Calendar years.					Per ct. in 1900.
		1896.	1897.	1898.	1899.	1900.	
	Pounds.	*Pounds.*	*Pounds.*	*Pounds.*	*Pounds.*	*Pounds.*	
Germany............	16,003,075	26,191,424	13,778,464	13,548,640	14,699,216	11,797,632	11.23
German West Africa.	1,208,458	682,416	1,285,200	528,864	164,528	3,381,280	3.22
Portuguese West Africa............	428,378	341,600	113,680	67,200	155,232	1,464,176	1.39
Liberia.............	b 596,400	(c)	399,840	387,408	248,752	1,349,600	1.28
French West Africa..	1,200,573	1,458,912	1,079,568	1,290,576	852,096	1,321,712	1.26
West Africa, n. e. s...	b 287,280	778,064	227,360	205,184	218,960	497,616	.47
Kongo Free State....	217,683	227,920	160,160	108,304	107,744	484,288	.46
Spanish West Africa.	181,440	22,848	71,456	250,208	123,648	439,040	.42
Belgium.............	348,656	235,200	19,040	426,720	1,059,744	2,576	} .26
France	41,485	134,176	60,144	6,384	5,376	1,344	
Other d	136,774	153,888	102,480	128,688	34,272	264,544	
Total foreign countries	20,629,078	30,226,448	17,297,392	16,948,176	17,669,568	21,003,808	19.99
BRITISH POSSESSIONS.							
Niger Protectorate ..	26,376,605	19,191,872	19,665,856	17,154,816	16,312,352	59,558,128	56.67
Lagos................	59,030,361	75,223,904	70,040,656	66,374,112	69,977,824	13,535,312	12.88
Gold Coast...........	3,186,848	1,871,744	1,101,296	1,103,088	1,472,128	10,385,984	9.88
Sierra Leone........	848,781	1,859,760	875,280	440,608	458,752	609,504	} .58
Other................	2,442	5,264	2,240	....	2,240	2,464	
Total British possessions ..	89,445,037	98,152,544	91,685,328	85,072,624	88,223,296	84,091,392	80.01
Total	110,074,115	128,378,992	108,982,720	102,020,800	105,892,864	105,095,200	100.00

SEED OIL (COTTON-SEED, LINSEED, ETC.). (e)

FOREIGN COUNTRIES.							
	Pounds.	*Pounds.*	*Pounds.*	*Pounds.*	*Pounds.*	*Pounds.*	
United States........	31,802,624	21,564,480	21,002,240	35,107,520	51,632,000	29,706,880	32.24
Belgium...............	22,093,568	16,517,760	26,196,800	24,628,800	22,796,480	20,328,000	22.06
Netherlands...,.....	8,225,728	5,738,880	4,813,760	4,856,320	8,951,040	16,768,640	18.20
Germany.............	9,884,224	16,334,080	5,382,720	5,725,440	8,538,880	13,440,000	14.59
France	11,419,968	14,349,440	15,305,920	9,069,760	10,093,440	8,281,280	8.99
Japan	228,032	....	371,840	(f)	....	768,320	.83
Brazil	145,600	....	....	2,240	....	725,760	.79
Denmark.............	251,328	230,720	49,280	109,760	488,320	378,560	.41
Other g	305,984	275,520	273,280	333,760	154,560	492,800	.54
Total foreign countries	84,357,056	75,010,880	73,395,840	79,833,600	102,654,720	90,890,240	98.65
BRITISH POSSESSIONS.							
Canada...............	487,424	2,240	358,400	143,360	909,440	1,023,680	1.11
British East Indies ..	339,136	271,040	483,840	490,560	244,160	206,080	.22
Other................	52,416	15,680	69,440	....	163,520	13,440	.02
Total British possessions ..	878,976	288,960	911,680	633,920	1,317,120	1,243,200	1.35
Total	85,236,032	75,299,840	74,307,520	80,467,520	103,971,840	92,133,440	100.00

a For values, see page 122.
b Annual average, 1897–1900.
c Included in "West Africa, n. e. s."
d In 1900 including 123,424 pounds from the United States.
e For values, see page 123.
f Less than 1,120 pounds (one-half ton).
g Including imports from Spain amounting to 13,440 pounds in 1897 and from Austria-Hungary 11,200 pounds in 1896.

Quantity of the agricultural imports of the United Kingdom (vegetable matter), etc.—Cont'd.

OPIUM. (a)

Countries from which imported.	Annual average, 1896–1900.	Calendar years.					Per ct. in 1900.
		1896.	1897.	1898.	1899.	1900.	
FOREIGN COUNTRIES.							
	Pounds.	Pounds.	Pounds.	Pounds.	Pounds.	Pounds.	
Turkey, European...	251,826	213,622	242,716	214,678	216,677	371,439	44.57
Turkey, Asiatic......	153,833	151,205	107,229	70,193	192,686	247,853	29.74
France	25,001	....	6,104	17,850	61,302	39,751	4.77
Persia	56,074	84,040	60,770	72,710	26,212	36,640	4.40
United States........	6,782	1,780	260	....	15,392	16,476	1.98
Netherlands........	4,131	3,620	2,100	5,420	1,540	7,973	.95
Belgium.............	3,649	....	1,750	5,740	5,615	5,140	.62
China	56	280	....	....	....	....	
Other b	4,074	1,428	2,150	4,895	4,392	7,504	.90
Total foreign countries....	505,426	455,975	423,079	391,486	523,816	732,776	87.93
BRITISH POSSESSIONS.							
British East Indies:							
Bengal	35,997	4,690	900	12,416	65,580	96,397	⎫
Straits Settlements	168	....	....	....	....	840	⎬ 11.67
Bombay	10,394	10,780	13,170	20,880	7,140	....	⎭
Hongkong.........	5,305	16,070	5,880	1,260	....	3,317	.40
New South Wales....	372	1,720	140	....	....	....	
Other...............	10	....	50	....	....	....	
Total British possessions ..	52,246	33,260	20,140	34,556	72,720	100,554	12.07
Total	557,672	489,235	443,219	426,042	596,536	833,330	100.00

RICE, RICE MEAL, AND RICE FLOUR.(a)

	Annual average	1896.	1897.	1898.	1899.	1900.	Per ct.
FOREIGN COUNTRIES.							
	Pounds.	Pounds.(c)	Pounds.(c)	Pounds.(c)	Pounds.(c)	Pounds.	
Netherlands........	51,939,059	46,657,296	45,477,376	51,812,208	51,148,384	64,600,032	9.17
French Indo-China..	43,457,143	....	110,018,720	9,923,200	47,053,440	50,290,352	7.14
Germany............	29,549,699	30,593,360	30,624,720	28,061,824	25,323,536	33,145,056	4.70
Turkey, Asiatic......	4,510,307	2,254,560	1,641,472	....	7,322,560	11,332,944	1.61
Italy...............	1,474,570	400,064	439,376	1,355,984	784,672	4,392,752	.62
France	741,776	916,608	21,504	9,632	257,936	2,503,200	.36
Japan	18,727,430	21,352,688	27,915,440	450,912	42,235,984	1,682,128	.24
Java...............	667,923	51,296	72,576	918,624	697,760	1,599,360	.23
United States........	1,271,088	1,272,320	1,008,784	1,782,592	820,960	1,470,784	.21
Siam	8,844,035	134,400	43,141,616	....	489,440	454,720	.06
Belgium.............	1,142,915	1,136,016	1,348,032	2,053,968	797,440	379,120	.05
Denmark............	609,885	2,204,832	145,824	469,952	228,480	336	⎫
Other...............	1,238,653	9,520	40,992	719,936	709,072	4,713,744	⎬ .67
Total foreign countries....	164,174,483	106,982,960	261,896,432	97,558,832	177,869,664	176,564,528	25.06
BRITISH POSSESSIONS.							
British East Indies:							
Burma	309,469,283	301,020,160	219,812,544	323,106,336	306,721,968	396,685,408	⎫
Bengal	105,123,111	96,065,200	72,322,880	83,784,624	157,202,192	116,240,656		
Straits Settlements	8,918,717	3,003,840	25,951,296	2,438,800	955,360	12,244,288	⎬ 74.56
Bombay	224,090	7,504	22,400	336,448	541,296	212,800		
Madras	46,592	....	....	....	232,960	....		
Ceylon	134	....	....	....	....	672	⎭
Natal..............	250,656	....	....	1,253,280	....	....	.38
Other d	855,747	450,352	26,656	721,056	399,280	2,681,392	
Total British possessions ..	424,888,330	400,547,056	318,135,776	411,640,544	466,053,728	528,064,544	74.94
Total	589,062,813	507,530,016	580,032,208	509,199,376	643,923,392	704,629,072	100.00

a For values, see page 124.
b Including imports from Egypt amounting to 1,372 pounds in 1896, 1,120 pounds in 1897, 1,755 pounds in 1898, and 2,260 pounds in 1899.
c Exclusive of rice meal and rice flour.
d In 1896 including 64,960 pounds from Aden.

uantity of the agricultural imports of the United Kingdom (vegetable matter), etc.—Cont'd.

SAFFLOWER.(a)

	Annual average, 1896–1900.	Calendar years.					Per ct. in 1900.
		1896.	1897.	1898.	1899.	1900.	
	Pounds.(b) 25,732	Pounds. 60,032	Pounds. 35,056	Pounds. 5,600	Pounds. 2,240	Pounds. (d)	e100.00

GARDEN SEEDS.(a)

	Annual average, 1896–1900.	1896.	1897.	1898.	1899.	1900.	Per ct. in 1900.
OREIGN COUNTRIES.	Pounds.	Pounds.	Pounds.	Pounds.	Pounds.	Pounds.	
rance	981,659	1,842,374	979,089	652,239	714,488	720,102	34.78
ermany	655,491	331,593	866,920	973,272	620,608	485,059	23.43
etherlands	207,836	213,011	162,787	135,585	209,042	318,757	15.39
aly	83,164	57,680	62,856	81,800	89,988	123,498	5.96
nited States	85,738	90,763	66,202	96,297	81,808	93,618	4.52
elgium	18,103	27,992	2,426	4,819	20,364	34,915	1.69
anary Islands	8,791	7,590	4,374	13,056	13,564	5,370	.26
ther f	51,385	12,537	67,256	50,541	57,208	69,385	3.35
Total foreign countries	2,092,167	2,583,540	2,211,910	2,007,609	1,807,070	1,850,704	89.38
BRITISH POSSESSIONS.							
Australasia g	170,549	52,572	238,840	116,496	227,573	217,266	10.50
British East Indies h	8,632	37,464	530	3,450	1,264	450	.02
Canada	22,632		93,440	17,250	2,472		
Other	1,432	1,480	791	1,966	825	2,098	.10
Total British possessions	203,245	91,516	333,601	139,162	232,134	219,814	10.62
Total	2,295,412	2,675,056	2,545,511	2,146,771	2,039,204	2,070,518	100.00

GRASS SEED, INCLUDING CLOVER SEED. (a)

	Annual average, 1896–1900.	1896.	1897.	1898.	1899.	1900.	Per ct. in 1900.
FOREIGN COUNTRIES.	Pounds.	Pounds.	Pounds.	Pounds.	Pounds.	Pounds.	
United States	14,009,990	10,992,128	13,422,080	17,411,296	16,088,912	12,135,536	41.36
France	8,620,953	14,630,560	7,727,664	8,128,288	7,545,888	5,072,368	17.29
Germany	6,238,893	11,161,360	6,673,744	5,313,952	3,887,968	4,157,440	14.17
Netherlands	1,496,656	1,683,696	1,433,600	1,649,424	1,359,344	1,357,216	4.63
Belgium	1,086,624	1,425,560	1,150,576	1,323,056	849,856	681,072	2.32
Chile	319,043	87,920	242,816	344,624	352,128	567,728	1.94
Italy	127,411	123,760	33,600	184,576	78,176	216,944	.74
Denmark	94,842	81,088	132,832	89,264	93,408	77,616	.26
Other	147,101	311,248	11,424	71,904	103,376	237,552	.81
Total foreign countries	32,141,513	40,500,320	30,828,336	34,516,384	30,359,056	24,503,472	83.52
BRITISH POSSESSIONS.							
Australasia:							
New Zealand	3,168,077	3,991,232	2,069,648	2,578,912	2,777,040	4,423,552	} 15.19
New South Wales	27,664	1,120	672		113,456	23,072	
Victoria	10,080				39,200	11,200	
Canada	705,286	929,712	694,848	1,295,280	228,704	377,888	1.29
Other i	1,546	6,720	448		560		
Total British possessions	3,912,653	4,928,784	2,765,616	3,874,192	3,158,960	4,835,712	16.48
Total	36,054,166	45,429,104	33,593,952	38,390,576	33,518,016	29,339,184	100.00

a For values, see page 125.
b Annual average, 1896–1899.
c Comprising in 1896, 46,256 pounds from Bengal and 13,776 pounds from Madras, and in 1897, 35,056 pounds from Bengal.
d Not stated.
e Per cent in 1899.
f Including imports from Denmark amounting to 670 pounds in 1896, 1,630 pounds in 1897, and 1,541 pounds in 1898.
g Including imports from New South Wales amounting to 23,510 pounds in 1896, 214,032 pounds in 1897, 69,786 pounds in 1898, 174,358 pounds in 1899, and 163,860 pounds in 1900.
h In 1896 including 35,840 pounds from Bombay.
i In 1896 comprising 6,720 pounds from Bombay.

Quantity of the agricultural imports of the United Kingdom (vegetable matter), etc.—Cont'd.

COTTON SEED.(a)

Countries from which imported.	Annual average, 1896–1900.	Calendar years.					Per ct. in 1900.
		1896.	1897.	1898.	1899.	1900.	
FOREIGN COUNTRIES.							
	Pounds.	*Pounds.*	*Pounds.*	*Pounds.*	*Pounds.*	*Pounds.*	
Egypt	796,790,848	749,454,720	854,703,360	885,864,000	711,473,280	782,458,880	85.94
Brazil	30,613,632	15,500,800	21,784,000	35,719,040	26,949,440	53,114,880	5.83
United States........	31,506,496	29,760,640	23,168,320	24,301,760	40,093,760	40,208,000	4.42
Turkey, Asiatic......	16,394,560	21,443,520	17,857,280	8,198,400	12,333,440	22,140,160	2.43
Peru.................	5,041,792	5,288,640	3,949,120	6,104,000	3,232,320	6,634,880	.73
Chile	1,001,280	461,440	1,113,280	947,520	488,320	1,995,840	.22
Colombia...........	1,019,200	1,055,040	409,920	1,429,120	969,920	1,232,000	.13
Germany	665,280	808,640	367,360	347,200	777,280	1,025,920	.11
France	1,053,696	286,720	387,520	394,240	3,454,080	745,920	.08
Pacific islands.......	288,064	448,000	282,240	347,200	232,960	129,920	} .02
Other...............	241,920	147,840	394,240	58,240	564,480	44,800	
Total foreign countries....	884,616,768	824,656,000	924,416,640	963,710,720	800,569,280	909,731,200	99.91
BRITISH POSSESSIONS.							
British West Indies..	517,888	598,080	338,240	443,520	530,880	678,720	.08
British East Indies ..	201,152	4,480	40,320	13,440	846,720	100,800	.01
Other...............	9,408	....	47,040	....	....	....	......
Total British possessions ..	728,448	602,560	425,600	456,960	1,377,600	779,520	.09
Total	885,345,216	825,258,560	924,842,240	964,167,680	801,946,880	910,510,720	100.00

FLAXSEED, OR LINSEED. (a)

	Annual average, 1896–1900.	1896.	1897.	1898.	1899.	1900.	Per ct. in 1900.
FOREIGN COUNTRIES.							
	Bushels.(b)	*Bushels.(b)*	*Bushels.(b)*	*Bushels.(b)*	*Bushels.(b)*	*Bushels.(b)*	
Russia...............	3,858,672	5,802,897	6,023,655	2,033,441	2,277,907	3,155,458	22.95
Argentina	3,508,643	6,266,816	3,585,733	2,165,020	2,962,047	2,563,599	18.65
Germany	405,990	479,540	385,616	230,066	307,065	627,664	4.57
United States........	903,213	2,060,376	864,463	307,734	747,062	536,429	3.90
Turkey, European ...	105,774	227,450	62,542	48,538	32,975	157,366	1.14
Netherlands........	94,244	156,375	67,658	64,836	41,417	140,936	1.03
France	31,280	55,033	668	990	1,576	98,133	.71
Turkey, Asiatic......	36,863	73,690	26,192	24,335	9,721	50,378	.37
Italy.................	18,248	19,037	36,474	18,815	5,867	11,049	.08
Cyprus	3,017	6,973	4,613	....	....	3,499	.03
Belgium.............	10,221	8,896	3,912	6,453	29,847	1,997	.01
Uruguay	5,635	5,224	9,523	206	12,601	619	} .01
Chile	3,813	4,019	14,276	50	314	404	
Roumania...........	77,282	28,965	312,503	44,940	....	....	......
Other...............	12,686	11,313	4,365	28,923	10,348	8,483	.06
Total foreign countries	9,075,581	15,206,604	11,402,193	4,974,347	6,438,747	7,356,014	53.51
BRITISH POSSESSIONS.							
British East Indies:							
Bengal	6,202,926	5,296,488	4,087,909	8,072,469	7,410,486	6,147,278	} 45.76
Bombay	266,850	743,613	37,233	140,730	286,608	126,066	
Madras	3,697	330	....	....	....	18,154	
Canada.....:	356,194	29,501	220,287	744,809	706,512	79,863	.58
Gibraltar...........	2,566	4,233	2,294	1,271	2,063	2,971	.02
Other...............	3,552	17	....	....	....	17,742	.13
Total British possessions ..	6,835,785	6,074,182	4,347,723	8,959,279	8,405,669	6,392,074	46.49
Total	15,911,366	21,280,786	15,749,916	13,933,626	14,844,416	13,748,088	100.00

a For values, see page 126.   *b* Winchester bushels.

uantity of the agricultural imports of the United Kingdom (vegetable matter), etc.—Cont'd.

RAPE SEED.(a)

ountries from which imported.	Annual average, 1896-1900.	Calendar years.					Per ct. in 1900.
		1896.	1897.	1898.	1899.	1900.	
OREIGN COUNTRIES.							
	Bushels.(b)	Bushels.(b)	Bushels.(b)	Bushels.(b)	Bushels.(b)	Bushels.(b)	
ussia	596,776	911,500	504,486	561,276	626,533	380,087	34.31
Belgium	37,352		44,148	1,791	51,682	89,138	8.05
Roumania	259,439	173,045	392,135	506,054	159,841	66,123	5.97
Netherlands	31,980	6,255	15,786	38,768	54,669	44,421	4.01
Germany	37,314	85,408	16,752	36,614	22,602	25,193	2.27
France	5,582	5,611	3,581	5,950	6,808	5,958	.54
Argentina	7,970	6,230	5,529	22,445		5,644	.51
United States	3,317		908	15,365	314		
Greece	1,502	6,189		1,320			
Other	340			1,395	83	223	.02
Total foreign countries	981,572	1,194,238	983,325	1,190,978	922,532	616,787	55.68
BRITISH POSSESSIONS.							
British East Indies ..							
Bengal	345,059	59,984	391,797	493,717	452,993	326,804	} 44.21
Bombay	196,663	125,521	153,272	341,509	205,632	157,382	
Madras	70,403	103,389		110,660	132,354	5,612	
Other	266		140			1,188	.11
Total British possessions ..	612,391	288,894	545,209	945,886	790,979	490,986	44.32
Total	1,593,963	1,483,132	1,528,534	2,136,864	1,713,511	1,107,773	100.00

OILSEEDS NOT ELSEWHERE SPECIFIED.(a)

FOREIGN COUNTRIES.	Bushels.(b)	Bushels.(b)	Bushels.(b)	Bushels.(b)	Bushels.(b)	Bushels.(b)	
Russia	172,338	202,686	138,031	97,704	196,538	226,732	14.41
Brazil	64,222	17	9,506	77,932	41,730	191,925	12.20
Netherlands	71,478	57,517	48,959	55,627	70,043	125,241	7.96
Germany	121,372	87,933	142,529	102,201	165,675	108,522	6.90
France	12,528	6,824	12,601	5,083	11,083	27,050	1.72
Turkey, Asiatic	11,536	7,806	8,227	9,787	10,348	21,513	1.37
Morocco	11,756	11,132	6,437	13,129	11,718	16,364	1.04
Belgium	5,684	462	11,974	1,155	2,294	12,535	.80
China	3,071		74	16	4,753	10,513	.67
Austria-Hungary	8,523	1,568	5,091	19,433	6,998	9,523	.61
Argentina	3,308	206	12,106	3,276	743	206	.01
Egypt	546	2,014		83	536	99	.01
Chile	5,093	21,076	4,365		25		
Other	8,800	3,416	6,255	5,306	16,050	12,972	.82
Total foreign countries	500,255	402,657	406,155	390,732	538,534	763,195	48.52
BRITISH POSSESSIONS.							
British East Indies:							
Bombay	509,670	261,200	700,372	486,563	652,386	447,828	} 51.19
Bengal	150,238	99,173	223,605	122,427	111,914	194,071	
Madras	263,783	59,043	391,978	411,659	293,573	162,663	
Ceylon	2,329	4,448	4,291	710	1,584	611	
Niger Protectorate ..	1,982	3,251	173	1,007	2,806	2,674	.17
Sierra Leone	1,406	3,746	223	908	1,320	833	.05
Lagos	1,140	322	3,713	1,559	91	16	} .07
Other	833	1,073	231	1,427	289	1,147	
Total British possessions ..	931,381	432,256	1,324,586	1,026,260	1,063,963	809,843	51.48
Total	1,431,636	834,913	1,730,741	1,416,992	1,602,497	1,573,038	100.00

a For values, see page 127.　　　　*b* Winchester bushels.

Quantity of the agricultural imports of the United Kingdom (vegetable matter), etc.—Cont'd.

SEEDS NOT ELSEWHERE SPECIFIED. (a)

Countries from which imported.	Annual average, 1896–1900.	Calendar years.					Per ct. in 1900.
		1896.	1897.	1898.	1899.	1900.	
FOREIGN COUNTRIES.							
	Pounds.	*Pounds.*	*Pounds.*	*Pounds.*	*Pounds.*	*Pounds.*	
Turkey, Asiatic......	19,419,321	25,366,320	21,051,072	13,050,912	12,108,432	25,519,872	39.47
Russia...............	5,190,304	4,750,704	3,253,152	2,121,168	6,808,368	9,018,128	13.95
Germany.............	4,245,203	2,638,160	3,837,904	4,747,008	4,950,064	5,052,880	7.81
Morocco.............	3,931,625	1,092,560	1,238,160	5,937,680	6,518,624	4,871,104	7.53
United States........	2,800,560	177,520	3,910,144	2,020,032	3,094,000	4,801,104	7.43
Netherlands.........	3,004,109	2,210,432	4,797,072	1,870,624	2,878,400	3,264,016	5.05
Turkey, European...	6,492,774	8,973,104	11,265,856	5,808,544	3,313,744	3,102,624	4.80
Egypt	1,569,344	1,092,336	930,496	2,082,976	677,488	3,063,424	4.74
Spain...............	2,185,949	1,488,816	2,415,728	3,769,584	1,751,456	1,504,160	2.33
France	1,432,928	1,176,224	1,565,760	2,012,080	1,128,848	1,281,728	1.98
Italy	625,565	533,344	694,960	696,864	376,096	826,560	1.28
Austria-Hungary	423,674	132,272	138,096	596,064	563,584	688,352	1.06
Tripoli	435,926	....	....	238,224	1,535,968	405,440	.63
Argentina...........	495,690	1,853,376	86,016	51,520	118,720	368,816	.57
Belgium.............	224,090	238,896	312,144	402,528	29,680	137,200	.21
Roumania............	7,698,589	....	4,952,080	19,689,488	13,719,216	132,160	.20
Bulgaria	210,560	....	....	1,052,800	....	....	
Portugal	42,493	141,344	....	14,560	56,560	....	
Other b	207,043	353,136	131,488	70,000	403,984	76,608	.12
Total foreign countries	60,635,747	52,218,544	60,580,128	66,232,656	60,033,232	64,114,176	99.16
BRITISH POSSESSIONS.							
British East Indies:							
Bombay.........	5,136,007	1,160,768	533,568	11,692,800	11,914,336	378,560	
Bengal	103,533	37,408	106,288	300,272	21,840	51,856	
Madras.........	37,677	53,312	23,296	36,064	53,760	21,952	
Ceylon	11,872	18,816	7,056	20,272	1,008	12,208	.72
Straits Settlements	22	....	....	112	....	....	
Gibraltar...........	44,979	21,168	8,960	187,040	3,808	3,920	.01
Other c	83,597	41,104	163,184	46,592	93,184	73,920	.11
Total British possessions ..	5,417,687	1,332,576	842,352	12,283,152	12,087,936	542,416	.84
Total	66,053,434	53,551,120	61,422,480	78,515,808	72,121,168	64,656,592	100.00

CINNAMON. (a)

	Annual average, 1896–1900.	1896.	1897.	1898.	1899.	1900.	Per ct. in 1900.
FOREIGN COUNTRIES.							
	Pounds.	*Pounds.*	*Pounds.*	*Pounds.*	*Pounds.*	*Pounds.*	
Germany.............	14,113	3,220	700	8,600	3,430	54,616	3.
France	4,608	14,780	200	....	2,460	5,600	
Japan	940	....	....	....	....	4,700	
Other d	11,448	43,280	2,790	2,258	3,146	5,766	.31
Total foreign countries	31,109	61,280	3,690	10,858	9,036	70,682	4.29
BRITISH POSSESSIONS.							
British East Indies:							
Ceylon	1,756,806	1,252,900	1,527,420	1,731,324	2,710,005	1,562,380	
Madras	3,560	....	....	6,500	....	11,300	
Bengal	12,358	....	....	20,000	37,800	3,990	
Burma	6,000	....	....	20,000	....	....	
Bombay.........	4,674	4,800	3,500	1,570	13,500	....	95.71
Straits Settlements	3,920	....	19,600	....	....	....	
Other...............	2,294	....	50	11,420	....	....	
Total British possessions ..	1,789,612	1,257,700	1,550,570	1,800,814	2,761,305	1,577,670	95.71
Total	1,820,721	1,318,980	1,554,260	1,811,672	2,770,341	1,648,352	100.00

a For values, see page 128.

b Including imports from Cyprus amounting to 166,880 pounds in 1896, 92,064 pounds in 1897, and 3,024 pounds in 1898; from Persia, 11,424 pounds in 1896 and 47,040 pounds in 1899; and from the Canary Islands, 11,200 pounds in 1896 and 24,640 pounds in 1898.

c Including imports from Malta and Gozo amounting to 4,480 pounds in 1896, 146,720 pounds in 1897, 29,680 pounds in 1898, and 40,320 pounds in 1899.

d Including imports from the Netherlands amounting to 41,770 pounds in 1896 and 2,340 pounds in 1897.

uantity of the agricultural imports of the United Kingdom (vegetable matter), etc.—Cont'd.

GINGER. (a)

	Annual average, 1896–1900.	Calendar years.					Per ct. in 1900.
		1896.	1897.	1898.	1899.	1900.	
'OREIGN COUNTRIES.	*Pounds.*	*Pounds.*	*Pounds.*	*Pounds.*	*Pounds.*	*Pounds.*	
'nited States.......	334,701	203,392	221,872	375,424	328,160	544,656	8.73
apan	608,743	726,208	1,598,800	360,640	22,848	335,216	5.37
ermany..........≈.	201,219	381,472	307,328	44,800	127,568	144,928	2.32
'est Africa, n. e. s ...	14,874	74,368	....	....	....	....	......
rance	9,318	32,480	9,520	4,592	....	....	......
ther...............	63,056	2,016	137,984	26,992	38,864	109,424	1.75
Total foreign countries	1,231,911	1,419,936	2,275,504	812,448	517,440	1,134,224	18.17
BRITISH POSSESSIONS.							
British East Indies:							
Bombay.........	3,176,768	2,692,256	2,427,712	3,942,064	4,721,584	2,100,224	⎫
Madras..........	1,541,209	1,629,152	2,901,584	2,151,968	534,016	489,328	⎪
Bengal	509,197	2,026,304	329,952	159,488	25,984	4,256	⎬ 41.55
Straits Settlements	31,808	....	58,240	95,200	5,600	....	⎪
Ceylon	3,114	....	....	4,928	10,640	....	⎭
British West Indies..	987,952	878,528	1,080,688	635,264	1,091,328	1,253,952	20.09
Sierra Leone	1,555,030	2,048,704	2,130,912	1,610,672	1,043,280	941,584	15.08
Canada..............	170,845	....	....	452,816	398,048	3,360	.05
Other b	135,968	81,424	68,432	69,440	144,592	315,952	5.06
Total British possessions ..	8,111,891	9,356,368	8,997,520	9,121,840	7,975,072	5,108,656	81.83
Total	9,343,802	10,776,304	11,273,024	9,934,288	8,492,512	6,242,880	100.00

PEPPER. (a)

	Annual average, 1896–1900.	1896.	1897.	1898.	1899.	1900.	Per ct. in 1900.
FOREIGN COUNTRIES.	*Pounds.*	*Pounds.*	*Pounds.*	*Pounds.*	*Pounds.*	*Pounds.*	
Java................	1,332,563	337,600	1,012,500	1,933,916	1,990,220	1,388,580	6.23
Netherlands........	1,179,750	623,262	2,138,872	1,277,290	693,224	1,166,104	5.24
France	357,773	114,692	176,724	428,980	309,826	758,642	3.41
Japan	214,576	235,600	114,390	319,500	173,420	229,970	1.03
Germany............	179,528	76,594	272,000	301,538	34,532	212,974	.96
United States........	64,037	....	22,400	71,500	72,054	154,230	.69
Spain..............	37,413	47,640	29,020	25,158	28,692	56,554	.25
Siam	27,122	67,200	50,400	....	....	18,010	⎫ .08
Belgium............	47,101	4,870	....	230,580	500	56	⎬
Denmark...........	108,939	....	....	143,625	401,070	....	......
Other c	39,223	24,680	61,928	24,952	44,626	39,930	.18
Total foreign countries	3,588,025	1,531,638	3,878,234	4,757,039	8,748,164	4,025,050	18.07
BRITISH POSSESSIONS.							
British East Indies:							
Straits Settlements	20,005,814	22,840,890	23,298,198	23,274,016	16,071,126	14,544,841	⎫
Madras..........	1,497,484	782,090	2,499,075	589,850	1,661,754	1,954,650	⎪
Bombay.........	1,030,478	264,600	864,490	634,960	1,950,366	1,437,973	⎬ 81.17
Bengal	45,254	3,040	10,370	17,000	91,320	104,539	⎪
Ceylon	40,901	46,870	2,940	6,630	108,576	39,490	⎭
Zanzibar and Pemba.	126,414	253,570	141,440	81,640	89,350	66,070	.29
Niger Protectorate ..	168,270	274,170	187,970	206,408	125,860	46,941	.21
Sierra Leone	87,230	107,343	127,977	142,502	27,448	30,882	.14
Natal..............	13,303	6,210	8,350	5,040	29,390	17,528	.08
Other...............	9,128	2,580	34,120	100	560	8,278	.01
Total British possessions ..	23,024,276	24,581,363	27,174,930	24,958,146	20,155,750	18,251,192	81.93
Total	26,612,301	26,113,001	31,053,164	29,715,185	23,903,914	22,276,242	100.00

a For values, see page 129.
b In 1896 including 35,952 pounds from Hongkong.
c Including imports from China amounting to 3,580 pounds in 1896 and 802 pounds in 1897.

Quantity of the agricultural imports of the United Kingdom (vegetable matter), etc.—Cont'd.

SPICES NOT ELSEWHERE SPECIFIED. (a)

Countries from which imported.	Annual average, 1896–1900.	Calendar years.					Per ct. in 1900.
		1896.	1897.	1898.	1899.	1900.	
FOREIGN COUNTRIES.							
	Pounds.	*Pounds.*	*Pounds.*	*Pounds.*	*Pounds.*	*Pounds.*	
Germany	1,056,950	1,060,648	1,610,784	644,083	672,908	1,296,326	13.65
Netherlands	430,515	155,514	291,296	207,545	504,350	993,873	10.47
United States	560,137	870,320	154,214	366,400	781,676	628,074	6.61
France	353,464	221,270	29,790	331,920	598,002	586,337	6.18
Japan	175,462	40,440	64,550	169,560	352,560	250,200	2.64
China	109,261	43,410	130,533	120,300	66,770	185,292	1.95
Spain	77,940	173,606	91,140	73,229	18,508	33,220	.35
Ecuador	91,928	433,540	9,100		17,000		
Colombia	23,588	87,940		30,000			
Other b	52,356	68,402	70,160	76,170	30,810	16,236	.17
Total foreign countries	2,931,601	3,155,090	2,451,567	2,019,207	3,042,584	3,989,558	42.02
BRITISH POSSESSIONS.							
British West Indies	3,543,655	3,490,972	2,723,288	2,990,322	5,284,145	3,229,549	01
Hongkong	486,873	14,000	381,970	911,184	292,360	834,850	79
Zanzibar and Pemba	1,372,968	2,123,260	2,420,447	591,750	971,530	757,850	34.98
British East Indies:							
Straits Settlements	1,121,148	1,672,160	1,426,770	1,110,752	921,248	474,811	
Bombay	192,185	249,720	221,380	227,140	102,188	160,498	
Ceylon	62,597	5,096	19,000	17,250	246,860	24,781	7.20
Madras	6,060	1,840	630	1,190	3,400	23,240	
Bengal	1,520	4,800	2,800				
Aden	78,922	420			394,190		
Canada	63,938	2,660	900	260,170	55,960		
Other	1,836	910	1,900	5,950	250	168	
Total British possessions	6,931,702	7,565,838	7,199,085	6,115,708	8,272,131	5,505,747	57.98
Total	9,863,303	10,720,928	9,650,652	8,134,915	11,314,715	9,495,305	100.00

BRANDY. (a)

	Proof gallons.(c)	Proof gallons.(c)	Proof gallons.(c)	Proof gallons.(c)	Proof gallons.(c)	Proof gallons.(c)	
FOREIGN COUNTRIES.							
France	2,909,773	3,026,372	3,349,336	2,650,678	2,711,503	2,810,978	90.20
Germany	128,590	84,856	130,488	194,109	98,875	134,624	4.32
Spain	55,840	65,793	47,480	62,027	56,103	47,796	1.53
Netherlands	33,275	40,825	42,918	26,486	29,203	26,942	.87
United States	19,045	23,682	34,221	7,032	10,068	20,225	.65
Cyprus	2,704	3,896	128		491	9,004	.29
Egypt	4,792	2,620	321	4,693	8,517	7,809	.25
Norway	2,425	3,639	79	2	769	7,638	.25
Greece	3,095	4,085	1,250	2,782	423	6,925	.22
Denmark	17,512	11,380	31,738	13,374	27,677	3,390	.11
Other	4,549	3,337	6,796	4,969	2,845	4,796	.15
Total foreign countries	3,181,600	3,270,485	3,644,755	2,966,152	2,946,474	3,080,137	98.84
BRITISH POSSESSIONS.							
Australasia:							
Victoria	35,844	28,846	57,931	48,594	10,062	33,786	
South Australia	1,346	20	3,035	1,615	443	1,619	1.14
New South Wales	360	370	1,236		191	2	
Other	1,271	653	1,091	2,140	1,716	753	.02
Total British possessions	28,821	29,889	63,293	52,349	12,412	36,160	1.16
Total	3,220,421	3,300,374	3,708,048	3,018,501	2,958,886	3,116,297	100.00

a For values, see page 130.
b Including in 1896, 310 pounds from Java and 20,640 pounds from the other Dutch East Indies, and in 1897, 1,830 pounds from Java.
c United States standard proof gallons.

Quantity of the agricultural imports of the United Kingdom (vegetable matter), etc.—Cont'd.

GIN. (a)

Countries from which imported.	Annual average, 1896–1900.	Calendar years.					Per ct. in 1900.
		1896.	1897.	1898.	1899.	1900.	
FOREIGN COUNTRIES.	*Proof gallons.(b)*	*Proof gallons.(b)*	*Proof gallons.(b)*	*Proof gallons.(b)*	*Proof gallons.(b)*	*Proof gallons.(b)*	
Netherlands	449,073	424,751	422,540	418,140	489,695	490,238	98.89
Belgium	4,947	5,840	6,434	4,440	3,768	4,256	.86
Germany	536	340	787	232	471	849	.17
United States	2				2	7	
Other	159	19	249	57	65	408	.08
Total foreign countries	454,717	430,950	430,010	422,871	494,006	495,751	100.00
BRITISH POSSESSIONS.							
Total British possessions	46	63	103	88	1	23	
Total	454,763	431,013	430,113	422,909	494,007	495,774	100.00

RUM. (a)

	Proof gallons.(b)	Proof gallons.(b)	Proof gallons.(b)	Proof gallons.(b)	Proof gallons.(b)	Proof gallons.(b)	
FOREIGN COUNTRIES.							
United States	565,412	565,693	414,526	559,028	205,455	1,082,361	14.55
Netherlands	158,122	214,196	61,057	36,275	130,049	349,033	4.69
France	152,626	1,908	3,368	85	531,237	226,532	3.05
Dutch Guiana	81,537	107,366	133,713	74,077	59,674	32,856	.44
Germany	37,185	77,340		5,592	76,670	26,322	.36
Azores	33,623		168,114				
Cuba and Porto Rico c	24,187		25		120,910		
Austria-Hungary	5,961	25,833	95	3,876			
Spain	1	4		1			
Other	6,645	67	324	2,137	26,275	4,422	.06
Total foreign countries	1,065,299	992,407	781,222	681,071	1,150,270	1,721,526	23.15
BRITISH POSSESSIONS.							
British Guiana	3,373,561	3,465,484	3,142,046	3,748,834	2,771,429	3,740,012	50.28
British West Indies	1,766,082	1,958,896	1,905,587	1,435,848	2,084,194	1,445,883	19.44
Mauritius	211,172		23,621	116,059	417,198	498,983	6.71
Australasia:							
Queensland	6,255		40	6	11,267	19,962	⎫
Victoria	245					1,227	⎬ .28
New South Wales	3,174	98		15,767		5	⎭
British East Indies:							
Madras	3,800			1,265	9,331	8,404	⎫
Straits Settlements	77		103			280	⎪
Bengal	23			4	11	101	⎬ .12
Burma						1	⎪
Bombay	8		9	28	4		⎭
Canada	169,730		51,211	565,669	230,762	1,006	⎫ .02
Other	4,521	1,815	44		20,421	325	⎭
Total British possessions	5,538,648	5,426,293	5,122,661	5,883,480	5,544,617	5,716,189	76.85
Total	6,603,947	6,418,700	5,903,883	6,564,551	6,694,887	7,437,715	100.00

a For values, see page 131.
b United States standard proof gallons.
c In 1899 the entire imports were credited to Cuba.

Quantity of the agricultural imports of the United Kingdom (vegetable matter), etc.—Cont'd.

IMITATION RUM.(a)

Countries from which imported.	Annual average. 1896–1900.	Calendar years.					Per ct. in 1900.
		1896.	1897.	1898.	1899.	1900.	
FOREIGN COUNTRIES.	*Proof gallons.(b)*	*Proof gallons.(b)*	*Proof gallons.(b)*	*Proof gallons.(b)*	*Proof gallons.(b)*	*Proof gallons.(b)*	
Germany............	37,866	30,403	32,999	19,040	58,427	48,458	94.69
United States........	418	....	177	20	52	1,839	3.59
Netherlands.........	289	403	98	378	115	453	.89
Other...............	930	772	1,116	1,323	1,038	402	.79
Total foreign countries....	39,503	31,578	34,390	20,761	59,632	51,152	99.96
BRITISH POSSESSIONS.							
Total British possessions	15	19	....	34	....	22	.04
Total	39,518	31,597	34,390	20,795	59,632	51,174	100.00

DISTILLED SPIRITS, N. E. S., NOT SWEETENED OR MIXED.(a)

	Annual average. 1896–1900.	1896.	1897.	1898.	1899.	1900.	Per ct. in 1900.
FOREIGN COUNTRIES.	*Proof gallons.(b)*	*Proof gallons.(b)*	*Proof gallons.(b)*	*Proof gallons.(b)*	*Proof gallons.(b)*	*Proof gallons.(b)*	
Germany.............	1,211,572	1,192,540	1,126,790	978,433	1,351,071	1,409,026	82.
Netherlands.........	65,559	43,384	28,965	45,242	32,469	177,738	10.
Denmark.............	82,382	157,159	132,598	25,218	45,700	51,238	2.
Belgium.............	19,535	3,109	420	21,535	29,047	43,563	2.
United States........	11,073	6,885	6,989	6,581	16,724	18,185	1.
France	44,073	15,261	90,578	87,504	17,815	9,205	.09
Norway	9,009	22,648	5,973	7,574	8,313	535	.00
Russia	82,267	144,893	238,770	27,603	57	13	.13
Other...............	2,866	2,267	2,428	4,941	2,479	2,215	
Total foreign countries....	1,528,336	1,588,146	1,633,511	1,204,631	1,503,675	1,711,718	99.73
BRITISH POSSESSIONS.							
Channel Islands.....	430	216	224	176	164	1,369	.08
Canada..............	5,149	6,307	3,715	11,544	3,025	1,155	.07
Australasia.........	2,112	77	4,005	2,281	3,145	1,055	.06
Other...............	724	1,053	507	624	410	1,024	.06
Total British possessions ..	8,415	7,653	8,451	14,625	6,744	4,603	.27
Total	1,536,751	1,595,799	1,641,962	1,219,256	1,510,419	1,716,321	100.00

DISTILLED SPIRITS, SWEETENED OR MIXED (TESTED).(c)

	Annual average. 1896–1900.	1896.	1897.	1898.	1899.	1900.	Per ct. in 1900.
FOREIGN COUNTRIES.	*Proof gallons.(b)*	*Proof gallons.(b)*	*Proof gallons.(b)*	*Proof gallons.(b)*	*Proof gallons.(b)*	*Proof gallons.(b)*	
France	51,728	38,082	46,112	59,303	64.277	50,866	41.57
Germany.............	18,850	15,909	19,835	19,739	17,174	21,591	17.65
United States........	14,540	13,385	14,122	12,697	15,527	16,969	13.87
Netherlands.........	9,392	9,594	9,928	9,329	9,361	8,749	7.15
Russia..............	6,393	5,549	5,996	7,677	7,988	4,754	3.89
Austria-Hungary....	3,770	3,416	4,263	3,670	3,888	3,612	2.95
Denmark............	4,061	4,435	4,191	3,749	4,409	3,522	2.88
Italy...............	1,011	391	451	1,107	798	2,305	1.88
Belgium............	957	361	619	1,300	1,595	849	.69
Sweden.............	224	216	191	341	210	163	.13
Norway	86	97	66	89	131	49	.04
Other...............	838	1,060	732	1,243	706	450	.37
Total foreign countries....	111,850	92,495	106,506	120,304	126,064	113,879	93.07
BRITISH POSSESSIONS.							
British West Indies..	9,004	8,109	9,097	9,780	9,635	8,401	6.87
Other...............	181	125	240	218	248	74	.06
Total British possessions ..	9,185	8,234	9,337	9,998	9,883	8,475	6.93
Total	121,035	100,729	115,843	130,302	135,947	122,354	100.00

a For values, see page 132.　　b United States standard proof gallons.　　c For values, see page 133.

uantity of the agricultural imports of the United Kingdom (vegetable matter), etc.—Cont'd.

LIQUEURS, CORDIALS, ETC. (NOT TESTED). (a)

Countries from which imported.	Annual average, 1896–1900.	Calendar years.					Per ct. in 1900.
		1896.	1897.	1898.	1899.	1900.	
FOREIGN COUNTRIES.	Gallons.(b)	Gallons.(b)	Gallons.(b)	Gallons.(b)	Gallons.(b)	Gallons.(b)	
France	9,710	9,006	8,700	8,304	10,910	11,632	63.71
United States........	1,513	1,312	1,347	1,192	1,701	2,015	11.04
Germany	2,150	2,450	2,771	2,248	1,967	1,312	7.19
Netherlands.........	1,375	1,446	1,703	1,311	1,414	1,003	5.49
Belgium..............	308	420	384	201	247	287	1.57
Denmark.............	412	625	449	498	393	94	.52
Russia...............	304	220	720	140	390	49	.27
Other................	444	706	275	522	217	501	2.74
Total foreign countries....	16,216	16,185	16,349	14,416	17,239	16,893	92.53
BRITISH POSSESSIONS.							
British West Indies..	388	179	181	243	77	1,259	6.90
Other................	290	239	117	814	176	105	.57
Total British possessions ..	678	418	298	1,057	253	1,364	7.47
Total	16,894	16,603	16,647	15,473	17,492	18,257	100.00

DISTILLED SPIRITS, PERFUMED.(c)

FOREIGN COUNTRIES.	Gallons.(b)	Gallons.(b)	Gallons.(b)	Gallons.(b)	Gallons.(b)	Gallons.(b)	
France	32,183	30,641	31,536	33,239	33,948	31,549	49.05
Netherlands.........	23,107	24,703	23,172	23,317	22,901	21,444	33.34
Belgium	6,205	5,169	5,626	6,088	6,306	7,837	12.18
United States........	1,847	1,418	1,923	1,976	2,255	1,665	2.59
Germany	1,191	1,635	1,305	1,078	982	953	1.48
Other................	27	42	37	7	13	35	.05
Total foreign countries....	64,560	63,608	63,599	65,705	66,405	63,483	98.69
BRITISH POSSESSIONS.							
Channel Islands.....	1,254	1,412	1,353	1,395	1,287	824	1.28
Other................	153	178	230	110	227	17	.03
Total British possessions ..	1,407	1,590	1,583	1,505	1,514	841	1.31
Total	65,967	65,198	65,182	67,210	67,919	64,324	100.00

STRAW.(c)

FOREIGN COUNTRIES.	Tons.(d)	Tons.(d)	Tons.(d)	Tons.(d)	Tons.(d)	Tons.(d)	
France	56,510	54,313	70,087	61,959	54,452	41,739	74.75
Netherlands.........	8,219	10,794	11,604	4,643	5,191	8,862	15.87
Germany	3,220	3,572	3,949	2,380	2,685	3,515	6.30
Belgium..............	3,089	3,843	4,648	2,871	2,439	1,643	2.94
United States........	114	22	472	7	4	65	.12
Denmark.............	407	1,209	681	80	56	11	.02
Other e	70	40	283	26	(f)	....	......
Total	71,629	73,793	91,724	71,966	64,827	55,835	100.00

a For values, see page 133.
b United States standard gallons.
c For values, see page 134.
d Tons of 2,240 pounds.
e In 1896 including 32 tons from Algeria.
f Less than one-half ton.

Quantity of the agricultural imports of the United Kingdom (vegetable matter), etc.—Cont'd.

MOLASSES.(a)

Countries from which imported.	Annual average, 1896–1900.	Calendar years.					Per ct. in 1900.
		1896.	1897.	1898.	1899.	1900.	
FOREIGN COUNTRIES.							
	Pounds.	*Pounds.*	*Pounds.*	*Pounds.*	*Pounds.*	*Pounds.*	
United States........	115,520,631	54,135,312	111,514,256	129,129,616	158,712,064	124,111,904	82.21
Egypt	15,828,848	28,670,432	15,030,400	6,743,072	14,773,472	13,926,864	9.23
Netherlands........	3,761,139	28,448	13,664	5,943,280	2,293,312	10,526,992	6.97
Germany............	2,892,848	2,221,072	2,108,064	6,900,768	2,299,472	934,864	.62
Belgium............	178,259	884,240	1,120	5,936	....	....	
Other b	328,944	184,800	234,976	787,472	371,280	66,192	.04
Total foreign countries....	138,510,669	86,124,304	128,902,480	149,510,144	178,449,600	149,566,816	99.07
BRITISH POSSESSIONS.							
British West Indies..	1,388,598	656,992	1,546,832	1,609,776	1,734,208	1,395,184	} .93
British Guiana	95,088	....	40,320	426,944	7,056	1,120	
Other...............	69,216	196,336	54,656	10,192	79,744	5,152	
Total British possessions ..	1,552,902	853,328	1,641,808	2,046,912	1,821,008	1,401,456	.93
Total	140,063,571	86,977,632	130,544,288	151,557,056	180,270,608	150,968,272	100.00

BEET SUGAR, UNREFINED. (c)

FOREIGN COUNTRIES.							
	Pounds.	*Pounds.*	*Pounds.*	*Pounds.*	*Pounds.*	*Pounds.*	
France	266,753,760	158,077,024	301,012,768	206,427,872	188,231,008	480,020,128	41.86
Germany............	520,682,557	560,314,944	488,589,136	629,303,696	567,612,304	357,592,704	31.18
Belgium............	172,895,117	124,180,336	130,239,648	166,752,208	211,151,360	232,152,032	20.24
Netherlands........	32,004,896	11,184,320	22,717,408	35,487,424	42,631,344	48,003,984	4.18
Austria-Hungary	17,407,779	9,012,192	6,613,376	15,966,272	34,456,016	20,991,040	1.83
Denmark............	8,019,312	12,710,880	10,479,280	6,187,440	5,251,120	5,467,840	.48
Russia..............	11,787,087	27,679,120	14,142,464	11,245,920	3,330,880	2,536,800	} .23
Egypt	13,149	....	....	....	....	65,744	
Other...............	13,126	....	....	....	65,632	....	
Total	1,029,576,733	903,158,816	973,794,080	1,071,370,832	1,052,729,664	1,146,830,272	100.00

SUGAR, CANE, ETC., UNREFINED. (c)

FOREIGN COUNTRIES.							
	Pounds.	*Pounds.*	*Pounds.*	*Pounds.*	*Pounds.*	*Pounds.*	
France	25,324,992	1,072,960	7,205,744	22,000,832	46,167,856	50,177,568	14.96
Peru................	72,949,721	93,778,160	94,937,808	112,246,064	36,894,592	26,891,984	8.02
Argentina	32,747,658	19,197,920	37,630,880	33,850,880	48,690,880	24,367,728	7.26
Philippine Islands d .	83,239,721	154,869,680	90,956,432	100,593,696	45,542,448	24,236,352	7.22
Java................	55,375,578	128,610,048	50,126,608	63,038,640	16,769,984	18,332,608	5.46
Brazil	31,272,662	44,275,056	36,398,544	49,568,512	14,184,240	11,936,960	3.56
Chile................	6,099,162	5,991,104	1,388,464	7,985,936	7,297,024	7,833,280	2.31
Egypt	16,948,355	39,804,240	22,293,488	10,041,920	6,277,376	6,324,752	1.89
French West Indies..	731,293	....	....	....	348,320	3,308,144	.99
Dutch Guiana	3,320,800	3,196,480	2,634,240	3,940,160	3,838,240	2,994,880	.89
Germany............	2,816,666	3,700,704	2,410,800	2,563,568	3,236,800	2,171,456	.65
Netherlands........	1,814,378	648,704	946,960	2,289,840	3,427,424	1,758,960	.52
Colombia............	316,064	....	....	795,200	....	784,000	.23
United States........	2,379,798	10,420,592	215,264	368,032	861,952	33,152	} .01
Denmark............	47,712	....	....	22,400	213,920	2,240	
Danish West Indies..	2,036,160	1,388,800	4,317,600	4,474,400	....	....	
Cuba and Porto Rico e	1,280,832	2,257,920	2,387,840	1,610,560	147,840	....	
Spain...............	717,158	1,512,000	739,200	208,320	1,126,272	....	
Ecuador............	591,136	256,480	....	2,699,200	....	....	
Mexico	364,269	1,410,544	380,800	....	....	....	
Belgium............	278,611	53,536	1,153,936	24,080	161,504	....	
Russia..............	114,688	....	....	336,000	237,440	....	
Other...............	152,544	....	15,680	582,400	156,800	7,840	
Total foreign countries....	340,919,958	512,474,928	356,140,288	419,240,640	235,582,032	181,161,904	51.00

a For values, see page 134.
  b Including imports from Sweden amounting to 16,352 pounds in 1896, 109,760 pounds in 1897, and 20,944 pounds in 1898.
  c For values, see page 135.
  d Including the Ladrone Islands.
  e In 1899 the entire imports were credited to Porto Rico.

Quantity of the agricultural imports of the United Kingdom (vegetable matter), etc.—Cont'd.

SUGAR, CANE, ETC., UNREFINED—Continued.

Countries from which imported.	Annual average, 1896–1900.	Calendar years.					Per ct. in 1900.
		1896.	1897.	1898.	1899.	1900.	
BRITISH POSSESSIONS.	*Pounds.*	*Pounds.*	*Pounds.*	*Pounds.*	*Pounds.*	*Pounds.*	
British West Indies..	61,567,319	85,811,264	62,145,888	41,391,056	63,543,088	54,945,296	16.38
British East Indies:							
Madras..........	62,589,789	152,667,760	48,886,880	29,944,320	51,972,480	29,477,504	
Straits Settlements	15,858,774	22,341,312	15,093,344	15,806,560	13,096,496	12,956,160	} 12.65
Bengal	1,276,285	6,381,424					
Ceylon	94,080			470,400			
British Guiana	52,752,694	76,118,448	56,339,920	60,102,784	33,021,520	38,180,800	11.38
Mauritius	10,135,216	3,881,584	5,445,888	7,012,768	15,588,160	18,747,680	5.59
Australasia:							
Queensland	591,808	2,240	112,000		2,844,800		
New South Wales	249,178			2,240	1,243,648		
Natal................	119,123	448,672		146,720	224		
Other a	36,243	5,264	36,736	117,152	9,296	12,768	....
Total British possessions ..	205,270,509	347,657,968	188,060,656	154,994,000	181,319,712	154,320,208	46.00
Total	546,190,467	860,132,896	544,200,944	574,234,640	416,901,744	335,482,112	100.00

UNREFINED SUGAR (TOTAL). (b)

FOREIGN COUNTRIES.	*Pounds.*	*Pounds.*	*Pounds.*	*Pounds.*	*Pounds.*	*Pounds.*	
France	292,078,752	159,149,984	308,218,512	228,428,704	234,398,864	530,197,696	35.77
Germany...........	523,499,223	564,015,648	490,999,936	631,867,264	570,849,104	359,764,160	24.27
Belgium...........	173,173,728	124,233,872	131,293,584	166,776,288	211,312,864	232,152,032	15.66
Netherlands........	33,819,274	11,833,024	23,664,368	37,777,264	46,058,768	49,762,944	3.36
Peru.................	72,949,721	93,778,160	94,937,808	112,246,064	36,894,592	26,891,984	1.81
Argentina..........	32,747,658	19,197,920	37,630,880	33,850,880	48,690,880	24,367,728	1.64
Philippine Islands c.	83,239,721	154,869,680	90,956,432	100,593,696	45,542,448	24,236,352	1.63
Austria-Hungary	17,407,779	9,012,192	6,613,376	15,966,272	34,456,016	20,991,040	1.42
Java.................	55,375,578	128,610,048	50,126,608	63,038,640	16,769,984	18,332,608	1.24
Brazil..............	31,272,662	44,275,056	36,398,544	49,568,512	14,184,240	11,936,960	.81
Chile.......,......	6,099,162	5,991,104	1,388,464	7,985,936	7,297,024	7,833,280	.53
Egypt	16,961,504	39,804,240	22,293,488	10,041,920	6,277,376	6,390,496	.43
Denmark...........	8,067,024	12,710,880	10,479,280	6,209,840	5,465,040	5,470,080	.37
French West Indies..	731,293				348,320	3,308,144	.22
Dutch Guiana	3,320,800	3,196,480	2,634,240	3,940,160	3,838,240	2,994,880	.20
Russia..............	11,901,725	27,679,120	14,142,464	11,581,920	3,568,320	2,536,800	.17
Colombia...........	316,064			795,200	1,120	784,000	} .06
United States........	2,379,798	10,420,592	215,264	368,032	861,952	33,152	
Danish West Indies..	2,036,160	1,888,800	4,317,600	4,470,400			
Cuba and Porto Rico d	1,280,832	2,257,920	2,387,840	1,610,560	147,840		
Spain................	717,158	1,512,000	739,200	208,320	1,126,272		
Ecuador.............	591,136	256,480		2,699,200			
Mexico..............	364,269	1,440,544	380,800				
Other...............	165,670		15,680	582,400	222,432	7,840	
Total foreign countries ...	1,370,496,691	1,415,633,744	1,329,934,368	1,490,611,472	1,288,311,696	1,327,992,176	89.59
BRITISH POSSESSIONS.							
British West Indies..	61,567,319	85,811,264	62,145,888	41,391,056	63,543,088	54,945,296	3.71
British East Indies:							
Madras..........	62,589,789	152,667,760	48,886,880	29,944,320	51,972,480	29,477,504	
Straits Settlements	15,858,774	22,341,312	15,093,344	15,806,560	13,096,496	12,956,160	} 2.86
Bengal	1,276,285	6,381,424					
Ceylon	94,080			470,400			
British Guiana	52,752,694	76,118,448	56,339,920	60,102,784	33,021,520	38,180,800	2.58
Mauritius	10,135,216	3,881,584	5,445,888	7,012,768	15,588,160	18,747,680	1.26
Australasia:							
Queensland	591,808	2,240	112,000		2,844,800		
New South Wales	249,178			2,240	1,243,648		
Natal................	119,123	448,672		146,720	224		
Other a	36,243	5,264	36,736	117,152	9,296	12,768	....
Total British possessions ..	205,270,509	347,657,968	188,060,656	154,994,000	181,319,712	154,320,208	10.41
Total	1,575,767,200	1,763,291,712	1,517,995,024	1,645,605,472	1,469,631,408	1,482,312,384	100.00

a Including imports from Canada amounting to 5,264 pounds in 1896, 14,336 pounds in 1897, and 116,032 pounds in 1898.
b For values, see page 136.
c Including the Ladrone Islands.
d In 1899 the entire imports were credited to Porto Rico.

Quantity of the agricultural imports of the United Kingdom (vegetable matter), etc.—Cont'd.

REFINED SUGAR. (a)

Countries from which imported.	Annual average, 1896–1900.	Calendar years.					Per ct. in 1900.
		1896.	1897.	1898.	1899.	1900.	
FOREIGN COUNTRIES.							
	Pounds.	*Pounds.*	*Pounds.*	*Pounds.*	*Pounds.*	*Pounds.*	
Germany	1,238,326,365	1,126,587,952	1,133,331,808	1,279,474,224	1,322,948,928	1,329,288,912	61.63
France	321,099,072	162,576,736	355,315,744	252,927,024	349,386,688	485,289,168	22.51
Netherlands	237,981,632	225,538,422	194,731,936	257,370,960	258,860,672	253,406,160	11.76
Belgium	65,068,864	71,083,712	84,243,488	52,243,856	50,189,664	67,583,600	3.14
Austria-Hungary	2,739,767		179,200		1,438,640	12,080,992	.56
Russia	18,378,842	67,281,088	3,505,600	5,093,760	9,281,440	6,732,320	.31
Egypt	414,982		32,480		1,000,384	1,042,048	.05
United States	931,728	1,075,586	1,552,432	858,592	962,416	209,664	} .01
Denmark	239,590	642,320	105,504	284,480	79,184	86,464	
Portugal	196,022	69,664	8,960	803,264	98,224		
Other	183,277	124,544	32,704	458,080	241,584	59,472	
Total foreign countries	1,885,560,141	1,654,979,984	1,773,039,856	1,849,514,240	1,994,487,824	2,155,778,800	100.00
BRITISH POSSESSIONS.							
Canada	44,531	22,624	2,016	61,152	121,296	15,568	
British West Indies	129,248			646,240			
Other	15,680	13,440	3,136	46,816	12,432	2,576	
Total British possessions	189,459	36,064	5,152	754,208	133,728	18,144	
Total	1,885,749,600	1,655,016,048	1,773,045,008	1,850,268,448	1,994,621,552	2,155,796,944	100.00

TEA. (a)

	Annual average, 1896–1900.	1896.	1897.	1898.	1899.	1900.	Per ct. in 1900.
FOREIGN COUNTRIES.							
	Pounds.	*Pounds.*	*Pounds.*	*Pounds.*	*Pounds.*	*Pounds.*	
China	25,990,087	31,115,707	25,130,786	24,154,197	30,673,136	18,876,358	6.30
Netherlands	4,753,347	4,616,116	3,496,963	3,737,661	5,321,806	6,594,187	2.20
United States	865,459	112,334	408,601	1,371,065	1,404,078	1,031,219	.34
Java	1,064,372	980,084	1,394,569	1,192,113	1,208,707	546,387	.18
France	822,664	1,520,917	1,255,506	472,081	322,748	512,069	.17
Germany	175,122	22,690	27,830	100,535	347,886	376,669	.13
Belgium	44,450	2,490	5,201	9,328	1,615	203,615	.07
Japan	122,711	143,863	96,277	115,714	159,429	98,271	.03
Macao	265,039	497,091	389,624	165,632	177,891	94,957	.03
Denmark	5,527	7,578	889	29	14,610	4,530	} .03
Other	75,333	10,570	26,087	186,150	84,758	69,099	
Total foreign countries	34,184,061	39,029,440	32,262,333	31,504,505	39,716,664	28,407,361	9.48
BRITISH POSSESSIONS.							
British East Indies:							
Bengal	136,942,288	125,343,752	131,836,024	136,622,498	140,116,795	150,792,370	
Ceylon	100,996,088	94,859,965	96,325,578	97,613,977	101,700,896	114,480,023	
Madras	2,124,398	1,835,929	1,866,441	2,125,500	2,017,422	2,776,699	
Bombay	957,963	528,980	1,013,714	1,146,147	1,376,911	724,063	} 89.72
Straits Settlements	36,545	1,470	4,896	51,262	88,526	36,570	
Burma	11,749	11,754	13,222	18,214	12,258	3,298	
Hongkong	3,198,445	3,686,932	3,239,887	2,757,930	3,963,254	2,344,223	.78
Canada	35,268	24,083	4,854	48,570	77,183	21,652	.01
Channel Islands	20,282	25,161	22,168	23,370	19,263	11,450	
Natal	24,084	3,378	75,639	31,474	5,974	3,956	
Australasia	36,594	31,820	132,386	8,440	6,513	3,808	} .01
Other	9,638	11,458	3,269	9,144	14,601	9,718	
Total British possessions	244,393,342	226,364,682	234,538,078	240,456,526	249,399,596	271,207,830	90.52
Total	278,577,403	265,394,122	266,800,411	271,961,031	289,116,260	299,615,191	100.00

a For values, see page 137.

Quantity of the agricultural imports of the United Kingdom (vegetable matter), etc.—Cont'd.

TOBACCO.(a)

Countries from which imported.	Annual average, 1896–1900.	Calendar years.					Per ct. in 1900.
		1896.	1897.	1898.	1899.	1900.	
FOREIGN COUNTRIES.							
	Pounds.	*Pounds.*	*Pounds.*	*Pounds.*	*Pounds.*	*Pounds.*	
United States........	82,272,275	74,163,042	69,203,341	69,740,450	109,450,021	88,804,522	90.30
Netherlands.........	5,653,457	4,689,770	5,707,761	6,182,781	5,958,357	5,728,615	5.82
Germany............	958,145	965,384	921,765	935,492	973,557	994,528	1.01
France	591,419	367,062	404,266	488,546	970,729	726,491	.74
Turkey, European...	369,877	479,102	443,124	324,876	110,023	492,260	.50
China	310,024	148,506	281,704	232,238	477,320	410,352	.42
Turkey, Asiatic......	464,972	666,754	313,324	508,462	455,393	380,928	.39
Belgium.............	387,294	450,598	334,615	415,307	428,694	307,257	.31
Japan ....'...	608,274	1,123,921	1,128,473	529,677	43,006	216,295	.22
Austria-Hungary	10,844	86,228				17,994	.02
Greece..............	35,975	133,830	17,627	8,888	4,656	14,872	} .02
Italy...............	8,878	43,062	111		571	644	
Philippine Islands b.	372,202	384	1,860,627				
Colombia............	13,889	67,358	124	339	1,622		
Argentina...........	5,692	26,569		1,890			
Other...............	63,609	9,239	86,571	181,537	15,867	24,829	.02
Total foreign countries	92,126,826	83,370,809	80,703,433	79,550,483	118,889,816	98,119,587	99.77
BRITISH POSSESSIONS.							
Australasia.........	77,179	26,977	3,782	15,910	157,103	182,123	.18
Canada.............	29,873	101,477	9,459	8,731	1,081	28,619	.03
British East Indies ..	13,777	42,203	2,587	16,493	5,264	2,338	}
Hongkong...........	3,049	4,787	8,229		1,633	594	.02
Other...............	17,802	12,504	942	40,338	19,988	15,239	
Total British possessions ..	141,680	187,948	24,999	81,472	185,069	228,913	.23
Total	92,268,506	83,558,757	80,728,432	79,631,955	119,074,885	98,348,500	100.00

ONIONS.(a)

FOREIGN COUNTRIES.	*Bushels.(c)*	*Bushels.(c)*	*Bushels.(c)*	*Bushels.(c)*	*Bushels.(c)*	*Bushels.(c)*	
Spain...............	2,025,159	1,868,477	1,808,826	1,776,982	2,277,178	2,394,381	32.75
Netherlands.........	1,729,262	1,631,200	1,795,869	1,534,049	1,797,955	1,887,240	25.82
Egypt	1,350,996	1,128,540	1,198,784	1,234,344	1,605,962	1,587,352	21.71
Belgium.............	362,581	313,987	396,295	352,538	293,727	456,357	6.24
France	481,427	482,110	407,393	494,630	569,158	453,845	6.21
Germany............	318,439	489,649	338,091	267,024	240,143	257,288	3.52
Portugal............	316,715	269,338	274,606	392,384	433,981	213,266	2.92
Italy	8,836	11,928	3,385	10,047	4,067	14,752	.20
Canary Islands.....	8,732	206		41,697	64	1,692	.02
Austria-Hungary....	3,245	611	13,057	58	2,476	23	}
Turkey, European...	2,400	1,144	5,852	5,001		3	.04
Other d	2,632	7,012	619	2,107	816	2,604	
Total foreign countries	6,610,424	6,204,202	6,242,777	6,110,811	7,225,527	7,268,803	99.43
BRITISH POSSESSIONS.							
Malta and Gozo	50,661	71,352	55,149	74,388	13,118	39,300	.54
Other e	3,178	3,089	3,429	6,395	730	2,246	.03
Total British possessions ..	53,839	74,441	58,578	80,783	13,848	41,546	.57
Total	6,664,263	6,278,643	6,301,355	6,191,594	7,239,375	7,310,349	100.00

a For values, see page 138.
b Including the Ladrone Islands.
c Winchester bushels.
d Including imports from the United States amounting to 1,754 bushels in 1896 and 2,517 bushels in 1900, and from Asiatic Turkey 3,847 bushels in 1896, 72 bushels in 1897, and 238 bushels in 1899.
e In 1896 comprising 3,089 bushels from the Channel Islands.

Quantity of the agricultural imports of the United Kingdom (vegetable matter), etc.—Cont'd.

POTATOES. (a)

Countries from which imported.	Annual average, 1896–1900.	Calendar years.					Per ct. in 1900.
		1896.	1897.	1898.	1899.	1900.	
FOREIGN COUNTRIES.							
	Bushels.(b)	*Bushels. (b)*	*Bushels.(b)*	*Bushels.(b)*	*Bushels.(b)*	*Bushels.(b)*	
Belgium..............	2,019,175	7,202	1,115,414	1,997,658	1,365,909	5,609,690	33.72
France	2,760,953	1,403,543	2,140,583	2,901,631	3,266,081	4,092,926	24.61
Germany.............	1,648,455	32,478	668,282	3,646,791	1,414,497	2,480,227	14.91
Netherlands........	977,740	90,268	1,049,197	1,223,693	581,829	1,943,711	11.69
Portugal	181,085	43,477	137,444	256,893	249,411	218,200	1.31
Canary Islands......	144,287	188,516	106,854	136,269	173,314	116,484	.70
Spain...............	25,501	9,212	54,126	1,988	21,194	40,983	.25
Algeria.............	7,075	5,031	2,753	2,768	6,642	18,183	.11
Egypt	4,169	6,089	7,913	4,351	547	1,945	.01
Norway	11,552	....	989	54,695	653	1,422	.01
Other c.............	18,593	2,206	6,104	39,056	8,915	36,686	.22
Total foreign countries....	7,798,585	1,788,022	5,289,659	10,265,793	7,088,992	14,560,457	87.54
BRITISH POSSESSIONS.							
Channel Islands.....	2,195,888	2,325,096	1,962,912	2,225,242	2,497,815	1,968,374	11.83
Malta and Gozo	79,987	76,414	65,574	111,952	42,470	103,524	.62
Other................	886	438	1,438	239	877	1,441	.01
Total British possessions ..	2,276,761	2,401,948	2,029,924	2,337,433	2,541,162	2,073,339	12.46
Total	10,075,346	4,189,970	7,319,583	12,603,226	9,630,154	16,633,796	100.00

TOMATOES.(a) (d)

Countries from which imported.	Calendar year 1900.	Per cent.	Countries from which imported.	Calendar year 1900.	Per cent.
FOREIGN COUNTRIES.			BRITISH POSSESSIONS.		
	Pounds.			*Pounds.*	
Spain.......................	22,588,944	24.21	Channel Islands	17,479,840	18.74
Canary Islands...............	20,979,952	22.49	Other	70,000	.07
France	15,963,024	17.11			
Italy.......................	6,683,824	7.16	Total British possessions................	17,549,840	18.81
United States...............	5,699,792	6.11			
Portugal....................	3,162,096	3.39	Total.................	93,299,360	100.00
Denmark....................	391,328	.42			
Netherlands.................	1,568	.30			
Other.......................	278,992				
Total foreign countries .	75,749,520	81.19			

a For values, see page 139.
b Bushels of 60 pounds.
c In 1900 including 385 bushels from the United States.
d Not stated prior to 1900.

antity of the agricultural imports of the United Kingdom (vegetable matter), etc.—Cont'd.

BEANS, DRIED. (a) (b)

	Annual average, 1896–1900.	Calendar years.					Per ct. in 1900.
		1896.	1897.	1898.	1899.	1900.	
REIGN COUNTRIES.	Bushels.(c)	Bushels.(c)	Bushels.(c)	Bushels.(c)	Bushels.(c)	Bushels.(c)	
ypt	1,552,376	2,289,859	1,503,899	868,149	2,057,253	1,042,720	32.52
rocco	391,948	585,947	114,856	301,000	227,267	730,669	22.79
rkey, Asiatic	875,721	998,592	1,408,774	952,933	343,691	674,613	21.04
rmany	502,717	591,024	508,965	566,371	504,952	342,272	10.67
ssia	162,026	111,701	160,608	215,077	182,933	139,813	4.36
rkey, European	57,643	56,000	75,600	53,947	28,560	74,107	2.31
therlands	38,587	68,077	34,851	14,390	34,496	41,123	1.28
ly	170,053	127,157	464,221	215,376	15,139	28,373	.88
stria-Hungary	7,605	2,651	1,195	9,912	9,333	14,933	.47
veden	23,085	38,808	23,427	27,552	12,880	12,507	.39
rprus	372,717	686,373	655,853	521,360	....	....	......
rtugal	195,216	184,427	304,005	487,648	....	....	......
exico	8,911	....	....	....	44,557	....	......
lgeria	3,136	....	....	15,680	....	....	......
ther d	20,322	6,328	17,192	23,696	25,947	28,448	.89
Total foreign countries	4,382,013	5,746,944	5,273,446	4,273,091	3,487,008	3,129,578	97.60
RITISH POSSESSIONS.							
ustralasia:							
New Zealand	27,877	25,947	21,579	747	14,765	76,347	} 2.38
New South Wales	448	....	....	....	2,240		
Canada	5,581	19,357	6,365	2,184	....	....	......
Other	1,124	....	37	4,891	131	560	.02
Total British possessions	35,030	45,304	27,981	7,822	17,136	76,907	2.40
Total	4,417,043	5,792,248	5,301,427	4,280,913	3,504,144	3,206,485	100.00

PEAS, DRIED. (e)

FOREIGN COUNTRIES.	Bushels.(c)	Bushels.(c)	Bushels.(c)	Bushels.(c)	Bushels.(c)	Bushels.(c)	
United States	984,018	714,429	1,169,821	1,060,584	890,157	1,085,099	25.85
Russia	1,000,575	1,876,710	1,643,078	553,355	504,093	425,637	10.14
Netherlands	236,773	194,413	151,461	198,035	302,611	337,344	8.03
Germany	162,843	173,021	87,588	148,853	226,263	178,491	4.25
Morocco	23,677	3,845	37	1,269	36,833	76,402	1.82
Chile	10,815	21,971	2,613	....	19,973	9,520	.23
Colombia	1,344	....	....	....	6,720	....	......
Other	11,423	12,651	5,326	6,039	22,583	10,517	.25
Total foreign countries	2,431,468	2,997,040	3,059,924	1,968,135	2,009,233	2,123,010	50.57
BRITISH POSSESSIONS.							
Canada	1,781,035	1,940,195	2,077,096	1,892,221	1,409,557	1,586,107	37.78
British East Indies:							
Bengal	593,118	617,381	96,320	188,272	1,665,002	398,617	} 9.50
Bombay	7,099	7,840	373	9,341	17,808	131	
Ceylon	75	....	373	....	....	....	
Australasia:							
New Zealand	31,961	37,464	28,206	9,856	36,120	48,160	}
Victoria	7,149	2,613	840	....	560	31,733	
Tasmania	2,091	....	....	....	......	10,453	} 2.15
New South Wales	149	....	....	....	560	187	
South Australia	6,496	32,293	187	....	....	....	
Other	202	....	933	....	....	75	
Total British possessions	2,429,375	2,637,786	2,204,328	2,099,690	3,129,607	2,075,463	49.43
Total	4,860,843	5,634,826	5,264,252	4,067,825	5,138,840	4,198,473	100.00

a For values, see page 140.
b Exclusive of kidney, haricot, and French beans; prior to 1899, including carob beans.
c Bushels of 60 pounds.
d Including imports from Spain amounting to 261 bushels in 1896 and 14,653 bushels in 1898, and from the United States 373 bushels in 1900.
e For values, see page 141.

Quantity of the agricultural imports of the United Kingdom (vegetable matter), etc.—Cont'd.

VETCHES AND LENTILS. (a)

Countries from which imported.	Annual average, 1896–1900.	Calendar years.					Per ct. in 1900.
		1896.	1897.	1898.	1899.	1900.	
FOREIGN COUNTRIES.							
	Bushels.(b)	Bushels.(b)	Bushels.(b)	Bushels.(b)	Bushels.(b)	Bushels.(b)	
Germany	132,434	110,708	103,227	92,296	137,164	218,776	53.64
Russia	70,992	72,292	50,715	67,779	100,986	63,191	15.49
Egypt	49,844	23,088	61,781	47,907	55,445	60,997	14.95
Turkey, Asiatic	7,959	13,752	6,856	10,342	497	8,347	2.05
Sweden	3,676	4,656	3,752	4,366	2,253	3,351	.82
Turkey, European	1,558	1,692	2,630	165	....	3,301	.81
Chile	8,028	13,794	10,587	11,647	970	3,143	.77
France	1,507	325	4,206	505	1,356	1,142	.28
Denmark	1,491	474	3,301	3,094	....	588	.14
Other	1,779	3,059	1,069	590	1,255	2,921	.72
Total foreign countries	279,268	243,840	248,124	238,691	299,926	365,757	89.67
BRITISH POSSESSIONS.							
British East Indies:							
Bombay	70,645	90,195	19,496	117,899	95,474	30,161	} 9.68
Bengal	22,478	70,961	....	71	32,053	9,304	
Other c	860	1,444	196	....	....	2,661	.65
Total British possessions	93,983	162,600	19,692	117,970	127,527	42,126	10.33
Total	373,251	406,440	267,816	356,661	427,453	407,883	100.00

VEGETABLES, PRESERVED IN SALT OR VINEGAR, INCLUDING PICKLES. (d)

FOREIGN COUNTRIES.							
	Gallons.(e)	Gallons.(e)	Gallons.(e)	Gallons.(e)	Gallons.(e)	Gallons.(e)	
Netherlands	1,760,538	1,443,099	1,405,519	1,633,947	2,080,389	2,239,737	62.22
France	835,858	873,329	889,354	714,879	785,613	916,117	25.45
Belgium	153,632	181,591	87,631	143,694	190,961	164,283	4.56
Italy	99,581	94,686	98,437	64,945	97,424	142,413	3.96
United States	112,952	66,464	38,052	74,963	283,130	102,149	2.84
Germany	23,334	23,024	24,221	19,229	22,821	27,376	.76
Other	3,413	4,303	4,485	5,275	1,049	1,954	.06
Total foreign countries	2,989,308	2,686,496	2,547,699	2,656,932	3,461,387	3,594,029	99.85
BRITISH POSSESSIONS.							
Total British possessions	10,338	7,934	9,400	21,229	7,595	5,531	.15
Total	2,999,646	2,694,430	2,557,099	2,678,161	3,468,982	3,599,560	100.00

SAUCES AND CONDIMENTS. (d) (f)

FOREIGN COUNTRIES.							
	Pounds.	Pounds.	Pounds.	Pounds.	Pounds.	Pounds.	
United States	771,856	465,090	1,032,074	982,419	962,184	417,514	7.16
Italy	351,163	168,852	353,516	427,800	458,936	346,713	5.94
Germany	462,446	990,843	238,559	239,884	530,767	312,176	5.35
France	334,619	335,203	331,790	375,625	332,487	297,991	5.11
Japan	115,892	122,484	63,340	72,636	80,150	240,850	4.13
Netherlands	18,663	6,062	13,406	21,268	25,818	26,761	.46
Russia	19,694	23,326	18,803	24,789	22,451	9,102	.15
Belgium	6,950	3,611	13,267	9,259	4,093	4,518	.08
China	43,766	28,620	23,200	122,500	44,510	....	......
Other	32,787	6,630	57,084	40,734	43,278	16,208	.28
Total foreign countries	2,157,836	2,150,721	2,145,039	2,316,914	2,504,674	1,671,833	28.66

a For values, see page 141.
b Winchester bushels.
c In 1896 comprising 1,444 bushels from New Zealand.
d For values, see page 142.
e United States standard gallons.
f Including table salt.

ntity of the agricultural imports of the United Kingdom (vegetable matter), etc.—Cont'd.

SAUCES AND CONDIMENTS—Continued.

ntries from which imported.	Annual average, 1896–1900.	Calendar years.					Per ct. in 1900.
		1896.	1897.	1898.	1899.	1900.	
TISH POSSESSIONS.							
	Pounds.	*Pounds.*	*Pounds.*	*Pounds.*	*Pounds.*	*Pounds.*	
ngkong............	1,691,492	1,280,110	1,348,490	1,277,300	1,949,650	2,601,910	44.61
tish East Indies:							
Bombay.........	865,283	695,771	707,050	1,009,563	942,053	971,978	
Madras	275,573	250,788	342,807	316,114	186,333	281,824	
Bengal	194,286	127,550	206,749	255,534	173,380	208,216	
Straits Settle-							} 26.46
ments	24,376	6,384	14,540	....	19,945	81,010	
Burma	107	....	....	90	256	188	
Ceylon	1,027	883	2,060	990	1,150	50	
her...............	12,695	11,404	4,022	15,346	16,860	15,846	.27
Total British possessions ..	3,064,839	2,372,890	2,625,718	2,874,937	3,289,627	4,161,022	71.34
Total.........	5,222,675	4,523,611	4.770,757	5,191,851	5,794,301	5,832,855	100.00

VINEGAR.(a)

'OREIGN COUNTRIES.							
	Gallons (b)	*Gallons.(b)*	*Gallons.(b)*	*Gallons.(b)*	*Gallons. (b)*	*Gallons.(b)*	
rance	86,486	77,095	92,925	81,010	97,049	84,350	36.34
elgium............	79,635	74,790	87,519	75,253	88,412	72,200	31.11
etherlands........	44,789	52,502	34,927	35,726	43,829	56,960	24.54
Germany............	15,447	17,215	23,418	10,476	17,127	8,999	3.88
Other c	4,448	1,938	667	5,531	4,533	9,574	4.13
Total foreign countries....	230,805	223,540	239,456	207,999	250,950	232,083	100.00
BRITISH POSSESSIONS.							
Total British posses- sions	382	....	....	420	1,489	....	....
Total.........	231,187	223,540	239,456	208,419	252,439	232,083	100.00

CHAMPAGNE AND OTHER SPARKLING WINES.(a)

FOREIGN COUNTRIES.							
	Gallons.(b)	*Gallons.(b)*	*Gallons.(b)*	*Gallons.(b)*	*Gallons.(b)*	*Gallons.(b)*	
France	2,107,240	2,091,132	2,349,700	2,354,819	1,873,427	1,867,123	93.82
Netherlands........	112,912	104,188	112,144	114,744	119,657	113,826	5.72
Belgium............	2,293	2,586	3,399	1,552	1,049	2,929	.15
Germany............	1,696	3,451	1,364	1,314	1,041	1,311	.06
Italy...............	688	657	557	392	943	890	.04
Portugal............	124	37	110	86	252	135	.01
Spain...............	155	85	126	508	41	13	} .03
Other d	6,199	26,415	1,154	2,602	305	521	
Total foreign countries....	2,231,307	2,228,501	2,468,554	2,476,017	1,996,715	1,986,748	99.83
BRITISH POSSESSIONS.							
Australasia..........	928	392	790	423	1,332	1,702	.08
Cape of Good Hope..	207	101	85	98	382	367	.02
Natal...............	58	....	....	72	98	118	.01
Other...............	1,147	904	1,113	1,711	867	1,143	.06
Total British possessions ..	2,340	1,397	1,990	2,304	2,679	3,330	.17
Total.........	2,233,647	2,229,898	2,470,544	2,478,321	1,999,394	1,990,078	100.00

a For values, see page 143.
b United States standard gallons.
c In 1900 including 2,153 gallons from the United States.
d In 1900 including 44 gallons from the United States.

Quantity of the agricultural imports of the United Kingdom (vegetable matter), etc.—Cont'd.

STILL WINES, BOTTLED. (a)

Countries from which imported.	Annual average, 1896–1900.	Calendar years.					Per ct. in 1900.
		1896.	1897.	1898.	1899.	1900.	
FOREIGN COUNTRIES.							
	Gallons. (b)	Gallons. (b)	Gallons. (b)	Gallons. (b)	Gallons. (b)	Gallons. (b)	
Netherlands.........	382,571	371,518	411,388	440,594	373,461	315,895	47.16
France	513,574	666,324	699,690	499,626	457,254	244,977	36.58
Germany	19,913	21,484	18,004	22,452	11,446	26,180	●3.91
Belgium	17,599	15,707	17,784	15,975	15,479	23·048	3.44
Italy................	33,679	47,133	31,975	38,759	28,161	22,367	3.34
Portugal............	16,858	17,772	19,797	20,178	14,110	12,435	1.86
Spain c	12,799	13,075	13,867	19,673	9,940	7,438	1.11
Other d	12,445	11,719	11,950	19,104	11,695	7,756	1.16
Total foreign countries....	1,009,438	1,164,732	1,224,455	1,076,361	921,546	660,096	98.56
BRITISH POSSESSIONS.							
Channel Islands.....	5,251	5,088	6,105	6,319	6,018	2,726	.41
Australasia..........	4,285	7,670	3,188	3,709	4,242	2,617	.39
Cape of Good Hope..	2,855	3,685	3,119	2,606	2,517	2,346	.35
Natal...............	212	270	259	214	319	....	......
Other...............	2,959	3,392	2,588	4,479	2,367	1,966	.29
Total British possessions ..	15,562	20,105	15,259	17,327	15,463	9,655	1.44
Total	1,025,000	1,184,837	1,239,714	1,093,688	937,009	669,751	100.00

STILL WINES, UNBOTTLED. (a)

	Annual average, 1896–1900.	1896.	1897.	1898.	1899.	1900.	Per ct. in 1900.
FOREIGN COUNTRIES.							
	Gallons. (b)	Gallons. (b)	Gallons. (b)	Gallons. (b)	Gallons. (b)	Gallons. (b)	
Spain e	5,134,609	4,455,916	5,126,957	5,274,771	5,333,166	5,482,238	31.31
Portugal............	4,742,842	4,269,087	4,730,286	5,346,885	4,745,046	4,622,905	26.40
France	4,848,751	5,328,627	4,878,684	4,813,660	4,874,024	4,348,760	24.84
Germany	539,955	463,880	517,944	531,300	563,626	623,025	3.56
Netherlands........	421,836	281,804	305,877	350,739	588,099	582,660	3.33
Italy	456,357	464,428	437,635	482,283	466,141	431,298	2.46
United States.......	245,676	257,762	211,753	291,027	270,422	197,416	1.13
Madeira Islands.....	89,079	72,806	149,225	77,994	62,107	83,264	.48
Belgium............	41,058	41,988	41,364	42,662	32,989	49,287	.28
Cyprus	13,918	7,268	4,466	4,908	15,316	37,634	.21
Turkey, Asiatic.....	7,846	1,090	1,148	1,790	18,500	16,701	.09
Canary Islands......	48,802	85,156	53,331	67,480	31,858	6,187	.03
Turkey, European...	7,617	20,919	6,413	7,987	1,476	1,289	.01
Other..............	28,764	17,491	28,213	34,614	28,685	34,815	.20
Total foreign countries....	16,627,710	15,768,222	16,493,296	17,328,100	17,031,455	16,517,479	94.33
BRITISH POSSESSIONS.							
Australasia:							
South Australia .	467,757	370,491	458,891	511,652	496,808	500,940	
Victoria	394,944	441,075	379,160	336,504	353,559	464,420	
New South Wales	20,308	23,100	14,742	9,032	37,560	17,108	5.61
New Zealand....	26	60	30	....	....	41	
Queensland	326	1,576	53	....	....	....	
Tasmania	36	178	....	....	....	....	
Cape of Good Hope..	6,659	7,696	8,725	4,650	5,992	6,231	.04
Natal...............	64	14	79	16	54	159	
Other...............	9,375	12,534	11,174	11,062	8,678	3,429	.02
Total British possessions ..	899,495	856,724	872,854	872,916	902,651	992,328	5.67
Total	17,527,205	16,624,946	17,366,150	18,201,016	17,934,106	17,509,807	100.00

a For values, see page 144.
b United States standard gallons.
c Of the imports from Spain, red wine comprised 7,354 gallons in 1896, 10,100 gallons in 1897, 13,334 gallons in 1898, 7,350 gallons in 1899, and 4,122 gallons in 1900; and white wine, 5,721 gallons in 1896, 3,767 gallons in 1897, 6,339 gallons in 1898, 2,590 gallons in 1899, and 3,316 gallons in 1900.
d In 1900 including 1,326 gallons from the United States.
e Of the imports from Spain, red wine comprised 2,300,801 gallons in 1896, 2,795,804 gallons in 1897, 2,986,508 gallons in 1898, 3,253,282 gallons in 1899, and 3,390,708 gallons in 1900; and white wine, 2,155,115 gallons in 1896, 2,331,153 gallons in 1897, 2,288,263 gallons in 1898, 2,079,884 gallons in 1899, and 2,091,580 gallons in 1900.

Quantity of the agricultural imports of the United Kingdom (vegetable matter), etc.—Cont'd.

WINES (TOTAL). (*a*)

Countries from which imported.	Annual average, 1896–1900.	Calendar years.					Per ct. in 1900.
		1896.	1897.	1898.	1899.	1900.	
FOREIGN COUNTRIES.							
	Gallons.(b)	Gallons.(b)	Gallons.(b)	Gallons.(b)	Gallons.(b)	Gallons.(b)	
France	7,469,565	8,086,083	7,928,074	7,668,105	7,204,705	6,460,860	32.03
Spain................	5,147,563	4,469,076	5,140,950	5,294,952	5,343,147	5,489,689	27.22
Portugal	4,759,824	4,286,896	4,750,193	5,367,149	4,759,408	4,635,475	22.98
Netherlands	917,319	757,510	829,409	906,077	1,081,217	1,012,381	5.02
Germany............	561,564	488,815	537,312	555,066	576,113	650,516	3.23
Italy	490,724	512,218	470,167	521,434	495,245	454,555	2.25
United States	253,101	286,109	214,300	293,640	272,669	198,786	.99
Madeira Islands.....	90,826	74,122	150,359	79,491	62,967	84,693	.42
Belgium.............	61,550	60,231	62,547	60,189	49,517	75,264	.87
Cyprus	14,046	7,535	4,819	4,908	15,335	37,634	.19
Turkey, Asiatic......	10,809	2,845	3,952	11,331	18,851	17,066	.08
Austria-Hungary....	11,344	1,695	11,343	13,818	14,318	15,544	.08
Greece...............	7,308	7,675	9,684	5,361	6,916	6,903	.03
Canary Islands......	49,155	85,614	53,751	68,028	32,120	6,263	.03
Turkey, European...	8,752	24,948	7,100	8,559	1,647	1,504	.01
Other................	15,506	10,083	12,345	22,370	15,541	17,190	.09
Total foreign countries....	19,868,456	19,161,455	20,186,305	20,880,478	19,949,716	19,164,323	95.02
BRITISH POSSESSIONS.							
Australasia:							
South Australia .	468,913	373,335	459,732	512,701	497,246	501,551	⎫
Victoria	396,358	442,103	379,734	337,481	356,992	465,480	⎪
New South Wales	22,365	25,762	16,884	10,892	38,641	19,647	⎬ 4.89
New Zealand....	385	597	450	188	551	139	⎪
Queensland	553	2,567	55	58	71	11	⎪
Tasmania	36	178	1	....	....	....	⎭
Cape of Good Hope..	9,721	11,482	11,929	7,354	8,891	8,944	.04
Channel Islands.....	7,069	5,912	9,800	8,906	7,377	3,353	.02
Malta and Gozo	2,927	3,786	3,464	2,423	3,172	1,790	.01
Gibraltar............	2,097	2,810	3,702	1,939	920	1,114	⎫
Natal................	334	284	338	302	471	277	⎬ .02
Other................	6,638	9,410	4,014	10,303	6,461	3,007	⎭
Total British possessions ..	917,396	878,226	890,103	892,547	920,793	1,005,313	4.98
Total	20,785,852	20,039,681	21,076,408	21,773,025	20,870,509	20,169,636	100.00

YEAST. (*a*)

FOREIGN COUNTRIES.							
	Pounds.	Pounds.	Pounds.	Pounds.	Pounds.	Pounds.	
Netherlands.........	10,942,512	11,673,872	11,656,848	10,987,312	10,566,080	9,828,448	63.25
France	3,940,742	4,041,744	3,673,040	3,982,720	3,731,056	4,275,152	27.51
Germany............	2,020,480	3,334,576	2,330,048	1,824,704	1,503,152	1,109,920	7.14
Denmark............	174,250	212,240	181,888	172,256	161,392	143,472	.93
Other c	53,088	44,912	22,624	24,752	53,312	119,840	.77
Total foreign countries....	17,131,072	19,307,344	17,864,448	16,991,744	16,014,992	15,476,832	99.60
BRITISH POSSESSIONS.							
Canada..............	34,586	11,200	10,304	59,696	29,792	61,936	.40
Total	17,165,658	19,318,544	17,874,752	17,051,440	16,044,784	15,538,768	100.00

a For values, see page 145.
b United States standard gallons.
c In 1900 including 108,080 pounds from the United States.

INDEX TO TABLES.

Index to tables—Continued.

Index to tables—Continued.